Fodor's First Edition

W9-AAX-306

Morocco

The complete guide, thoroughly up-to-date

Packed with details that will make your trip

The must-see sights, off and on the beaten path

What to see, what to skip

Mix-and-match vacation itineraries

City strolls, countryside adventures

Smart lodging and dining options

Essential local do's and taboos

Transportation tips, distances and directions

Key contacts, savvy travel tips

When to go, what to pack

Clear, accurate, easy-to-use maps

Fodor's Travel Publications • New York, Toronto, London, Sydney, Auckland
www.fodors.com

Fodor's Morocco

EDITOR: Christine Cipriani

Editorial Contributors: Dr. Jonathan Bell, Eileen Colucci, David Crawford, Katherine Hoffman, Angela Scarfino, George Semler, Pamela Windo

Editorial Production: Nicole Revere

Maps: David Lindroth, *cartographer*; Rebecca Baer, Robert Blake, *map editors*

Design: Fabrizio La Rocca, *creative director*; Guido Caroti, *art director*; Jolie Novak, *photo editor*; Melanie Marin, *photo researcher*

Cover Design: Pentagram

Production/Manufacturing: Bob Shields

Cover Photograph: Simon Russell

Copyright

Copyright © 2000 by Fodor's Travel Publications

Fodor's is a registered trademark of Random House, Inc.

All rights reserved under International and Pan-American Copyright Conventions. Published in the United States by Fodor's Travel Publications, a division of Random House, Inc., New York, and simultaneously in Canada by Random House of Canada Limited, Toronto. Distributed by Random House, Inc., New York.

No maps, illustrations, or other portions of this book may be reproduced in any form without written permission from the publisher.

First Edition

ISBN 0–679–00393–2

ISSN 1527–4829

Poetry on page 254 from *The Prophet,* by Kahlil Gibran (Alfred A. Knopf, a division of Random House, Inc., 1923)

Special Sales

Fodor's Travel Publications are available at special discounts for bulk purchases for sales promotions or premiums. Special editions, including personalized covers, excerpts of existing guides, and corporate imprints, can be created in large quantities for special needs. For more information, contact your local bookseller or write to Special Markets, Fodor's Travel Publications, 201 East 50th Street, New York, NY 10022. Inquiries from Canada should be directed to your local Canadian bookseller or sent to Random House of Canada, Ltd., Marketing Department, 2775 Matheson Blvd. E, Mississauga, Ontario L4W 4P7. Inquiries from the United Kingdom should be sent to Fodor's Travel Publications, 20 Vauxhall Bridge Road, London SW1V 2SA, England.

PRINTED IN THE UNITED STATES OF AMERICA

10 9 8 7 6 5 4 3 2 1

Important Tip

Although all prices, opening times, and other details in this book are based on information supplied to us at press time, changes occur all the time in the travel world, and Fodor's cannot accept responsibility for facts that become outdated or for inadvertent errors or omissions. So **always confirm information when it matters,** especially if you're making a detour to visit a specific place.

CONTENTS

IV

Contents

Maps

ON THE ROAD WITH FODOR'S

WE'VE PULLED OUT ALL STOPS in preparing *Fodor's Morocco*. To guide you in putting together your Moroccan experience, we've created multiday itineraries and neighborhood walks. And to direct you to the places that are truly worth your time and money, we've rallied the team of endearingly picky know-it-alls we're pleased to call our writers. Having seen all corners of the regions they cover for us, they're real experts. If you knew them, you'd poll them for tips yourself.

Dr. Jonathan Bell, a specialist on disease control in African village poultry, has lived on the Atlantic coast of Morocco for 18 years. His work has taken him around Morocco and other parts of Africa, and he has organized international conferences in Rabat. The author of more than 20 articles in his field, he is currently writing an adventure story for children.

Native New Yorker **Eileen Colucci** has lived in Morocco for the past 20 years. Formerly an assistant director of the American Language Center in Rabat, she is currently a French-English translator at the American Embassy. She lives in Rabat with her husband, a Moroccan architect, and their two sons, Driss and Amine.

David Crawford is a doctoral student in anthropology at the University of California, Santa Barbara. He recently completed his dissertation fieldwork, which focuses on social organization and identity among High Atlas farmers.

Katherine Hoffman is an anthropologist who received her Ph.D. from Columbia University. She spent four years in northern and southern Morocco conducting a study of language, song, and community and consulting for a joint Moroccan-American educational project to improve rural schools. She has also researched for several documentary film productions. Hoffman currently teaches at UCLA.

A native of St. Charles, Missouri, **Angela Scarfino** recently lived in Morocco for four years, first as a U.S. Peace Corps volunteer working in disease control in the rural south, then as a health advisor for USAID's population and health program in Rabat. Proficient in both Moroccan Arabic and the Berber languages, she likes to think she left no Moroccan stone unturned. Now based in New York, she is a manager of Heritage Tours, specializing, sure enough, in trips to Morocco.

A Barcelona-based specialist on the Mediterranean, journalist **George Semler** has written about Morocco for the better part of a decade. From automotive breakdowns in Atlas-mountain villages to dawn camel treks in the Sahara to adventures in the medieval labyrinth of Fez el Bali, Semler has reported on nearly every aspect of Morocco's various peoples and places.

A native of Brighton, England, **Pamela Windo** came to the United States in 1979 and moved to Morocco in 1989, where she taught English to the children of the governor of Tiznit and wrote for the *Marrakech Echo* and *British Airways* Magazine. Later, as a publicist for Moroccan tourism, she was chosen to present Morocco to the U.N. community, and served as location assistant to Martin Scorsese in the Ouarzazate-based filming of *Kundun*. Since returning to the U.S. Windo has contributed to the Sunday *Daily News* and British *Condé Nast Traveller* and written Fodor's *Escape to Morocco*.

We'd also like to thank Benjafaar Marrakshi, director of the Moroccan National Tourist Office, New York, and Royal Air Maroc for their kind assistance.

Don't Forget to Write

Keeping a travel guide fresh and up-to-date is a big job. So we love your feedback—positive and negative—and follow up on all suggestions. Contact the Morocco editor at editors@fodors.com or c/o Fodor's, 201 East 50th Street, New York, New York 10022. And have a wonderful trip!

Karen Cure
Editorial Director

VI

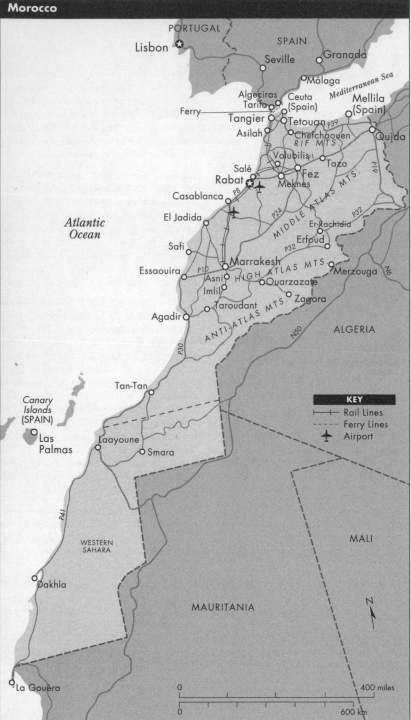

Morocco

PORTUGAL

Lisbon

SPAIN

Seville

Granada

Málaga

Mediterranean Sea

Algeciras
Tarifa

Ceuta
(Spain)

Mellila
(Spain)

Ferry

Tangier

Tetouan

P39

Oujda

Asilah

Chefchaouen

RIF MTS.

P19

Volubilis

Taza

Salé

Fez

Rabat

Meknes

Casablanca

P8

El Jadida

P24

MIDDLE ATLAS MTS.

Er-Rachidia

P32

Atlantic
Ocean

Safi

Erfoud

P32

Marrakesh

HIGH ATLAS MTS.

Merzouga

N6

Essaouira

P10

Asni

Ouarzazate

Imlil

Zagora

Taroudant

ANTI-ATLAS MTS.

Agadir

N50

ALGERIA

P30

Tan-Tan

Canary
Islands
(SPAIN)

Las
Palmas

Laayoune

KEY

Rail Lines

Ferry Lines

Airport

Smara

P41

WESTERN
SAHARA

MALI

Dakhla

MAURITANIA

N

La Gouéra

0   400 miles

0   600 km

SMART TRAVEL TIPS A TO Z

AIR TRAVEL

From North America the only carrier with direct flights to Morocco is **Royal Air Maroc (RAM)** (☎ 800/344–6726), which departs New York and Montreal for Casablanca. For schedules *see* Web Sites, *below*. In partnership with TWA, RAM offers connecting flights from other North American cities. Generally speaking, you'll get a better fare if you use the same carrier for the whole trip.

Between RAM, British Airways, Iberia, KLM, Lufthansa, Sabena, and Swissair there are direct flights to Casablanca daily from nearly all Western European countries. One of the cheapest points of departure is London; here the **Air Travel Advisory Bureau** (☎ 207/636–5000) can give you the names of agencies offering discounted fares. **Royal Air Maroc** (☎ 207/439–4361) flies from London to Casablanca.

From Australasia and the Far East, Gulf Air, Kuwait Airways, EgyptAir, and Royal Jordanian run connecting flights, as do the European airlines. Lufthansa has good connections from Sydney.

From South Africa, RAM has a direct flight from Johannesburg once weekly, and European airlines such as Swissair and British Airways also offer well-priced connections. Egypt, Tunisia, Algeria, Mauritania, Senegal, Mali, and the Côte d'Ivoire also have direct flights to Morocco.

For destinations other than Casablanca, there are scheduled flights from Paris to Rabat, Tangier, Fez, Marrakesh, and Agadir, and from London to Tangier and Marrakesh. In addition, many European charter flights head for Agadir, and some for Tangier. Domestic flights from Casablanca to other Moroccan cities are operated by **Royal Air Maroc** and **Regional Air Lines.**

Fares *from* Morocco are getting more competitive, and all the airlines mentioned above offer special unpublished fares outside the high season (July–September and the Christmas–New Year period) for travel with one carrier. These fares are not available outside Morocco.

Most airline offices in Casablanca are in or near the Tour Habous building, opposite the Sheraton Hotel on Avenue FAR (Avenue des Forces Armées Royales). To reconfirm your seat, simply call the airline; you don't need to present yourself at the office as you do in some African countries.

BOOKING YOUR FLIGHT

When you reserve, **look for nonstop flights** and **remember that "direct" flights stop at least once.** Try to avoid connecting flights, which require a change of plane.

CHECK-IN & BOARDING

Check-in for international flights usually starts two hours before departure; the latest possible check-in time is 70 minutes before departure for African flights, 60 minutes for European flights. You cannot check in at the departure gate unless you have no luggage. Your baggage will be checked by customs after check-in, and you'll need to fill out a departure card before going through passport control. Assuming that not everyone with a ticket will show up, airlines routinely overbook planes; when that happens, airlines ask for volunteers to give up their seats. In return these volunteers usually get a certificate for a free flight and are rebooked on the next flight out. If there are not enough volunteers, the airline must choose who will be denied boarding, and the first to get bumped are passengers who checked in late and those holding discounted tickets—so get to the gate and **check in as early as possible,** especially during peak periods.

THE GOLD GUIDE / SMART TRAVEL TIPS

Always **bring a government-issued photo I.D. to the airport.** You may be asked to show it before you're allowed to check in.

CUTTING COSTS

On domestic flights, Royal Air Maroc offers a 50% discount for one member of a married couple traveling together, as well as additional discounts for children in family groups of three or more (not counting infants in the three). The airline also gives 50% discounts to young people between the ages of 12 and 22 and students 31 or younger. Both Royal Air Maroc and the domestic company Regional Airlines also offer annual subscription plans that discount all internal flights.

The least expensive tickets to Morocco are nonrefundable and usually must be purchased in advance. It's smart to **call a number of airlines, and if you're quoted a good price, reserve on the spot**—the same fare may not be available the next day. Always **check different routes** and look into using different airports. Travel agents, especially low-fare specialists (☞ Discounts & Deals, *below*), can be helpful.

Consolidators are another good source. They buy tickets for scheduled international flights from the airlines at reduced rates, then sell them at prices that beat the best fares available directly from the airlines, usually without restrictions. Sometimes you can even get your money back if you need to return the ticket. Carefully read the fine print detailing penalties for changes and cancellations, and **confirm your consolidator reservation with the airline.**

When you **fly as a courier,** you trade your checked-luggage space for a ticket deeply subsidized by a courier service. There are restrictions on when you can book and how long you can stay.

➤ CONSOLIDATORS: **Cheap Tickets** (☎ 800/377–1000). **Discount Airline Ticket Service** (☎ 800/576–1600). **Unitravel** (☎ 800/325–2222). **Up & Away Travel** (☎ 212/889–2345). **World Travel Network** (☎ 800/409–6753).

ENJOYING THE FLIGHT

For more legroom, **request an emergency-aisle seat.** Try not to be seated in front of the emergency aisle or in front of a bulkhead, as the seats may not recline. If you have vegetarian, low-cholesterol, kosher, or other dietary requirements, **ask for special meals when booking.** To avoid jet lag after long flights, try to maintain a normal routine: **get some sleep** at night; by day, **eat light meals, drink water (not alcohol), and move around the cabin** to stretch your legs.

HOW TO COMPLAIN

If your baggage goes astray or your flight goes awry, complain right away. Most carriers require that you **file a claim immediately.**

➤ AIRLINE COMPLAINTS: U.S. Department of Transportation **Aviation Consumer Protection Division** (✉ C-75, Room 4107, Washington, DC 20590, ☎ 202/366–2220). **Federal Aviation Administration Consumer Hotline** (☎ 800/322–7873).

RECONFIRMING

Domestic Moroccan carriers may require reconfirmation to hold your seat. If yours does, remember to place this call ahead of time. (Sometimes your hotel can do it for you.)

AIRPORTS

By far the best way to enter Morocco is to fly into **Casablanca** (Mohammed V Airport; international code CMN). The airports at Rabat, Tangier, Tetouan, Al Hoceima, Oujda, Nador, Fez, Marrakesh, Ouarzazate, Essaouira, Agadir, Laayoune, and Dakhla have only domestic flights or limited international service (☞ Air Travel, *above*). You can often arrange connecting flights to these cities from Casablanca.

BIKE TRAVEL

You can cycle on quiet roads in rural parts of Morocco, but it's dangerous to ride a bike on any major road, as bicycles are almost as low as pedestrians on the traffic totem pole. All major towns have bike-repair shops and/or shops with spare parts. There are no bike maps in print; the next best thing is a detailed topographical map, available from the **Division de la Cartographie** (⌂ 31, Avenue Moulay Hassan, Rabat), although these are not usually up to date. Bike rental is generally not an option—plan to bring your own.

BIKES IN FLIGHT

Most airlines accommodate bikes as luggage, provided they're dismantled and boxed. For bike boxes, often free at bike shops, you'll pay the airline about $5 (as compared to at least $100 for bike bags). You can sometimes substitute a bike for a piece of checked luggage at no charge; otherwise, the cost is about $100.

BOAT & FERRY TRAVEL

Unfortunately, disembarking in Tangier's port as a pedestrian is the worst way to arrive in Morocco. You're likely to be greeted, the moment you set foot on Moroccan soil, by an unpleasant character who will not cease harassing you until you have parted company with some money, or at best suffered some verbal abuse. To avoid this unpleasant and totally unrepresentative experience, fly into Casablanca if at all possible and see Tangier and the north later on. If you do arrive by ferry, do not admit to the brigands in Tangier that you're visiting Morocco for the first time. Beware also of people who approach you on trains leaving Tangier.

For details on ferries from Spain and elsewhere, ☞ Tangier, Tetouan, and the Mediterranean A to Z *in* Chapter 2.

BUS TRAVEL

Buses serve most towns in Morocco, and bus fares are inexpensive. The national bus company, C.T.M., serves all major cities, and there are many smaller companies. C.T.M. buses and some others are comfortable, but they also include French-language television; so if you'd rather ride in peace than travel through Morocco to the tune of French films, you might be better off with one of the less luxurious bus lines. In each city the bus station—known as the *gare routière*—is generally near the edge of town. Some larger cities have separate C.T.M. stations.

CITY BUSES

Since city buses were privatized, supply and demand for them has pretty much reached equilibrium, and they're a safe and feasible way to get around. Fares are very cheap and are independent of the distance traveled. When appropriate, we indicate bus numbers within our suggested sightseeing tours.

FARES & SCHEDULES

Buy tickets at the bus station prior to departure; payment is by cash only. Tickets are only sold for the seats available, so once you have a ticket, you have a seat. Other than tickets, there are no reservations. Often tickets only go on sale an hour before departure. For schedules, inquire at the bus station.

In rural areas people often stop buses en route and simply pay on the bus.

SMOKING

In theory, smoking is not allowed on public transportation. In practice, local buses may contain some lawbreakers.

BUSINESS HOURS

Banks and post offices open and close punctually, but hours for all other institutions are only approximate.

BANKS & OFFICES

Moroccan banks are open weekdays from 8:15 to 11:30 and 2:15 to 4:30. Post offices are open Monday through Thursday from 8:30 to noon and 2:30 to 6:30, Friday 8:30 to 11:30 and 3 to 6:30. Government offices are accessible weekdays from about 9 to 11:30 and 3 to 6 (9 to 11 and 3:30 to 6 on Friday).

In summer—early July to mid-September, corresponding to school vacations—hours for banks, post offices, and government offices are continuous: from 8 or 8:30 to 1:30 or 3. During Ramadan (☞ When to Go, *below*), everything changes again; hours are roughly 9 to 2, with banks closing slightly earlier than 2.

Private businesses are generally open from 8:30 to 12:30 and 2:30 to 6:30 year-round; during Ramadan, they're generally open from 9 to 4.

GAS STATIONS

Moroccan gas stations tend to hover on the edges of cities, catering to those heading out of town; but there are plenty in cities and on the highways as well. Many are open 24 hours.

MUSEUMS & SIGHTS

Museums are generally open from about 9 to noon and 2:30 to 6 (from 9 to 4 during Ramadan).

SHOPS

Shops are open every day except Sunday from about 9 to 1 and from 3 or 4 to 7. Shops in medinas are often closed on Friday instead of Sunday. Food stores are open daily and keep longer hours. During Ramadan shops are open from about 9 to 4, with food stores staying open until just before sunset.

CAMERAS & PHOTOGRAPHY

Morocco is highly fertile ground for photography, from magnificent landscapes in the High Atlas to colorful urban souk scenes. Photographing Moroccans themselves is generally no problem, but it's best to ask first, particularly in rural areas. The best time of year for photography is spring, after the rain, when the sky is a beautiful, deep blue and wildflowers abound. Sunsets on the Atlantic coast are most brilliant in October. At some tourist attractions a self-appointed photographer will snap a Polaroid picture for you if you've forgotten your camera.

➤ PHOTO HELP: **Kodak Information Center** (☎ 800/242–2424). *Kodak Guide to Shooting Great Travel Pictures,* available in bookstores or from Fodor's Travel Publications (☎ 800/533–6478; $16.50 plus $4 shipping).

EQUIPMENT PRECAUTIONS

In the summer, when things get a bit dusty, it might be helpful to have a clear or ultraviolet filter to protect your lens.

Always **keep your film and tape out of the sun.** Carry an extra supply of batteries, and **be prepared to turn on your camera or camcorder** in transit to prove to security personnel that the device is real. Always **ask for hand inspection of film,** as it becomes clouded after successive exposures to airport X-ray machines, and **keep videotapes away from metal detectors.**

FILM & DEVELOPING

Kodak, Konica, Fuji, and other film brands are available all over Morocco, as is film processing. A roll of 36-exposure color-print film costs about 40DH. Processing is normally done within half a day. The standard prints are 3 x 5 inches.

VIDEOS

Morocco uses the VHS system. A 120-minute cassette costs about 30DH.

CAR RENTAL

The cars most commonly available in Morocco are Renaults, Peugeots, and Fiats. Many companies also rent four-wheel-drive vehicles, a boon for touring the Atlas mountains and oasis valleys. A 20% VAT (value-added tax) is levied on rental rates.

Note that you can negotiate the rental of a taxi with driver just about anywhere in Morocco for no more than the cost of a rental car from a major agency. Normally you negotiate an inclusive price for a given itinerary. The advantage is that you don't have to navigate; the disadvantage is that the driver may have his own ideas about where you should go.

➤ MAJOR AGENCIES: **Alamo** (☎ 800/ 522–9696; 020/8759–6200 in the U.K.). **Avis** (☎ 800/331–1084; 800/ 879–2847 in Canada; 02/9353–9000 in Australia; 09/525–1982 in New Zealand). **Budget** (☎ 800/527–0700; 0144/227–6266 in the U.K.). **Dollar** (☎ 800/800–6000; 020/8897–0811 in the U.K., where it is known as Eurodollar; 02/9223–1444 in Australia). **Hertz** (☎ 800/654–3001; 800/263–0600 in Canada; 0990/906090 in the U.K.; 02/9669–2444 in Australia; 03/ 358–6777 in New Zealand). **National InterRent** (☎ 800/227–3876; 0345/ 222525 in the U.K., where it is known as Europcar InterRent).

CUTTING COSTS

The best place to rent a car is Casablanca's airport, as the rental market is very competitive here—

most of the cars are new, and you can often negotiate a discount. Local companies will give you a much better price for the same car than the international agencies (even after the latter have offered "discounts"). We list the agencies with offices at Casablanca's airport; most have other branches in Casablanca itself, as well as in Rabat and Marrakesh. To get the best deal, **book through a travel agent who will shop around.**

Do **look into wholesalers,** companies that do not own fleets but rent in bulk from those that do and often offer better rates than traditional rental agencies. Payment must be completed before you leave home.

➤ LOCAL AGENCIES: Where two numbers are given, the first is for central reservations. **Always Rent a Car** (☎ 02/22–59–60, airport ☎ 02/53–81–86). **Atis-Car** (airport ☎ 02/53–81–86). **Ennasr Car** (☎ 02/22 08–13, airport ☎ 02/53–82–66). **Express Location** (☎ 02/33–94–13). **First Car International** (☎ 02/31–87–88, airport ☎ 02/53–91–77). **Janoub Tours** (☎ 02/31–87–48, airport ☎ 02/53–91–48). **Jet Car** (☎ 02/30–44–42). **Loca-Car** (airport ☎ 02/53–86–92). **Nava Tour** (☎ 02/22–06–07, airport ☎ 02/53–99–40). **Prince Car** (☎ 02/30–69–45, airport ☎ 02/53–94–92). **Renaissance Car** (☎ 02/30–03–01, airport ☎ 02/33–95–34). **Siaha Car** (airport ☎ 02/53–80–85). **Tourist Cars** (airport ☎ 02/53–97–59). **Visa Car** (☎ 07/70–97–24, airport ☎ 02/53–99–34).

➤ WHOLESALERS: **Auto Europe** (☎ 207/842–2000 or 800/223–5555, FAX 800–235–6321). **Kemwel Holiday Autos** (☎ 914/825–3000 or 800/678–0678, FAX 914/381–8847).

INSURANCE

Insurance is included in the price of a rental, with an additional charge for collision damage. Payment of a daily collision-damage waiver provides complete coverage. This is recommended in Morocco, as the risk of collision is not insignificant.

When driving a rented car, you are generally responsible for any damage to or loss of the vehicle, as well as for any property damage or personal injury you may cause. Before rent, see what coverage your personal auto-insurance policy and credit card already provide.

REQUIREMENTS & RESTRICTIONS

Most companies require drivers to be at least 25 years old and to have held a license for at least one year.

SURCHARGES

Before you pick up a car in one city and leave it in another, **ask about drop-off charges or one-way service fees,** which can be substantial. Note, too, that some rental agencies charge extra if you return the car *before* the time specified in your contract. To avoid a hefty refueling fee, **fill the tank just before you turn in the car** (bearing in mind, of course, that gas stations near the rental outlet may overcharge).

CHILDREN IN MOROCCO

Morocco is a child-friendly destination. Virtually all adults in Morocco have children, so everyone appreciates them. Having children with you will be an asset, an easy way for the locals to relate to you. It's not unusual for shopkeepers to give presents to young children while their parents are shopping.

Features that will appeal to kids include the beaches, the Temara Zoo, calèche rides in Marrakesh, and swimming pools. If you have toddlers and plan to rent a car, don't forget to **arrange for a car seat** when you reserve.

FOOD

Pizza and hamburger joints are common in major cities, but nowhere else.

FLYING

If your children are two or older, **ask about children's airfares.** As a general rule, infants under two not occupying a seat fly at greatly reduced fares or even free. If you're traveling with infants, **confirm carry-on allowances** when booking. In general, for babies charged 10% of the adult fare, you're allowed one carry-on bag and a collapsible stroller; if the flight is full, the stroller may have to be checked, or you may be limited to less baggage.

THE GOLD GUIDE / SMART TRAVEL

...d idea to use
...ildren weigh-
...ls. Airlines set
...S. carriers usu-
...child be ticketed,
...oung enough to
...eat must be
...ular seat. **Check
...y about using
safety seats d...g takeoff and land-
ing,** and since safety seats are not
allowed everywhere in the plane, get
your seat assignments early.

When reserving, **request children's
meals or a freestanding bassinet** if
you need them. Note that bulkhead
seats, where you must sit to use the
bassinet, may lack an overhead bin or
floor space for storage.

LODGING

Some hotels allow young children to
stay in their parents' room without
additional charge, and many hotel
restaurants serve lower-priced kids'
meals. Many hotels have pools and
gardens, which can help keep children
amused, and some have suites with
adjoining children's rooms.

SIGHTS & ATTRACTIONS

We indicate places that are especially
good for kids with a rubber duck in
the margin.

SUPPLIES & EQUIPMENT

Powdered baby formula is readily
available from pharmacies at 70DH–
95DH per kilogram (32DH–43DH
per pound). There are several brands;
the main one is Nestlé. Good-quality
disposable diapers are available from
supermarkets and general stores for
about 2DH each.

TRANSPORTATION

All the airlines serving Morocco offer
a standard 33% discount for children
between 2 and 12. Royal Air Maroc
and Swissair have special children's
meals and toys. Domestic flights offer
supplementary discounts for children
traveling with their families (☞ Air
Travel, *above*), and kids travel at half
price on Moroccan trains.

CONSUMER PROTECTION

Whenever shopping or buying travel
services, **pay with a major credit card**
so you can cancel payment or get

reimbursed if there's a problem. If
you're doing business with a particular company for the first time, **contact
your local Better Business Bureau and
the attorney general's offices** in your
state and the company's home state,
as well. Have any complaints been
filed? Finally, if you're buying a
package or tour, always **consider
travel insurance** that includes default
coverage (☞ Insurance, *below*).

➤ LOCATING YOUR BBB: **Council of
Better Business Bureaus** (✉ 4200
Wilson Blvd., Suite 800, Arlington,
VA 22203, ☎ 703/276–0100, FAX
703/525–8277).

CUSTOMS & DUTIES

When shopping, **keep receipts** for all
purchases. Upon reentering your
home country, **be prepared to show
customs officials what you've bought.**
If you feel a duty is incorrect or if you
object to the way your clearance was
handled, note the inspector's badge
number and ask to see a supervisor. If
the problem isn't resolved, write to
the customs authorities, beginning
with the port director at your point of
entry.

IN MOROCCO

Customs duties are very high in
Morocco, with many items subject to
various taxes that can total 80%.
You'll have no problem bringing in
personal effects, a reasonable amount
of alcoholic drinks, cigarettes, food,
or a laptop computer; there are no
hard-and-fast rules for these things,
though a friendly attitude always
helps. Large electronic items will be
taxed. (It is possible to temporarily
import large electronics—such as
laptop computers—without tax, but
the event will be marked in your
passport, and the next time you leave
the country you must take the equipment with you, even if you're only
going on a short trip to, say, Spain.)
Note that it's always easier to bring
things in person than to have them
sent to you and cleared through
customs at the post office, where even
the smallest items, such as individual
items of clothing, will be taxed.

IN AUSTRALIA

Australia residents 18 or older may
bring home $A400 worth of sou-

venirs and gifts (including jewelry), 250 cigarettes or 250 grams of tobacco, and 1,125 milliliters of alcohol (including wine, beer, and spirits). Residents under 18 may bring back $A200 worth of goods. Seeds, plants, and fruits must be declared upon arrival. Prohibited items include meat products.

➤ INFORMATION: **Australian Customs Service** (Regional Director, ✉ Box 8, Sydney, NSW 2001, ☎ 02/9213–2000, ℻ 02/9213–4000).

IN CANADA

Canadian residents who have been out of Canada for at least seven days may bring home C$500 worth of goods duty-free. If you've been away less than seven days but more than 48 hours, the duty-free allowance drops to C$200; if your trip lasts 24–48 hours, the allowance is C$50. You may not pool allowances with family members. Goods claimed under the C$500 exemption may follow you by mail; those claimed under the lesser exemptions must accompany you. Alcohol and tobacco products may be included in the seven-day and 48-hour exemptions but not in the 24-hour exemption. If you meet the age requirements of the province or territory through which you reenter Canada, you may bring in, duty-free, 1.14 liters (40 imperial ounces) of wine or liquor *or* 24 12-ounce cans or bottles of beer or ale. If you are 16 or older, you may bring in, duty-free, 200 cigarettes and 50 cigars. Check ahead of time with Revenue Canada or the Department of Agriculture for policies regarding meat products, seeds, plants, and fruits.

You may send an unlimited number of gifts worth up to C$60 each duty-free to Canada. Label the package UNSOLICITED GIFT—VALUE UNDER $60. Alcohol and tobacco are excluded.

➤ INFORMATION: **Revenue Canada** (✉ 2265 St. Laurent Blvd. S, Ottawa, Ontario K1G 4K3, ☎ 613/993–0534; 800/461–9999 in Canada).

IN NEW ZEALAND

Kiwis 17 or older may bring home $700 worth of souvenirs and gifts. Your duty-free allowance also includes 4.5 liters of wine or beer; one 1,125-milliliter bottle of spirits; and either 200 cigarettes, 250 grams of tobacco, 50 cigars, or a combination of the three up to 250 grams. Prohibited items include meat products, seeds, plants, and fruits.

➤ INFORMATION: **New Zealand Customs** (Custom House, ✉ 50 Anzac Ave., Box 29, Auckland, New Zealand, ☎ 09/359–6655, ℻ 09/359–6732).

IN THE U.K.

From countries outside the EU, including Morocco, you may bring home, duty-free, 200 cigarettes or 50 cigars; 1 liter of spirits or 2 liters of fortified or sparkling wine or liqueurs; 2 liters of still table wine; 60 milliliters of perfume; 250 milliliters of toilet water; plus £136 worth of other goods, including gifts and souvenirs. Prohibited items (from outside the EU) include meat products, seeds, plants, and fruits.

➤ INFORMATION: **HM Customs and Excise** (✉ Dorset House, Stamford St., Bromley Kent BR1 1XX, ☎ 020/7202–4227).

IN THE U.S.

U.S. residents who have been out of the country for at least 48 hours (and who have not used their $400 allowance or any part of it in the past 30 days) may bring home $400 worth of foreign goods duty-free.

U.S. residents 21 and older may bring back 1 liter of alcohol duty-free. In addition, regardless of your age, you are allowed 200 cigarettes and 100 non-Cuban cigars. Antiques, which the U.S. Customs Service defines as objects more than 100 years old, enter duty-free, as do original works of art done entirely by hand, including paintings, drawings, and sculptures.

You may also send packages home duty-free: up to $200 worth of goods for personal use, with a limit of one parcel per addressee per day (and no alcohol or tobacco products or perfume worth more than $5); label the package PERSONAL USE and attach a list of its contents and their retail value. Do not label the package UNSOLICITED GIFT, or your duty-free exemption will drop to $100. Mailed items do not affect your duty-free allowance upon your return.

➤ INFORMATION: **U.S. Customs Service** (inquiries, ✉ 1300 Pennsylvania Ave. NW, Washington, DC 20229, ☎ 202/927–6724; complaints, ✉ Office of Regulations and Rulings, 1300 Pennsylvania Ave. NW, Washington, DC 20229; registration of equipment, ✉ Registration Information, 1300 Pennsylvania Ave. NW, Washington, DC 20229, ☎ 202/927–0540).

DINING

The best of Moroccan cuisine is delectable, and French fare and seafood are widely available. Moroccan dining establishments range from outdoor food stalls to elegant restaurants, the latter of which are disproportionately expensive, with prices approaching those in Europe. Simpler, much cheaper restaurants abound. Between cities, roadside restaurants commonly offer grilled meat with bread and salad; on the coast, fried fish is an excellent buy, and you can choose your own specimen from the daily catch. Moroccans often buy meat separately at a neighboring butcher's stall, then take it to be grilled; fruit is also purchased separately. (Beverages are available wherever you eat.) The major cities have pizzerias and other non-Moroccan, non-French cuisines such as Chinese.

MEALTIMES

Moroccan hotels normally serve a Continental breakfast: coffee or tea, fruit juice, croissants, bread, butter, and jam. You can buy an equivalent meal at any of numerous cafés at a much lower price. (Many urban Moroccans have the same breakfast, with the addition of olive oil and Moroccan pancakes. In rural areas, people have soup or a kind of porridge.) The more expensive hotels have elaborate buffets. Breakfast is usually served from about 7 AM.

Lunch in Morocco tends to be a large meal, as in France. A typical lunch menu consists of salad, a main course with meat, and fruit or crème caramel. It's usually served between noon and 2:30

At home, people tend to have afternoon tea, then a light supper, often with soup, around 8. In hotels dinner is usually served from 7:30, with a menu similar to that offered at lunchtime.

During Ramadan (☞ When to Go, *below*) everything changes. All cafés and nearly all restaurants are closed during the day; the *ftir*, or breakfast, is served precisely at sunset, and most people take their main meal of the night, the *soukhour*, at about 2 AM. The main hotels, however, continue to serve meals to non-Muslim guests as usual.

PAYING

Only the pricier restaurants take credit cards. Of the major cards, MasterCard and Visa are the most widely accepted, American Express the least. It's customary to tip your server, but there are no hard-and-fast rules, as in the United States; all tips are gratefully received. Think 10DH at a cheap place, up to 10% at a posh one.

RESERVATIONS & DRESS

Reservations are always a good idea; we mention them only when they're essential. Book as far in advance as you can and reconfirm as soon as you arrive. Jacket and tie are never required.

WINE, BEER & SPIRITS

The more expensive restaurants are licensed for alcoholic drinks. Morocco produces some red wines in the vicinity of Meknes, and the national beer is Flag Special. Heineken is produced under license in Casablanca. Apart from restaurants, drinks are available at the bars of hotels classified by the government with three stars or more; you can also buy them in the alcoholic-drink sections of large supermarkets (except during Ramadan, when they're replaced with tasteful displays of dates and chocolates) and in seedy little shops in small towns.

DISABILITIES & ACCESSIBILITY

Morocco has very few special facilities for travelers with disabilities, beyond a few low-rise telephones. People are always willing to help, however, so while sightseeing is difficult, a traveler will never be left stranded.

LODGING

When discussing accessibility with a tour operator or reservations agent, **ask hard questions.** Are there any stairs, inside *or* out? Are there grab bars next to the toilet *and* in the shower/tub? How wide is the doorway to the room? To the bathroom? For the most extensive facilities, **opt for newer accommodations.**

➤ COMPLAINTS: **Disability Rights Section** (✉ U.S. Department of Justice, Civil Rights Division, Box 66738, Washington, DC 20035-6738, ☎ 202/514–0301; 800/514–0301; 202/514–0301 TTY; 800/514–0301 TTY, FAX 202/307–1198) for general complaints. **Aviation Consumer Protection Division** (☞ Air Travel, *above*) for airline-related problems. **Civil Rights Office** (✉ U.S. Department of Transportation, Departmental Office of Civil Rights, S-30, 400 7th St. SW, Room 10215, Washington, DC 20590, ☎ 202/366–4648, FAX 202/366–9371) for problems with surface transportation.

TRAVEL AGENCIES

In the United States, the Americans with Disabilities Act requires that travel firms serve the needs of all travelers, but some agencies specialize in working with people with disabilities.

➤ TRAVELERS WITH MOBILITY PROBLEMS: **Access Adventures** (✉ 206 Chestnut Ridge Rd., Rochester, NY 14624, ☎ 716/889–9096), run by a former physical-rehabilitation counselor. **Accessible Journeys** (✉ 35 W. Sellers Ave., Ridley Park, PA 19078, ☎ 610/521–0339 or 800/846–4537, FAX 610/521–6959). **Flying Wheels Travel** (✉ 143 W. Bridge St., Box 382, Owatonna, MN 55060, ☎ 507/451–5005 or 800/535–6790, FAX 507/451–1685). **Hinsdale Travel Service** (✉ 201 E. Ogden Ave., Suite 100, Hinsdale, IL 60521, ☎ 630/325–1335, FAX 630/325–1342).

DISCOUNTS & DEALS

Be a smart shopper: **compare all your options** before making decisions. A plane ticket bought with a promotional coupon from travel clubs, coupon books, and direct-mail offers may not be cheaper than the least expensive fare from a discount ticket agency. And always keep in mind that what you get is just as important as what you save.

DISCOUNT RESERVATIONS

Look into discount-reservation services with toll-free numbers, which use their buying power to get a better price on hotels, airline tickets, even car rentals. Always ask about special packages or corporate rates.

While shopping for accommodations and car rentals, **look for guaranteed exchange rates,** which protect you against a falling dollar. With your rate locked in, you won't pay more even if the price goes up in the local currency.

➤ AIRLINE TICKETS: ☎ **800/FLY–4–LESS.**

➤ HOTEL ROOMS: **Hotel Reservations Network** (☎ 800/964–6835).

PACKAGE DEALS

Don't confuse packages with guided tours. When you buy a package, you travel on your own, just as though you had planned the trip yourself. Fly/drive packages, which combine airfare and car rental, are often a good deal.

DRIVING

A car is not necessary if your trip is confined to major cities, but it's the best and sometimes the only way to explore Morocco's mountainous areas or small coastal towns. You can rent a car here (☞ *above*) or bring one into the country for up to three months. On penalty of imprisonment, you *must* have third-party insurance that's valid in Morocco in case of accident.

AUTO CLUBS

➤ IN AUSTRALIA: **Australian Automobile Association** (☎ 02/6247–7311).

➤ IN CANADA: **Canadian Automobile Association** (CAA, ☎ 613/247–0117).

➤ IN NEW ZEALAND: **New Zealand Automobile Association** (☎ 09/377–4660).

THE GOLD GUIDE / SMART TRAVEL TIPS

➤ IN THE U.K.: **Automobile Association** (AA, ☎ 0990/500–600). **Royal Automobile Club** (RAC, ☎ 0990/722–722 for membership; 0345/121–345 for insurance).

➤ IN THE U.S.: **American Automobile Association** (☎ 800/564–6222).

EMERGENCIES

In case of accident on the road, dial **177** outside cities and **19** in urban areas for police assistance. In case of fire, dial **15.** The European subscription outfit **Mondial Assistance** (☎ 02/31–31–50) is well represented in Morocco.

GASOLINE

Gas is easily available, if relatively expensive. It's heavily taxed, but the price is fixed within regions (making comparison shopping unnecessary). The gas that most cars use is known as *"super,"* the lower-octane variety as *"essence."* Unleaded fuel (*sans plomb*) is widely available but not currently necessary for local cars. Diesel fuel (*diesel*) is significantly cheaper. All gas stations provide full service; tipping is optional. If you want a receipt, ask for *un bon*. Some stations take credit cards.

ROAD CONDITIONS

Road conditions are generally very good. A network of toll freeways (*autoroutes*) runs from Casablanca north through Rabat to Larache (near Tangier) and east from Rabat to Meknes and Fez. An autoroute is under construction from Casablanca to Settat (south toward Marrakesh). These freeways are strongly recommended as they're much safer than the lesser roads.

Rush hours in the major cities are from about 8 to 9, noon to 12:30, 2:30 to 3, and 6:30 to 7. Of these, the most intense is the noon hour, followed by the evening rush.

The idea of cooperation on the road is not very well developed in Morocco; and flashing of headlights nearly always means "Give way to me" rather than the opposite. Road markings are not usually taken literally—*never* assume that oncoming traffic will not cross a white line. Most drivers are responsible enough, but the other 40% are truly dangerous. Beware of inadequate or unfamiliar lighting at night, particularly on trucks—it's not uncommon for trucks to have red lights in the front or white lights in the rear.

ROAD MAPS

Try to get a road map before you leave home, as road maps are hard to find in Morocco outside major tourist centers. Bear in mind that your map may not show the new freeways.

RULES OF THE ROAD

Traffic moves on the right side of the road. There are two main rules in Morocco; the first is "Priority to the right," an old French rule meaning that on traffic circles (roundabouts), you must always give way to traffic entering from the right.

The second is "Every man for himself."

You must carry your car registration and insurance certificate at all time so you can produce them on request (these documents are always supplied with rental cars). Morocco's speed limits, enforced by radar, are 120 kph (74 mph) on the freeway and 40 or 60 kph (25 or 37 mph) in towns. The penalty for speeding is a 400DH fine or confiscation of your driver's license.

In parking lots, give the *guardien* one or two dirhams (three at weekly markets) upon leaving. Some cities have introduced the European system of prepaid tickets from a machine, valid for a certain duration. Illegally parked cars can be wheel-clamped or towed.

WARNING

If you bring a car into Morocco, this will be noted on your passport, and you will not be able to leave the country by plane with the same passport for any reason—even in an emergency—until you complete a complicated customs procedure involving visits to various officials and the collection of various documents, none of which are available on weekdays.

ELECTRICITY

The electrical current in Morocco is 220 volts, with 50 cycles of alternating current (AC). To use electric equipment purchased in the United States, **bring a converter and adapter.** Wall outlets take the two-pin plug found in continental Europe. Power surges do occur.

If your appliances are dual-voltage, or come from the United Kingdom, you'll need only an adapter for the plug. Most laptop computers, for instance, operate equally well on 110 and 220 volts. Don't use 110-volt outlets, marked FOR SHAVERS ONLY, for high-wattage appliances such as hair dryers.

EMBASSIES

The British embassy handles consular affairs for New Zealand.

➤ CANADA: ⊠ 13 bis, Rue Jaafar As-Saddik, Agdal, Rabat, ☎ 07/67–28-80, FAX 07/77–21–87.

➤ UNITED KINGDOM: ⊠ 17, Boulevard Tour Hassan, Rabat (next to Tour Hassan), ☎ 07/72–09–05, FAX 07/70–45–31.

➤ UNITED STATES: ⊠ Avenue de Marrakech, Rabat, ☎ 07/76–22–65, FAX 07/76–23–52.

EMERGENCIES

Fire: ☎ 15. **Police:** in cities, ☎ 19. In the country (where they're known as gendarmes), ☎ 177.

ENGLISH-LANGUAGE MEDIA

BOOKS

Most bookstores in Morocco carry only French and Arabic books. We list the few that sell English-language books in the A to Z sections at the end of the Rabat and Marrakesh chapters.

NEWSPAPERS & MAGAZINES

The *International Herald Tribune* is on sale from around 6 PM on the day of its publication; pick it up at the newsstands in large hotels and major railway stations. The American magazines *Time* and *Newsweek* are available, as are the British *Daily Telegraph, Times,* and *Guardian* a day or two after publication. The English-language *Saudi Gazette* is less expensive, but it doesn't arrive in Morocco until a few days after publication.

TELEVISION & RADIO

Morocco has two TV stations, Royale Télévision Marocaine and 2M, both broadcasting in French and Arabic. On the radio, BBC World Service can be received on shortwave at about 12 MHz. Satellite TV stations such as CNN are available at the more expensive hotels.

ETIQUETTE & BEHAVIOR

Everyone is polite in Morocco, even to their sworn enemies. Moroccans shake hands with each other every time they meet. Nothing can happen without politeness: If you have a problem and you lose your temper, you give up hope of solving it. A combination of courtesy and persistence is the best approach. **Open transactions with the proper greetings** (☞ Language, *below,* and the French and Arabic Vocabulary) before getting down to business, and remember that people come first; the actions to be accomplished are secondary. Status is another key concept. Morocco is a very hierarchical society; people are dealt with according to their position in the hierarchy, not the order in which they happen to arrive. In markets, this phenomenon is modified: someone selling vegetables will deal with several customers at once, rather than one after another. If you wait meekly to be served in turn, you'll wait a long time. Finally, Moroccans do not always say what they mean: what they say can be governed by other considerations, such as the desire to please, or in the case of less charitable characters, the perception of what will work to their advantage. You don't need to take all these guidelines into account for simple transactions like buying train tickets, but they'll help in more complicated situations.

If you're invited to someone's home, do not enter until invited to do so. In more traditional homes, you'll have to leave your shoes at the door. Greet the assembled company in turn, starting with the person on your right. For all food served in a communal dish and meant to be eaten by hand, be sure to use only your right hand. Warning: Moroccan hospitality can be extremely generous, and you may need to pace your eating. It's not unusual to have two main meat dishes. Sometimes you can determine the number of courses to come by counting the number of tablecloths; one is removed with each course. It's customary to socialize before the meal rather than afterwards, so food is not served upon guests' arrival, and it's acceptable to leave immediately after tea at the end of the meal. For more on socializing with the locals in highly traditional rural areas, *see* Exploring the High Atlas *in* Chapter 7.

Regarding dress: Barring only the beach, shorts are not acceptable for either sex anywhere in Morocco, even in the hottest weather. Apart from this, casual clothing is quite acceptable.

With the exception of the Hassan II Mosque in Casablanca, non-Muslims may not enter mosques.

BUSINESS ETIQUETTE

Business appointments are not usually scheduled more than a week in advance and should be reconfirmed by phone the day before. Schedules are often changed at the last moment if something of higher priority comes up, so the prudent business traveler will always have contingency plans in case meetings don't materialize. Punctuality is not a virtue: Whatever time you're given is approximate. Don't expect to keep a series of tightly scheduled appointments. Never start a meeting by coming immediately to the point of business; always start with general conversation. Sensitive questions are approached politely and indirectly. Debt recovery in particular must be approached in a tactful way. Business cards are always appreciated.

GAY & LESBIAN TRAVEL

Despite famous gay enclaves in the Tangier and Marrakesh of yore, homosexual acts are strictly illegal in Morocco, and travelers have been imprisoned as a consequence.

➤ GAY- AND LESBIAN-FRIENDLY TRAVEL AGENCIES (U.S.): **Different Roads Travel** (⊠ 8383 Wilshire Blvd., Suite 902, Beverly Hills, CA 90211, ☎ 323/651–5557 or 800/429–8747, FAX 323/651–3678). **Kennedy Travel** (⊠ 314 Jericho Turnpike, Floral Park, NY 11001, ☎ 516/352–4888 or 800/

237–7433, FAX 516/354–8849). **Now Voyager** (⊠ 4406 18th St., San Francisco, CA 94114, ☎ 415/626–1169 or 800/255–6951, FAX 415/626–8626). **Skylink Travel and Tour** (⊠ 1006 Mendocino Ave., Santa Rosa, CA 95401, ☎ 707/546–9888 or 800/225–5759, FAX 707/546–9891) serves lesbian travelers.

HEALTH

Morocco poses few serious health hazards; there is no malaria or yellow fever. Hepatitis, however, does crop up.

If you're fair-skinned, **use sunscreen before prolonged spells in the sun,** especially in the mountains.

➤ HEALTH WARNINGS: **National Centers for Disease Control** (CDC, National Center for Infectious Diseases, Division of Quarantine, Traveler's Health Section, ⊠ 1600 Clifton Rd. NE, M/S E-03, Atlanta, GA 30333, ☎ 888/232–3228, FAX 888/232–3299, www.cdc.gov/travel).

FOOD & DRINK

The tap water in cities is safe to drink. The quality of taste varies by city; it's good in Fez, for example, while in Rabat it's heavily chlorinated. Mineral water is available everywhere.

Food should not pose a health problem, though people unaccustomed to traveling might require a temporary adjustment to the local microbial flora. The only thing to watch out for in this regard is undercooked meat at roadside restaurants.

Mild cases of traveler's diarrhea may respond to Imodium (known generically as loperamide) or Pepto-Bismol (not as strong), both of which can be purchased over the counter. The local brand Metagliz is another digestive aid. Drink plenty of purified water or tea—chamomile (*camomile*) is a good folk remedy. In severe cases, rehydrate yourself with a salt-sugar solution (½ teaspoon salt [*sel*] and 4 tablespoons sugar [*sucre*] per quart of water).

MEDICAL PLANS

No one plans to get sick while traveling, but it happens, so **consider sign-**

THE GOLD GUIDE / SMART TRAVEL TIPS

ing up with a medical-assistance
company. Members get doctor referrals, emergency evacuation or repatri-
ation, hot lines for medical
consultation, cash for emergencies,
and other assistance.

➤ MEDICAL-ASSISTANCE COMPANIES:
AEA International SOS (✉ 8 Ne-
shaminy Interplex, Suite 207,
Trevose, PA 19053, ☎ 215/245–4707
or 800/523–6586, FAX 215/244–9617;
✉ 12 Chemin Riantbosson, 1217
Meyrin 1, Geneva, Switzerland, ☎
4122/785–6464, FAX 4122/785–6424;
✉ 331 N. Bridge Rd., 17-00, Odeon
Towers, Singapore 188720, ☎ 65/
338–7800, FAX 65/338–7611).

OVER-THE-COUNTER REMEDIES

Nearly all medicines, including antibi-
otics and painkillers, are available
over the counter at Moroccan pharmacies. (The sole exceptions are
psychoactive drugs such as Valium,
which are strictly controlled.) Aspirin
is sold as Aspro; ibuprofen is sold as
Analgyl, Algantyl, or Tabalon. Ac-
etaminophen, the generic equivalent
of Tylenol, is not available.

Pharmacies, which are ubiquitous, are
marked PHARMACIE in green and are
easily recognizable by a green crescent
or cross.

PESTS

Mosquitoes can be a nuisance in
summer, but they're not a health
hazard. The same is true of cock-
roaches.

HOLIDAYS

The two most important religious
holidays in Morocco are **Aïd el Fitr**
(early January), which marks the end
of the monthlong Ramadan fast, and
Aïd el Adha (mid-March), the sheep-
sacrifice feast commemorating the
prophet Ibrahim (Abraham)'s absolu-
tion from the obligation to sacrifice
his son. Both are two-day festivals
during which all offices, banks, and
museums are closed. Many craftsmen
and private traders take even longer
holidays. Public transportation is very
busy around these periods; hotels
operate as they normally do. The
other religious holiday is the one-day
Aïd el Mouloud (early to mid-June),

commemorating the birthday of the
prophet Mohammed. Ramadan is not
a holiday in this round-the-clock
sense, but it does change the pace of
life; for details, *see* Business Hours,
above, and When to Go, *below.*
Because the Muslim calendar is lunar,
the dates for Ramadan and other
religious holidays shift back 11 days
each year.

The most important political holiday
is **Aïd el Arch,** or Throne Day (July
30), which commemorates the coronation of King Mohammed VI.
Throne Day is a good time to see a
fantasia (☞ Chapter 6), a fine display
of horsemanship performed around
the kingdom that day. Morocco's
other holidays are: **January 1,** New
Year's Day; **January 11,** anniversary
of the proclamation of Moroccan
independence; **May 1,** Labor Day;
May 23, National Day; **July 9,** Youth
Day; **August 14,** Oued ed Dahab,
otherwise known as Allegiance Day;
August 20, anniversary of the revolu-
tion of the king and the people
(against the French); **November 6,**
commemoration of the Green March,
Morocco's reclamation of the western
Sahara in 1975; **November 18,** Independence Day.

INSURANCE

The most useful travel insurance is a
comprehensive policy that includes
coverage for trip cancellation and
interruption, default, trip delay, and
medical expenses (with a waiver for
preexisting conditions).

Without insurance you will lose all or
most of your money if you cancel
your trip, regardless of the reason.
Default insurance covers you if your
tour operator, airline, or cruise line
goes out of business. Trip-delay
insurance covers expenses that arise
because of bad weather or mechanical
delays. When comparing policies,
study the fine print.

If you're traveling internationally, a
key component of travel insurance is
coverage for medical bills incurred if
you get sick on the road. Such expenses are not generally covered by
Medicare or private policies. British
and Australian citizens need extra
medical coverage when traveling

THE GOLD GUIDE / SMART TRAVEL TIPS

overseas; U.K. residents can buy a policy valid for most vacations taken that year (but check coverage for preexisting conditions).

Always **buy a travel policy directly from the insurance company.** If you buy it from a cruise line, airline, or tour operator that goes out of business, you probably will not be covered for the agency or operator's default, a major risk. Before you make any purchase, **review your existing health and homeowner's policies** to find what they cover away from home.

➤ TRAVEL INSURERS: In the U.S.: **Access America** (✉ 6600 W. Broad St., Richmond, VA 23230, ☎ 804/285–3300 or 800/284–8300), **Travel Guard International** (✉ 1145 Clark St., Stevens Point, WI 54481, ☎ 715/345–0505 or 800/826–1300). In Canada: **Voyager Insurance** (✉ 44 Peel Center Dr., Brampton, Ontario L6T 4M8, ☎ 800/668–4342 in Canada).

➤ INSURANCE INFORMATION: In the U.K.: the **Association of British Insurers** (✉ 51–55 Gresham St., London EC2V 7HQ, ☎ 020/7600–3333, FAX 020/7696–8999). In Australia: the **Insurance Council of Australia** (☎ 03/9614–1077, FAX 03/9614–7924).

LANGUAGE

The main spoken language in Morocco is Moroccan Arabic, a compacted Arabic that has fewer vowels than other dialects and includes a number of Spanish and French words. There are also three Berber languages—Tarifit, in the northern Rif; Tamazight, in the Middle Atlas and eastern High Atlas; and Tashelhit, in the western High Atlas, Souss Valley, and Anti-Atlas—none of which is written. French is very widely spoken. There is no difference between the French spoken here and that used in France, except perhaps the presence of fewer colloquialisms, so any standard French phrase book will serve you well. English is more and more widely spoken; there is usually no problem communicating in English at hotels in trafficked areas.

The official written languages are Arabic and French, and most signs

are written in both, so you don't need to know Arabic script to find your way around. Numerals within Arabic script are the same Arabic numerals we use in English (unlike those used in Middle Eastern countries).

It's difficult to learn Moroccan Arabic on location, because unless you look like a Moroccan, you will nearly always be addressed in French. Still, it's useful to know some key words for proper greetings and for situations where no one speaks French. For a primer, *see* the French and Arabic Vocabulary at the end of this book.

SELF-STUDY

If you want to learn or brush up on French, a phrase book and set of language tapes can get you started.

➤ PHRASE BOOKS & CASSETTES: *Fodor's French for Travelers* (☎ 800/733–3000 in the U.S.; 800/668–4247 in Canada; $7 for phrase book, $16.95 for audio set).

LANGUAGE PROGRAMS

Courses in Moroccan Arabic are taught at the **American Language Center** in Rabat, Casablanca, Fez, and Marrakesh. The center in Fez, in collaboration with some American universities, also teaches classical Arabic through its ALIF (Arabic Language in Fez—*alif* is the first letter of the Arabic alphabet) program.

The **Centre Culturel Français** offers French courses in all major cities.

➤ LANGUAGE PROGRAMS: **American Language Center** (✉ 4, Rue Tanger, Rabat, ☎ 07/76–71–03; ✉ 1, Place de la Fraternité, Casablanca, ☎ 02/48–61–01; ✉ 2, Rue Ahmed Hiba, Fez, ☎ 05/62–48–50; ✉ 3, Impasse du Moulin, Gueliz, Marrakesh, ☎ 04/44–72–59). **Centre Culturel Français** (✉ 123, Boulevard Zerktouni, Casablanca, ☎ 02/23–79–14).

LODGING

We always list a hotel's facilities, but we don't specify whether they cost extra: when pricing accommodations, always ask what's included and what carries additional fees. Assume that hotels operate on the European Plan (with no meals) unless we note that breakfast or half-board (*demi-*

pension; two out of three meals) is included.

APARTMENT & VILLA RENTALS

If you want a home base that's roomy enough for a family and comes with cooking facilities, **consider a furnished rental.** These can save you money, especially if you're traveling with a group. Home-exchange directories sometimes list rentals as well as exchanges.

➤ INTERNATIONAL AGENTS: **Rent-a-Home International** (⊠ 7200 34th Ave. NW, Seattle, WA 98117, ☎ 206/789–9377 or 800/964–1891, FAX 206/789–9379). **Villas and Apartments Abroad** (⊠ 1270 Avenue of the Americas, 15th floor, New York, NY 10020, ☎ 212/759–1025 or 800/433–3020, FAX 212/897–5039). **Villas International** (⊠ 950 Northgate Dr., Suite 206, San Rafael, CA 94903, ☎ 415/499–9490 or 800/221–2260, FAX 415/499–9491). **Hideaways International** (⊠ 767 Islington St., Portsmouth, NH 03801, ☎ 603/430–4433 or 800/843–4433, FAX 603/430–4444; membership $99).

CAMPING

There are campgrounds at many coastal resorts and near some of the major cities. Sanitary facilities can be very rudimentary. Note that local use of campgrounds is highly seasonal: Massive numbers of people use them in July and August, and nobody uses them the rest of the year. Off-season, the scene can be very tasteful.

Camping in uninhabited parts of the Atlas mountains in the summer can be an exhilarating experience.

HOSTELS

Regardless of your age, you can **save on lodging costs by staying at hostels.** In some 5,000 locations in more than 70 countries around the world, Hostelling International (HI), the umbrella group for a number of national youth-hostel associations, offers single-sex, dorm-style beds and, at many hostels, couples rooms and family accommodations. Membership in any HI national hostel association, open to travelers of all ages, allows you to stay in HI-affiliated hostels at member rates (one-year membership

is about $25 for adults; hostels run about U.S.$10–$25 per night). Members also have priority if the hostel is full; they're eligible for discounts around the world, even on rail and bus travel in some countries.

➤ ORGANIZATIONS: **Australian Youth Hostel Association** (⊠ 10 Mallett St., Camperdown, NSW 2050, ☎ 02/9565–1699, FAX 02/9565–1325). **Hostelling International—American Youth Hostels** (⊠ 733 15th St. NW, Suite 840, Washington, DC 20005, ☎ 202/783–6161, FAX 202/783–6171). **Hostelling International—Canada** (⊠ 400–205 Catherine St., Ottawa, Ontario K2P 1C3, ☎ 613/237–7884, FAX 613/237–7868). **Youth Hostel Association of England and Wales** (⊠ Trevelyan House, 8 St. Stephen's Hill, St. Albans, Hertfordshire AL1 2DY, ☎ 01727/855215 or 01727/845047, FAX 01727/844126). **Youth Hostels Association of New Zealand** (⊠ Box 436, Christchurch, New Zealand, ☎ 03/379–9970, FAX 03/365–4476). Membership in the U.S. is $25, in Canada C$26.75, in the U.K. £9.30, in Australia $44, and in New Zealand $24.

HOTELS

Hotels are classified by the Moroccan government with one to five stars, plus an added category for five-star luxury hotels. In hotels with three or more stars, all rooms have private bathrooms, and there is a bar on-site. Air-conditioning is common in three-star hotels in Fez and Marrakesh and in all five-star hotels. Standards do vary, though; it's possible to find a nice two-star hotel or, occasionally, a four-star hotel without hot water. In the same vein, hotels that are beneath the star system altogether—"unclassified"—can also be satisfactory.

Prices for each government category are fixed within each region of the country and are generally very reasonable (except in the five-star luxury hotels, which have no price ceilings). Note that the large business hotels of this category in Casablanca and Rabat will systematically discount their published rates by applying "corporate rates" on the mention of the name of a company. It may be possible to negotiate a discount at

THE GOLD GUIDE / SMART TRAVEL TIPS

other hotels for a long stay out of season or for a large group. The most famous luxury hotels are the **Palais Jamai,** which overlooks the medina in Fez, and **La Mamounia,** residence of the rich and famous, in Marrakesh.

The hotels we list are the cream of the crop in each of our price categories (which do *not* parallel the Moroccan government's star system). Because prices vary so widely from region to region, each chapter in this book has its own price chart. All hotels have private bath unless otherwise noted.

Hotels in Marrakesh tend to fill up around Christmas and the New Year. Lodging throughout the country is heavily booked around Easter, when Europeans appear in droves.

HOUSE RENTALS

In Marrakesh you can rent well-furnished traditional houses (*riads*) in the medina, a unique opportunity to experience traditional Moroccan architecture. Contact **Marrakech Medina** (✉ 72, Derb Arssat Aouzal [Bab Doukala], Marrakesh, ☎ 04/44–24–48, FAX 04/39–10–71; ☞ Web sites, *below*).

MAIL & SHIPPING

Outgoing airmail is completely reliable. Note that if you mail letters at the main sorting office of any city (usually situated on Avenue Mohamed V), they will arrive several days sooner than if you mail them from elsewhere, sometimes in as little as three days to Europe. Airmail letters to North America take between 5 and 12 days; to Europe, between 3 and 10 days; and to Australasia, about two weeks.

E-MAIL

In major cities, particularly Casablanca and Rabat, you can check Web-based E-mail in various cyber-cafés for a surprisingly small fee, usually about 15DH.

OVERNIGHT SERVICES

Within Morocco, the Express Mail Service (**EMS,** or **Poste Rapide**) offers overnight delivery from main post offices to major cities. There is also same-day service between Rabat and Casablanca. The international EMS,

or Poste Rapide, takes three to five days from Morocco to Europe. **DHL** (✉ 40, Avenue France, Agdal, Rabat, ☎ 07/77–14–57 and ✉ 52, Boulevard Abdelmoumen, Casablanca, ☎ 02/23–15–23) is quicker but more than double the price. **United Parcel Service** operates in Casablanca (✉ 210, Boulevard Mohamed Zerktouni, ☎ 02/48–36–36).

When sending packages to Morocco by courier, bear in mind that only two courier services are represented outside Casablanca: the post office's **Express Mail Service** and **DHL** (☞ *above*). If you use another service, you may find (regardless of whatever the office tells you) that your recipient is only informed of the arrival of a package via postcard from Casablanca—and is then expected to show up in Casa to collect it. Note that if anything other than documents is sent to Morocco via courier, the package will be delayed, and the recipient will have to pay a customs broker and customs duty. The minimum time for a courier package to arrive is three days from the United Kingdom, five days from North America.

POSTAL RATES

For a 20-gram airmail letter or postcard, rates are 9.8DH to the United States or Canada, 6DH to the United Kingdom, and 13DH to Australia or New Zealand.

RECEIVING MAIL

You can have letters sent to poste restante—just note that about 2% of incoming mail gets lost, and letters with cash in them always get lost. Receiving packages by mail is not recommended, since you often have to pay customs duties almost equal to the value of the goods (☞ Customs & Duties, *above*).

SHIPPING PARCELS

Sending packages *out* of the country is easy enough. Go to the Colis Postaux (parcel post office; one in each town), where you can also buy boxes. You'll need to fill in some forms and show the package to customs officials before wrapping it. Airmail parcels reach North America in about two weeks, Europe in about 10 days. For surface mail count on from three to six months to North America, from one to three months to Europe. Airmail is more reliable. DHL offers a special rate for handicraft items shipped overseas, and some carpet stores can arrange shipping.

MONEY

Costs in Morocco are low compared to both North America and Europe. Fruit and vegetables, public transportation, and labor are very cheap. (Cars, gasoline, and electronic goods, on the other hand, are relatively pricey.) Sample costs are in U.S. dollars:

Meal in cheap restaurant, $5; meal in expensive restaurant, $25; cup of coffee in café, 50¢; double room in three-star hotel, $35; liter of gasoline 70¢; train from Casablanca to Marrakesh (230 km [142 mi]) $15 first class, $11 second class; short urban taxi ride, $1. Prices throughout this guide are given for adults; reduced fees are usually available for children, but not students or seniors. For information on taxes, *see* Taxes, *below.*

ATMS

Automatic teller machines (ATMs) are attached to banks in major cities, and there's one in the arrivals hall at Casablanca's airport. **BMCE** and **Wafabank** belong to the Cirrus and Plus networks. The machines also give cash advances on Visa and MasterCard. ATM withdrawals impose a slight premium on the exchange rate compared to cash or traveler's checks.

CREDIT CARDS

Credit cards are accepted at the pricier hotels, restaurants, and souvenir shops. In all but the top hotels, however, the vendor occasionally has problems obtaining authorization or forms, so it's prudent to have an alternative form of payment available at all times. The most widely accepted cards are MasterCard and Visa; American Express is less widespread.

We use the following abbreviations throughout this book: **AE,** American Express; **DC,** Diner's Club; **MC,** MasterCard; and **V,** Visa.

CURRENCY

The national currency is the dirham (DH), which is divided into 100 centimes. There are bills for 20, 50, 100, and 200 dirhams, and coins for 1, 5, and 10 dirhams and 5, 10, and 20 centimes. You might hear some people refer to centimes as francs; others count money in *"rials,"* which are equivalent to 5 centimes each. A *"million"* is a million centimes, or 10,000 dirhams.

CURRENCY EXCHANGE

At press time, one U.S. dollar was equivalent to about 9.5 dirhams, one pound sterling to about 15.5 dirhams. The exchange rate is the same at all banks, including those at the airport. Moroccan law prohibits the exportation of dirhams, and the few places that sell dirhams outside the country are likely to have less favorable rates. You can change dirhams back into U.S. dollars or French francs (only) at the airport upon departure, as long as you've kept the exchange receipts from your time of entry.

➤ EXCHANGE SERVICES: **International Currency Express** (☎ 888/842–0880 on East Coast; 888/278–6628 on West Coast). **Thomas Cook Currency Services** (☎ 800/287–7362 for phone orders and store locations).

TRAVELER'S CHECKS

Traveler's checks are best used in cities. They can be exchanged for dirhams at major banks and at the airport.

Lost or stolen traveler's checks can usually be replaced within 24 hours; to ensure a speedy refund, buy your own traveler's checks—don't let someone else pay for them. The person who bought the checks should make the call to request a refund, and irregularities can cause delays.

OUTDOOR ACTIVITIES & SPORTS

CAVING

Morocco has one of the largest underground complexes of caverns in Africa, in the Friouato Caves National Park just southwest of Taza. Guides are available at the site; ☞ Chapter 4.

THE GOLD GUIDE / SMART TRAVEL TIPS

GOLF

Golf is a royal sport here, with the result that excellent golf courses dot the kingdom. Most can rent you clubs and caddies. The **Royal Moroccan Golf Federation** is headquartered at Rabat's Royal Golf Dar Es-Salam (☏ 07/75–56–36).

HIKING AND TREKKING

The High Atlas mountains are ground zero for Moroccan trekking. The range runs from Agadir to Taza, and you can walk this entire way. The steep mountains are separated by deep valleys, which often hide Berber villages, and there is an extensive network of paths. You can hire mules to carry your packs if you like, and stay in villages along the way rather than camp; in summer you can camp in wild high places such as the Tichka Plateau, bathe in beautiful mountain rivers, and at night see the stars as you've never seen them before. Djebel Toubkal, the highest mountain in North Africa, presents a relatively straightforward ascent; some other peaks are more challenging. For gentler walks the Middle Atlas is ideal—you can easily arrange day walks on beautiful hills and plateaus and through cedar forests. Detailed topographical maps are available from the **Division de la Cartographie** (✉ 31, Avenue Moulay Hassan, Rabat).

HORSEBACK RIDING

Like golf, horseback riding is a royal sport. Many equestrian clubs are for members only, but not all; and several hotels can arrange rides for their guests. This is a lovely way to explore just about any of Morocco's various terrains.

RUNNING

A winter marathon, the Marathon des Sables, is run every year in the desert, and Rabat hosts a half-marathon in the spring. The long, sandy beaches of the Atlantic coast make an excellent training ground.

SKIING

Unbeknownst to many, Morocco has several ski resorts, one at **Oukaimeden,** in the High Atlas near Marrakesh, and a few near **Ifrane,** in the Middle Atlas. The season comprises roughly January and February, but in a good year it can start in December. It's usually longer in Oukaimeden. Both resorts have chairlifts and rent toboggans as well as skis.

SURFING

Surfing waves are excellent along much of the Atlantic coast, particularly at Skhirat Plage (Skhirat Beach) and near Agadir and El Oualidia.

TENNIS

Tennis is popular with both Moroccans and visitors. Many larger hotels have their own courts.

PACKING

Demand for baggage carts in airports is often greater than supply. You won't find them in train and bus stations, but porters are often available. As is true anywhere, traveling light gives you more flexibility.

Casual clothes are fine in Morocco; there's no need to bring formal apparel. Everywhere but the beach, however, you'll need to wear trousers or long skirts rather than shorts.

In summer, the heaviest thing you'll need is a light sweater, unless you're bringing full hiking gear to the mountains. Bring sunscreen year-round. In winter Morocco is not terribly hot, and since the season is short, many buildings are not heated—bring warm clothes.

In your carry-on luggage **bring an extra pair of eyeglasses or contact lenses and enough of any medication you take** to last the entire trip. You may also want your doctor to write a spare prescription using the drug's generic name, since brand names may vary from country to country. In luggage to be checked, **never pack prescription drugs or valuables,** and to avoid customs delays, carry medications in their original packaging. And don't forget to copy down and carry the appropriate contacts for refunds of lost traveler's checks.

CHECKING LUGGAGE

The number of carry-on bags you can take with you is up to your airline; most allow two. Make sure that everything you want to carry on board will fit under your seat, and get to the gate early. If you're assigned a seat at the back of the plane, you'll probably board first, while the overhead bins are still empty.

On international flights, baggage allowances may be determined not by piece but by weight—generally 88 pounds (40 kilograms) in first class, 66 pounds (30 kilograms) in business class, and 44 pounds (20 kilograms) in economy.

Airline liability for baggage on international flights is limited to $9.07 per pound ($20 per kilogram) for checked baggage (roughly $640 per 70-pound bag) and $400 per passenger for unchecked baggage. You can buy additional coverage when you check in for about $10 per $1,000 of coverage, but this excludes a rather extensive list of items, shown on your airline ticket.

Before departure **itemize your bags' contents** and their worth, and label the bags with your name, address, and phone number (if you use your home address, cover it so potential thieves can't see it readily). **Pack a copy of your itinerary inside each bag.** Before you check in, **make sure each bag is correctly tagged** with the destination airport's three-letter code (Casablanca, CMN; Rabat, RBA; Marrakesh, RAK; Fez, FEZ; Tangier, TNG; Ouarzazate, OZZ; Oujda, OUD; Agadir, AGA; Laayoune, EUN). If your bags arrive damaged or fail to arrive at all, file a written report with the airline before leaving the airport.

PASSPORTS & VISAS

Make two photocopies of your passport's data page, one for someone at home and another for you, carried separately from your passport. If you lose your passport, promptly call your nearest embassy or consulate and the local police.

ENTERING MOROCCO

Australian, British Canadian, New Zealand, and U.S. citizens with a valid passport can enter Morocco and stay up to 90 days without a visa.

PASSPORT OFFICES

The best times to apply for or renew a passport are fall and winter. Before

any trip, check your passport's expiration date and renew it as soon as possible if necessary.

➤ AUSTRALIAN CITIZENS: **Australian Passport Office** (☎ 131–232).

➤ CANADIAN CITIZENS: **Passport Office** (☎ 819/994–3500 or 800/567–6868).

➤ NEW ZEALAND CITIZENS: **New Zealand Passport Office** (☎ 04/494–0700 for information on how to apply; 04/474–8000 or 0800/225–050 in New Zealand for information on applications already submitted).

➤ U.K. CITIZENS: **London Passport Office** (☎ 0990/210–410) for fees and documentation requirements and to request an emergency passport.

➤ U.S. CITIZENS: **National Passport Information Center** (☎ 900/225–5674; calls are 35¢ per minute for automated service, $1.05 per minute for operator service).

REST ROOMS

All train stations and freeway service stations have toilets, which are normally well maintained. It's customary to tip the attendant one dirham. Gas stations have toilets, but these are of variable quality. All cafés are obliged to have them as well. Bring your own toilet paper in all these cases—it's easy to find in stores, but only hotels can be counted on to provide it in bathrooms.

SAFETY

Morocco is a safe destination. Violent crime is relatively rare, particularly compared to the United States. People who pester you to hire them as guides in places like Fez are a nuisance, but not a threat to your safety.

WOMEN TRAVELERS

Women traveling without men should not be at any substantive risk if they dress modestly and take the same precautions they would take in any large and foreign city. Unwanted attention is almost inevitable, but you can decrease the irritation level by avoiding shorts and miniskirts completely, anywhere other than the beach. Stick to long-sleeve shirts, loose-fitting pants, and long skirts or dresses.

THE GOLD GUIDE / SMART TRAVEL TIPS

SENIOR-CITIZEN TRAVEL

To qualify for age-related discounts with international car-rental agencies or chain hotels, **mention your senior-citizen status up front** when making reservations, not when checking out.

➤ EDUCATIONAL PROGRAMS: **Elderhostel** (✉ 75 Federal St., 3rd floor, Boston, MA 02110, ☎ 877/426–8056, FAX 877/426–2166). **Interhostel** (✉ University of New Hampshire, 6 Garrison Ave., Durham, NH 03824, ☎ 603/862–1147 or 800/733–9753, FAX 603/862–1113).

SHOPPING

You *must* negotiate when purchasing Moroccan specialties like carpets, pottery, brassware, and leather goods. There's no rule for the percentage by which you should aim to reduce the price, because some vendors start with a decent price and can only be reasonably expected to reduce the price by 10% or 20%, whereas others start by inflating the price ten- or twenty-fold. The only way to be confident is to have an idea of the market price before you start. An average-quality 3 x 6 carpet sells for around $100–$140, *not* $1,000. A good-quality leather jacket might cost $300, a cheaper one half that. For more on bargaining, *see* "The Moroccan Zen of Bargaining" box *in* Chapter 6.

Guides take a commission of about 30% on items purchased in their presence, a scheme that has a correspondingly inflationary effect on the price. Any kind of intermediary will in fact inflate the price; only when you deal directly with the proprietor can you expect a fair deal. Beware of people who try to bring you to a shop on another pretext, such as "Come see my brother's workshop."

KEY DESTINATIONS

Marrakesh has endless tempting souks in its medina. Fez is stuffed to the gills with handicrafts, but it's harder here to avoid intermediaries. You may find it easier to shop in places that are not such tourist magnets, like Rabat.

Once you've honed your bargaining skills, you can get the best prices for carpets at the Tuesday carpet souks in

Khemisset and Azrou (Khemisset has a better selection). For the best values in pottery, go to Safi. Salé also has pottery, and Fez makes a finer blue variety.

SMART SOUVENIRS

You'll find no shortage of temptations, but some particularly authentic items are: a brass plate engraved with a traditional geometric design (not a camel); a beautiful blue Fassi ceramic bowl; an embroidered tablecloth; and something leather—a bag, case, or belt.

WATCH OUT

Americans on package tours to the Imperial Cities are systematically taken the day after arrival (when they're still jet-lagged) to a large house in Fez piled high with Moroccan carpets. Here they are encouraged to buy carpets at the same prices in dollars for which they usually sell in dirhams—*10 times* the market rate. The price is often charged to a credit card, and buyers can be made to sign a form saying they won't complain later (that is, when they learn the market price). Keep your eyes wide open for this swindle.

SIGHTSEEING GUIDES

There are two kinds of guides: official and unofficial. Official guides have a badge to prove it and cost about 300DH a day. Your hotel can arrange an official guide for you. Unofficial guides will approach you when you emerge from your hotel or around popular tourist sights; their rate is negotiable, and you should fix it in advance. In places like Fez you'll find you need a guide just to protect you from being approached by other guides. In smaller towns no guide is necessary. Remember that all guides take a commission on any durable goods you buy in their presence.

STUDENT TRAVELERS

➤ STUDENT IDs & SERVICES: In the U.S.: **Council on International Educational Exchange** (CIEE; ✉ 205 E. 42nd St., 14th floor, New York, NY 10017, ☎ 212/822–2600 or 888/268–6245, FAX 212/822–2699), for mail orders only. In Canada: **Travel Cuts** (✉ 187 College St., Toronto,

Ontario M5T 1P7, ☎ 416/979–2406 or 800/667–2887).

TAXES

Hotel taxes are low, currently 12DH per person per night at four-star hotels, less at cheaper hotels.

There are no airport taxes above those originally levied on the ticket price.

VALUE-ADDED TAX (VAT)

The VAT (called TVA in Morocco) is generally 20%. It is not refundable.

TAXIS

Moroccan taxis take two forms: *petits taxis,* small taxis confined to city limits, and *grands taxis,* large taxis that travel between cities.

Petits taxis are color-coded according to city and cannot go outside city limits—in Casablanca and Fez they're red, in Rabat they're blue, in Marrakesh they're beige, and so on. These can be hailed anywhere but can only take a maximum of three passengers, including infants. The fare is metered and not expensive: usually 5DH–30DH for a short- or medium-length trip. Taxis often pick up additional passengers en route (up to the limit of three), so if you can't find an empty cab, try hailing a taxi with one or two people in it and see if your destination is near theirs. At busy train stations drivers sometimes wait until they have three people going to similar destinations.

Grands taxis are usually old Mercedes cars. Called "grand taxis" in English by Morocco's anglophone community, they travel fixed routes between cities and in the country. Two people sit in front with the driver, and four sit, a little cramped, in the back. The worst seat is the one next to the driver, as there's no backrest and no security in case of an accident. Fares for these shared rides are inexpensive, sometimes as little as 5DH per person for a short trip. Drivers usually wait until the taxi is full before departing. You can also charter a grand taxi for trips between cities, in which case there's no limit on the price—it needs to be negotiated in advance and can be somewhat expensive. For trips within cities, petits taxis are all you need.

TELEPHONES

Morocco has an efficient phone system; you can call anywhere without difficulty.

COUNTRY & AREA CODES

The country code for Morocco is 212. The area codes are: Casablanca, 02; Settat and El Jadida, 03; Marrakesh, 04; Fez and Meknes, 05; Oujda, 06; Rabat, 07; Laayoune, 08; Tangier, 09; mobile phones, 01. When dialing a Moroccan number from overseas, drop the initial 0 from the area code. To call locally, within the area code, just dial the number.

For international calls *from* Morocco, dial **00** followed by the country code. Country codes: U.S. and Canada, 1; U.K., 44; Australia, 61; New Zealand, 64. Note that the cost of an international call dialed directly from a hotel room (as opposed to one made with a phone card or through a *téléboutique*) is ridiculously inflated, sometimes threefold.

DIRECTORY & OPERATOR INFORMATION

Access directory assistance by dialing **16** from anywhere in the country. Many operators speak English, and they all speak French. Phone numbers are given in French as a series of three two-digit numbers.

Four printed directories divide the country by area codes, but these are not published annually, so they tend to be out of date. The annual **Télécontact**, available from some bookstalls and the directory's office at 402, Boulevard Zerktouni, Casablanca (☎ 02/20–92–83), lists businesses in the area between El Jadida to Kenitra, the country's main business and industrial area. It's not complete, but it's a good starting point.

LONG-DISTANCE SERVICES

AT&T and MCI access codes make international calls relatively convenient, but you may find the local access number for your phone card blocked in some hotel rooms (since the hotel profits handsomely when you dial direct). If this happens, ask the hotel operator to connect you. If the hotel operator can't comply, ask for an international operator or dial the international operator yourself. One way to improve your odds of getting connected to your long-distance carrier is to travel with more than one company's calling card (a hotel may block AT&T, for example, but not MCI). As an alternative, you can use a *téléboutique* (☞ *below*) or pay phone.

➤ ACCESS CODES: **AT&T Direct** (☎ 002–11–0011). **MCI WorldCom** (☎ 00–211–0012). Sprint does not serve Morocco.

PUBLIC PHONES

Téléboutiques are all over Morocco. These little blue shops provide well-maintained pay phones and, if you don't have a phone card, change. The cheapest way for you and your loved ones to connect: call from a téléboutique, give your hotel phone number and room number, and take the call back at the hotel. Rates from the United States and United Kingdom are much less than rates from Morocco.

Some private companies provide European-style card phones in the centers of Marrakesh and Casablanca and at Casablanca's airport. Some train stations also have card phones; you can buy cards for these at the ticket windows.

GSM cellular phones with international roaming capability work well in the cities and along major communication routes.

TIME

Morocco observes Greenwich mean time year-round (five hours ahead of eastern standard time), so most of the year it's on the same clock as the United Kingdom: five hours ahead of New York and one hour behind Continental Europe. In the summer, during daylight savings time, Morocco is one hour behind the United Kingdom, four hours ahead of New York, and two hours behind Continental Europe.

TIPPING

Waiters in proper restaurants are always tipped up to 10% of the bill. At informal cafés, the tip is normally one or two dirhams per person in the dining party. Porters, hotel or other-

wise, will appreciate 5 or 10 dirhams. It's customary to give small tips of one or two dirhams to people such as parking and rest-room attendants. When in doubt, you can't go wrong by tipping; the cash is always appreciated.

TOURS & PACKAGES

On a guided tour or independent package vacation, everything is prearranged, so you'll spend less time planning—and often get a good price.

BOOKING WITH AN AGENT

Travel agents are excellent resources. Collect brochures from several agencies, as some agents' suggestions may be influenced by relationships with tour and package firms that reward them for volume sales. If you have a special interest, **find an agent with expertise in that area**; ASTA (☞ Travel Agencies, *below*) has a database of specialists worldwide.

Make sure your travel agent is familiar with rooms and other services in any lodging he or she recommends. Ask about a hotel's location, room size, beds, and whether it has a pool, room service, or programs for children if these matter to you. Has your agent been there in person, or sent others whom you can contact?

Do some homework on your own, too: Local tourist boards can provide information on lesser-known and small-niche operators, some of which may sell only direct.

BUYER BEWARE

Each year consumers are stranded or lose their money when tour operators—even big ones with excellent reputations—go out of business. So **check out the operator.** Ask several travel agents about its reputation, and try to **book with a company that has a consumer-protection program** (look for information in the company's brochure). In the United States, members of the National Tour Association and United States Tour Operators Association are required to set aside funds to cover your payments and travel arrangements in case the company defaults. It's also a good idea to choose a firm that participates in the American Society of Travel Agent's

Tour Operator Program (TOP); ASTA will act as mediator in any disputes between you and your operator.

Remember that the more your package or tour includes, the better you can predict the ultimate cost of your vacation. Make sure you know exactly what's covered, and **beware of hidden costs.** Are taxes, tips, and transfers included? Entertainment and excursions? These can add up.

➤ TOUR-OPERATOR RECOMMENDATIONS: **American Society of Travel Agents** (☞ Travel Agencies, *below*). **National Tour Association** (NTA, ✉ 546 E. Main St., Lexington, KY 40508, ☎ 606/226–4444 or 800/682–8886). **United States Tour Operators Association** (USTOA, ✉ 342 Madison Ave., Suite 1522, New York, NY 10173, ☎ 212/599–6599 or 800/468–7862, FAX 212/599–6744).

TRAIN TRAVEL

Morocco's rail system, **ONCF** (Office National de Chemins de Fer, or National Rail Office) is excellent, albeit limited in the south. Most trains are air-conditioned, and many have telephones. From Casablanca and Rabat the network runs east via Meknes and Fez to Oujda, north to Tangier, and south to Marrakesh. A rapid shuttle service connects Casablanca's Port station with Rabat, and Casablanca's airport with the city itself. Trains east toward Oujda have couchettes. Bus connections link trains with Tetouan, Nador, and Agadir, and you can buy through tickets covering both segments before you leave.

CLASSES

Trains are divided into first class (*première classe*) and second class (*deuxième classe*). First class is a very good buy compared to its counterpart in Europe, but second class is comfortable, too. Long-distance trains seat six people to a compartment in first class, eight to a compartment in second class.

FARES & SCHEDULES

Fares are relatively inexpensive compared to those in Europe. A first-class ticket from Casablanca to Marrakesh might cost 150DH first class, 110DH second class. You can buy train tickets up to six days in advance; payment is by cash only. It costs 6% more to buy your ticket on the train. Seats are not reserved, but overnight couchettes are.

To plot your trip before you even leave home, consult ONCF's Web site for schedules (☞ Web Sites, *below*).

SMOKING

Smoking is prohibited by law on public transport, but in practice people smoke in the corridors or in the areas between coaches.

TRANSPORTATION
WITHIN MOROCCO

The best form of domestic transport depends on your itinerary. If you're sticking mainly to the four Imperial Cities—Fez, Meknes, Rabat, and Marrakesh—you're best off taking the train and using petits taxis in the cities. Taxis release you from finding the way, braving Moroccan traffic, memorizing one-way streets, and parking.

For cities not served by train (mainly those in the south), buses are a good option. They're relatively frequent, and seats are usually available.

If you're headed for rural areas, such as the Middle Atlas or High Atlas, or the smaller coastal towns, a car is extremely useful. There's a lot to be said for renting a car at an airport, as compared to bringing one in: you skip border delays, and you're free to leave by plane at any time if necessary (☞ Driving, *above*). From the United Kingdom in particular, when you add the cost of ferries and perhaps accommodations en route, it's probably no cheaper to come to Morocco by car than by plane.

Hiring a taxi with driver will not be more expensive than renting your own car if you negotiate the price well, but you might find your itinerary modified by the driver. If you want to see rural areas but your budget doesn't cover the cost of a car, you can still go practically everywhere by shared grand taxi, bus, or, in some mountainous areas, truck; you'll just lose some speed and flexibility.

For long distances within Morocco, consider flying. If, for instance, you want to concentrate on the southern oasis valleys, land in Casablanca, fly to Ouarzazate, and rent a car there.

TRAVEL AGENCIES

A good travel agent puts your needs first. Look for an agency that has been in business at least five years, emphasizes customer service, and has someone on staff who specializes in Morocco. In addition **make sure your agency belongs to a professional trade organization.** The American Society of Travel Agents (ASTA), with 27,000 agents in some 170 countries, is the largest and most influential in the field. Operating under the motto "Integrity in Travel," it maintains and enforces a strict code of ethics and will step in to help mediate any agent-client disputes if necessary. ASTA also maintains a Web site that includes a directory of agents. If your travel agency is also your tour operator, *see* Buyer Beware *in* Tours & Packages, *above*.

➤ LOCAL AGENT REFERRALS: **American Society of Travel Agents** (ASTA; ☎ 800/965–2782 24-hr hot line, FAX 703/ 684–8319, www.astanet.com). **Association of British Travel Agents** (✉ 68– 271 Newman St., London W1P 4AH, ☎ 020/7637–2444, FAX 020/7637– 0713). **Association of Canadian Travel Agents** (✉ 1729 Bank St., Suite 201, Ottawa, Ontario K1V 7Z5, ☎ 613/521–0474, FAX 613/521–0805). **Australian Federation of Travel Agents** (✉ Level 3, 309 Pitt St., Sydney 2000, ☎ 02/9264–3299, FAX 02/ 9264–1085). **Travel Agents' Association of New Zealand** (✉ Box 1888, Wellington 10033, ☎ 04/499–0104, FAX 04/499–0786).

VISITOR INFORMATION

For general information and brochures before you leave home, contact the offices below.

➤ MOROCCAN NATIONAL TOURIST OFFICE: **New York** (✉ 20 E. 46th St., Suite 1201, New York, NY 10017, ☎ 212/557–2520, FAX 212/949– 8148). **Orlando** (✉ Box 2263, Lake Buena Vista, FL 32831, ☎ 407/827– 5337, FAX 407/827–5129). **London** (✉ 205 Regent St., London W1 R7DE, ☎ 207/437–0073, FAX 207/

734–8172). **Sydney** (✉ 11 West St. N, North Sydney NSW 2060–DX10641, ☎ 612/922–4999, FAX 612/923– 1053).

➤ U.S. GOVERNMENT ADVISORIES: For information from the U.S. **Department of State** (✉ Overseas Citizens Services Office, Room 4811 N.S., 2201 C St. NW, Washington, DC 20520; ☎ 202/647–5225), enclose a self-addressed, stamped business envelope.

WEB SITES

Check out the World Wide Web when you're planning any trip. You'll find everything from up-to-date weather forecasts to virtual tours of famous cities. Fodor's Web site (www.fodors.com) is a great place to start your online travels. For more information on Morocco:

The Moroccan government's comprehensive travel site is **www.mincom.gov.ma**. The Moroccan National Tourist Office maintains **www.tourism-in-morocco.com**. Royal Air Maroc posts flight schedules on **www.royalairmaroc.com**. The French-language ONCF site, **www.oncf.org.ma**, has train schedules—click on "Voyageurs," then "Horaires." See **www. marrakech-medina.com** to explore renting a house in Marrakesh. At **www.multimania.com/ moulaybousselham** you'll find a description of the Merdja Zerga bird reserve at Moulay Bousselham.

WHEN TO GO

The best times to come to Morocco are spring and fall, specifically, March, April, and October. Spring may be ideal—the sky is a beautiful deep blue, washed clear by the winter rain, and beautiful spring flowers blanket the landscape. Winter is the best time to see the desert and most of the south; summer is the best time to explore the High Atlas.

The Atlantic and Mediterranean coastal resorts are crowded during the summer school vacation, which covers July, August, and the first half of September. It's best to see the coast another time; June is still warm, and the beaches are much less crowded.

Non-Muslim travelers will probably want to **avoid coming to Morocco during Ramadan.** During this month-long fast, all cafés and nearly all restaurants are closed during the day, and the pace of work is reduced. Ramadan starts in late November in 2000 and 2001 and lasts for 29 or 30 days.

CLIMATE

Morocco enjoys a Mediterranean climate. Inland, temperatures are high in the summer—sometimes in excess of 104°F (40°C)—and cool in the winter. The coastal regions have a more temperate climate, warmer in the winter and less brutally hot in the summer. Rain falls mainly in the winter, from October through March, often with more in November and March. Interestingly, as soon as it stops raining, the sun comes out. Northern Morocco, especially the Rif mountains, gets more rain than the south.

➤ FORECASTS: **Weather Channel Connection** (☎ 900/932–8437), 95¢ per minute from a Touch-Tone phone.

The following are average daily maximum and minimum temperatures for Marrakesh and Rabat, a comparison of which reveals the tempering effects of the ocean on coastal destinations. Climate varies widely throughout Morocco, so consult the appropriate chapters for details on each region you'll be visiting.

MARRAKESH

Jan.	65F	18C	May	84F	29C	Sept.	92F	33C
	40	4		57	14		63	17
Feb.	68F	20C	June	92F	33C	Oct.	83F	28C
	43	6		62	17		57	14
Mar.	74F	23C	July	101F	38C	Nov.	73F	23C
	48	9		67	19		49	9
Apr.	79F	26C	Aug.	100F	38C	Dec.	66F	19C
	52	11		68	20		42	6

RABAT

Jan.	63F	17C	May	74F	23C	Sept.	81F	27C
	46	8		55	13		62	17
Feb.	65F	18C	June	78F	26C	Oct.	77F	25C
	47	8		60	16		58	14
Mar.	68F	20C	July	82F	28C	Nov.	70F	21C
	49	9		63	17		53	12
Apr.	71F	22C	Aug.	83F	28C	Dec.	65F	18C
	52	11		64	18		48	9

WORSHIP

The Moroccan kingdom has an official policy of freedom of worship. There are Catholic churches, Protestant churches, and synagogues in the main cities, and mosques throughout the country.

1 DESTINATION: MOROCCO

GATEWAY TO NORTH AFRICA

WESTERNERS HAVE BEEN fascinated by Morocco since the middle of the 19th century. The country's vivid colors, dramatic light, and sensuous labyrinthine medinas (whitewashed medieval quarters) drew painters like Matisse and Delacroix, and its mysterious culture and perceived social freedoms—whose allure came as much from French colonial culture as from Morocco itself—drew a generation of anglophone writers in the first half of the 20th century, most notably the New York novelist and composer Paul Bowles, William Burroughs, Tennessee Williams, Allen Ginsberg, Jack Kerouac, Edith Wharton, and Federico García Lorca. And contemporary western jazz and rock musicians have found inspiration in the sensuous Gnaoua music of the Marrakesh and Essaouira regions, rooted in West Africa.

But independent travelers who, rather than seek out the exotic, let themselves be taken in by sights, sounds, and smells that feel hospitable will be better rewarded. Morocco's tourism industry is a primary source of state income, topped only by revenues from emigrant workers—meaning that you're unlikely to be the first foreigner ever to set foot just about anywhere you go. Rather than fight the omnipresent bazaar economy of roadside minerals, sun-"aged" rugs, and eager unofficial guides, seize opportunities for interaction with Moroccans. Sights may entice you to come here—snow-peaked mountains on a sunny day, a palm-studded desert expanse, intricate Islamic architecture—but it's impossible not to be intrigued by daily life as well.

There is a certain pleasure in traveling among people who love their country. Moroccans rightly complain of unemployment, rising costs, and the changing expectations that plague many developing countries, but they love the same aspects of Morocco that make traveling here a pleasure: the immediacy of human warmth and generosity, the availability of transportation, geographic and cultural variety, fresh and nutritious food, and an Islam-inspired sense of charity that ensures that no one goes hungry.

Morocco's demographics reflect its position as a crossroads between Africa and Europe, the East and the West. Andalusian, Berber, African, Eastern Arab, and French elements combine in different measures according to the tides of various local histories. Racial and ethnic categorizations fail to capture the diversity of the contemporary population (of more than 30 million); speakers of Moroccan Arabic may be dark, light, or medium-skinned, just like their compatriots who speak one of the regional varieties of Berber. Many Moroccans trace their ancestry to the Beni Hillal, 11th-century invaders from the Arab East whose numbers solidified a substantial Arab and Islamic presence in Morocco. Others have roots in Mali and Senegal; their ancestors were slaves in the Moroccan sultans' courts. The majority of Moroccans are indigenous Imazighen (Berbers), primarily sedentary and sometimes nomadic farmers and shepherds dispersed through mountains and valleys but sharing certain sociopolitical, linguistic, and cultural traits. Intermarriage and migration have decreased the certainty with which most Moroccans can claim exclusively Arab or Amazigh (Berber) roots; even in small towns and villages, people's features reflect a variety of ancestries.

A Moroccan's most significant social characteristic is whether he or she is urban or rural. In the Habbous quarter of industrial Casablanca—an enclave built during the French Protectorate to reflect an Arab aesthetic—Ishelhin (Tashelhit-speaking Berbers) from the southern Anti-Atlas mountains sell their wares. In a rural weekly market north of Sidi Kacem, Arab women hawk electronics from blankets laid out on the ground, while in the deep-southern palmery of Tata, women shield their faces with the passing of each car. Many professors of Islamic sciences at prestigious Kairaouine University, in the heart of the Andalusian Arab city of Fez, go home to obscure mountain villages. The administrative official for a High Atlas valley may hail from Tangier. Despite their strong regionalism, Moroccans defy easy categorization.

Much of this geographic mobility is the result of post-independence state policies designed to integrate people from different regions into a united nation. It also reflects increased communication, expanded transportation routes, and shifting economic constraints. Morocco's history is often cast as a succession of conquests from outside, but internal conflict was plenty fierce until well into the 20th century, when the remaining *caids,* or local dignitaries, finally ceded control over massive parts of the country. Their grip on the Moroccan population had arguably been more pervasive than that of the foreign invaders, whose influence had tended to be restricted to urban and coastal locales, with occasional tax-collecting incursions into the hinterlands.

The Phoenicians established coastal commercial posts; the Romans' ruins and mosaics survive; and the Portuguese left stoic ramparts framing Essaouira and El Jadida. None of these groups, however, made nearly the mark on the indigenous Berber populations that the Gulf Arabs did when they arrived in the late 7th century. Arabs brought the religion of Islam and its holy language, Arabic, both of which took hold (to varying degrees) in various regions of Morocco. A Berber chieftain seized with the new religion led the charge into Spain, which remained under Almoravid and then Almohad rule for the next seven centuries. The Moors, as they were often called, were Muslim Berbers whose scribes, along with Andalusian Jews and Christian monks, saved Greek and Latin scientific and philosophical manuscripts from oblivion during Europe's Dark Ages, profoundly affecting the course of world history. When the Spanish Inquisition put a stop to this scholarly effervescence, the Muslims and Jews who fled to Morocco reinvigorated urban life and shaped the character of what came to be thought of as Arab Morocco.

Over the next few centuries, Portuguese, French, and even German attempts to colonize parts of Morocco were short-lived (or restricted to fishing enclaves such as Ceuta, on the Mediterranean, and Sidi Ifni, in the deep south). In the early 20th century, however, the Moroccan sultan's financial debt to the French grew large enough for the French to convince him to sign a Protectorate agreement. Legally governing under the name of the Moroccan sultanate from 1912 to 1956, French marshal Hubert Lyautey swore off the kind of failed assimilation experiments imposed in the French "province" of Algeria, and discouraged oversettlement by French agriculturalists. An idealist who proposed creating an indigenous Moroccan elite that would eventually take over the administrative duties of a modern state, Lyautey was eventually replaced and his visions aborted as brute force and excessive bureaucracy were increasingly used to preserve French interests. In retrospect, the French made less of a mark on Moroccan politics, economics, culture, and ideology than they made on the same institutions in Algeria. The colonial administration fought resistance from some far-flung areas of Morocco until the early 1930s, rendering the impact of colonial power less significant in rural areas.

Islamization of the indigenous Berber population seems to have been a rapid process. The Berbers of the 7th century seem to have practiced primarily the other monotheisms, Christianity and Judaism, in local forms. Islam has long been riddled with conflict over the precise form its practice should take and what relationship religion should have to political power. *Salafism,* or purification movements, characterize several critical moments. In the 11th century Ibn Tumert attempted to oppose imperial rule from Marrakesh by violently consolidating a High Atlas army of Muslims behind his radical reformist teachings of the individual's responsibility for the *umma,* the body of believers. In the early 20th century, the budding nationalist movement in both Morocco and France rallied around the conviction that French occupation could be overthrown only with the spiritual purification of colonized believers. Throughout the centuries, the orthodoxy of local saints (*waliyin* or *salahin*) has aroused fierce passions. Wali tombs—square stone structures, some with white domes—dot the landscape across North Africa—but contemporary political Islamists (so-called fundamentalists) oppose belief in these saints as intercessors since Islamic doctrine forbids mediators between God and the individual. Pious saints remain an integral part of local consciousness and normative morality, however, as expressed in commemorative ritual, song, and everyday proverbs. Often a mosque and a saint's tomb stand adjacent to each other, and religious practices integrate spaces and concepts: men gather in the mosques for Friday prayers, while women visit saints' tombs in times of hardship or to seek female companionship.

Despite their conversion to Islam from Christianity, Judaism, or animism, most Moroccans retained their Berber vernaculars rather than adopt the language of the conqueror. Berber can be roughly divided into three geolects (regional varieties): Tarifit, in the northern Rif; Tamàzight, in the Middle Atlas and eastern High Atlas; and Tashelhit, in the western High Atlas, Souss Valley, and Anti-Atlas. In contrast to these mountain regions, the cities and other parts of the plains adapted a vernacular form of Arabic for everyday use. Both populations maintained classical Arabic as the language of literacy and religion. The bulk of religious training continued to take place, however, in rural Koranic schools (*medersa*s), which still train community religious leaders today. The prevalence of a primarily oral culture has helped preserve the Berber geolects to this day.

Sultan Hassan II was the political head of Morocco from the death of his father, Mohammed V—father of independence, the "Moroccan Gandhi"—in 1961 to his own death in 1999. The new king, Mohammed VI, 32 years old, has promised to modernize the country, stressing territorial integrity, educational reform, and increased public freedom, including women's rights. Because their Alaouite dynasty traces its roots back to the prophet Mohammed—they are *shorfa*—the royals have special spiritual authority. (The Alaouites came into power in the 17th century, after Morocco's economic power had declined; it was no longer a major thoroughfare for gold, sugar, and slaves across the Sahara, and its population had been decimated by plague.) Coup attempts in the 1970s led to a decade of crackdown, particularly imprisonment of critics of the monarchy, including Marxist student leaders, popular musicians, and outspoken intellectuals generally. Although the sultan retains absolute political authority,

political reforms in the late 1990s showed a new openness: a bipartite parliament has been created to encourage broader representation and ensure veritable political opposition; the socialist former political prisoner Youssoufi has been named prime minister; and the press has gained more freedom. Unlike in Algeria and Tunisia, Islamist political parties have no legal role in elections here; their influence is strongest among students and the educated unemployed.

Education and the economy are the most obvious problems for contemporary Morocco. The state sector is no longer able to employ large numbers of educated graduates, as it did in the 1950s and 1960s, but the private sector remains stunted by government policies such as high taxation. Moreover, many educated Moroccans no longer want to work the agricultural and manual positions available, preferring instead the scarce white-collar office jobs. This situation has led to an educational crisis, for people have lost faith in the rewards of schooling as a means to economic mobility or even sustenance. The "generalization" (democratization) of education in Morocco began soon after independence from the French in 1956, when Moroccan authorities declared an educational policy of generalization, unification, Moroccanization, and Arabization. Generalization meant increased access to primary education for the whole population. Unification meant adoption of a uniform curriculum. Moroccanization meant replacing Syrian and French instructors with newly qualified Moroccan instructors. Arabization meant phasing out instruction in French in favor of instruction in Arabic. At the turn of the 21st century, however, many rural areas are still building their first primary schools. With rural female literacy at about 5% and the percentage of young Casablanca children in school at 95%, the rift between rural and urban education is acute. The Arabization of the state system defies the demand for technological know-how, which Moroccans obtain in French-language courses taught on a fee basis and geared toward the increasingly global economy. In these rapidly changing times, networks of families and friends typically include people from a variety of socioeconomic classes, rural and urban, schooled and unschooled, with varying language skills. For many Moroccans the shifting domains of economic opportunity are perceived not so much as Westernization as ways to perpetuate their own way of life more comfortably.

What does all this social and political change mean for women in Morocco? With two women in the royal cabinet and another in parliament, educated urban women are making some small inroads to greater political participation. Women have been accepted with open arms as professionals, civil servants, and especially doctors—their presence makes medical care more accessible to modest women fearful of male doctors. As in most countries, however, women are entering the labor force primarily in service, factory, secretarial, and domestic jobs, where their salaries help secure their families' well-being but their wages are lower than those of men. In many agricultural areas, women continue to perform as much (if not more) manual labor and animal husbandry as men. In elite and poor circles in both city and country, women retain domestic duties regardless of whether they have paying jobs outside the home. The *mutadawana*—the Moroccan family legal code grounded in Islamic *sharia* law—stipulates that a husband must provide financially for his wife, who in turn must maintain the home and raise the children. This norm prevails, despite individual constraints. Polygamy is legal, if uncommon; a late 1990s reform now requires a first wife's consent to an additional wife, and it grants the first wife the right to divorce her husband if she objects. More and more educated women are marrying later, even in their thirties, if at all; and women who take advantage of educational and employment opportunities face the additional burden of protecting their honor in mixed-sex company with unfamiliar men. The extent to which the sexes mingle is actually greater in many rural contexts than in urban ones. Increased public freedoms for women in towns are paired with the plague of sexual harassment and unwanted attention for both foreign and Moroccan women. Inside the family home, however, whether urban or rural—away from the anonymity of the city street—Moroccan and foreign women alike generally find men respectful and friedly. Like other aspects of social interaction in Morocco, the context dictates the rules.

In the process of facilitating the movement of people, goods, and information throughout the country and abroad, Morocco's vastly improved infrastructure has made more corners of the country accessible to travelers than ever before. There are now regional airports in Tangier, Tetouan, Al Hoceima, Oujda, Fez, Marrakesh, Essaouira, Agadir, Laayoune, and Dakhla in addition to the international airport at Casablanca. Major intercity roads have been paved (even if the pavement in many areas is only 1½ cars wide, requiring one or both vehicles to pull off the pavement when meeting from opposite directions). New gas and service stations open every month, serving almost every patch of the country except a few mountain passes. The privatization of intercity bus lines has led to significant competition from newer ones, some of which are now only slightly less reliable than the excellent train service in the north. Communications have expanded, too: just about every town has a public fax machine, and Internet cafés have sprouted in the cities, following the introduction of the information superhighway here in 1996.

Morocco's geographic diversity is one of its greatest attractions. The Mediterranean Sea, on the north coast, and the Atlantic Ocean, on the west coast, pair with desert in the east and south to enclose alternating series of mountain peaks—the highest of which, Mt. Toubkal, reaches almost 14,000 ft—and plains, some fertile, some desolate. The proximity of contrasting terrains is striking: you can watch the sun rise over the Merzouga dunes by the Algerian border, pass through a snowy cedar forest in the Middle Atlas by afternoon, and take in the medina lights of the Imperial City of Fez by bedtime.

— By Katherine E. Hoffman

PLEASURES AND PASTIMES

Architecture and Ornament

Refined Islamic architecture graces the Imperial Cities of Fez, Meknes, Marrakesh, and Rabat. Mosques and *madrasas* (schools of Islamic science) dating from the Middle Ages, as well as 19th-century palaces in the Andalusian style, are decorated with colorful geometric tiles, bands of Koranic verses in marble or plaster, stalactite crevices, and carved wooden ceilings. Outside these holds of Arab influence are the mud *pisé* (mud-and-clay) Kasbahs in the Ouarzazate–Er-Rachidia region, where structures built with local soil range from deep pink to burgundy to shades of brown. Rural pisé homes throughout the southern plains are decorated with cheerful, white-painted barley stalks, the staff of rural life.

Beaches

With coasts on both the Mediterranean Sea and the Atlantic Ocean, Morocco has hundred of miles of sandy beaches, many of them little developed. Dangerous currents and national-park preservation explain some why some beaches are unused, but gems abound on both the sea and the ocean sides. The port towns of Essaouira, Sifi Ifni, Asilah, and Al Hoceima make peaceful, low-key coastal getaways, and Agadir is a major destination for the European package-tour tanning crowd. Those familiar with Tunisia's topless beaches may be struck by the modesty that reigns on Moroccan beaches, where picnicking local families spend their holidays. Many beaches have a rugged feel to them, and are accessible only by four-wheel-drive transportation.

Dining

Like Morocco itself, Moroccan cuisine mixes tastes and ingredients in surprising ways. Sweet-and-salty combinations such as *pastilla de pigeon* (pigeon in a flaky phyllo pastry—a sort of pigeon potpie) and lemon and olives with *tagine de poulet* (stewed chicken) are common. Tagines, which you'll find throughout the country, are refined spiced stews cooked in cone-lidded earthenware pots of the same name; the classic pastilla is a phyllo-pastry pie made of pigeon, hard-boiled eggs, and almonds and dusted with sugar and cinnamon. Dishes are based on a wide range of spices and vegetables and tend away from thick sauces. For simple street fare, you can grab a bowl of *harira* (chickpea, lentil, and meat soup) at a nominal cost in any souk (market). Brochettes and beef or lamb kebabs may cost as much as 10DH, just over a U.S. dollar. Restaurant fare varies widely. The standard Moroccan menu is nearly always composed of hors d'oeuvres followed by pastilla, tagine, couscous, and, for dessert, another flaky pastilla with sweet cream. After sampling the traditional menu, order à la carte to try new dishes. *Mechoui*, roast lamb, must be ordered before you arrive at the restaurant. The best wines are the red Medaillon, Cuvée du Président, Ksar, and the white Coquillage, all from around Meknes. Mint tea (known affectionately as Moroccan whiskey, though it's nonalcoholic) is the standard hot beverage.

Music

Music is integral to daily and ritual life in Morocco, both for enjoyment and as a form of social commentary. It emanates from homes, stores, markets, and public squares everywhere you go, and various musical genres set the mood for each region. In the Rif you'll hear men singing poetry accompanied by guitar and high-pitched women's choruses; in Casablanca, *rai* (opinion) music, born of social protest, keeps young men company on the streets; cobblers in the Meknes medina may work to the sounds of violin-based Andalusian classical music or the more folksy Arabic *melhoun,* sung poetry; and you know you've reached the south when you hear the banjo of the roving storytelling *rawais* in Marrakesh. Gnaoua music is best known for its use in trance rituals, but it has become popular street entertainment; the performer's brass *qaraqa* hand cymbals and cowry shell–adorned hat reveal the music's sub-Saharan origins. A few high-end urban Moroccan restaurants, such as the one in Fez's Palais Jamai, have superb Andalusian and melhoun dinner accompaniment. Many large hotels also arrange for folkloric "Berbère" performances that range from the outstanding to the crummy and chaotic; you're better off seeking out live music at public squares such as Marrakesh's Djemâa el Fna, or attending a festival, a regional *moussem* (pilgrimage festival), or even a rural market to see the performances locals enjoy. Cassette sellers throughout the country will let you sample selections; if you visit one during a lull in business, you can learn quite a bit by listening to a few different tapes before buying.

Shopping

Moroccan rugs vary tremendously in quality and design. Deep-red Middle Atlas rugs are among the most widely available; Khemisset is an excellent place to buy them at wholesale prices. *Goundafi* rugs, with their alternating plush pile and intricate woven motifs of mustard, orange-brown, and black are most plentiful in Taznacht and the Tifnout Valley, north of Aouluz. Simpler, sparser geometric details distinguish rugs from the Chiadma and Bou Sbaa regions of the Haouz plains. Short-pile Rabat carpets recall their Iranian counterparts. The newly popular (pseudo-) Toureg rugs are mostly a response to Western tourists' tastes. Toureg-motif silver jewelry has also become a hot item with visitors. Older pieces are usually collected by silver merchants from rural women who need cash, so used-jewelry selections tend to reflect regional traditions. Silver bracelets and necklaces should be priced by the gram; earrings are usually priced according to intricacy and metal quality. Ask the silver merchant to test the piece in front of you for its silver content. As with any other purchases, decide what the piece is worth to you before bargaining; an "old" item might be anywhere from 5 to 50 years old. Merchants know that Westerners have a weak spot for antiques when in fact many recently manufactured pieces are of just as high quality.

Textile **embroidery** details are highly valued in everyday clothes; you can buy exquisite kaftans and linens in Tetouan, Fez, and Chefchaouen. The best ceramics are made in Fez and Salé, but the Marrakesh medina has a good selection as well. Lacquered mirrors come in all sizes, colors, and motifs, either reminiscent of Iranian illustrated manuscripts or in Moroccan geometric patterns. Leather and suede *belgha* from Fez are the ultimate house slipper. Don't forget the local culinary accents at the spice seller's stand, such as saffron and pungent cumin; merchants also sell bulk lavender, assortments of incense, and fragrant oils such as jasmine.

Sports and Outdoor Activities

A range of eye-popping landscapes combined with a reliance on tourist revenues has made Morocco a real destination for rugged outdoor sporting challenges and adventure travel. The 1998 Eco-Challenge brought 500 teams from around the world for a month of rock climbing, kayaking, and camel riding through the mountains, ocean, and deserts of the south. The weeklong Marathon des Sables, organized by the French-run Atlantide Organisation International, has sponsored competitions in the Ouarzazate outback since the 1980s. Events that combine sportsmanship and scenery in a hospitable climate reflect what many independent travelers have already discovered: that Morocco's peaks, cliffs, and waterways lend themselves to tests of strength and endurance. The country is expanding its national-parks system as well, seeks to encourage ecotourism as a source of revenue for preservation efforts.

Much of Morocco's natural beauty lies in its mountains, where the famous Berber hospitality can make hiking an unforgettable experience. Day hikes are an option from just about any place with a mule path, and you can organize longer hikes in the High Atlas, usually with mule and guide accompaniment. Rock climbing is possible in the Todra and Dadès gorges, and the caves around Taza invite spelunking. Oukaimeden has facilities for skiing, and a few other long, liftless runs await the more athletic. Golf is available in Rabat, Casablanca, Marrakesh, Agadir, and an increasing number of other scenic spots. Several High Atlas rivers are suitable for fishing. A number of American and British outfits organize increasingly popular adventure trips here, integrating hiking, biking, and other activities, but you can arrange most outdoor excursions by yourself or with the help of tourist offices in the bigger cities.

WHAT'S WHERE

Tangier, Tetouan, and the Mediterranean

Best known for its harvest and exportation of *kif* (a preparation of hemp leaves whose name comes from the Arabic word for "pleasure") and its importation of expensive German cars, the Rif Mountain region along the Mediterranean Sea is one of Morocco's most scenic and under-explored. Mediterranean beaches are low-key destinations for those weary of the city. The Rif Mountains are some of the most striking in Morocco, rendered all the more mysterious by the perfunctory police stops along kif-smuggling routes. A drive through the rolling hills takes you past harvesting women in Spanish-style hats, tied with a scarf under the chin. Rifis have a reputation for regional allegiance and fierceness, and their history belies more than a few attempts to strengthen Rifi autonomy. Spanish influence is most palpable in the coastal cities of Tangier and Tetouan, with their seaside medinas.

Casablanca, Rabat, and the Northern Atlantic Coast

Morocco's economic capital, Casablanca, and political capital, Rabat, are lively colonial cities on the move. Boulevards designed by French architects to highlight buildings inspired by Islamic architecture run alongside mazelike medinas. University students and merchants from all corners of the country flood both of these cities in pursuit of a more prosperous future than they might have back home. Commuting Rabati bureaucrats pack the streets for the morning, lunchtime, and evening rush hours, but Rabat's streets are empty at night while Casablanca seems consistently rushed. Both cities attract travelers with a combination of colonial architecture in the New City (or Ville Nouvelle) and a colorful, less harried medina with vegetable stalls, live-chicken sellers, and entrepreneurial women selling home-baked goods on the streets. The magnificent Hassan II Mosque is set apart on the Casablanca Corniche, jutting into the Atlantic Ocean, its spires rising to a height matched only by the pilgrimage center in Mecca. The building's architectural polish reflects both its subtle French design and its detailed Moroccan craftsmanship.

Fez and Meknes

The Arab-Islamic chapters in Morocco's history are most evident in these two Imperial Cities, with their centuries-old *biban,* or arched gates, built to be locked against invaders during uncertain times. The Fez medina contains the world's oldest university, the Kairaouine, attached to the mosque of the same name and nestled in the heart of the most exciting maze of shops, covered spice markets, tanneries, textile-weaving crannies, and food stalls in all of Morocco. The intrigue of what seems at first glance a slice of medieval life is not dampened by Fez's film stalls and Coke distributors, for this is an utterly lived-in medina, a first stop for rural migrant families crowded into single rooms inside mansions once owned by wealthy Fassis. UNESCO has invested in renovations here, in an attempt both to repair crumbling buildings and walkways and to rejuvenate traditional handicrafts and religious education. Meknes is a more relaxed version of Fez, making up for its lack of intensity with livability and hassle-free sightseeing.

The Middle Atlas

Often passed through on the way to more dramatic destinations, the Middle Atlas is an underrated mountain range of great natural beauty. Its contrast with the bustling Imperial Cities is immediate: one heaves a sigh of relief upon reaching the low-lying hills outside Midelt. Vast expanses of rolling hills, valleys, high peaks, and Kasbahs reward the rambler. Immouzer and the surrounding area offer rare North African fall foliage and a cool break from the heat of Fez. Middle Atlas Berbers manufacture some of the country's most popular and sturdy deep-red carpets and delicate wool-embroidered straw mats and sell them in regional weekly markets for half what they command in Marrakesh. Haunting call-and-response Tamazight music rings throughout gathering places here, hinting at the rough living conditions in the mountains above. Poverty is particularly acute here, yet the Middle Atlas people show resilience in their festivities and their gracious hospitality.

Marrakesh

Marrakesh is the turning point between Morocco's north and south, Arab and Berber, big city and small town. If you can see only one city in Morocco, make it Marrakesh. The legendary Djemâa el Fna Square is a sensorial feast, a highlight of any trip to this country: in late afternoon Moroccans as well as foreigners crowd the square to hear storytellers and musicians perform, be wooed by herbalists and acrobats, and sip some of the country's best orange juice, sold by rows of vendors. As the sun sets, smoke rises from the outdoor food stalls as they whip up traditional Moroccan fare (tagine and couscous), fried fish, and simple bowls of harira with dates on the side. Djemâa el Fna can be overwhelming, but the medina beyond is a pleasure, with its relatively wide walkways and its children playing among adult

Marrakshis going about their lives. The understated Almoravid *koubba* (saint's tomb) contains the oldest traces of distinctive Moroccan architectural and decorative motifs, and its underground water conduit hints at the city's technological centrality in earlier times. The snowcapped High Atlas mountains, rising beyond the lush gardens sprinkled throughout town, tempt you to forge on and out, and indeed the city is an ideal base for High Atlas day trips.

The High Atlas

Although parts of the High Atlas are veritably mobbed with hikers, you can still get off the beaten path by foot or mule and taste rural Morocco at its most colorful and hospitable. Here, unlike in more conservative corners, the occasional shepherd or the woman tending her fields is more likely to want to talk to you than to flee from you. These are some of Morocco's most densely populated areas; the presence of many humans on the landscape contrasts sharply with the more remote areas south and east. Free-flowing rivers and abundant underground springs keep the High Atlas verdant for much of the year, and a stroll through villages and countryside takes you past groves of walnut, pomegranate, fig, and almond as well as fields of corn, barley, and various vegetables. Respite from the beating sun comes in the shade of thick-trunk trees. Ribbons of mountain peaks layer into the distance as you hike; Mt. Toubkal is the highest peak in North Africa, retaining snow into August. Decent roads offer pleasant rides to destinations popular with Marrakshis as well as foreigners, such as Setti Fatma, Sidi Chamarouch, and the ski resort Oukaimeden.

The Great Oasis Valleys

Some of Morocco's most exotic scenery is in the southeast, where rock-dry hills and winding oases cling to the few rivers that sustain this region. Oases of date palms and apricot trees line the banks of the Oued Ziz, running north from Er-Rachidia to Rich and farther up. The single road down from Meknes makes the Tafilalt (source of the ruling Alaouite dynasty) accessible in a day's drive through the Middle Atlas. The narrow road between Er-Rachidia and Ouarzazate runs through some of the sleepiest picturesque villages,

with homes decorated in a distinctive lace pattern that has become ubiquitous in representative images of the Berber south. The Zagora Valley, south of Ouarzazate, is known for its distinctive green-glazed pottery; and the silver jewelry of Rissani is renowned for its original designs and high quality. The road is particularly beautiful in late winter, when almond trees bloom amid date palms, and deep orange sunsets over dry hills create unforgettable views.

Essaouira, the Souss Valley, and the Anti-Atlas

The southwest brings together Arab and Berber, ocean and mountain, luxury accommodations and guest facilities in rural homes. The coastal towns of Essaouira and Sidi Ifni are temperate year-round, whereas the Souss plains and Anti-Atlas mountains have intensely hot summers and cool winters. The triangle formed by Agadir, Tafraoute, and Tiznit is formed by curvy but manageable mountain roads studded with deserted hilltop Kasbahs, villages, and centuries-old rural Koranic schools. People-watching is interesting here, as women's wraps vary widely within the region, from austere black or navy full-body coverings in Taroudant to the white *haik* of Essaouira to brightly flowered sheetlike garments along the southern coast.

The Southern Coast and Western Sahara

In 1975 nearly 400,000 Moroccans walked south to the former Spanish Sahara in the Green March, taking possession of what are now officially called the Southern Provinces and locally called the Sahara. Since then, however, the civil war between the Polisario (Saharan separatists) and the Moroccan military has been off and on; elections to determine the province's political future have been postponed numerous times. There is currently a truce. The region is primarily a military zone, fishing port, and phosphorus-rich industrial zone whose residents enjoy subsidized food and lodging to compensate for the distance between them and the rest of the country. The main attraction for the traveler is a chance to set foot in the Sahara, as the cities are new and charmless and the military presence pervasive. You cannot drive through the western Sahara to Mauritania without a

Mauritanian visa and a Moroccan police escort.

GREAT ITINERARIES

Morocco is a feast for the eyes, and driving is the most exciting way to see it. Maddening, however, is the careless and reckless manner in which many Moroccan drivers cover their territory. Patience, a good eye, and good brakes are prerequisites for any driving tour. Blinding sunrises and sunsets mean you should time west- and eastbound tours accordingly. Beyond these challenges, the only real difficulty is keeping your eyes on the road, as surprising sights and breathtaking views open off every turn. Motorists are advised to travel in pairs at the very least, if possible, and women will find they encounter fewer hassles when accompanied by a man. Women traveling without male companions should drive and walk as they would on any urban street in the world—purposefully, avoiding eye contact with men.

5 Days: Classic Morocco

Fly to ▥ **Marrakesh** and spend two days there. On day three, rent a car and drive over the High Atlas to **Ouarzazate** for lunch at Chez Dimitri. That afternoon, drive the spectacular Kasbah route through the **Dadès Valley** to Erfoud. Spend the night alongside the ▥ **Merzouga dunes,** then watch the sun rise over the desert before driving north through the Azrou Cedar Forest. Spend day five exploring the medina in ▥ **Fez.**

7 Days: Southern Idyll

Fly to Agadir and rent a car. Drive inland to **Taroudant** and spend a day exploring the low-key markets and the ramparts. Have dinner and spend the night at the Palais Salam before starting off to Inezgane and turning south towards Tafraoute. The morning of day three, leave for the **date palmeries** before it gets too hot. Return to town in the late afternoon, driving on to spend the night at the Hotel Kerdous, overlooking a dramatic valley on the road to Tiznit. On day four, hit **Tiznit** by late morning for silver and wool-blanket shopping, then turn south. Arrive in

Sidi Ifni late in the afternoon to catch the sunset over the ocean and enjoy a fish dinner at Loca Suerte. The morning of day five, head straight north, stopping off at the **Souss Massa National Park** for some bird-watching. Enjoy the gorgeous drive from Agadir to Essaouira, and arrive by nightfall. Spend days six and seven relaxing in **Essaouira.**

14 Days: Grand Tour

In two weeks you can see just about all of Morocco: the Atlantic coast, the High Atlas mountains, pre-Saharan palmeries, Berber architecture, hillside towns, and an exquisite Imperial City. Arrive in **Tangier** and rent a car; drive south to the Rif Mountains and the white-and-blue hillside town of ▥ **Chefchaouen.** Spend half a day walking the hill overlooking the valley and navigating the labyrinth of whitewashed lanes. On day two, drive through Ouazzane en route to Fez, and stop off at the Roman ruins of **Moulay Idriss.** Arrive in ▥ **Fez** by nightfall and splurge on a refined Fassi meal at an upscale medina restaurant. Spend day three exploring the Fez medina, taking care to absorb the view from one of the rooftop cafés overlooking this ancient maze. Day four takes you south through the **Azrou Cedar Forest** to Erfoud. Rise early on day five to catch the sunrise over the ▥ **Merzouga dunes,** then get on the road to Tinerhir. Spend the night in the Todra Gorges and day six exploring the Kasbah route on the road to ▥ **Ouarzazate.** Treat yourself to the Berbère Palace that night—if only to fuel up on its breakfast smorgasbord, unmatched in the country. Devote day seven to the **Tizi-n-Tichka Pass** to Marrakesh, stopping off at the *ksour* (fortified villages) of Aït-Benhaddou and Telouet. Settle into a ▥ **Marrakesh** hotel by nightfall, and spend day nine storming the medina, architectural monuments, and Djemâa el Fna. On day nine, head west to ▥ **Essaouira** and treat yourself to a few days in a calm port town. Day 11 can take you north along the coast to **Safi** for pottery shopping, then on to the Portuguese port town of ▥ **El Jadida.** On Day 12, pop into the stunning oceanside Hassan II Mosque in ▥ **Casablanca** before heading up to ▥ **Rabat.** Wander through Rabat's Rue des Consuls for last-minute purchases on your way to the 12th-century Kasbah des Oudayas, savoring your last taste of imperial Morocco.

FODOR'S CHOICE

Architecture

★ **Abou el Hassan Medersa, Salé.** It's small, but this medieval Koranic school has lovely ornamentation, a fine mihrab (prayer niche) with carvings representing the cosmos, and preserved student cells— all capped by a stunning rooftop view of Salé and Rabat.

★ **Aït-Benhaddou, near Ouarzazate.** Strewn across a hillside, the red-pisé towers of this village fortress resemble a melting sand castle. Crenellated and topped with blocky towers, it's one of the most sumptuous sights in the Atlas mountains.

★ **Bou Inania and Attarin medersas, Fez.** The most celebrated of the Kairaouine University's 14th-century residential colleges, Bou Inania has a roof of green tile, a ceiling of carved cedar, stalactites of white marble, and ribbons of Arabic inscription. The Attarin Medersa has graceful proportions and elegant, geometrical cedar ornamentation in a superior state of preservation.

★ **Chefchaouen.** Near fields of wildflowers at the edge of the gray Rif Mountains, the white- and bluewashed houses of this calm northern town line a warren of steep, narrow streets.

★ **El Bahia Palace, Marrakesh.** Built as a harem's residence, El Bahia has the key Moroccan elements—light, symmetry, decoration, and water. Interspersed with cypress-filled courtyards, the building is filled with smooth arches, ceramic-tile walls and fountains, marbled finishes, stucco cornices, and brightly colored, intricately patterned ceilings of carved cedar.

The Outdoors

★ **Azrou Cedar Forest.** This Middle Atlas woodland is a unique habitat in Morocco. Even in Fez you can sense a breath of fresh air when it's is mentioned, usually as the source of some intricate cedar carving. Moroccan cedars grow to heights of close to 200 ft.

★ **Beaches, Sidi Ifni and Essaouira.** Well off the beaten beach paths, Ifni and Essaouira offer, respectively, burgundy rock formations and some of the hardest surfing winds in all of Africa.

★ **High Atlas.** People come from around the world to trek in these mountains, drawn by the rugged scenery, bracing air, and rural Berber culture. Hiking is easily combined with mule riding, trout fishing, and vertiginous alpine drives.

★ **Merzouga dunes.** Southeast of Erfoud, beyond Morocco's great oasis valleys, these waves of sand mark the beginning of the Sahara Desert. Brilliantly orange in the late-afternoon sun, they can be gloriously desolate at sunrise.

★ **Palm oases near Tafraoute.** A striking tropical contrast to the barren Anti-Atlas mountains and the plains farther north, the oases are scattered with massive, pink cement houses built by wealthy urban merchants native to this area.

Shopping

★ **Essaouira.** The craftsmen and merchants in the woodcarvers' souk specialize in fragrant thuya wood, usually in the forms of boxes, trays, and photo frames inlaid with shells or mother-of-pearl.

★ **Fez.** The medina is a living museum of artisans creating some of the finest ceramic, copper, leather, wood, and embroidered crafts in the world. Pressure to purchase can be high, but there's no better place to assess the state of a particular art.

★ **Marrakesh.** Stretching north through the medina from the Djemâa el Fna, the souk is a vast and flourishing labyrinth of narrow alleyways—some covered and dark, some open-air—stuffed with colorful, highly specialized handicrafts workshops and bazaars.

★ **Rabat.** Hassles are minimal on Rue des Consuls, a pedestrian-only shopping street rich in crafts. Browse Berber jewelry, leather goods, wood and brass items, traditional clothing, slippers, and, on Monday and Thursday mornings especially, carpets.

★ **Tiznit.** The silver markets of Tiznit sell more—and better—silver per square foot than any other market in Morocco. Some vendors also sell handwoven cream-color blankets, traded in by local women for a few pieces of new silver.

People-Watching

★ **Djemâa el Fna, Marrakesh.** This cacophonous market square is unlike anything else on earth. Settle into a rooftop café for an unobstructed view of the acrobats, storytellers, musicians, dancers, fortune-tellers, juice carts, and general organized chaos.

⭐ **Fez el Bali.** Packed with mosques, medersas, souks, and fondouks (medieval inns), Fez's medina has changed little in the last thousand years. With no cars and some 1,000 dead-end lanes, this artisans' quarter is a microcosm of daily Moroccan life.

⭐ **Place Moulay Hassan, Essaouira.** Locals, temporary locals, and fishermen are all welcome to linger in this laid-back plaza, watching the world go by from an outdoor café. Try a cup of *louisa*—warm milk with fresh verveine leaves.

Dining

⭐ **La Gazelle d'Or, Taroudant.** Favored by French President Jacques Chirac for his springtime holidays, this bungalow hotel serves a superb poolside lunch buffet of both salads and hot dishes. $$$–$$$$

⭐ **La Maison Bleue, Fez.** The former home of a famous astrologer and adviser to King Mohammed V is now an exquisite setting for Moroccan dining and music, its high ceilings and intricately carved stucco and cedar walls surrounding a patio and fountain. $$$$

⭐ **Le Yacout, Marrakesh.** You're led to this palatial medina home by a guardian with a lantern, and served rooftop aperitifs to the strains of Gnaouan music. The Moroccan feast is served in several settings, including a lush, cushion-filled salon and the rim of a turquoise pool. $$$$

⭐ **Port, Essaouira.** Find a dockside table and savor the daily catch of sardines, calamari, and skate next to the deep-fishing rigs and bright blue and green wooden

sailboats that brought them in. Grilled fish is the specialty. $

⭐ **Restaurant Populaire La Saveur du Poisson, Tangier.** This minuscule stall is one of Tangier's best-kept secrets. Focusing on seafood, the owner creates a simple menu of succulent dishes. The restaurant is filled with dried and fresh herbs, flowers, and mounds of produce. $$

Lodging

⭐ **Auberge Tengaro, Diabat.** Separated from the Atlantic Ocean by a eucalyptus forest, the rooms and grounds of this rustic-yet-refined inn south of Essaouira are lit by candlelight and lantern only. The fabulous meals are four-course French-provincial with a Mediterranean twist. $$$

⭐ **El Minzah, Tangier.** This classic hotel near the medina has studded wooden doors, beautiful gardens, an elegant patio, the constant sound of falling water, and fine views over the Straits of Gibraltar to Spain. $$$$

⭐ **Riad Enija, Marrakesh.** Original Moroccan detail blends with modern sculpture in this gorgeous *riad* mansion. The bathrooms are works of art in themselves, and peacocks roam the plant-filled courtyard. $$$$

⭐ **Palais Jamai, Fez.** A lap of luxury astride one of the world's most fascinating medinas, this Place to Be is both lavishly decorated and endowed with one of the country's best Moroccan restaurants. Dinner is served to the strains of classical Andalusian music. $$$$

⭐ **Villa Maroc, Essaouira.** Tucked into a side street and intricately laid out, this house is so brilliantly decorated that designers and photographers hold it up as a model. White is abundant, but trimmings include textiles, metalwork, and ceramics. $$$

FESTIVALS AND SEASONAL EVENTS

There are hundreds of festivals throughout the year, most neatly classifiable as religious (either Islamic or commemorating a local patron saint) or secular. Some of the biggest festivals began as small religious affairs but have taken on a fairlike quality over the years. The smallest local *moussem*s hold little interest for the passing traveler, but the larger festivals are worth planning your trip around. Exact dates shift from year to year, according to the Muslim lunar calendar, harvest seasons, or local school schedules and organizing officials. It's best to ask locals for exact dates a few weeks before the festival; they're unlikely to know the specifics any farther in advance. Dates noted are based on the year 2000; Islamic holidays move 11 days earlier each year.

Some traditional Moroccan celebrations occur spontaneously. Moroccan marriage ceremonies last a week, beginning with street processions of family, friends, and musicians following a mule-drawn cart bearing gifts of a sheep, sugar, flour, and sequined slippers to the bride's house. Circumcision ceremonies also manifest themselves in street processions to bear the young boy, dressed in green velvet, to and from the ceremony on a horse. The act itself is traditionally performed by a barber.

AUTUMN

Sept.➤ The infamous but still picturesque **Imilchil Brides' Fair** is held every September in the Middle Atlas. Now so popular with tourists that TV journalists interview them as part of the event, the fair was originally a public occasion for young women to select their spouses, with whom they were usually familiar prior to the fair. Prospective partners would size each other up and agree on their union within an elaborate song-and-dance format. The fair has been misrepresented as evidence of Berber women's freedom on the pretext that they selected their spouses rather than vice-versa; in these communities, multiple, sequential marriages for both men and women are common, starting at a very young age. Forced marriage is a rarity.

The moussem of **Moulay Idriss II** honors the patron saint of Fez. An elaborate procession weaves through the medina in the afternoon en route to the saint's centrally located tomb.

Oct.➤ The **date festival** in Erfoud celebrates this local delicacy with an extensive market.

Nov.➤ **Ramadan** is the Islamic month of fasting, an idea that draws travelers in search of lively nocturnal street life and keeps other travelers well away. Fasting requires that Muslims abstain not only from eating, drinking, and smoking during daylight hours, but also from carnal pleasures such as sex, makeup, and perfume and vices such as gossip. Foreigners are not expected to observe these proscriptions, but eating, drinking, and especially smoking in public are received with either glares or outright hostility. Travelers engaging a Muslim guide for outdoor tours during Ramadan should keep in mind the physical and logistical limitations that fasting involves. In many communities the 15th day of Ramadan merits special attention; one example is the all-women's outdoor market, called Tamsrit, held in Taroudant. The 28th day commemorates the day God delivered the Koran to Jibril (Gabriel)—pious men spend this night in the mosque, while women send large plates of couscous to those asking for alms at the mosque's doors. The end of Ramadan is marked by the **Id el Fitr** (break fast holiday), also called Id Sghir (small holiday).

Nov.➤ The commemoration of the **Green March** (November 6) against Spain is a national holiday that can stretch into as many as five days. Parades fill the streets, and TV programs recall the march.

FEB.➤ After the winter rains, pink and white buds blossom on **almond trees** throughout the country, and Tafraoute celebrates with a festival. This is an ideal time to tour the south, both east and west.

SPRING

MAR.–APR.➤ Two months and 10 days after the end of Ramadan, Muslims celebrate their biggest annual holiday, **Id Lkbir,** the "Great Feast." To commemorate the story of God's redemption for Ibrahim (Abraham) after Ibrahim offered to sacrifice his son as a sign of his obedience, each family that is able slaughters a sheep or, in poorer mountain communities, a goat. In the weeks leading up to the Id, markets are full of livestock, and even in the cities you can hear the echoes of bleating sheep across the rooftops. Every part of the sheep is used: the meat is eaten immediately or salted and preserved, and the woolly skins become small rugs. The holiday occasions a rush for public transportation a few days before and after, so expect to pay double for a seat in a collective taxi (if you can find one).

On **Ashura,** the day of tithing (*ashur* means "one-tenth"), the more fortunate give cash offerings to those who ask for

alms. Many businesses close for a day or two to prevent solicitations. Ashura has become a sort of children's holiday as well: adults give gifts of musical instruments, especially drums, to children, a few weeks in advance, and the sound of children drumming in the street and of boys setting off firecrackers pierces the night. Boys traditionally light bonfires and jump through the flames, though this practice is in decline; political Islamists have become more vocal in their critique of what they consider pre-Islamic or un-Islamic practices.

Aïd el Arch, or Throne Day (July 30) is a national holiday commemorating the coronation of King Mohammed VI. The country takes on a festive atmosphere (that may last for two or three days) as local communities pay tribute to the monarchy through elaborate musical, dance, and dramatic performances.

MAY–JUNE➤ Fragrant rosewater fills the air during the **Rose Festival** held in El Kelâa M'Gouna in early May. Meknes hosts an annual moussem for the saint **Ben Aïssa,** replicated in less elaborate form in smaller communities throughout the country during the spring and fall. The saint's disciples, the Aïssaoua, are one of many Sufi orders throughout North Africa and the Middle East, known for their ability to fall into trances and perform superhuman feats such as swallowing fire, walking on glass, or eating scorpions. The curiosity quotient is just as high for the Moroccan audience, some of whom themselves fall

into trances and sway to the drumbeats.

The **Id el Mouloud,** celebrating the birthday of the prophet Mohammed, may have been a 16th-century invention to counter the appeal of Christmas, but there is no trace of this in local memory. Salé has the most striking commemoration: an elaborate **candle procession** in which descendants of the corsairs, dressed in finery, wind through the streets with candles to the zaouia of Sidi Abdellah ben Hassoun.

SUMMER

JUNE➤ Fez's weeklong **Sacred Music Festival** has been drawing musicians from around the world since 1997. "Sacred music" is broadly defined here, including whirling Turkish dervishes, African soloists, American gospel, European philharmonic orchestras, and Israeli pop in addition to Moroccan melhoun, Andalusian, Gnaoua, and Aissaoua acts. Tickets must be purchased in advance.

Independence Day in Sidi Ifni is a weeklong oceanside party marking the end of colonial rule in this Spanish enclave in 1975. A large field in the center of town is taken over by merchants, storytellers, and acrobats in the morning and afternoon, and in the evening *ahawash* music and *fantasia* performances by horse cavalcades are the main attractions. The *almuggar,* as it is locally called, holds ethnographic and historical interest; local organizations dedicated to public education about local history erect elaborate displays of domestic and agricultural implements from days past as well as reports on local customs as researched by amateur historians.

The **Marrakesh Popular Arts Festival** is a week-long catalog of music and dance performances by troupes, especially Berber troupes, from throughout the country.

Essaouira hosts a **Gnaoua festival** in the summer, several days packed with performances of a musical genre rooted in West Africa that has become something of a cathartic, trance-inducing ritual in wealthy Rabat and Marrakesh homes, as well as the more modest communities in which the music was born. Popularized in the West by Hassan Hakmoun and Keith Richards of the Rolling Stones, Gnaoua draws large crowds: book a room early, plan to camp, or prepare to beg a local family for space.

JULY➤ Two festivals that have grown from saint visitations into extravagant national festivals are the moussems of **Moulay Brahim** (south of Marrakesh) and **Sidi Hmed u Moussa** in Tazeroualt (east of Tiznit). Aspects of these moussems replicate rural markets, and merchants travel from distant regions in hopes of finding customers for their homespun wool *djellabas* and *silhams,* rugs, blankets, leather slippers, silver, and copper kitchenware. Entertainment includes a range of music representing both local and more distant Moroccan customs. Sidi Hmed u Moussa represented a formidable Berber political power in the southwest until the end of the 19th century, when their power shifted increasingly from political to spiritual. All moussems are open to the public, although foreigners—especially those exploring rural locales and those toting cameras—should be prepared for gendarmes (policemen) to ask them what they're doing there.

AUG.➤ The **Asilah Arts Festival** showcases talented painters and sculptors from Morocco and abroad in this pleasant coastal town.

El Jadida hosts a **Fantasia Festival.**

2 TANGIER, TETOUAN, AND THE MEDITERRANEAN

Many travelers catch their first glimpse of Morocco in legendary Tangier—after the longest short ferry ride on the globe, replacing 21st-century Spain with timeless and tumultuous North Africa in less than 2 hours. Beyond Tangier are the ancient city of Tetouan, the alpine town of Chefchaouen, the Rif Mountains, Mediterranean beaches, Spanish enclaves, and verdant fields and valleys, all tinged with a mixture of Arabic, Berber, and European culture.

ESTLED BETWEEN THE SHORES of the Mediterranean Sea and the backbone of the Rif Mountains are the figurative golden gates through which most travelers enter Morocco. Though not associated with the *maroc typique* of deserts and oases, this northern region is one of the most naturally varied in the country. The ancient cities of Tangier and Tetouan, the mountain jewel of Chefchaouen, the eastern beaches of Al Hoceima and Saïdia, and the Spanish enclaves of Ceuta and Melilla are worlds in themselves. More than 480 km (300 mi) of coastline, both rustic and developed, the vast and wild Rif Mountains, and the lush hillsides, valleys, and fields in between create a constantly changing landscape.

Northern Morocco has a tumultuous history of invasion and revolt. Phoenician settlements dotted the coastline as early as 1200 BC and were later taken over by Carthaginians; eventually they became an important part of the Roman province of Mauretania Tingitana, one of the Roman Empire's foremost agricultural production centers. Germanic Vandals and, later, Byzantine troops made claims to the area until Arab Muslim invaders entered the region in AD 682. The dawn of Islam in Morocco began more than 1,000 years of conflict, which reached through the north into Spain, involving the native Berber tribes, Arab dynasties, Moors, and Saharan tribes.

Recent Moroccan history is, of course, marked by European imperialism. Until Moroccan independence in 1956, northern Morocco was under the control of the Spanish and the French, a colonial legacy now evident in everything from architecture to gastronomy, from divergent languages to blue-eyed Rifi Berbers.

A trip through Morocco's Mediterranean region gives a sense of the variation within Moroccan culture. The cities of Tangier and Tetouan offer a glimpse of evolving urban Morocco with their Arab-inspired sophistication, European languages, palm-lined boulevards, and copious amenities for travelers. In sharp contrast are the villages and small towns along the Rif Mountain routes, where the regional dress and a traditional, often agricultural way of life create a strong sense of timelessness. As you travel farther east, the language shifts from Arabic to Rifi Berber, mingling with Spanish and French around the cities.

As diverse as these cultures may seem, the landscape keeps up with them. Morocco's vast Mediterranean coastline supports substantive fishing, and the rocky coastal outcroppings provide perfect places for natives both old and young to cast lines from long bamboo poles. In contrast, the Rif valleys and plateaus, extremely fertile from the region's reliable annual rainfall, yield some of the country's finest agricultural products, including olives, wheat, barley, and honey. The large cities of Tangier and Tetouan bear little tactile resemblance to the timeless town of Chefchaouen or the villages that dot hillsides across the region. This close-range variety makes a journey through the north an ongoing feast for the senses.

Pleasures and Pastimes

Beaches

The one constant across the northern Moroccan outdoors is outstanding beaches. From crowded city beaches to miles of empty space, from fine sand to high cliffs, you'll find whatever combination of leisure, civilization, and scenery you have in mind on these shores.

On the far-northern Atlantic coast west of Tangier, Robinson Beach offers several uninterrupted miles of fine sand and good waves. This is the last beach on the Atlantic Ocean before its waters merge with those of the Mediterranean Sea up at Cap Spartel.

The northern Mediterranean beaches, centered on Cap Malabata, between Tangier and Ceuta, are known as some of the finest in the region. Their water is classic Mediterranean turquoise, and quiet spots are easy to come by. The road from Ceuta south to Martil passes over 32 km (20 mi) of newly developed beach resorts that offer a wide array of sports and activities.

Farther east, on the road to Al Hoceima, you'll have sweeping views along the Mediterranean coast. The water is calm here, and the beaches range from slightly pebbly to long stretches of golden sand. The tiny fishing villages of Torres de Alcalá and Kalah Iris make good afternoon stops en route to the natural sights of the east.

The area around Al Hoceima has some of the finest beaches in the north. Quemado Beach, in Al Hoceima proper, is a cove tucked between large hills, with fine sand and crystal water—during a simple swim you can see coral and schools of fish below. A kilometer (½ mile) west of the city, the beach at Asfiha comprises long stretches of sand wrapped around the bay. Farther east, the beaches along the towns of Nador, Kariet Arkmane, Ras-el-Mar, and Saïdia are also good choices.

Dining

As much of a mosaic as the region itself, northern Moroccan cuisine combines influences from several other cultures with native ingredients. Tagine is made with particular flair in the north, where olives, spices, and produce are all grown locally. *Barrogog b'basela* (lamb tagine with prunes), *djej m'qualli* (chicken tagine with lemons and olives), and *tagine b'lhout* (fish tagine) are all regional specialties.

The abundance of fresh seafood makes it a natural choice in coastal areas. Fresh grilled sardines, shrimp, and calamari are standard fare here, and any one of them makes a wonderful lunch in a small seaside village.

The finer Moroccan restaurants serve delicacies usually reserved within Moroccan culture for special occasions. Pastilla, *mechoui* (roast lamb), and *tangia* (a meat dish roasted in clay pots over fire for more than 10 hours) are well worth a try here. More common but also enjoyable is Morocco's famous couscous, combined happily in the north with fresh local produce, *za'alook* (a cold, spicy eggplant-based side dish), and a multitude of other soups and salads available at all types of restaurants.

Restaurants range from sophisticated in the larger cities to very simple in smaller towns. Be aware that generally credit cards are only accepted at the pricier venues, and that in Ceuta and Melilla you may be asked to pay in Spanish pesetas.

CATEGORY	COST*
$$$$	over 300DH
$$$	200–300DH
$$	100–200DH
$	under 100DH

per person for a three-course meal, excluding drinks, service, and tax.

Lodging

Accommodations in the north vary from opulent to downright sparse, with everything in between. You'll have a range of options in most areas. Hotels in Tangier, an area hard hit by tourists, are on a par with those of Europe, but the farther you venture off the beaten path, the farther you might feel from Tangier's five-star welcome. Particularly in some of the smaller cities east of Chefchaouen and Tetouan, hotels in this region lack the amenities to call themselves top tier. Look a bit closer, though—what they lack in luxury these hotels often make up in charm, character, and, most of all, scenic locale.

In major cities (Tangier and Tetouan) and in cities with few rated hotels, such as Chefchaouen and Al Hoceima, advance reservations are a must if you want decent accommodations. Note that prices rise in July and August and that if you'll be staying anywhere other than a five-star hotel, you may want to inquire in advance (quite seriously) about the state of the hotel's credit-card machine. Paying cash in Ceuta and Melilla may mean paying in Spanish pesetas.

CATEGORY	COST*
$$$$	over 900DH
$$$	500–900DH
$$	300–500DH
$	under 300DH

All prices are for a standard double room, excluding tax.

Exploring Tangier, Tetouan, and the Mediterranean

Great Itineraries

Numbers in the text correspond to numbers in the margin and on the maps of Tangier, Tetouan, and the Mediterranean and Tangier: The Medina.

IF YOU HAVE 3 DAYS

Save Tangier for your last day. If you arrive in Morocco via Tangier, head immediately south to 🔛 **Chefchaouen** ⑰, making a quick stop in Tetouan en route if you've gotten an early start. Spend the afternoon wandering the Kasbah, medina, and hillsides of Chefchaouen, and spend the night in the charming Casa Hassan. The next day head north via the coastal road from Tetouan to Ceuta. Stop for lunch in the **Kabila** ⑬ marina and roam the beaches around **Restinga-Smir** ⑫ before continuing north to **Ceuta** ⑪. Spend the afternoon wandering the ramparts and plazas of Ceuta; then follow the beautiful coastal road from Ceuta past Cap Malabata to 🔛 **Tangier** ①–⑨. Spend your third day wandering Tangier's medina and Kasbah area, stopping for a late lunch at the eclectic Restaurant de Saveur des Poisson.

IF YOU HAVE 5 DAYS

Spend your first full day in 🔛 **Tangier** ①–⑨, exploring the medina and other sights. The next day head south to see **Tetouan** ⑯ and continue on to 🔛 **Chefchaouen** ⑰. Take a leisurely walk through the medina and over the nearby hillsides, and enjoy dinner and an overnight stay at Casa Hassan. On day three grab lunch for the road in Chefchaouen's Place el Mahkzen (sandwiches from the cafés, fruit from the outdoor vendors) and devote the day to a drive through the hills and forests east of Chefchaouen. Follow P39 east, then take the 8500N mountain road from east of **Ketama** ⑱ to El Jebha and enjoy lunch on the beach. Follow the coastal road west toward Ceuta, stopping if you like for a swim at any of the small beaches en route. Settle into 🔛 **Kabila** ⑬ for dinner and the night. Day four takes you farther up the northern road and across into the Spanish enclave of 🔛 **Ceuta** ⑪. Explore the city and ramparts and enjoy fresh seafood for dinner. On day five travel west to Tangier via Cap Malabata. Continue out to the Caves of Hercules and **Cap Spartel** ⑩ before returning to Tangier in time for a late lunch.

Tangier, Tetouan, and the Mediterranean

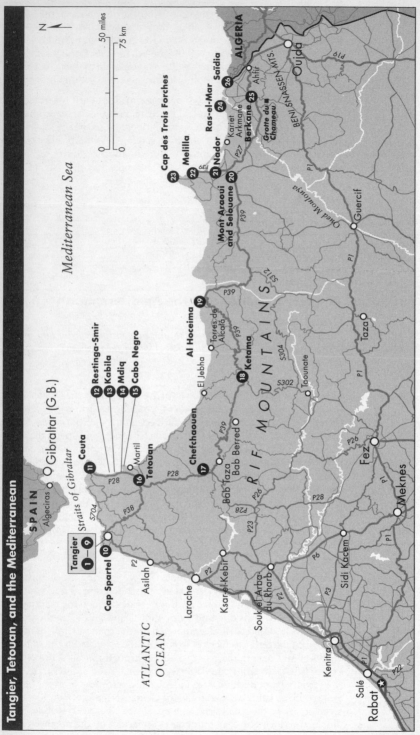

Start with a full day and night in ⊡ **Tangier** ①–⑨, with perhaps a quick sunset trip to **Cap Spartel** ⑩. Travel via Cap Malabata to ⊡ **Ceuta** ⑪ for the next day and night. On day three head south from Ceuta through the beach towns of **Kabila** ⑬, **Mdiq** ⑭, Oued Laou, and, finally, El Jebha, where Route 8500 winds south to emerge east of **Ketama** ⑱. Continue on to ⊡ **Al Hoceima** ⑲ for the night. Spend the morning of the fourth day wandering this small Rifi city and perhaps hitting some beaches before heading east to **Nador** ㉑, stopping en route for lunch at Restaurant Brabo, in **Selouane** ⑳. Cross over to **Melilla** ㉒ to explore the Medina Sidonia and take part in the evening *paseo* (promenade), dipping into some of the tapas bars in the city center. Spend day five exploring the natural sights in this area: Pack a picnic lunch and head up to the **Cap des Trois Forches** ㉓ and east to Kariet Arkmane and **Ras-el-Mar** ㉔, where you can pick up the southern route to ⊡ **Berkane** ㉕. Overnight at the Hotel Zaki, enjoying dinner by its creative chef. Spend the morning of day six exploring the Zezel Gorge route, reserving the afternoon for a trip up to the beach at **Saïdia** ㉖ via Ahfir. Spend the night in Saïdia or return to Berkane for the evening.

The next day return west from Berkane to Selouane, where you can pick up the route to Al Hoceima. Stop at sites not visited on the first leg of the journey. Spend the night in Al Hoceima. On day eight go south from Al Hoceima, passing through the green mountains around Ketama en route to ⊡ **Chefchaouen** ⑰. Spend the night at Casa Hassan, savoring a dinner prepared in its excellent kitchen. Spend day nine wandering Chefchaouen's medina and hillsides, departing in the afternoon for the short trip north to **Tetouan** ⑯. Try to visit the city sights in the afternoon so you're free to wander the medina in the bustling early evening. The last day takes you back to Tangier, with plenty of time to travel to the nearby **Cap Spartel** ⑩ and Caves of Hercules. Return to Tangier in the afternoon and consider a last-night splurge on dinner in El Korsan, at the famous Hotel El Minzah.

When to Tour Tangier, Tetouan, and the Mediterranean

The presence of the sea keeps this region temperate throughout the year. Inland, the Rif Mountain areas see rain in winter and spring, and the high peaks are often snowcapped through April.

The month of May is the region's finest hour: The wildflowers on its hillsides are in full bloom then. The traditional high season is from late July to the end of August; beaches teem with vacationing Moroccan families as well as substantial numbers of Europeans. Extensive beach campgrounds—full-fledged tent towns, really—stretch for miles in the summer. During this time prices are higher, rooms hard to find, beaches packed, and roads crowded. The fall months are quiet and peaceful.

TANGIER TO TETOUAN

To explore this tip of the top of Morocco is only to scratch the surface geographically, yet there's plenty of variety between these these two metropolitan bookends alone, including a Spanish enclave, a lighthouse surveying the end of the Mediterranean Sea, several beaches, and simple resort towns.

Tangier

15 km (9 mi) across Straits of Gibraltar from Algeciras, Spain, 350 km (220 mi) north of Casablanca.

Set dramatically against the backdrop of the turquoise Mediterranean, Tangier is a whitewashed city dappled with jolts of color from ancient walls, tiled roofs, blooming vines, and the markets that dot the streets. It's a melting pot: Sophisticated Moroccans share the sidewalks with Rifi Berbers wrapped in traditional striped *mehndis,* American and European expats, Saudi princes, and the boatloads and busloads of tourists who flock to Tangier from Spain to sip quickly from a cultural cup that took centuries to fill. Perched on the country's northernmost promontory, Tangier has always been and remains Morocco's premier threshold.

Tangier is a legendary city steeped in nostalgia: a birthplace of heroes, the home shore of ancient cultures and conquerors ranging from prehistoric man to Phoenicians, Romans, and Arabs, and later the playground of the international jet set. The name *Tangier* is derived from the mythical Labors of Hercules. One of the hero's labors was to capture a golden apple from the Garden of the Hesperides (believed to be near the ancient site of Lixus, outside modern-day Larache). In so doing, Hercules killed the giant Anteus, married his widow, Tingis, and had a son with her. As a gift to their offspring, who would later become King Sophix, Hercules grasped the rock of Gibralter with one hand and Djebel (Mt.) Musa, near Tangier, with the other, and pulled Africa and Spain apart to give his son a city protected by the sea. Sophix named this city Tingis, in honor of his mother. Thousands of years later Tingis has become Tangier, and the mythical land—although it does retain much of its magic—has evolved into a modern city.

Tangier's strategic position at the juncture of sea and ocean has long been hotly contested. Following ancient Phoenician, Roman, and then Arab conquerors, Portugal seized Tangier in the 15th century, only to hand it over to Britain in the 17th century as a part of the dowry in Catherine of Braganza's marriage to King Charles II (a dowry that also included Bombay). England's control of Tangier was short-lived; in 1685 it fell into the hands of the Arab Moulay Ismail. The French came to Tangier in 1912, but not without disputes from England and continued scurries over control, so that by 1923 Tangier was governed by a international authority. The city's international status, complete with special tax laws and loose governance, attracted international crowds. Tangier in the first half of the 20th century was a sumptuous, rather anarchic sensory feast that drew artists, writers, diplomats, heiresses, and fun seekers from all over the world.

With Moroccan independence from French rule in 1956, Tangier was incorporated into Moroccan governance. The international population—and the investors—dwindled, and the city's magnificence retreated to the realm of myth. Modern-day Tangier is much more subdued than the sybaritic haven of the glory days, yet it still has immeasurable appeal. Like Morocco's distinctive *zellij* (mosaic) tiles, the city is an amalgam—in this case of various periods and nationalities—that appears to change shape depending on the angle from which it's viewed.

At first glance, Tangier can be a very intimidating place. Particularly in the port area, its streets play host to some very hard characters, who seem to have an inexhaustible appetite for annoying passersby. But beyond this frustrating first impression, Tangier has a charm that echoes off the crumbling Kasbah walls, lurks around corners in the serpentine medina, grows through vines of bougainvillea, and bounces gently off French balconies, Spanish cafés, and other remnants of times gone by.

A Good Walk

Tangier can be divided into two parts: the medina and the Ville Nouvelle (New City). A stroll through the city should begin on Boulevard Pasteur, the thriving Ville Nouvelle thoroughfare that crawls north toward the medina. The belvedere at the top of the boulevard has a fine view over the city and the sea. From there walk to the **Place de la France** ①, passing the French consulate and the glorious El Minzah hotel as you snake your way down to the bustling **Grand Socco** ②. West of the Grand Socco, visit **St. Andrew's Church** ③; then reenter the Socco and head north—following the red-and-yellow signs to the right—to the Kasbah. To the left as you walk are the **Mendoubia Gardens** ④; to the right, stores bursting with merchandise. At every turn of this living labyrinth, you can see the city from a different angle, adding another tile to the mosaic that is Tangier.

From the gardens follow Rue d'Italie, which dips and then climbs, turning into Rue de la Kasbah as it rises. At the top of the street, pass through the Bab el Kasbah to enter the **Kasbah** ⑤ itself. Explore the Kasbah area and **Dar el Makhzen** ⑥; then stop for a drink at the Café Détroit, whose stairway appears as you exit the Dar el Makhzen. Leaving the café, stop and take in the sea view from the belvedere. Exit the Kasbah area through Bab el Assa, off the Place de la Kasbah, and descend slowly past a maze of medina streets. Look on the left for **Villa Hosni** ⑦. Continuing downhill, stop at a few of the most impressive stores selling traditional Tangerine goods along the Rue des Chrétiens.

The route winds to the Petit Socco and left through the medina's main drag, Rue de la Marine, past numerous vendors. The **Grand Mosque** ⑧ will appear on the right, after which the street ends—here you can either climb down a set of stairs to the port area or walk uphill on Rue Portugal. The latter route leads to the **American Legation** ⑨ and continues past Berber women selling sundries and various vegetable souks. Climbing the stairs at the end of the vegetable market, you'll emerge back on Rue de la Liberté at the foot of the Hotel El Minzah. Follow the street up to Place de la France to come full circle.

TIMING

This walk takes at least five or six hours.

NEED A BREAK?

Occupying the upper floors of a medina home with floor-to-ceiling windows is the fine tearoom **Salon de Thé/Restaurant le Détroit** (☎ 09/93-80-80), known as "Café Détroit." Established during the international era by beat writer Brion Gysin, it's the perfect place for the weary wanderer to sit and take in panoramic views of the Mediterranean Sea and palace gardens along with fabulous Moroccan cookies and mint tea.

Sights to See

⑨ **American Legation.** Following Rue de Portugal as it climbs upward, look for a set of double stairs on the right, leading to an archway. When you find yourself under a balcony with a tile underside, walk up the stairs, go through the archway, and follow the winding street until you see the seal of the United States. The Legation is housed in a typical Tangerine medina home with carved wooden doors, ornate plaster finishings, and high walls surrounding an outdoor courtyard. Preserved today as an American Historic Landmark, this property was given to the United States by the Moroccan sultan in 1821. Morocco was the first nation in the world to recognize the independent United States, and this building was the first American ambassadorial residence, established in 1777. Displays include the history of Tangier, correspondence between the sultan and George Washington, and artwork. The

24

Tangier: The Medina

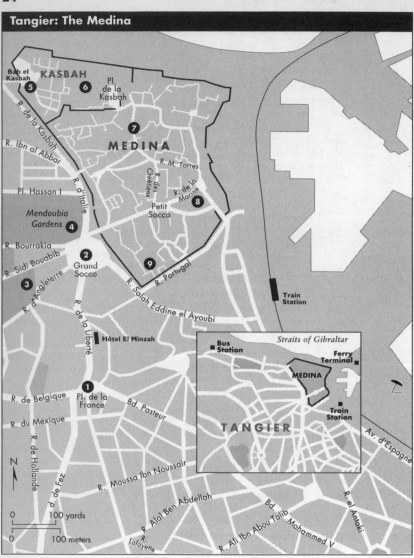

American Legation, **9**

Dar el Makhzen, **6**

Grand Mosque, **8**

Grand Socco, **2**

Kasbah, **5**

Mendoubia
Gardens, **4**

Place de la France, **1**

St. Andrew's
Church, **3**

Villa Hosni, **7**

library has a small but interesting collection of English-language books, augmented by photos and historical documents on the walls. ⊠ *8, Zankat d'Amerique,* ☎ *09/93–53–17.* ⊙ *Mon., Wed., and Thurs. 10–1 and 3–5; and by appointment.*

⑥ Dar el Makhzen. Constructed by the 17th-century sultan Moulay Ismail, this was the Kasbah's palace. The sultan's former apartments now house an interesting museum of Moroccan arts, with historic, finely crafted examples of carved cedar ceilings painted in the *zouak* style, mosaic floors, carpets, traditional Fez furniture, jewelry, ceramics, leather, daggers, illuminated manuscripts, and textiles.

The marble columns in the courtyard were taken from the ancient Roman city of Volubilis. Don't miss the mosaic *Voyage of Venus* or the life-size Carthaginian tomb. Exit the palace via the former treasury of Moulay Ismail, the Bit el Mal; look for the giant wooden boxes once used to hold gold and precious gems. ☎ *09/93–20–97.* ⊙ *Wed.–Mon. 9:30–1 and 3–6.*

⑧ Grand Mosque. Look for the beautiful green-and-white minaret. The mosque was built by Moulay Ismail upon the return of Tangier to Arab rule in 1685. Entrance is strictly forbidden to non-Muslims.

② Grand Socco. Tangier's chief market area in times past, the Great Souk has dwindled to a collection of cafés and now serves as a local transportation hub.

⑤ Kasbah. Sprawling across the highest point of the ancient medina, Tangier's Kasbah has been tinkered with since the Roman era. During early Arab rule it was the traditional residence of the sultan and his harem. Since then the Kasbah has become a fashionable residential area—particularly in the international era, but even so today. Stop at the overlook off the main Kasbah square for wonderful views across the straits to Gibraltar and Spain's Costa del Sol, accompanied by the roar of the ocean below.

④ Mendoubia Gardens. The former residence of the Mendoub—the sultan's representative on the governing commission during the international years—is now a quiet, shady park. To the right of the entrance is a large banyan tree that locals claim is more than 800 years old. Farther into the park is a small terrace with several bronze cannons from European warships and good views of the sea. ⊠ *Rue Bourrakia.* ⊙ *Sun. 9–6; Mon.–Thurs. and Sat. 3–6.*

① Place de la France. Famous for its café scene in the international era, the Place de la France is the center of Tangier. It fills up during the nightly promenade, after about 6 PM.

③ St. Andrew's Church. This 19th-century Anglican church is one of the purest vestiges of Tangier's international days. The architecture and interior are both Moorish in flavor (the "Our Father" and "Gloria" are inscribed in Arabic above the altar), while the cemetery, with graves of famous Britons who spent time in Morocco, recalls the English countryside. ⊠ *50, Rue d'Angleterre,* ☎ *09/93–46–33.* ⊙ *Daily 9–6 except during Sun. services (8:30 and 11 AM).*

⑦ Villa Hosni. A former home of the actress Barbara Hutton, this address was known in the international era for Hutton's lavish parties and eclectic crowd. It was said she had the medina streets widened to allow her Rolls-Royce to enter the villa's gates.

Dining and Lodging

$$$ ✕ **El Korsan.** Tangier's top restaurant serves traditional Moroccan cuisine in the most sumptuous possible manner. Specialties include suc-

culent mechoui, slow-cooked tagines, seafood, and couscous. The decor is classically Moroccan, with soaring arches and handicrafts; the staff is attentive; and Andalusian music is performed nightly. The environment makes your meal a true experience. ⊠ *Hotel El Minzah, 85, Rue de la Liberté,* ☏ *09/93–58–85. MC, V.*

$$$ ✕ **Hammadi.** Decorated in an over-the-top Moroccan style, with banquette seating and lush pillows and brocades, Hammadi is not to be missed if you have two evenings in Tangier and can spend the first at El Korsan. Complete with a slightly outdated feel, it has a comfortable charm and ambience, and is slightly less expensive than its competitor. Try the house pastilla, chicken tagine, or *kefta* (beef patties). ⊠ *2, Rue de la Kasbah,* ☏ *09/93–45–14. MC, V.*

$$ ✕ **Restaurant Populaire La Saveur du Poisson.** Who'd have thought
★   such an unassuming little eatery could be so good? Housed in a stall on the stairs leading down from Rue de la Liberté to the Berber market, this is one of Tangier's best-kept secrets. Owner Mohamed Belhadj combines his knowledge of herbs and spices (brought from his native Rif Mountains) with seafood and produce from the rest of the region to create a simple menu of succulent dishes. The restaurant is filled with dried and fresh herbs, flowers, and mounds of fresh produce. Try the fish soup, the fish brochettes, or the seafood tagine; you'll also be served special fruit juices and water infused with flowers, as well as powders said to "aid in digestion." Don't pass up the dessert mixture of strawberries, walnuts, and honey. The flavors are exquisite and the vibe relaxed. ⊠ *2, Escalier Waller (on right side, halfway down the stairs from Hotel El Minzah),* ☏ *09/33–63–26. No credit cards.*

$$ ✕ **Restaurant Raihani.** This is one of Tangier's finest Moroccan restaurants, and there's an excellent French menu as well. Try the pastilla, couscous, or brochettes. Classically understated, the Moroccan decor is simple and tasteful. ⊠ *10, Rue Ahmed Chaouki (off Boulevard Pasteur),* ☏ *09/93–48–66.*

$$ ✕ **Rubis Grill.** Decorated in warm wood and originally run by an English couple, the Rubis serves fresh grilled meats and seafood as well as a full international menu. A guitarist entertains most evenings, and the bar fills up with a mix of locals and expats, creating a cordial environment. ⊠ *3, Ibn Rochd,* ☏ *09/93–14–43.*

$ ✕🛏 **Hotel/Restaurant El Djenina.** This lovely restaurant serves soups, fresh grilled meats, and seafood as well as a number of tagines and international dishes. The bar is well stocked, and freshly made crepes make delicious desserts. The patio tables look out over Tangier's harbor and a very pleasant garden. Upstairs are some simple, clean guest rooms; ask for one with a balcony. ⊠ *8, Rue el Antaki,* ☏ *09/94–22–44.* 𝔽𝔸𝕏 *09/94–22–46. MC, V.*

$$$$ 🛏 **El Minzah.** Tangier's premier hotel was built in 1930 by the English
★   lord Bute. Decorated in Moorish style, it has extensive gardens yet is close by the entrance to the medina. Studded wooden doors, a helpful staff in Ottoman costume, beautiful gardens, an elegant patio, the constant sound of falling water (a music much cherished by Moroccans), and fine views over the Straits of Gibraltar to Spain make it a classic experience. The spacious rooms are carpeted and decorated with rich fabrics, brass light fixtures, and traditional Moroccan tables, pottery, and artwork. ⊠ *85, Rue de la Liberté,* ☏ *09/93–58–85 or 08/00–37–44,* 𝔽𝔸𝕏 *09/93–45–46. 142 rooms, 14 suites. 2 restaurants, 3 bars, piano bar, air-conditioning, in-room safes, no-smoking rooms, pool, beauty salon, massage, sauna, 18-hole golf course, 5 tennis courts, health club, horseback riding, baby-sitting, meeting rooms, laundry service, free parking. AE, DC, MC, V.*

$$$ ⊡ **Rembrandt.** A somewhat less expensive option in the Ville Nouvelle, Rembrandt offers simple rooms with little in the way of style. It has a nostalgic, understated, 1940s sort of charm, and its central location makes it a good all-around choice. Many package tours stay here. ⊠ *Boulevard Pasteur,* ☎ *09/93–78–70,* FAX *09/93–04–43. 63 rooms, 6 suites. Restaurant, pool, free parking. MC, V.*

$$$ ⊡ **Sheherazade.** This beachfront hotel has a private beach that makes surfing and other water sports a breeze. Rooms are standard modern. The rooftop terrace has good views over the beach and city. ⊠ *11, Avenue des FAR,* ☎ *09/94–08–03,* FAX *09/94–08–01. 656 rooms. Bar, dance club. MC, V.*

$$$ ⊡ **Solazur.** The best of Tangier's beachfront hotels, Solazur offers direct beach access and many rooms with good sea views. The late Tangier resident Malcolm Forbes held his 70th-birthday party here. ⊠ *Avenue des FAR,* ☎ *09/94–01–64,* FAX *09/94–52–86. 360 rooms. 2 restaurants, sauna, tennis court, dance club. DC, MC, V.*

$$$ ⊡ **Tanjah Flandria.** Well situated on the main thoroughfare in the Ville Nouvelle, this modern hotel has a rooftop pool, a Moroccan lounge, and an adjoining art gallery. The large, carpeted rooms have large beds, good light from large windows, and relaxing earth-toned color schemes, blending classy functionality with such Moroccan touches as pottery, brass mirrors, and paintings. ⊠ *6, Boulevard Mohammed V (off Boulevard Pasteur),* ☎ *09/93–32–79,* FAX *09/93–43–47. 153 rooms, 4 suites, 18 apartments. 2 restaurants, piano bar, snack bar, air-conditioning, pool, dance club, travel services, free parking. AE, DC, MC, V.*

$ ⊡ **Hotel Continental.** Morocco's very first hotel was built in 1865 in the Victorian style, and Victoria's son Alfred was the first official guest, in 1885. The yellowed pages of the 19th-century guest book also contain the simple quilled entry "Degas: Paris." Kept strictly to Victorian style until 1990, the Continental has made some changes since then, adding Moroccan arches and crafts. Imbued with a slightly threadbare charm, it's nostalgic, romantic, and stately, perched over the old port. You can relax at will in a variety of small parlors, reading rooms, sunrooms, nooks, and crannies. Each of the 70 rooms is uniquely decorated; Numbers 108 and 208 have the best sea views. With breakfast included, it's a good value. ⊠ *36, Dar Baroud,* ☎ *09/93–10–24,* FAX *09/93–11–43. Restaurant, café, steam room, free parking. No credit cards.*

$ ⊡ **Hotel El Muniria.** Made famous as the hotel of choice for the 1950s beat generation, El Muniria still offers basic but very clean accommodations and a garden. Famous former guests include Allen Ginsburg, Jack Kerouac, and William Burroughs, who wrote *Naked Lunch* in Room 9. Several rooms have private bathrooms, but most share facilities. The hotel's legendary late-night bar, the Tanger Inn, still draws both locals and beatniks. ⊠ *1, Rue Magellan,* ☎ *09/93–53–37. 8 rooms. Restaurant, bar. No credit cards.*

Nightlife and the Arts

Tangier's nightlife begins with the early evening promenade and café hour, from about 6 to 9, when the streets teem with locals and expats alike. In the summer many beachfront cafés are full well into the night. Dining is another mainstay of Tangerine entertainment, with many restaurants open well past 10 PM—rare in Morocco.

Discos, of which there is no shortage in Tangier, begin to fill around 11 and thump well into the morning. Some of the better clubs in town: **Borsalino** (⊠ 30, Avenue du Prince de Moulay Abdellah). **Regine Club** (⊠ Rue El Mansour Dahbi). **Up 2000** (⊠ Hotel les Almohades, Avenue des FAR).

Morocco Palace (⊠ 11, Avenue Prince Moulay Abdellah, ☎ 09/93–86–14) offers quality belly-dancing shows until 1 AM, at which point it turns into a disco.

Performances of traditional Moroccan music are periodically sponsored by the American Legation, the French Consulate, and the Institut Français de Tanger. The tourist office can provide information on concerts; the **Galerie Delacroix** (⊠ 86, Rue de la Liberté) has information on French-sponsored events and hosts interesting contemporary-art exhibitions.

Several cinemas show French films and, on occasion, original-version American films. Try the **Cinema Flandria** (⊠ Rue Ibn Rochd), near the hotel of the same name.

Shopping

Tangier can be an intense place to shop; proprietors are accustomed to inflicting their hard sell on day-trippers from Spain. The boutiques in the Ville Nouvelle offer standard Moroccan items, such as carpets, brass, leather, ceramics, and clothing at higher—but fixed—prices. The more unique and creative high-quality items, however, are mostly in the specialty shops throughout the medina. Don't be afraid to stop at small, unnamed stores, as these often stock real off-the-beaten-path treasures.

The name **Art de la Reliure** (⊠ Rue de Belgique, ☎ 09/93–25–80) means "the art of binding," and this tiny store specializes in handmade detailed leather goods—folders, desk sets, and address books in addition to bags. One of the finest antiques shops in Morocco, **Boutique Majid** (⊠ 66, Rue des Chrétiens, ☎ 09/93–88–92) has an amazing collection of antique textiles, silks, rich embroideries, rugs, and Berber jewelry (often silver with coral and amber) as well as wooden boxes, household items, copper, and brass. Prices are high, but the quality of the items is indisputable. As proprietor Abdelmajid says, "It's an investment!" The simple **Boutique Marouaini** (⊠ 65, Rue des Chrétiens, ☎ 09/33–60–67) sells ceramics, wood, rugs, clothing, and metal ware, as well as paintings by local artists at very reasonable prices. The extensive collection of rugs at **Coin de l'Arts Berbères** (⊠ 66, Rue des Chrétiens, ☎ 09/93–80–94) includes samples from the Middle and High Atlas regions, made by Saharan and southern Berber tribes. Check out the collection of doors, locks, windows, and boxes from southern Morocco and the Sahara Desert. You'll need to bargain here. The fixed-price, government-regulated **Ensemble Artisanal** (⊠ Rue de Belgique, ☎ 09/93–15–89) offers handicrafts from all over Morocco. If nothing else, it's a good place to develop an eye for quality items and their market prices before you hit the medina shops. **Galerie Tindouf** (⊠ 72, Rue de la Liberté, ☎ 09/93–86–00) is a pricey antiques shop specializing in clothing, home furnishings, and period pieces from old Tangier. The owners also run the Bazar Tindouf, right down the street, which sells modern Moroccan crafts of ceramic, wood, iron, brass, and silver plus embroidery and rugs. Attached to the Tanjah Flandria hotel, the **Tanjah Flandria** art gallery (⊠ Rue Ibn Rochd, ☎ 09/93–31–64) sells sculpture, paintings, and other works inspired by Tangier, featuring both Moroccan and expatriate artists. It's open later than most shops: Monday through Saturday from 10 to 1 and 5 to 8.

Cap Spartel

10 *16 km (10 mi) west of Tangier.*

Minutes from Tangier is the jutting Cap Spartel, the extreme northwest corner of the African continent. Known to Romans as Ampelusium (Cape of the Vines), this fertile area sits high above the rocky coast. A shady, tree-lined road leads up to the summit, where a large lighthouse has wonderful views out over the Mediterranean at the very point where it meets the Atlantic; ask the kindly gatekeeper to show you around. Stop for tea at the Café-Bar Sol and browse the various wares available from outdoor vendors.

Five kilometers (3 miles) south of the Cap are the **Caves of Hercules.** Inhabited since prehistoric times, the caves were used more recently to cut millstones, hence the hundreds of round indentations on their walls and ceiling. The caves are known for their windowlike opening in the shape of Africa, through which the surf comes crashing into the lagoon and lower cave. Stairs lead down to a viewing platform with a great vantage point and just a touch of sea spray. The caves are open daily from 9 to 1 and 3 to 6, with an admission fee of 10 DH.

Above and to the right of the caves' entrance, follow the blue-tile wall down to a path leading to a small platform café. Run by Abdelkader, this tiny café is the prime spot from which to view the caves from the outside. Its small wicker seats are ideal places to take in the stunning views down nearby Robinson Beach and to look down on local fisherman trying their luck on the rocks below. Besides these features, the tiny café offers a hidden secret. The small gray door near the café's kitchen opens into a two-story dining room inside Abdelkader's own personal cave; he will serve up one of his wonderful tagines while the sound of the surf echoes off the cool cave walls.

Leaving the caves and following the road straight for about 2 km (1 mi), look down toward the beach, and you'll see the ruins of the 3rd-century (AD) Roman town of **Cotta** in the middle of the fields. Cotta was known for its production of garum, an anchovy paste that was exported throughout the Roman Empire; all that remains of it now are the foundations of buildings, baths, and villas. You can walk to the site from the road or, more easily, from Robinson Beach.

Lodging

$$$$ ☷ **Hotel Mirage.** This modern cliff-top complex directly above the Caves of Hercules has appropriately stunning sea views in season. The atmosphere is relaxed, and the restaurant serves excellent seafood and international cuisine. ⊠ *Grotte de Hercules, Route de Cap Spartel,* ☎ *09/33–33–31,* ℻ *09/33–34–92. 30 bungalows. Restaurant, pool, free parking. MC, V. Closed Oct.–Mar.*

En Route   The drive northeast from Tangier to the Spanish enclave of Ceuta follows the area's other cape, Cap Malabata. The coastal road passes through several small seaside towns, many of which have small cafés serving fresh fish. The road turns inland on the approach to Fndiq, the unremarkable border town, snaking through the edge of the Rif Mountains before opening up to panoramic views over Ceuta.

Ceuta

⑪   *94 km (58 mi) northeast of Tangier.*

When it was incorporated into Spanish rule in 1580, Ceuta was one of the finest cities in northern Morocco. Thriving under its Arab conquerors, the city was extolled in 14th-century documents for its busy harbors, fine educational institutions, ornate mosques, and sprawling villas. Smelling prosperity, the Portuguese seized Ceuta in 1415; the city passed to Spain when Portugal itself became part of Spain in 1580, and it remains under Spanish rule today.

Ceuta's strategic position on the Straits of Gibraltar explains its ongoing use as a Spanish military town (many of the large buildings around the city are military properties). Walls built by the Portuguese surround the city itself and, together with the ramparts, are impressive legacies of the town's historic importance on European–Near Eastern trade routes.

Now serving mainly as a port of entry or departure between Spain and Morocco, Ceuta has scant attractions for travelers. The most interesting sights are in the upper city, away from the bustle of the port. Start your walk in the **Plaza de Nuestra Señora de Africa,** centered on a **war memorial** to the Spanish invasion of Morocco in 1859. The square is flanked by a pair of impressive churches: to the north, the church of **Nuestra Señora de Africa** (Our Lady of Africa), and to the south, the **cathedral.** Both were built in 18th-century Baroque style on the sites of former mosques.

Wander west out from the plaza to the **Foso de San Felipe** (St. Philip's Moat), built in 1530 by Portuguese crusaders to strengthen the town's fortifications. Crossing the moat gives you grand views of the ramparts, including their inner walls and structures.

For more ambitious strollers, an hour's walk leads onto the rocky peninsula known as **Monte Hacho.** Wandering east along the Avenida de la Marina Española, you'll pass the former Spanish **Ermita de San Antonio** (St. Anthony's Convent) and its statue of General Francisco Franco, and see the walls of Fort Hacho. Continue out to the **Castillo des Desnarigade**— a walled coastal fort that now houses a military museum—for one of the best views in town. From the onetime castle you can look out across Ceuta's port and, on clear days, drink in a stunning view of Gibraltar.

Crossing into Ceuta from Morocco involves a roughly 30-minute process of having your passport stamped by customs authorities and being shuffled through several checkpoints. Note that Spanish pesetas are the standard currency here, with dirhams accepted only in some establishments. Cash machines are readily available downtown; try the **Banco de España** (⊠ Plaza de España). Large hotels will also change money for their guests.

Dining and Lodging
When calling Ceuta from Morocco or from overseas, use the country code for Spain, 34.

$$$$ ✕ **La Torre.** Ceuta's best restaurant serves classic Andalusian dishes, sumptuous seafood, and creative daily specials in an open room in the city's oldest quarter. Reservations are advisable. ⊠ *Gran Hotel Parador–La Muralla, 15, Plaza Nuestra Señora de Africa,* ☎ *956/51–49–49. No lunch. MC, V.*

$$$ ✕ **Casa Silva.** This tiny, charming restaurant feels like the dining room of an old Spanish home. The kitchen cooks up delicious seafood, Spanish specialties with an Andalusian flavor, and savory meat dishes; the house specialty by far is a lovely seafood paella. There's also an extensive wine list. ⊠ *87, Calle Real,* ☎ *956/51–37–15.*

$$ ✕ **Club Nautico.** Overlooking the harbor, this small seafood place specializes in fish, calamari, and shrimp. The decor is nothing remarkable, but the Club makes a nice lunch stop. ⊠ *Calle Edrissis,* ☎ *956/51–44–00.*

$$$$ ▦ **Gran Hotel Parador–La Muralla.** The top lodging in Ceuta, La Muralla is conveniently located on the main square, with views of the garden, sea, or the plaza itself. Rooms are large and modern, with ample windows. ⊠ *15, Plaza Nuestra Señora de Africa,* ☎ *956/51–49–40,* FAX *956/51–49–47. 77 rooms, 29 suites. Restaurant, bar, minibars, pool, free parking. AE, DC, MC, V.*

$$$ ▦ **Melia Confort.** On a busy street in Ceuta's commercial center, the Melia offers comfort and amenities within walking distance of the main sights. The rooms are simply decorated in calming earth tones, and the airy, sunny lobby is adjoined by some small boutiques. The restaurant

serves international cuisine. ⊠ *3, Alcalde Sanchez Prado,* ☎ *956/51–12–00,* FAX *956/51–15–01. 120 rooms. Restaurant, pub, pool, exercise room, free parking. AE, MC, V.*

$$ ▣ **La Rociera.** A short walk from the Plaza Nuestra Señora de Africa, and thus near restaurants and shopping, this simple hotel offers basic, clean rooms with showers. The staff is polite and helpful. ⊠ *Calle Real,* ☎ *956/51–35–59. 12 rooms. MC, V.*

En Route Winding south out of Ceuta, back into Morocco, the P28 follows the coast toward Martil. The road gives you easy access to a string of well-developed beach resorts that combine sophisticated amenities with gorgeous Mediterranean beaches.

Restinga-Smir

⑫ *18 km (11 mi) south of Ceuta.*

Until recently, Restinga-Smir was a small fishing village. Development has come quickly: It's now one of the region's priciest summering spots, rimmed by a long, uninterrupted beach. Diversions include windsurfing, horseback riding, miniature golf, tennis, and camping, all of which your hotel can arrange. The port, Marina Smir, is lined with shops, cafés, and small restaurants. Most upscale restaurants are in the hotels, but the seafood places on the marina are all good bets, grilling up the catch of the day in a pleasant outdoor atmosphere.

Lodging

$$$$ ▣ **Hyatt Regency/Marina Smir.** Right on the beach, this luxurious all-suite hotel provides every comfort you can dream up. Every one of the spacious suites has a balcony facing the pool and the private beach. The restaurant features Moroccan and Spanish-inspired cuisine, the snack bar serves light grilled lunches poolside, and the bar has a patio with sea views. Outdoor activities are easily arranged. The staff is attentive, and the atmosphere breathes relaxation. Prices rise substantially in the summer. ⊠ *Route de Ceuta via Tetuoan, 93200,* ☎ *09/97–12–34,* FAX *09/97–12–35. 59 suites. Restaurant, bar, snack bar, air-conditioning, in-room safes, pool, sauna, spa, exercise room, jet skiing, windsurfing, beach, free parking. MC, V.*

$$ ▣ **Hotel Karabou.** The Karabou is small and quaint, with a distinctly maritime feel. The rooms are simple rather than plush, but the staff is friendly, and you're a quick walk from the beach. It's a steal for the price, so reserve ahead in the summer months. ⊠ *Route de Ceuta, Km 27,* ☎ *09/97–70–70,* FAX *09/97–70–48. 24 rooms. Restaurant, bar, pool, 4 tennis courts, dance club, free parking. MC, V.*

Kabila

⑬ *2 km (1 mi) south of Restinga-Smir.*

Kabila is quite literally a tourist village—a sprawling tourist complex complete with hotel, villas (some for rent), a helpful staff, a shopping center, and a marina with restaurants. The beaches are spotless (if a bit grainier than those farther north and south), and the majority of the sand is reserved for resort guests. Well-kept grounds and plenty of flowers keep the area green. Think California, with Moroccan food.

Dining and Lodging

$$$$ ✕ **El Pueblo Restaurant.** Dine indoors or out at this charming marina restaurant, decorated with Moroccan lanterns, pottery, and Tangerine paintings. The extensive menu features exotic salads and creative seafood and meat dishes and is augmented by a good wine list. Portions are large. ⊠ *Marina,* ☎ *09/97–71–94. MC, V.*

$$$ 🏨 **Hotel Kabila.** No expense was spared in creating this full-blown tourist package. The room are furnished with a distinctively Rifi Berber flair, featuring regional handicrafts, and each has a patio (or, on upper floors, a balcony) with footpaths leading to the hotel's private beach. The grounds are well-maintained gardens with blooming flowers and clean paths. The restaurant serves both regional Moroccan and Spanish dishes and backs them with live music most evenings. ⊠ *Route de Ceuta, Km 20,* ☎ *09/66–60–13, 66–60–71, or 66–60–90,* 🆎 *09/66–62–03. 82 rooms, 14 suites. Restaurant, bar, snack bar, pool, golf, 4 tennis courts, exercise room, beach. MC, V.*

Mdiq

🚩 *2 km (1 mi) south of Kabila.*

Mdiq is a charming, friendly seaside town with an appealingly lived-in feel. Unlike those in the more touristy towns just north, Mdiq's hotels are more or less confined to the beachfronts, with the result that Mdiq is a functioning town in its own right. The main streets are lined with small stores and cafés, and there are plenty of side streets to explore. The hillside behind town is dotted with whitewashed and colorfully painted homes. At the port fresh seafood is served both in a restaurant and at food stalls within plain view of fishing boats and the ongoing activity of local fishermen.

Lodging

$$$ 🏨 **Hotel Golden Beach.** This well-run waterfront hotel offers comfortable lodging in airy, simple, modern rooms. The location is both scenic and central, near the bus station. Many of the guests are on package holidays. ⊠ *Route de Ceuta,* ☎ *09/97–50–77,* 🆎 *09/97–50–96. 86 rooms. Restaurant, bar, café, pool, nightclub, free parking. MC, V.*

Cabo Negro

🚩 *3½ km (2 mi) east of P28 (turnoff 4 km south of Mdiq).*

The beach here is more rugged and hilly than those around it, leaving Cabo Negro less developed than its neighboring towns. Horseback riding is one of the main attractions in this area, with several stables offering rentals in the town center. Try La Ferma—besides arranging rides, it has a good, largely French restaurant. There's also the 18-hole Cabo Negro Royal Golf Course (☞ Outdoor Activities and Sports *in* Tangier, Tetouan, and the Mediterranean A to Z, *below*).

Known as "Tetouan's beach," **Martil** comes alive mainly in the summer, when it fills with Moroccans and feels more crowded than Cabo Negro. The rest of the year it's a good place to take a walk on the sand or enjoy lunch at a beachfront café.

Dining and Lodging

$$$$ ✕🏨 **Club Mediterannie Yasmina.** This beautiful seaside resort complex has comfortable rooms, an attentive staff, and beautiful surroundings from May through September. You're near both the beach and the golf course. The popular restaurant serves international cuisine. ⊠ *Cabo Negro,* ☎ *09/97–82–65, 97–82–66, or 97–82–98,* 🆎 *09/97–81–99. Restaurant, bar, pool, 18-hole golf course, 12 tennis courts, nightclub, free parking. MC, V. Closed Oct.–Apr.*

Tetouan

16 *40 km (24 mi) south of Ceuta.*

Nestled in a valley between the Mediterranean Sea and the backbone of the Rif Mountains, the city of Tetouan was founded in the 3rd century BC by Berbers, who called it Tamuda. Romans destroyed the city in the 1st century AD and built their own in its place, the ruins of which you can still see on the edge of town. The Merenids built a city in the 13th century, which flourished for a century and was then destroyed by Spanish forces, who ruled intermittently from the 14th to 17th centuries. The medina and Kasbah that you see today were built in the 15th and 16th centuries and improved upon in the centuries thereafter: Moulay Ismail took Tetouan back in the 17th century and traded with the Spanish throughout the 18th. Tetouan's proximity to Spain, and especially to the enclave of Ceuta, kept its Moroccan population in close contact with the Spanish throughout the 20th century. Spanish religious orders set up schools here and established trading links between mainland Tetouan, Ceuta, and mainland Spain. Their presence infused the city with Spanish architecture (notice the balconies and iron work on homes) and culture (Moroccan girls in private-school uniforms fill the streets at lunchtime). This Andalusian flavor mingles with the strong Rifi Berber and traditional Arab identities of the majority to make Tetouan a kind of modern Moroccan mélange of sights, sounds, and society.

A leisurely stroll through Tetouan begins most naturally in the **Place Moulay el Mehdi,** a large plaza ringed with cafés and lighted by strings of lights in the evening. Follow Boulevard Mohammed V—past Spanish-inspired houses with wrought-iron balconies—to **Place Hassan II,** the open square near the Royal Palace. West of Place Hassan II, off Place Al-Jala, the **Archaeological Museum** (⊠ Boulevard Aljazaer, ☎ 09/96–71–03) holds a large collection of Roman mosaics, coins, bronze, and pottery found at various sites in northern Morocco. It's open weekdays from 9 to noon and 2 to 6, and admission is 10DH. From the southeastern corner of Place Hassan II, across from the palace, follow Rue Terrafin through Bab er Rouah to enter the **medina.** The street follows a more or less straight path through the craft, food, clothing, and houseware souks. Tetouan's medina is fairly straightforward, so don't hesitate to deviate from the main path in your explorations; it's hard to get lost. As you exit the medina through the Bab el Okla, visit the **Museum of Moroccan Arts** (⊠ Avenue Hassan II, in medina wall, ☎ 09/97–05–05), open weekdays 8:30–noon and 2:30–5:30, with free admission. Housed in a former sultan's fortress surrounded by an Andalusian garden, the museum has a wonderful collection of traditional Moroccan costumes, embroidery, weapons, and musical instruments. The **Artisan School** nearby has craftsmen working in stalls on zellij tiles, embroidery, and leather goods.

Dining and Lodging

Considering its size, Tetouan has very few good restaurants and hotels. The ones listed below are clean and comfortable.

$$ ✕ **Restaurant Restinga.** Here you'll find an excellent value and well-made Moroccan dishes in a simple and quaint atmosphere. Try the house tagine or the mixed platter of fried fish. Dining is available inside or in the breezy courtyard. Service is friendly, and beer is occasionally available. ⊠ *21, Boulevard Mohammed V,* ☎ *no phone. No credit cards.*

$$ ✕ **Restaurant Saigon.** This oddly named restaurant is very popular with locals. Standard Moroccan and Spanish fare is served in a charming environment, with pottery and taped music for ambience. Try the

chicken tagine or the house paella. ✉ *2, Rue Mohammed Ben Larbi Torres.*, ☎ *no phone. No credit cards.*

$ ✕ **Pâtisserie Dallas.** Perfect at breakfast or teatime, this cozy spot serves homemade cookies, cakes, pastries, and other delicacies. Fresh-squeezed fruit juices take the beverage menu beyond coffee, tea, and soft drinks. ✉ *11, Rue Ben Youseff*, ☎ *09/96–60–69. No credit cards.*

$ ✕ **Snack Taos.** The atmosphere is entirely casual at this great little luncheon diner. Fill up on sandwiches, salads, brochettes, fried seafood, tagines, and couscous here or take it on the road. ✉ *3, Rue 10 Mai*, ☎ *no phone. No credit cards.*

$$$ ⊡ **Hotel Safir.** Tetouan's finest hotel is a mile from its center. Part of a large chain of Moroccan hotels, it has classic Moroccan decor and well-furnished rooms, many with balconies. The garden has some pleasantly shady places to sit, and the restaurant serves well-regarded fixed-price Moroccan meals. ✉ *Avenue Kennedy*, ☎ *09/97–01–44*, FAX *09/98–06–92. 88 rooms, 4 suites. Restaurant, pool, nightclub. MC, V.*

$$ ⊡ **Hôtel Champs.** On the outskirts of the north side of town, this hotel offerslarge, airy rooms with lovely views of the hillsides and valley around Tetouan. ✉ *Route de Martil, Km 2.3*, ☎ *09/99–09–01, 09/99–09–02, or 09/99–09–03*, FAX *09/99–09–07. 68 rooms, 12 suites. Restaurant, air-conditioning, pool, parking. MC, V.*

$ ⊡ **Hotel Oumaima.** Moments from Place Moulay el Mehdi, this is one of the few clean and respectable budget hotels in the center of Tetouan. Private bathrooms with showers are the only luxury, but what the hotel lacks in amenities it makes up for in convenience. ✉ *Rue Achra Mai*, ☎ *09/96–34–73. No credit cards.*

$ ⊡ **Paris Hôtel.** The Paris is the best hotel downtown. True, that's not saying much, but you should still call here first. Rooms are basic to the point of drabness, but they're very clean and perfectly comfortable, and each has a private shower. ✉ *11, Rue Chkil Arssalane*, ☎ *09/96–67–50. 40 rooms. Café. No credit cards.*

INTO THE RIF: CHEFCHAOUEN TO AL HOCEIMA AND BEYOND

The trip south from Tetouan to Chefchaouen takes you through fertile valleys where locals sell produce along the road, sheep graze in golden sunshine, and the pace of life slows remarkably from that of the regions just north. The route from Chefchaouen to Al Hoceima winds through the highest mountains in northern Morocco, finally emerging on long strips of uninterrupted Mediterranean coast.

Chefchaouen

★ ⑰ *59 km (37 mi) south of Tetouan.*

Nestled high in the gray Rif Mountains, Chefchaouen, known as the Blue City, is built on a hillside and is a world apart from its larger, Spanish-style neighbors. The pace of life here seems somehow in tune with the abundant natural springs, wildflowers, and low-lying clouds of the surrounding mountainsides. Chefchaouen is unlike any other place in Morocco, from its Rifi Berbers dressed in earth-tone wool *djellabas* and sweaters (ideal for cold, wet Rif winters) to the signature blue-washed houses lining its narrow streets. The medina, walled since its earliest days, is still off-limits to cars, and even the burgeoning tourist shops don't tarnish the feeling of everyday life in motion. Chaouen, as it's sometimes called, is an ideal place to wander a tiny medina, walk up into the looming mountains, and sip mint tea in an open square.

A stroll through Chefchaouen should start in the Nouvelle Ville (New City), in the **Place Mohammed V**—a circular park filled with flowers, vines, and shady spots. Walk up Avenue Hassan II, the palm-lined main avenue, and you'll see the old medina walls on your left; streets wind down to modern-day street markets on your right. Enter the **medina** through Bab l'Ain. Follow the steep path to the right, up past multifarious vendors, until you reach a flight of stairs. These lead to the heart of the old city, the **Place Uta el Hammam.** Cafés line the main plaza, across which is the 15th-century **Grand Mosque,** with its octagonal minaret. Also on the plaza is the **Kasbah.** Built in the 17th century by Moulay Ismail, it was used as everything from an Arab stronghold to the center of Berber resistance to a prison during the Spanish period. It has beautiful gardens, and its walls have elaborate walkways on several levels. The dungeon, with shackles still attached to the walls, is a grim and mazelike place to wander. Take a quick tour through the Kasbah museum. It has wonderful collections of old photographs, musical instruments, handicrafts and furniture from the region, as well as an exhibit on the various and very diverse dress of the region.

Leave the plaza by following Rue Targui northeast, a charming street whose overarching trellises are covered with grapevines. Back in the heart of the medina, feel free to take any turn; Chaouen's medina is very manageable, and all roads lead back to the Place Uta el Hammam. For a stroll up to the hills, leave the square by its southeastern corner and climb to Place el Mahkzen. Follow Avenue Hassan II downhill until you see a set of stairs on the left; these lead to a road above the river. Follow the river and spend the afternoon wandering around the **natural springs, waterfalls, and pathways** that climb the mountain and overlook Chefchaouen. Following a trail that starts at the southeastern edge of town, you can walk up to an old, white hillside mosque known as the **Spanish Mosque,** and from here the views over the town and the entire verdant valley are truly amazing.

Dining and Lodging

$$ ✕ **Restaurant El Baraka.** Set in a 150-year-old medina home and named for the Muslim concept of auspicious divine protection, this restaurant serves traditional Moroccan dishes in the salon of a typical medina home. The staff is charming, and the price makes the experience a real bargain. ✉ *Just off Place Kharrazine (near Pension Andaluz),* ☎ *09/98–69–88. No credit cards.*

$ ✕🍴 **Hotel-Restaurant Tissemlal (Casa Hassan).** Renowned throughout
★ Morocco, this 350-year-old family home combines an excellent restaurant with an intimate number of guest rooms. Both of the gorgeous suites are unique, decorated with the best of local craftsmanship: zellij tiles, hand-wrought iron, hand-painted wood furniture, local wool products. Ask for the suite on the left; it has a canopy bed, fireplace, and wonderfully simple elegance. The rooftop terrace is a tranquil sitting area, with carpets, richly covered banquettes, and lantern light in the evenings, all with views of the Rif Mountains. The restaurant serves homemade soups, salads, tagines, slow-roasted meats, and succulent chicken, not to mention lemon tarts and sweet cakes for desert. A classy establishment and a real bargain (the room rate includes half board), Casa Hassan is a must if you're in Chefchaouen for more than a few hours. ✉ *22, Rue Targui,* ☎ *09/98–61–53,* 🖷 *09/98–81–96. 6 rooms, 2 suites. Restaurant. MC, V.*

$$ 🍴 **Hotel Parador.** Ideally situated on the edge of the medina, within eyeshot of Place Uta el Hammam, the Hotel Parador is frequented by tour groups. Guest rooms are comfortable, and some, along with the public terrace, have wonderful views over the valley. ✉ *Place El*

Mahkzen, ☎ *09/98–63–24,* FAX *09/98–70–33. 34 rooms, 4 suites. Restaurant, bar, pool (in season). No credit cards.*

$ 🏨 **Hostal Gernika.** This charming Spanish-run pension in the heart of the medina centers on an indoor courtyard. Built with Andalusian archways and moldings and decorated with regional crafts, it feels more like a house than hotel. Guest rooms are cheery, simple, and clean; ask for one with a valley view. The plant-lined roof, with both covered and open-air patios, is perched above the medina's snaking streets and myriad rooftops, providing sweeping views across the valley and old town. Spanish lunches and dinners are available if you place an order in the morning. ⊠ *49, Rue Onssar,* ☎ *09/98–74–34. 10 rooms, some with shower. Restaurant. No credit cards.*

$ 🏨 **Hotel Madrid.** A quick stroll from the medina walls, this airy, spacious hotel has traditional Moroccan decor, accented by the works of local photographers in each hallway. In the lobby, greenery and canary song fill an area commanded by a hand-tiled fountain. There's no restaurant, but there's a breakfast buffet. The owners are cheerful locals. ⊠ *Avenue Hassan II,* ☎ *09/98–74–96,* FAX *09/98–74–98. 22 rooms. MC, V.*

Shopping

Chefchouen is one of the best places in the north to shop for quality traditional crafts. Wool items are the main local export: Look in small medina stores for thick wool blankets, djellabas, and rugs. **Abdellah Alami** (⊠ 257, Onsar Rasselma, ☎ 09/98–73–03) sells nothing but bronze products, made by a family of bronze workers who produce some of the finest handmade plates, bowls, and trays in this region. Prices are reasonable, and the selection is vast. The small workshop **Artisanal Chefchaouen** (⊠ Place el Mahkzen, in parking lot of Hotel Parador) produces beautiful, inexpensive hand-painted wood boxes, shelves, birdcages, chests, and mirrors of extremely high quality. Accredited by the Moroccan Ministry of Industry and Artisanal Commerce, **Casa Marbella/Coin de l'Artisanat** (⊠ 40, Rue Grandade Hay Andalouss, ☎ 09/98–71–20) creates some of the finest zellij work in the country, as well as metalwork, pottery, silver filigree, and bronze. Traditional henna application is also available for women. Prices are reasonable, and orders can be shipped via airmail around the world.

Around Ketama

🔞 *Ketama is 78 km (48 mi) southeast of Chefchaouen.*

Heading southeast from Chefchaouen toward Al Hoceima, the P39 road passes through the villages of **Bab Taza** and **Cheferat.** Both are small and spring fed, with substantial floral growth and greenery, and both have small cafés for stops along the route. Continuing along the road as it snakes progressively upward, the stunning drive on to Ketama rewards you with sweeping views across valleys and down into gorges and ravines. Lush, green farming valleys grow progressively browner as they give way to rocky gorges dotted with sparse trees and plant life.

The small village of **Bab Berred,** 30 km (19 mi) west of Ketama, marks the beginning of what is known as Kif Country and what appear to be acres and acres of marijuana plants. The agricultural mainstay of this region, kif (a preparation of hemp leaves) has created a climate that demands a certain degree of caution from travelers. Locals will try to sell you cheap bags of the stuff, sometimes aggressively, so it's best not to stop in this area at all—just stick to the P39. This is unfortunate, as Ketama, the regional kif capital, is a beautiful place. Long-term, the regional government plans to turn the town into a resort devoted to hunting and hiking, perfect activities for its clouded mountaintops and thick cedar forests. For now, however, lodging is limited and not recommended.

Twelve kilometers (7 miles) east of Ketama, Route 8500 turns north, from which point it's a 60-km (37-mi) drive to the northern coastal village of **El Jebha.** This small fishing community has some basic cafés and empty pebble beaches. A better bet for a nice lunch is to wait until Route 8501 branches north 37 km (23 mi) east of Ketama—this road leads to Torres de Alcalá and the beaches of **Kalah Iris.** These are among the finest beaches in the Mediterranean, with a long spit of sand connecting the shore with a small island. A second island lies unconnected to the beach, and the whole area feels private thanks to the surrounding cliffs. A small café and a small campground with rustic bungalows are open here year-round.

To continue to Al Hoceima, go back south and pick up the P39 near **Targuist.** Cedar forests surround this small town and are much safer to hike and explore than those near Ketama.

Al Hoceima

⑲ *112 km (69 mi) northeast of Ketama.*

Surrounded on three sides by the foothills of the Rif Mountains and rimmed on the fourth by emerald Mediterranean waters, Al Hoceima has a striking coastal site. From its perch in rolling hills, the town looks directly down on a stunning bay. It's not nearly as developed as Tangier and Tetouan, and its natural sights and exquisite coastline make it the perfect place to relax for a day or two.

Established by the Spanish in 1925 as Villa Sanjuro, Al Hoceima was built as a stronghold against Rifi Berber rebellions. Al Hoceima is now a proudly Berber place, but its Spanish architecture and atmosphere have remained. The finest Spanish edifice is the beautifully tiled **Collège Espagnol** (Spanish College) at the end of Boulevard Mohammed V. The old town is centered on the rather dingy **Place du Rif.** There are few sights here, but you can wander the town's markets, kick back at a café, and just enjoy the relative quietude. In the Ville Nouvelle, the cliff-top **Place Massira,** just above the main beach, is the focal point of the evening promenade. Festivals are held here in the summer; the **tourist office** (⊠ Avenue Tariq Ibn Ziad, ☎ 09/98–28–30) has information on events.

The real reasons to come to Hoceima are the beaches. The main city beach, **Quemado,** sits in a natural bay formed by mountains on each side. The water is crystal clear—perfect for snorkeling and scuba diving, and you can rent equipment from a very obvious stall on the beach. Near Quemado Beach is Al Hoceima's **port,** where several restaurants cook up wonderful seafood. The coastline outside town is equally scenic; the beach at **Asfiha** stretches around the bay with miles of uninterrupted fine sand.

Dining and Lodging

$$ ✕ **Hotel Karim.** Simple in appearance, this downtown hotel is better known for its restaurant than its rooms: the creative menu combines Moroccan, French, and Spanish dishes. Locals are fond of the seafood dishes. ⊠ *25, Avenue Hassan II,* ☎ *09/98–21–84. MC, V.*

$ ✕ **Restaurant La Belle Vue.** This small café operates as a restaurant in the summer, serving modest portions of salads and grilled fish. The bay views from the outdoor tables are stunning. ⊠ *Avenue Mohammed V,* ☎ *no phone. No credit cards.*

$ ✕ **Restaurant Karim.** The best of several restaurants in Al Hoceima's port, Karim serves excellent and varied seafood. Come early for tapas or a drink at the bar; then dine indoors or outdoors. ✉ *Port area,* ☎ *09/98–23–10. No credit cards.*

$$ ✕⛱ **Hotel Maghred el Jadid.** Downtown, within walking distance of the beaches, this clean, comfortable, tasteful hotel has simple guest rooms and can often arrange jet skiing or scuba diving. The best option downtown for both dining and lodging, it also has a top-notch, top-floor restaurant (with bar) serving a largely Moroccan and Spanish menu. ✉ *56, Avenue Mohammed V,* ☎ *09/98–25–04. 40 rooms. Restaurant, bar. MC, V.*

$$$ ⛱ **Hotel Quemado.** This seafront complex offers rooms, bungalows, and villas with fabulous views and direct beach access. Prices soar—and reservations are scarce—in the summer. ✉ *Plage de Quemado,* ☎ *09/98–33–15,* FAX *09/98–48–87. 22 rooms, 10 bungalows, 2 villas. Restaurant, bar, 2 tennis courts, beach, boating, jet skiing, nightclub. MC, V. Closed Nov.–Mar.*

$$ ⛱ **Hotel Mohammed V.** Al Hoceima's grand old hotel is no longer state-run, and its remodeled rooms and bungalows are classy: sparsely decorated, with simple beds, earth-tone tables, and quiet artwork. Centrally located, on the Place Massira, you're steps from the stairs down to the beach and port. The terrace and many of the rooms have lovely sea views. ✉ *Place Massira,* ☎ *09/98–22–33,* FAX *09/98–33–14. 30 rooms. MC, V.*

Mont Araoui and Selouane

⑳ *Mont Araoui is 144 km (89 mi) east of Al Hoceima; Selouane is 11 km (7 mi) east of Mont Araoui.*

The drive east from Al Hoceima to Nador takes you through rolling hills and small villages. Few of these call out for a stop, but the village of **Mont Araoui,** 20 km (12 mi) before Nador, attracts lively storytellers to its Sunday souk, as well as mountain crafts and public games.

A key stop in these parts, however, is lunch at Restaurant Brabo in **Selouane.** While in Selouane have a look at the **Kasbah of Moulay Ismail,** built in the late 17th century. (It's now a storage facility.)

Dining

$$$ ✕ **Restaurant Brabo.** Run by a Belgian chef, this charming place is a
★ frequent weekend destination for Spaniards living in Melilla. The French-style cuisine includes succulent meats and chicken in rich sauces, and the open, airy dining room is adorned with fresh flowers. One of the finest restaurants in northern Morocco, it's a must on this route. ✉ *110, Avenue Mohammed V, Selouane,* ☎ *06/60–90–33. MC, V. Closed Mon. No dinner Sun. MC, V.*

NADOR, MELILLA, AND THE WILDLIFE

The Spanish enclave of Melilla, together with its border town of Nador, provides a mellow, distinctly Spanish environment. East of Nador, the coastal road passes lagoons rich in plant and bird life near the mouth of the Moulouya River.

Nador

㉑ *20 km (12 mi) west of Mont Araoui, 145 km (90 mi) east of Al Hoceima.*

Controlled by the Spanish until 1957, Nador is the frontier to the Spanish enclave of Melilla. In many ways it's a typical Moroccan border town, complete with contraband products and multilingual young boys, and today it's very much an industrial center as well. Iron from nearby mines is forged into steel here, and the port is a bustling enterprise in its own right.

Still, Nador has a certain Spanish air, and a walk around this grid-patterned town is pleasant enough. The most attractive area surrounds **Boulevard Mohammed V**—open plazas lead off to Spanish-style churches, climbing bouganvillea, and homes trimmed with iron-grille windows and flower boxes. Few travelers feel the need to stay here overnight, but because hotels are expensive in Melilla, Nador is a logical base for a day trip across the border (the border-crossing post is at Beni Enzar, a few miles out of town).

Lodging

$$$ 🏨 **Hotel Rif.** This large, upscale hotel near the seaside has comfortable rooms with floral motifs, good lighting, and spacious bathrooms. Ask for a sea view. ⊠ *1, Boulevard Youssef Ben Tachfine,* ☎ *06/60–65–35,* FAX *06/33–33–84. 54 rooms, 3 suites. Restaurant, pool, 2 tennis courts, nightclub, free parking. MC, V.*

$$$ 🏨 **Hotel Ryad.** This modern luxury hotel in the center of Nador offers plush accommodations, including well-furnished suites. You enter via a large salon, and encounter Moroccan art and pottery throughout. ⊠ *Avenue Mohammed V,* ☎ *06/60–77–15,* FAX *06/60–77–19. 22 rooms, 18 suites. Restaurant, 2 bars, parking. MC, V.*

$$ 🏨 **Hotel Mediterranie.** An economical choice, this airy seaside hotel has clean, simple rooms, some with balconies. The restaurant's charming cook makes tasty Moroccan cuisine. ⊠ *2–4, Boulevard Youssef Ben Tachfine,* ☎ *06/60–64–95,* FAX *06/60–66–11. 24 rooms. Restaurant. MC, V.*

Melilla

㉒   *Border is 12 km (7 mi) north of Nador.*

Well worth a day trip, this charming Spanish enclave beckons with small-town charm, good shopping, and a handful of interesting sights. Settled by Phoenicians as the port of Rusadir, the strategic site was also inhabited by Greeks and Romans. The Spanish conquered the region from Rifi Berbers in the late 15th century.

The ancient city center, **Medina Sidonia,** is on the eastern promontory and makes a good starting point for a walk through town. Its imposing walled structure surrounds a series of three forts separated by drawbridges and gates. Enter on foot via the Puerta de la Marina, where you'll see the Chapel of St. James. The area's main square, the **Plaza Maestranza,** positions you to explore the forts and barracks. The beautiful **Puerta de Santiago,** near the ramparts, bears the coat of arms of Spain's King Charles V. Across from the Puerta de Santiago, the **Museo Municipal** has a fine collection of local archaeological and historical treasures, most notably those from the Carthaginian and Roman eras. The museum is open Sunday through Friday from 10 to 1 and 5 to 7; admission is free. Approach the **Iglesia de la Concepción** (Church of the Immaculate Conception) via Calle de la Concepción; built in the 17th century, the church holds some interesting Baroque artwork and decoration and looks onto a cave cut into the rock below.

Outside the Medina Sidonia, all roads lead to the **Plaza de España,** center of the new city and site of the *paseo* (evening promenade). The nearby **Parque Hernandez** is a lovely place for an afternoon stroll. Restaurants and tapas bars line the main artery, **Avenue Juan Carlos I Rey,** between the plaza and the lively municipal market—when you decide it's time for dinner, simply join the paseo and follow the crowds.

Dining and Lodging

When calling Melilla from Morocco or from overseas, use the country code for Spain, 34. Spanish pesetas are the standard currency here, but dirhams are widely accepted. There are plenty of banks around.

$$$$ ✕ **Restaurant La Muralla.** With its prime position on the old town's southern ramparts, La Muralla is remarkable mainly for its great views but does have lovely, rich wooden decor. The seafood is excellent, particularly in paella, and the salads are good. ⊠ *1, Calle Fiorentina, Medina Sidonia,* ☎ *no phone. MC, V.*

$$ ✕ **Zayka.** This Spanish menu centers on seafood and meat—roast pork, grilled chicken, sautéed shrimp, and calamari are all excellent choices. The atmosphere is cheerful, and the staff is attentive. ⊠ *32, Montemar,* ☎ *952/68–10–37.*

$$$$ 🏨 **Parador de Melilla.** It's a bit of a walk from the center of town, but this is the best of Melilla's higher-priced hotels. The rooms have sweeping views over the town and the nearby Parque Lobera. You can exchange currency at the front desk. ⊠ *Avenida de Candido Lobera,* ☎ *952/68–49–40,* 𝔽𝔸𝕏 *952/68–34–86. 40 rooms. Restaurant, bar, café, air-conditioning, in-room safes, minibars, pool, parking. AE, DC, MC, V.*

$$$ 🏨 **Hostal-Residencia Anfora.** This simple downtown hotel is not luxurious; its comfortable, basic rooms have a sort of mismatched charm. The top-floor restaurant serves good meals and even better views. You're well situated for the evening *paseo.* ⊠ *8, Calle Pablo Vellesca,* ☎ *952/68–33–40,* 𝔽𝔸𝕏 *952/68–33–44. 140 rooms. Restaurant, bar, café, air-conditioning, free parking. MC, V.*

$$$ 🏨 **Hotel Avenida.** Ideally situated on Melilla's main avenue, this charming hotel retains a kind of distinguished antique air. Warm and cozy, with off-white colors and wooden furnishings, the rooms are spacious, carpeted, and very clean. Beds are large and firm. ⊠ *24, Avenida Juan Carlos I Rey,* ☎ *952/68–49–49,* 𝔽𝔸𝕏 *952/68–32–26. 70 rooms. Bar, air-conditioning. MC, V.*

Cap des Trois Forches

㉓ *30 km (19 mi) north of Nador.*

North of the Spanish enclave, this long peninsula juts into the sea, rocky, windswept, and wild. The name means "Cape of Three Forks," referring to the peninsula's three-pronged tip. Civilization here consists of a lighthouse and a few small dwellings. The scenery en route to the tip is gorgeous, and small pockets of calm beach appear between the rocks. If you want to linger and swim, try the beaches at **Cala Tramontana,** 4 km (2 mi) past the cape village of Taourirt.

En Route   Heading southeast of Nador, the coastal road threads along the spit of a lagoon. **Kariet Arkmane,** 30 km (19 mi) east of Nador, is a salt-marsh area rich in migratory birds and insect life. A small shell beach here makes a lovely spot for an afternoon picnic.

Ras-el-Mar

㉔ *40 km (24 mi) east of Kariet Arkmane, 70 km (43 mi) east of Nador.*

The drive between Kariet Arkmane and the town of Ras-el-Mar (also known as Ras Kebdana) takes you through the Rif foothills along the sea. A walk east of the town center gets you a glimpse of some sand dunes and the topographical succession of plants in the harsh environment. Migratory birds and many varieties of gulls, including the rare Audouin's gull, frequent this region. The beaches are pleasant and never crowded.

From the beach three Spanish Islands, the **Islas Chafarinas,** come into focus in the distance. These are important ecological sites: In addition to extensive plant and bird life, they're home to one of only 500 pairs of monk seals in the world.

THE NORTHEASTERN CIRCUIT

Far from the imperial and colonial capitals and way off the tourist track, Morocco's far northeast is all about pristine natural sights. The P27 winds south from Nador to Berkane's Zezel Gorge and Beni Snassen Mountains, with other routes leading north to the stunning 12-km (7-mi) beach at Saïdia. Lodging in this region is simple and scarce; Berkane is the recommended base, with Saïdia an added option in summer.

From Nador follow the P39 south to P27, the main road to Oujda. The road passes through the stark Kebdana foothills, offering sweeping views east toward the Algerian border, then winds through agricultural parts of the Mouloya River basin, with the dark Beni Snassen Mountains rising to the south.

En route to Berkane you'll cross the Oued Moulouya, Morocco's longest river (446 km/279 mi). The river is harnessed by the Mechra Klila Dam for use in regional agriculture, but its mouth—farther north, near Saïdia—is home to exquisite bird life. Twenty kilometers (12 miles) after the river crossing, take Route S404 south to Taforalt: This road winds south through limestone mountains and oak forests to ancient cave sites, of which the **Grotte du Chameau** (Camel Grotto), with vast stalactites and tunnels, and the **Grottes de Plombo** (Plombo Caves), with prehistoric drawings, are highlights. They're administered only by guardians and have no reliable daily schedule, so drop by and see what you can see.

About 1 km (½ mi) beyond the caves, pick up the **Zezel Gorge** route north to Berkane, passing through orange groves and vineyards, both of which cover the slopes of the Beni Snassen Mountains. Planted years ago by the French and cultivated now by local farmers, these vineyards produce the Vins des Beni Snassen (Beni Snassen Wines), served in upscale restaurants nationwide. As the route winds higher, dwarf oaks and cedars replace the citrus trees. The route finally straightens out on the Berkane plain.

Berkane

㉕ *30 km (19 mi) south of Ras-el-Mar.*

Berkane is a pleasant, modern agricultural town with several (mostly unclassified) hotels. Berkane also has banks, pharmacies, and gas stations, the latter a good idea before trips north to Saïdia.

Lodging

$–$$ 🏨 **Hotel Zaki.** Berkane's only 3-star hotel is an adorable little place with attentive reception staff and general small-inn charm. Rooms are large and simple, with comfortable beds, thick carpets, and nice views; ask for a view of the street out front. Prices are flexible. The kitchen prepares creative, inexpensive meals, such as omelets and tagines, upon request. ✉ *27, Route Principal d'Oujda,* ☎ *06/61–37–43,* FAX *06/61–46–65. 30 rooms. No credit cards.*

En Route You can pick up a northern road to Saïdia right in Berkane, but the most direct route follows the P27 east of Berkane to Afnir, where the P18 safely climbs along the Algerian border and drops you in Saïdia.

Saïdia

㉖ *79 km (49 mi) east and north of Berkane.*

One of northeastern Morocco's most pleasant areas, Saïdia combines extensive beaches with a 17th-century fortress, nearby forested mountains, and a generally calm atmosphere. The beach, known as one of the finest in the Mediterranean, stretches for 12 km (7 mi) around a tranquil bay. The town is arranged in a simple grid that makes walking around easy, but most people find themselves staying within view of the beach. Festivities peak in August, when the town's annual **music festival** brings large crowds to hear everything from traditional Moroccan tunes to Algerian-influenced Räi music, Andalusian strains, and even rock-n-roll. Parts of the beach fill up with family tents. Reservations are a must throughout the summer.

Dining and Lodging

Because the sea is the main attraction, many of Saïdia's hotels and restaurants operate only from May through October only. (The ones listed below are open year-round.) Saïdia has no bank, so credit cards are generally not accepted here.

$$$$ ✕ **Café/Restaurant Al Nassim.** This airy dining room has panoramic views over the sea. Fresh fish is the specialty, and it deserves its top billing. ⊠ *Rue Bir Anzarane. No credit cards.*

$$ 🏨 **Hotel Hannour.** The center of Saïdia's off-season nightlife, this fine hotel offers basic accommodations, a good restaurant, and a popular bar. The rooms are carpeted, spacious, and standard modern in style. ⊠ *20, Place Août,* ☎ *06/62–51–15. Restaurant, bar. No credit cards.*

$$ 🏨 **Hotel Paco.** Run by a kind family, the Paco is a charming choice. Guest rooms are very basic, but they're clean, safe, and close to the beach. The restaurant serves homemade meals. ⊠ *Boulevard Hassan II,* ☎ *06/62–51–10. 15 rooms. Restaurant. No credit cards.*

TANGIER, TETOUAN, AND THE MEDITERRANEAN A TO Z

Arriving and Departing

By Boat

All ferries to Morocco arrive at Tangier, Ceuta, or Melilla. Car ferries make the 2-hr trip between Algeciras (Spain) and Tangier daily, and ferries connect Gibraltar with Tangier twice weekly. The number of daily crossings is higher in the summer, but you'll have plenty of options year-round. Tickets should only be purchased through accredited travel agents or at the counters in the ports. Bus trips between Europe and Morocco include ferry service. Passport control takes place on the boat; have your passport stamped before arrival to avoid delays. You can walk to Tangier's train stations from the port. Note that huge numbers of Moroccans working in Europe return for their summer vacations in July and August, so if you're traveling with a car between Algeciras and Tangier or Ceuta during that period, expect long delays.

The well-established Spanish company **Transmediterrania** (⊠ 31, Avenue de la Resistance, Tangier, ☎ 09/94–11–01, ᶠᵃˣ 09/94–38–63) handles most ferry routes between Morocco and Spain. The Moroccan firm **Comarit Ferry** (⊠ 7, Rue de Mexique, Tangier, ☎ 09/93–12–20, ᶠᵃˣ 09/93–67–84) also connects the two countries, and in the warmer months adds a 1-hr hydrofoil trip to its ferry options. A car ferry with cabin accommodation runs from Sète (southern France) to Tangier every four days, a 36-hour trip; for schedules and fares, contact **Southern Ferries Ltd** in London (✉ 179 Piccadilly, ☎ 207/491–4968, ℻ 207/491–3502).

Credit cards are accepted in the offices of the ferry companies, but not at the port terminals themselves. You pay in pesetas if you're coming from Spain, dirhams if you're leaving Morocco; we list fares in U.S. dollars as guidelines.

TANGIER

Daily ferries connect Tangier with the Spanish port of Algeciras (two hours; $30 passenger, $100 car) and Gibraltar (two hours; $30 passenger, $75 car). Weekly ferries serve the French port of Sète (38 hours; prices vary with season) and the Portuguese port of Faro (10 hours; prices vary).

Passenger-only hydrofoil service connects Tangier with the Spanish ports of La Linea (which serves Gibraltar) and Algeciras once or twice daily (one hour; $30).

CEUTA

Ceuta has ferry service to and from the Spanish port of Algeciras (1½ hours; $20 passenger, $70 car).

MELILLA

Daily ferries connect Melilla with the Spanish ports of Malaga (eight hours; $30 passenger, $80 car) and Almería (seven hours; $25 passenger, $75 car).

By Plane

Northern Morocco has four airports, each with domestic and international flights. Tangier's **Boukhalef Airport** (☎ 09/93–51–29), 15 km (9 mi) from the city center, is linked to Tangier by a bus to the Grand Socco (Numbers 17 and 70) and taxis. **Royal Air Maroc** (✉ 1, Place de la France, ☎ 09/93–47–22) and **GB Airways** (✉ 83, Rue de Liberté, ☎ 09/93–52–11) offer daily domestic and international flights.

Tetouan's small **Aéroport de Sania R'Mel** (☎ 09/97–12–33), 5 km (3 mi) outside town, has domestic flights to Rabat, Casablanca, and Al Hoceima.

Al Hoceima's **Aéoport Côte du Rif** (☎ 09/98—20–05), 17 km (11 mi) southeast of town, offers daily flights on **Royal Air Maroc** (☎ 09/98–20–63) to Tangier, Tetouan, Casablanca, and Rabat, as well as weekly flights to Europe.

The airport in **Melilla** (☎ 952/68–99–47 or 952/68–99–48) is a 10-minute ride from the town center. Daily flights link the enclave to various cities in Spain, with connecting flights to other points in Europe.

Getting Around

By Bus

The national **C.T.M.** line, with offices in all major cities, runs several buses daily between Tangier, Tetouan, Chefchaouen, Al Hoceima, and Nador. Tourist offices in the larger cities can direct you to the local C.T.M. office and/or assist you in arranging bus trips.

By Car

Driving is by far the best means of transportation if you want to explore the Rif and the Mediterranean beyond Tangier. Many of the most scenic routes in northern Morocco are not served by public transportation, and day trips in particular are most efficiently taken in a car.

Roads range from significant routes—the P38 and P28 connecting Tangier, Ceuta, Tetouan, and the beaches, P39 cutting east to Al Hoceima and Melilla, and P27 stretching east past Berkane to Oujda—to smaller mountain routes. Use caution on the back roads; watch for donkeys, loose edges on mountains roads, trucks, and crazy drivers.

To rent a car in Tangier, contact: **Avis** (⊠ 54, Boulevard Pasteur, ☎ 09/93–30–31). **Europcar/InterRent** (⊠ 87, Boulevard Mohammed V, ☎ 09/94–19–38). **Hertz** (⊠ 36, Boulevard Mohammed V, ☎ 09/93–33–22). All three agencies also have desks at Tangier's airport.

By Train
The only northern city served by **ONCF,** the Moroccan rail service, is Tangier (station: ☎ 09/95–25–55). The main track runs from Casablanca to Oujda, substantially south of most destinations in this chapter.

Contacts and Resources

Consulates
United Kingdom (⊠ 9, Rue Amerique du Sud, Tangier, ☎ 09/93–58–95). **United States** (⊠ 29, Rue El Achouak, Tangier, ☎ 09/93–59–04).

Emergencies and Late-Night Pharmacies
Ambulance: In Tangier, Tetouan, and Al Hoceima, dial 15 from any phone. In Ceuta, dial 51–45–48; in Melilla, 67–22–22. **Hospitals:** Hospital Al Kortobi (⊠ Tangier, ☎ 09/93–10–73), Hospital Mohammed V (⊠ Al Hoceima). **Police:** Dial 19. In Ceuta and Melilla, dial 92.

In Tangier, the **Pharmacie Jamilla "Depôt de Nuit"** (⊠ 10, Rue de Fès, ☎ 09/94–96–76) is open 24 hours. In Tetouan, the Pharmacie Al Ouahada (⊠ Rue Al-Ouahada, ☎ 09/96–67–77) is also open 'round the clock.

Guided Tours
Contact the nearest tourist office (☞ Visitor Information, *below*) for a multilingual local guide.

Sports and Outdoor Activities
GOLF

Golf, the favorite sport of the late King Hassan II, is quickly spreading throughout Morocco. The premier courses in the north: **Royal Club de Golf** (⊠ Tangier, ☎ 09/94–44–84, 18 holes). **Cabo Negro Royal Golf Club** (⊠ Cabo Negro, ☎ 09/97–83–03), 18 holes.

HORSEBACK RIDING

La Ferma (⊠ Cabo Negro, ☎ 09/97–80–75). **Martine Catena** (⊠ Ceuta, ☎ 956/51–10–48).

SAILING

The many ports and marinas on Morocco's Mediterranean coast take advantage of ideal sailing conditions. Local tourist offices have up-to-date lists of rental outfits. **Kabila** (contact: ⊠ Kabila Hotel, ☎ 09/66–60–90). **Mdiq** (⊠ Port, ☎ 09/97–76–94). **Melilla** (⊠ Marina Club Marítimo, Calle Muelle, Melilla, ☎ 952/68–36–59). **Tangier** (Tangier Yacht Club, ⊠ Port, ☎ 09/93–85–75).

Travel Agencies
Local travel agencies can be very helpful in planning transport, reserving hotel rooms, and arranging guided tours. Many take credit cards and have English-speakers on staff. **Akersan Voyages** (⊠ Avenue FAR, Tetouan, ☎ 09/96–30–34). **Andalucía Travel** (⊠ Avenida de la Democracia, Melilla, ☎ 952/67–07–30). **Kemata Voyages** (⊠ 146, Boulevard Mohammed V, Nador, ☎ 09/98–23–76). **Viajes Dato** (⊠ Muelle Canonero Dato, Ceuta, ☎ 956/50–74–57). **Voyages Marco Polo** (⊠ 72, Avenue d'Espagne, Tangier, ☎ 09/93–43–45).

Visitor Information

Information on the region as a whole is hard to come by in the north; most tourist offices specialize in their respective cities. **Al Hoceima** (✉ Rue Tarik Ibn Zyad, ☎ 09/98–11–85). **Ceuta** (✉ Booth across from town hall, Avenida de la Marina Española). **Chefchaouen** (✉ Place de Mohammed V). **Melilla** (✉ Avenida General Aizpuru, ☎ 952/67–40–13). **Nador** (✉ 80, Boulevard Ibn Rochd, ☎ 06/33–03–48). **Tangier** (✉ 29, Boulevard Pasteur, ☎ 09/94–86–61). **Tetouan** (✉ 30, Avenue Mohammed V, ☎ 09/96–19–15).

3 FEZ AND MEKNES

Synonymous with the Arabic and Islamic culture introduced to Morocco in the 8th century, the labyrinthine medieval city of Fez is one of the most fascinating places in the world. Pressed tight with donkey traffic and colored by the din of commerce, its endless narrow alleys look like film clips about the Old Testament. Nearby Meknes, with its miles of concentric sets of walls, is a lovely and calmer experience, as are the ancient Roman ruins at Volubilis.

FEZ AND MEKNES ARE, respectively, the Arab and Berber capitals of Morocco, ancient centers of learning, culture, and craftsmanship. Long recognized as Morocco's intellectual and spiritual nerve center, Fez boasts the oldest university in the West and the world's largest still-functioning medieval quarter, with a population of 60,000 (one-tenth of the city's total) and no transport beyond donkeys. Built in the fertile basin of the Fez River—the Oued Fez, also known as Oued el-Yawahir, the River of Pearls—Fez el Bali (literally, Fez the Old) was founded in AD 808 by Moulay Idriss II, son of the founder of Morocco, Moulay Idriss I. The original and the most imperial of Morocco's Imperial Cities, Fez was the nation's capital in the 9th, 12th–14th, and 16th centuries. Fez el Djedid (New Fez) was founded in 1276 by the Merenid rulers, who needed extra space for their palaces as well as a sense of distance from the population itself. The Ville Nouvelle was built by the French after they established their protectorate in 1912.

By George
Semler

With its many mosques, *medersas* (Koranic schools), souks (markets), *fondouks* (lodging and trading houses), and myriad practicing artisans and artisanal collectives and guilds, Fez el Bali is essentially a gigantic crafts workshop and market that has changed little in the past millennium. With no cars and some 1,000 *derbs* (dead-end alleys), it beckons the walker on an endless and absorbing odyssey. Craftsmen lathing wood, tanning hides, soldering copper pots, or engraving brass plates produce an exciting and chaotic range of sounds and aromas. The food-produce souks are staggeringly beautiful, with pyramids of perfectly stacked olives, immense spice displays, fruit stands, and butcher shops selling everything from goat to camel meat.

Meknes, unjustly eclipsed by Fez, has been called the Moroccan Versailles, surrounded as it is by some 40 km (25 mi) of lime-and-earth walls built by the formidable Moulay Ismail, Sultan of Morocco from 1672 to 1727. Surrounded and threatened by 45 regional Berber tribes, Moulay Ismail was obsessed with defense to a degree virtually unparalleled in world history. Meknes was developed to withstand a hypothetical 20-year siege, with protected granaries, a reservoir, and three concentric systems of ramparts surrounding the 9th-century medina, the 13th-century Imperial City, and the Royal Palace. In addition, Ismail was known to have maintained 500 concubines and a standing army, the Abid regiment, of 150,000 crack troops (the infamous Black Guard) originally purchased from the Sudan. Handed Arab and Berber women as wives, Ismail's army lived in a special camp where male offspring were impressed into service at an early age, officially 15. Two hundred palace eunuchs, a 12,000-horse cavalry, and a labor force of 60,000 slaves (largely prisoners of war, condemned criminals, and random captives) completed Moulay Ismail's extraordinary personal staff. Somewhat surprisingly, Ismail is remembered and revered for his unique achievements rather than reviled for his equally unique excesses: under his leadership Morocco was united under government control for the first time in five centuries and experienced its last golden age to date.

As if sapped of strength after Ismail's reign of terror, Meknes crumbled during the late 18th and early 19th centuries. The Lisbon earthquake of 1755 destroyed part of the Imperial City, and even Ismail's son tore down a palace or two before moving Morocco's capital to Marrakesh. For the traveler, though, Meknes offers a chance to experience all the sights, sounds, and smells of Fez on a somewhat smaller, more manageable scale. Declared a World Heritage Site by UNESCO in 1996, Meknes now seems likely to take its place alongside Fez and Marrakesh as one of the most authentic and fascinating cities in Morocco.

Volubilis and Moulay Idriss are easy side trips from Meknes, just a 30-minute drive north. Volubilis was the farthest-flung capital of the ancient Roman empire, and Moulay Idriss has Morocco's most sacred shrine, the tomb of founding father Moulay Idriss I. Both sites are key to an understanding of Moroccan history.

Pleasures and Pastimes

Crafts

Fez el Bali is a living museum of artisans creating some of the finest ceramics, copper engravings, leatherwork, embroidery, wood carvings, and carpets in the world. The traditional techniques, skills, and methods these master craftsmen keep alive are as fascinating as the work they produce. All of Fez's major emporiums and workshops, especially the carpet shops, have English-speaking guides who give excellent and detailed explanations. The pressure to purchase varies from shop to shop, but if you're accompanied by an official guide from the tourist office, he will generally allow you to extricate yourself from what can seem like endless negotiations. Although Fez is the most exciting place in Morocco to watch artisans at work, salesmen here are known for their prowess in haggling. If you find Fez daunting, you can still buy high-quality crafts in Meknes or the surrounding countryside—and usually at lower prices.

Dining

Every Moroccan city has its own way of preparing the national dishes. *Harira,* the hearty bean-based soup with vegetables and meat, may be designated as Fassi (from Fez) or Meknessi (from Meknes) and vary slightly in texture and ingredients. *Tagines,* stewed combinations of vegetables and meat (or fish) cooked in conical earthenware vessels, are nearly always delicious, as is couscous. *Pastilla de pigeon,* a phyllo-pastry pie with pigeon meat, is a Fez specialty; it's cloyingly sweet, with sugar and cinnamon. *Mechoui,* roast lamb, must usually be ordered either a day or several hours in advance. *Kebabs* are brochettes of meat. Some of the best and cheapest food in Morocco is sold in the souks, where you can grab an excellent harira for 2DH (about 40 U.S. cents) and spicy meat sandwiches in Moroccan bread for 5DH.

Note that few medina restaurants in Fez and Meknes are licensed to serve wine. Proprietors generally allow oenophiles to bring their own, as long as they do it discreetly.

CATEGORY	COST*
$$$$	over 200DH
$$$	150–200DH
$$	100–150DH
$	under 100DH

per person for a three-course meal, excluding drinks, service, and tax

Festivals

Throne Day, or Aïd el Arch, the anniversary of the king's coronation (July 30), is always an impressive display of the nation's devotion to the king and the Alaouite dynasty. Fez's *moussem* of **Moulay Idriss II,** held in September, is a major celebration, with a lengthy procession through the medina to the tomb of the city's major historical figure. May's **Festival of Sacred Music** is becoming a major draw, with music representing every faith from Judaism to Hinduism to Buddhism, Taoism, and West African animism. In Meknes the moussem of **Ben Aïssa** includes a wild *fantasia* (a Berber cavalry charge with muskets blazing) and the annual exhibition of the Aissaoua, a Sufi order, who go into prayerful trances and voluntarily endure such ordeals as walking on hot coals and slicing themselves with knives.

Lodging

Hotels in Fez range from the luxurious and the comprehensively comfortable, such as the Palais Jamai, the Merenides, and the Jnan Palace, to more friendly but fallible choices like the Zalagh. Meknes hotels generally start at the latter level and descend from there. In Fez, hotels nearest Fez el Bali are best, as the medina is almost exclusively what you have come to see. The Palais Jamai and the Batha are the only options right over the medieval city, but the Merenides and the Zalagh, while farther away, have more panoramic views. In Meknes, the "Transat" (Hôtel Transatlantique) is the best combination of old-world digs overlooking the walls of the Imperial City, with the Hôtel Rif as a second, more modern option.

CATEGORY	COST*
$$$$	over 400DH
$$$	300–400DH
$$	200–300DH
$	under 200DH

All prices are for a standard double room, excluding service and tax.

Exploring Fez and Meknes

Together with Marrakesh, Fez and Meknes are the richest cities in Morocco both architecturally and culturally. Of the two, Fez is by far the more rewarding visit, but Meknes's maze of defensive walls, its immense Royal Granary, and the brilliantly decorative Bab Mansour are some of Morocco's most treasured monuments.

Numbers in the text correspond to numbers in the margin and on the Fez and Meknes maps.

Great Itineraries

An unhurried exploration of Fez's medina takes two or three nights and as many days. Meknes is perennially overshadowed by its larger and historically more important neighbor, but it, too, merits two or three days for both its varied sights and the exquisite wares in its relatively low-key souk. You can easily explore Volubilis and Moulay Idriss from Meknes, as they each take only a few hours each, but there is a good hotel just above Volubilis in case you prefer not to backtrack.

IF YOU HAVE 3 DAYS

If your time is limited, spend two full days wandering the ☒ **Fez** medina, preferably with a good guide from the tourist office. Start early the next day to see ☒ **Meknes,** as many national monuments close at 11 or 12. The afternoon of day three can easily embrace an hour or two at the ruins of Roman **Volubilis** and, if there's time, the town of **Moulay Idriss.**

IF YOU HAVE 6 DAYS

Spend three days in ☒ **Fez** exploring the medina and its various souks, mosques, and medersas. With two days in ☒ **Meknes,** you can see the major sights, navigate the souks with enough time to haggle properly, and have lunch at Moulay Ismail's great-great-great grandson's lovely *riad* (historic mansion) restaurant. On day six venture out of Meknes to wander the ruins of Roman **Volubilis** and visit the sacred town of **Moulay Idriss.**

When to Tour Fez and Meknes

Busloads of tourists tend to suppress the romance of just about anything. Try to visit Fez and Meknes between October and early March, before the high season kicks in. Note that, as with everything in Morocco, travel commodities like hotel rooms and local car rentals are negotiable, and you have more bargaining power in the low season.

FEZ

Alternately dubbed the Baghdad of the Maghreb and the Athens of Africa, Fez is a living work of art, one of the great religious and cultural centers of the world since the Middle Ages. Fez has been at the heart of the Arabic and Islamic development of Morocco since shortly after the arrival of the first religious refugees from the Middle East in AD 788. Founded in 808 by Moulay Idriss II, Fez el Bali—the medina—is divided into two quarters on either side of the Fez River. The Andalusian Quarter originally housed refugees from Moorish Spain, who had begun to flee the Christian Reconquest; the Kairaouine Quarter originally housed refugees from Kairaouine, Tunisia, who fled westward in search of a purer form of Islamic worship. Always the more important of the two demographically and commercially, the Kairaouine Quarter was especially expanded under the Merenid dynasty, during Fez's 14th-century golden age.

Passing through one of the *babs* (gates) into Fez el Bali is like entering a time warp, the occasional television antenna your only reminder that you're entering the third, not the second, millennium AD. A maelstrom of seemingly chaotic commercial and artistic activity, it's the perfect medieval labyrinth—mysterious, bewildering, fascinating. Each neighborhood within Old Fez has seven traditional elements: mosque, medersa, fondouk, Koranic school, fountain, *hammam,* and bakery. The din of hammering coppersmiths and the cries of *"Balek!"* ("Watch out!") from donkey drivers pushing through crowded alleys mingle with the smells of cooking, spices, mint, dung, decay, leather, and cedar wood, all dramatically illuminated by shafts of sunlight bursting down through the thatched roof of the *kissaria* (covered markets).

Fez el Bali

Exploring this honeycomb of 9th-century alleys and passageways is a real adventure. Hiring an official guide from the tourist office on your first day will save you a lot of confusion and hassle and is definitely recommended. Fez is not really yours, however, until you've tackled it on your own, become hopelessly lost a few times, and survived to tell the tale. Once you have a sense of the place, about the worst that can happen is that a nine-year-old hustler will offer to take you wherever you want to go. Five or 10 dirhams will more than satisfy his commercial instincts; and for another five and a clear explanation that you would now prefer to continue alone, he'll vanish.

A Good Walk

Start at **Bab Boujeloud** ①, often called the Porte Bleue (Blue Gate) for its blue-tile outer facade. Walk down and hook right through the cafés and harira, kebab, sausage, and meat-sandwich cookeries that line the main artery down into the medina. Bear left around the first corner, and you'll be descending Talâa Seghira (Small Street), the smaller of the two streets down into the medina. Talâa Kebira (Big Street), one block west, is slightly larger and covered. Both of these arteries make for fascinating browsing, though Talâa Kebira can be more aggressively commercial. A cut left at the first corner of Talâa Seghira will take you over to Talâa Kebira, where the door of the 14th-century **Bou Inania Medersa** ②, the most famous student residence at the Kairaouine University, is just to the left.

Leaving the medersa, a wooden scaffold to the left conceals the site of the mid-14th-century water clock **Dar el Magana** (House of the Clock). Consisting of cymbals and mechanical birds, this clepsydra, or water-operated clock—a sort of hydraulic carillon—is presently being restored by a master clocksmith said to have rediscovered the lost knowledge of its mechanics.

A cut to the right through the next small street downhill will take you back from the Talâa Kebira to the Talâa Seghira. Near the bottom of Talâa Seghira, a small stairway to the right leads down into the **Place Nejjarine** (Carpenters' Square). Here, the Nejjarine Fountain and the lovely wooden gateway leading into the imposingly grand and intricately carved Fondouk Nejjarine, along with the wooden-door cafés—especially the handsome cedar doors of the Café La Fontaine, at Number 11—add up to one of the prettiest squares in the medina. The **Musée Nejjarine des Arts et Métiers du Bois** ③, on your right as you arrive in the square, is one of the loveliest and best-restored monuments in Fez el Bali. Near the bottom of the stairs on the right is the best known of the medina's 80 fountains, the **Fontaine Nejjarine,** a 14th-century covered fountain with ceramic roof tiles, carved cedar eaves, and stucco and ceramic-tile walls.

From your entrance to the Place Nejjarine, the street out to the left leads down to the **Souk el Attarin** (the perfume and spice vendors' souk) and the **Souk el Henna** ④. Nearby is Place Achabin, center of the produce and salt souks. In the vicinity is the fragrant Rue Hormis, lined with some of the cheapest and best places to eat in North Africa. Rue Hormis leads up to Bab Guissa and the Palais Jamais.

From Souk el Attarin, duck under the wooden beam marking the entrance to the **zaouia of Moulay Idriss II** ⑤, the sanctuary containing the saint's tomb. Non-Muslims cannot enter the *zaouia* (sanctuary), but they can enter the *horm,* the sacred area that surrounds it. Moving right around the zaouia, turn left at the corner, and you'll pass the worn brass slot for alms to the Idrissid cult. The intricately carved wall and the polychrome carved ceiling mark the outside of the tomb.

Passing under the bar marking the far side of the horm, turn left into the **Chemaîne souk,** originally a candle makers' and wax vendors' market, now an open space where dates and dried fruits are sold. Walk straight down to the side door of the Kairaouine Mosque, the most important mosque in Fez (out of 785 in the medina alone).

Another 100 ft to the left, just past the street that turns right at the corner of the mosque, is the **Attarin Medersa** ⑥. Moving back to the corner of the mosque, turn left and walk about 100 ft down to the ornate, blue-and-white-stucco main entrance to the **Kairaouine Mosque** ⑦.

The next corner has a public bakery on the right, where you might see little kids delivering dough from their homes to be baked in the wood ovens. Just to the left of the cigarette and candy salesman (a single cigarette costs a single dirham) is the entrance to the **Maison de l'Artisanat Travaux de Cuivre et de Bronze** (Copper and Bronze Artisans' Guild), from which emerge pungent aromas of soldering copper being heated and shaped. Left up the tunnel (following the arrows and signs through all seven turns) is the best rug, kilim, and carpet emporium in the medina, **Aux Merveilles du Tapis** ⑧.

52

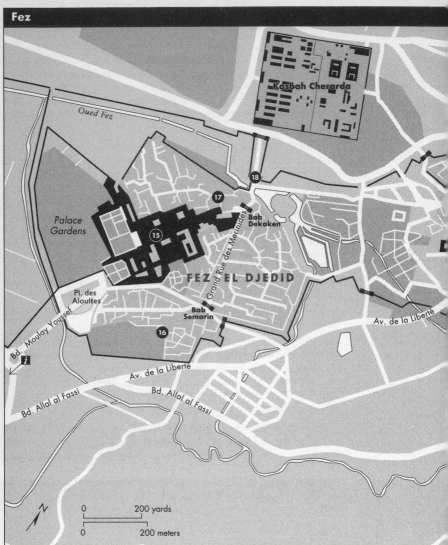

Andalusian Mosque, **12**

Attarin Medersa, **6**

Aux Merveilles du Tapis, **8**

Bab Boujeloud, **1**

Bab es Seba, **18**

Bou Inania Medersa, **2**

Cherratin Medersa, **14**

Dar Batha, **19**

Dar el Makhzen, **15**

Fondouk Tsetouanien, **9**

Kairaouine Mosque, **7**

Mellah, **16**

Moulay Abdellah Quarter, **17**

Musée Nejjarine des Arts et Métiers du Bois, **3**

Place Seffarine, **10**

Sahrij Medersa, **13**

Souk el Henna, **4**

Terrasse des Tanneurs, **11**

Zaouia of Moulay Idriss II, **5**

Merenid
Tombs

Bab
Guissa

R. Talãa Kebira

1

2

R. Talãa Seghira

Souk el Attarin

4

3

5

6

8

19

14

7

9

11

10

F E Z   E L   B A L I

R. Sidi Youssef

13 12

R. Sidi Ali Boughaleb

R. Kaïd Khammar

Bd. Ahmed ben Mohammed el Alaoui

Oued Fez

Oued Fez

Bab
Ftouh

Bd. Allal al Fassi

Back out on the street bordering the Kairaouine Mosque, a small sign announces the **Fondouk Tsetouanien** ⑨, the best preserved of all the medina's fondouks, of which there were once 200. The next courtyard along the back wall of the mosque is known for its frequent secondhand-book market. Following the courtyard is the Mohammed Bouchareeb wood and marquetry store, next to the tragically burned Palais de Fez carpet emporium and restaurant (scheduled to reopen in 2001).

Place Seffarine ⑩, the coppersmiths' souk, is the major opening off Boutouil Kairaouine. The Kairaouine University library is on the right. The street leading out of the square, Rue Mechatine (a sharp left on your way in), leads to the **Terrasse des Tanneurs** ⑪, one of the most beautiful and unforgettable spots in Fez el Bali. From the tanneries back down Rue Mechatine to Beyin el Moudoun (literally, the area "between the cities"), the bridge across the Fez River leads into the Andalusian Quarter. Walk up Rue Nekhaline to the **Andalusian Mosque** ⑫.

A few steps to the right of the Andalusian Mosque is the **Sebayine Medersa** ("of the Seven"), so named for its teaching of the seven ways of reading the Koran. Nearby is the **Sahrij Medersa** ⑬ ("the Pool").

Leaving the Sahrij Medersa, walk downhill into the busy Rue Michline, usually easily identifiable by its roaring flow of humanity. Continue down through the dyers' souk, **Souk des Teinturiers,** where dyes form puddles under dripping skins and fabrics, and through intimate Place Aouadine, with its brass workers' shops, to the edge of Place Seffarine. Rue Cherratin leads back left toward the center of the medina and the zaouia of Moulay Idriss II, passing the **Cherratin Medersa** ⑭, built in 1670 by Moulay er Rachid, founder of the Alaouite dynasty.

Not far from the zaouia of Moulay Idriss II, near the Tijani restaurant, is the **zaouia of Sidi Ahmed Tijani,** dedicated to an African missionary (1150–1230) much revered by pilgrims from black Africa. From here you can walk up either Talâa Seghira or Talâa Kebira (whichever you didn't take on the way down) back to Bab Boujeloud. If you take Talâa Seghira, about halfway up on the right you'll see an intricately carved wooden door surrounded by *zellij* tiles—this is the **Dar M'Nebhi,** a sumptuous palace and now a fine restaurant. Built in the mid-19th century, it was once the home of General Hubert Lyautey, commander of the French Protectorate.

TIMING

Allow six to eight hours for this walk.

Sights to See

⑫ **Andalusian Mosque.** This mosque was built in AD 859 by Myriam, sister of the Fatima who had erected the Kairaouine Mosque on the other side of the river two years earlier. The gate was built by the Almohads in the 12th century. The detailed wood carvings in the eaves, which bear a striking resemblance to those in the Fondouk Nejjarine, are the main thing to see here, as the mosque itself is set back and elevated, making it hard to examine from outside. ⊠ *Rue Nekhaline.*

★ ⑥ **Attarin Medersa.** The Attarin Medersa (Koranic school) was named for local spice merchants known as *attar.* Founded by Sultan Abou Saïd in the 14th century as a dormitory for students at the Kairaouine Mosque next door, it is arguably the loveliest medersa in Fez for its graceful proportions and elegant, geometrical carved-cedar ornamentation as well as its excellent state of preservation. ⊠ *Boutouil Kairaouine.* ☺ *Daily 9–1, 3–6:30.*

★ ⑧ **Aux Merveilles du Tapis.** Here, proprietor Hamid Hakim, brother of a university lecturer in 16th-century English literature (whose linguistic and oratory skills he seems to share), gives an impeccably polished, humorous, and erudite presentation of Moroccan rugs and carpets as well as the architecture and traditional life of a Moroccan town house. This ornate 14th-century medina palace has exquisite ceilings of carved cedar restored and enriched with olive oil. Mr. Hakim's assistants roll and unroll rugs with great flair and precision while serving an excellent mint tea, and, remarkably, the establishment applies no pressure at all. The store takes credit cards and ships rugs overseas—and they really arrive. ⊠ *Sebaâ Louyet*, ☎ *05/63–87–35.* ⊙ *Daily 8–7.*

❶ Bab Boujeloud. Built in 1913 by General Hubert Lyautey, Moroccan commander under the French Protectorate, this gate is 1,000 years younger than the rest of the medina yet generally considered its most beautiful point of entry. The side facing out is covered with blue ceramic tiles painted with flowers and calligraphy; the inside is green, the official color of Islam—or of peace, depending on the interpretation. (The famous Marche Verte, or Green March, that King Hassan II led into the Spanish Sahara in 1975 was so named for its pacific character: its several hundred thousand Moroccan participants marched unarmed to reclaim their natural borders.) ⊠ *Place Boujeloud.*

★ **❷ Bou Inania Medersa.** From outside Bab Boujeloud you will have seen the green-tile tower of this medersa, generally considered the most beautiful of the Kairaouine University's 14th-century residential colleges. First organized in the 10th century, the university is, unbeknownst to many, the Western world's first center of higher education, predating Oxford, La Sorbonne, and Bologna. The word *medersa* comes from *madrasa,* a classical Arabic word for "school"—which meant, of course, Koranic school, in which the only subject was the memorization of the Koran. The medersas housed students while they learned to recite the Koran and the Hadith, the words and deeds of the prophet; and once they had mastered these, they were passed on to more analytical studies. The Kairaouine University has always enrolled some 2,000 students, and its library of 30,000 volumes (including 10 manuscripts), one of the greatest in the world in the Middle Ages, is still one of the most significant Arab collections.

The Bou Inania Medersa was built by order of Abou Inan, the first ruler of the Merenid dynasty, which would become the most decisive ruling clan in the development of Fez. (Nearly all the medersas were built by the Merenids, with the exception of the Moulay Rachid Medersa, built by the Alaouites.) The main components of the medersa's stunningly intricate decorative artwork are the green-tile roofing; the cedar eaves and upper patio walls, carved in floral and geometrical motifs; the carved-stucco mid-level walls, the ceramic-tile lower walls covered with calligraphy (Kufi script; essentially cursive Arabic) and geometrical patterns, and, finally, the marble floor.

The most dazzling display is the carved cedar, each square inch a masterpiece of handcrafted sculpture involving long hours of the kind of concentration required to memorize the Koran—no doubt precisely the message this decoration was designed to convey. The stucco is made of plaster toughened with egg white (a technique that, after more than 1,000 years, must be pronounced effective). The black belt of ceramic tile around the courtyard bears Arabic script reading THIS IS A PLACE OF LEARNING and other such exhortatory academic messages. ⊠ *Talâa Kebira.* ▣ *10DH.* ⊙ *Daily 9–7.*

⓮ Cherratin Medersa. Constructed in 1670 by Moulay er Rachid, this is Fez's only Alaouite medersa. Less ornate than the 14th-century medersas of the Merenids, this one is more functional, designed to hold more than 200 students. It's interesting primarily as a contrast to the intricate craftsmanship and decorative intent of the Merenid models. ⊠ *Derb Zaouia.* 🎫 *10DH.* 🕙 *Daily 9–1, 3–6:30.*

❾ Fondouk Tsetouanien. Named for the traders from Tetouan who traded and lodged here, this fondouk is the most original and lifelike of all those in the medina. With its jumble of balconies, ground-floor scales, and rug and leather dealers, it seems to come closest to the look of the fondouks in Delacroix and Fortuny paintings. With their transient traders and occasional students, fondouks were great centers of ribaldry and intrigue in the Middle Ages, and some sense of this vitality somehow remains. ⊠ *Boutouil Kairaouine.* 🕙 *Daily 24 hrs.*

❼ Kairaouine Mosque. One look through the doorway will give you an idea of the immensity of this place. With about 10,760 square ft, the Kairaouine was the largest mosque in Morocco until Casablanca's Hassan II Mosque came along in the early 1990s. Stand at the left side of the door for a peek through the dozen horseshoe arches into the mihrab (marked by a hanging light). An east-facing alcove or niche used for leading prayer, the mihrab is rounded and covered with an arch designed to project sound back through the mosque. Lean in and look up to the brightly painted and intricately carved ceiling. Built by the Kairaouine Fatima in 857, the Kairaouine Mosque became the home of the first university in the West and the world's foremost center of learning at the beginning of the second millennium. Averroës, Maimonides, and Pope Sylvester II were among the celebrated scholars and teachers who studied and taught in Fez. Sylvester II (a Frenchman from the Auvergne, originally named Gerbert), who was pope from 999 to 1003, was also and a legendary mathematician who introduced Europe to Arabic mathematical concepts, most notably the zero. ⊠ *Boutouil Kairaouine.* 🎫 *Free; entrance restricted to Muslims.* 🕙 *Daily.*

❸ Musée Nejjarine des Arts et Métiers du Bois (Nejjarine Museum of Wood Arts and Crafts). Reopened in 1998, this former 14th-century fondouk is without a doubt the most modern restored monument in the medina. The three-story patio displays Morocco's various native woods, some forestry-management schemes, 18th- and 19th-century woodworking tools, and a series of antique wooden doors and pieces of furniture. The rooftop tearoom has panoramic views over the medina. For the traveler, however, the museum's best feature may be its palatial, cedar-ceiling public bathrooms, certainly the finest of their kind in Fez. Don't miss the former jail cell on the ground floor, or the large scales—a reminder of the building's original functions, commerce on the patio floor and lodging on the three levels above. ⊠ *Place Nejjarine,* ☎ *05/74–05–80.* 🎫 *10DH.* 🕙 *Daily 10–7.*

❿ Place Seffarine. The wide, triangular souk of the *dinandiers,* or coppersmiths, is one of the largest open spaces in the medina, a comfortable break from tight crags and corners. Donkeys and their masters wait for transport work here, and a couple of plain trees are welcome reminders that this was once a fertile valley alongside the clear-running Fez River. Copper bowls are wrought and hammered over fires around the market's edge, and the smells of donkey droppings and soldering irons blend nicely in the sun. Looking into the Kairaouine Mosque at the top of the square is the Kairaouine University library, once one of the best book collections in the world but not presently open to the public. Opposite the library and facing away from it is the **Seffarine Medersa.**

⓭ Sahrij Medersa. Built by the Merenids in the 14th century, the medina's third-finest medersa is named for the pool (*sahrij*) on which its patio is centered. The cedar carvings here seem a particularly rich chocolate color late in the afternoon, and the birds in the eaves seem

especially numerous. The medersa provides rooms for Koranic studies sponsored by the Kairaouine Mosque, so you might hear students
chanting the Koran's verses from a room over the central patio. ⊠ *Andalusian Quarter.* 🏛 *10DH.* ⊙ *Daily 9–1, 3–6:30.*

❹ Souk el Henna. This little henna market is one of the most picturesque
squares in the medina, with a massive, gnarled fig tree in the center
and rows and ranks of spices, hennas, kohls, and aphrodisiacs for sale
in the stalls and shops around the edges. The ceramic shops on the way
into the henna souk sell a wide variety of typically blue Fassi pottery.
At the end of the square is a plaque dedicated to the Maristan Sidi Frej,
a medical center and psychiatric and teaching hospital built by the
Merenid ruler Youssef Ibn Yakoub in 1286. Used as a model for the
world's first mental hospital—founded in Valencia, Spain, in 1410—
the Maristan operated until 1944.

⓫ Terrasse des Tanneurs. The medieval tanneries are at once beautiful,
for their ancient dyeing vats of reds, yellows, and blues, and unforgettable, for the nauseating smell of rotting animal flesh on curing sheep,
goat, cow, and camel skins. The terrace overlooking the dyeing vats is
high enough to escape the full fetid power of the place and get a spectacular view over the multicolor vats. Absorb both the process and the
finished product at No. 2 Chouara Lablida, just past Rue Mechatine
(named for the combs made from animals' horns): the store is filled
with leather goods of all kinds, all of which smell terrific. One of the
shopkeepers will explain to you what's going on in the tanneries
below—how the skins are placed successively in saline solution, lime,
pigeon droppings, and then any of several natural dyes: antimony for
black, poppies for red, saffron for yellow, mint for green, and indigo
for blue. Barefoot workers in shorts pick up skins from the bottoms
of the dyeing vats with their feet, then work them manually. Though
this may look like the world's least desirable job, the work is actually
very well paid and somewhat in demand. Studies on the health of tan-
nery workers have shown that tanners live, if anything, longer and health-
ier lives than workers in most other collectives. This might be because
they need to be fit to do the work in the first place; or perhaps the foul-
smelling liquids contain some as-yet-undefined curative properties.

❺ Zaouia of Moulay Idriss II. Originally built by the Idriss dynasty in the
9th century in honor of the city's founder—just 33 at the time of his
death—this zaouia was restored by the Merenid dynasty in the 13th
century and has became one of the holiest shrines in the medina. Particularly known for his *baraka* (divine protection), Moulay Idriss II has
an especially strong cult among women seeking fertility and pilgrims
hoping for a turn in their luck. The wooden beam at the entrance, about
6 ft from the ground, was originally placed there to keep Jews, Christians, and donkeys out of the horm, the sacred area surrounding the
shrine itself. Inside the horm, Moroccans have historically enjoyed official sanctuary—they cannot be arrested if sought by the law. Look
through the doorway and you'll see the tomb of the saint at the far
right corner, with the fervently faithful burning candles and incense and
touching the tomb's silk-brocade covering. Note the rough wooden doors
themselves, worn smooth with hundreds of years of kissing and caressing
the wood for baraka. ⊙ *Daily 24 hrs. Restricted to Muslims.*

Fez el Djedid

Fez el Djedid (Fez the New) lies southwest of Bab Boujeloud between
Fez el Bali and the Ville Nouvelle. Built after 1273 by the Merenid dynasty as a government seat and stronghold, it seems at once flat and
monumental after the intensity of the medina.

A Good Walk

Starting from the tourist office on Place de la Résistance, in the Ville Nouvelle, a 15-minute walk east down Avenue Moulay Youssef leads to the Place des Alaouites. The closed and rarely used Royal Palace, **Dar el Makhzen** ⑮, rises behind walls to the left. The gardens surrounding the palace are among the loveliest in Morocco, but they're not currently open to the public. Continue down Grande Rue des Merenids through the **Mellah** ⑯, the medieval Jewish quarter, now inhabited almost completely by poor rural migrants to Fez. Upon reaching Bab Semarin, Grande Rue des Merenids veers off through rows of shops and street restaurants with the Royal Palace on the left and Fez el Djedid on the right. Bab Dekaken (Gate of the Benches) is the next major portal; to the left of here is the **Moulay Abdellah Quarter** ⑰, the seat of Morocco's government until the capital was moved to Rabat in 1912. **Bab es Seba** ⑱ leads into the **Petit Méchouar** (Small Arms Square). Just north are a former parade ground, the **Vieux Méchouar** (Old Arms Square), and, on the left, the massive Makina, once an arms factory and now a rug and carpet workshop. If you continued north from here, you'd come to the Kasbah Cherarda, a late-17th-century fortress built by Moulay Rashid to defend against Berber tribes. Even farther uphill, a 20-minute climb around to the right takes you to the Merenid tombs, from which you have an excellent view over Fez el Bali. Back at Bab Dekaken, walk east and downhill on the small pathway that eventually crosses the river, passing the entrance to La Noria (the Waterwheel), a peaceful café and restaurant overlooking the surprisingly clear stream and the wooden wheel that once irrigated the Bab Boujeloud gardens. Continuing right and through the gardens, you'll arrive at **Dar Batha** ⑲, which houses an excellent Moroccan art museum. From here it's just a few steps left (northwest) to Bab Boujeloud and Fez el Bali.

TIMING

Depending on how long you linger in Dar Batha, this walk should take two to three hours.

Sights to See

⑱ **Bab es Seba.** Named for the seven brothers of Moulay Abdellah who reigned during the 18th century, the Gate of Seven connects two open spaces originally designed for military parades and royal ceremonies, the Petit Méchouar and Vieux Méchouar. It was from this gate that Prince Ferdinand, brother of Duarte, king of Portugal, was hung head-down for four days in 1437. (He had been captured during a failed Portuguese invasion of Tangier, and Portugal had failed to raise the ransom for his release.) His remains were subsequently stuffed and displayed here for 29 years.

⑲ **Dar Batha.** Built in the late 19th century by Moulay el Hassan, this Andalusian palace houses the **Museum of Moroccan Arts,** one of Morocco's finest collections of craft works. The display of ceramics, for which Fez is particularly famous, includes rural earthenware crockery as well as elaborately ornate and colorful china painted with intricate geometrical patterns. Other displays feature embroidery stitched with real gold, astrolabes from the 11th to the 18th centuries, illuminated Korans, and Berber carpets and kilims. ⊠ *Place de l'Istiqlal,* ☎ *05/ 63–41–16.* ⌨ *10DH.* ☉ *Wed.–Mon. (except national holidays) 8:30– 11:45 and 2:30–6.*

⑮ **Dar el Makhzen.** Fez's Royal Palace and gardens are strictly closed to the public, but they're an impressive sight even from the outside. From Place des Alaouites you can take a close look at the door's giant brass knockers, made by artisans from Fez el Bali, as well as the brass doors themselves. Inside are various palaces, gardens, and *Places des Armes* (arms squares or parade grounds), as well as a medersa founded in 1320. One of the palaces, Dar el Qimma, one of the wonders of Dar el Makhzen, has intricately engraved and painted ceilings. The street running along the southeast side of the palace is Rue Bou Khessissat, one side of which is lined with typically ornate residential facades from the edge of the Mellah.

⑯ **Mellah.** The Mellah, with its characteristically ornate balconies and forged-iron windows (Arab facades are plain outside and decorated inside), was created in the 15th century when the Jews, forced out of the medina in one of Morocco's recurrent pogroms, were removed from their previous ghetto near Bab Guissa and set up as royal financial consultants and buffers between the Merenid rulers and the people. Derived from the Arabic word for salt (*melh*), the Mellah was so named for the Jewish task of salting the decapitated heads of bandits and rebels before they were publicly displayed around the walls. Fez's Jewish community suffered repressive measures until the beginning of the French Protectorate in 1912. Faced with an uncertain future after Morocco gained independence in 1956, nearly all of Fez's Jews migrated to Israel, the United States, or Casablanca.

⑰ **Moulay Abdellah Quarter.** Built by the Merenids as a seat of government and a stronghold against their subjects, this area lost its purpose when Rabat became the Moroccan capital under the French Protectorate. Subsequently a red-light district filled with brothels and dance halls, the quarter was closed to foreigners for years. Historic highlights include the vertically green-striped **Moulay Abdellah Mosque** and the **Great Mosque Abu Haq,** built by the Merenid sultan in 1276.

NEED A BREAK?   The quiet café **La Noria** (⊠ 43, Batha, ☎ 05/62–54–22), just down to the right of Bab Dekaken by the Fez River, at the southwest corner of the Bab Boujeloud gardens, is a welcome respite from the turbulent streets of either Fez El Bali or Fez el Djedid. Hamid Idriss, the fourth-generation owner, speaks fine English and is happy to chat. Mint tea or tagines are available.

Dining and Lodging

$$$ ✕ **Al Firdaous.** Moroccan tagines, pastillas, and couscous are just the beginning here: Al Firdaous (Arabic for "paradise") offers Moroccan art, belly dancing, and Berber Gnaoua music along with excellent cuisine and service. Occasional tour groups notwithstanding, it delivers a complete evening of Moroccan cuisine and culture. ⊠ 10, Rue Zenjfour, ☎ 05/ 63–43–43. AE, DC, MC, V.

$$$ ✕ **Dar Saada.** This 16th-century mid-medina palace is one of Fez's great traditional treats and retreats. The kitchen is known for the quality and quantity of everything from beef tagines to pigeon pastilla to mechoui (roast lamb), which must be ordered a day in advance. High ceilings, carved stucco, and elaborate woodwork all add to the sensorial rush of the place. ⊠ 21, Souk el Attarin, ☎ 05/63–73–70. Reservations essential. AE, DC, MC, V.

$$$ ✕ **La Maison Bleue.** The former home of a famous Moroccan as-
★ trologer and adviser to King Mohammed V is now an exquisite setting for both dining and music, with high ceilings and intricately carved stucco and cedar walls surrounding a central patio and fountain. Monsieur Abaddi, the owner, will graciously show you the upstairs rooms, library, and rooftop terrace upon request. The classic Moroccan dishes are carefully prepared and invariably tasty; try the *chwa'k dar*, a Fassi beef tagine. ⊠ 2, Place de l'Istiqlal Batha, ☎ 05/74–18–43. Reservations essential. AE, DC, MC, V.

$$$ ✕ **Zagora.** This Ville Nouvelle standout is known and respected for its classic Moroccan cuisine. The beef and lamb tagines are especially good, and the *briouates* (spicy meatballs) are nonpareil. The wine list is an anthology of Moroccan vineyards, and the service is first-rate. ✉ *5, Boulevard Mohamed V,* ☎ *05/94–06–86. Reservations essential. AE, DC, MC, V.*

$$ ✕ **Restaurant du Centre.** This unpretentious Ville Nouvelle place serves large portions of top-quality Moroccan dishes, including delicious tagines. The decor is unmemorable but authentic, and the service is excellent. All in all, it's a great value. ✉ *105, Boulevard Mohamed V,* ☎ *05/60–34–15. No credit cards.*

$–$$ ✕ **Palais Tijani.** Near the Tijani Mosque in Fez el Bali, this simple but commendable restaurant serves real Moroccan food to both locals and foreigners. Warmth and authenticity are the strong suits: *briouates au kefta* (ground-beef dumplings), *tagines d'agneau aux pruneaux* (lamb stewed in prunes), and mechoui (roast lamb) are staples. The only drawback is the absence of wine. ✉ *51–53, Derb ben Chekroune–La Blida,* ☎ *05/63–33–35. MC, V.*

$$$$ ✕⌧ **Jnan Palace.** For sheer comfort and service, this modern structure is unsurpassed among the new hotels in the Ville Nouvelle. Aesthetically it seems to have little in common with the city around it, but the tranquility around the pool and the quietly cosmopolitan bar, café, and atmosphere are a welcome relief from the wildness of Fez el Bali. ✉ *Avenue Ahmed Chaouki,* ☎ *05/65–39–65,* ⌧ *05/65–19–17. 165 rooms. 2 restaurants, 2 bars, pool, free parking. AE, DC, MC, V.*

$$$$ ✕⌧ **Merinides.** Strategically placed to overlook Fez, the Merinides is deservedly popular, so reserve well in advance. The views of Fez el Bali from the pool—nicely raised above the fray—are the best in town. The building is a clean-lined modern structure of glass and steel, and the spotless rooms are at once simple and luxurious. ✉ *Borj Nord,* ☎ *05/64–60–40,* ⌧ *05/64–52–25. 79 rooms, 11 suites. 2 restaurants, 2 bars, pool. AE, DC, MC, V.*

$$$$ ✕⌧ **Palais Jamai.** With an unbeatable combination of elegance, com-
★   fort, and proximity to the medina, the Palais Jamai is *the* place to stay in Fez. Built over 120 years ago, this former residence of the Vizier Jamai (prime minister under Sultan Moulay elHassan in the late 19th century) was just lavishly renovated in 1999. Decorated in typical Moroccan cedar painted with bright geometrical motifs, guest rooms overlook the gardens and the medina. The two restaurants serve fine Moroccan and international cuisine, accompanied by stellar performances of classical Andalusian music. ✉ *Bab Guissa,* ☎ *05/63–43–31,* ⌧ *05/63–50–96. 123 rooms, 14 suites. 2 restaurants, piano bar, pool, hammam, 4 tennis courts. AE, DC, MC, V.*

$$$ ✕⌧ **Hôtel Menzeh Zalagh.** Endowed with luxuriant Andalusian gardens and a pool that overlooks the medina, the Zalagh is close to the Ville Nouvelle restaurants and just a 20-minute walk from Fez el Bali. Guest rooms vary wildly, from lovely cedar-carved upper-floor suites, to rooms with balconies overlooking the gardens, the pool, and Fez el Bali, to somewhat undistinguished chambers on the Ville Nouvelle side. The staff is thrilled to help you in any way they can, so don't hesitate to call upon them; even the receptionists seem to hold graduate degrees in literature. Fires burn regularly in the fireplaces in winter. ✉ *10, Rue Mohamed Diouri,* ☎ *05/62–55–31,* ⌧ *05/65–19–95. 143 rooms, 6 suites. 3 restaurants, 3 bars, pool, dance club, free parking. AE, DC, MC, V.*

$$–$$$ ✕⌧ **Hôtel Batha.** Near Bab Boujeloud on the edge of the medina, the Batha is a great choice for its proximity to Fez el Bali combined with reasonable prices. The rooms are comfortable, if not especially elegant; and the staff is warm, willing, and fluent in English. ✉ *Place Batha,*

☎ 05/74–10–77, ℻ 05/74–10–78. 62 rooms. Restaurant, pool, parking (fee). AE, DC, MC, V.

Nightlife and the Arts

All of Fez's nightlife unfolds in the Ville Nouvelle. The disco in the **Hotel Sofia** (✉ 3, Rue de Pakistan, ☎ 05/62–42–65) gets active around 10 and, depending to the general level of frenzy, may stay open until 3 or 4. Other spots to investigate include the bar at the **Jnan Palace** hotel, where there's often a live performance (usually on the quiet side) and the nightclub at the **Hôtel Menzeh Zalagh** (☞ Lodging, *above*).

Shopping

Fez el Bali is one large souk. Woodworking, embroidery, ceramics, leather goods, rugs and carpets, copper plates, jewelry, textiles, and spices are all of exceptional quality and sold at comparatively low prices, considering the craftsmanship. Get used to the bargaining process: decide what the item is worth to you (which may come down to the question of whether or not you really want it) and stick with it as closely as you can. For copper, gold, and silver, stop into **Argenterie Fès** (✉ 6, Aouadine Bab Sensla, ☎ 05/63–39–55). **Au Bleu de Fès** (✉ Boutouil i Safarine, ☎ 05/63–35–79) specializes in Fassi pottery. For the best rugs-and-carpets discussion in Fez and a good mint tea, make a trip to **Aux Merveilles du Tapis** (✉ 22, Sebaâ Louyet [Seven Turns], ☎ 05/63–87–35); ☞ Fez el Bali, *above*. **Herboriste Ibn Sina** (✉ 6, Foundouk Lihoudi Derb Zaouia, ☎ 05/63–74–17) sells herbal remedies and homeopathic cures. **Maison Sahara** (✉ 9, Place Nejjarine, ☎ 05/63–45–22) has pottery and other assorted goods. **Belmajdoub Mohamed** (✉ 270, Talâa Lakbira, ☎ 05/64–11–12) features wood crafted with traditional lathes. **Bouchareb Mohamed** (✉ 8, Boutouil Kairaouine, ☎ 05/63–57–69) crafts marquetry and other wood products. **Fès Art Gallery** (✉ 2, Boutouil Kairaouine, ☎ 05/63–46–63) has miscellaneous arts and crafts. **Akessbi Fouad** (✉ 23, Rue Nejjarine, Souk Sekatine, ☎ no phone) is a master of the art of damascene (watered steel or silver inlay work) and the officially proclaimed "Best Artisan of Fez." For bronze, copper, and jewels, visit **La Maison Bouanania** (✉ 6, Derb ben Azahoum, Talâa Kebira, ☎ 05/63–65–66). For jewels and antiques try **Perle du Rif** (✉ 34, Boutouil Kairaouine, ☎ 05/63–37–49). **Terrasse des Tanneurs** (✉ 2, Chouara Lablida, ☎ 05/74–08–42), overlooking the tanneries, sells a variety of fragrant leather goods.

MEKNES

60 km (37 mi) west of Fez, 138 km (85 mi) east of Rabat.

Founded in the 10th century by the Zénète Meknassa tribe from the eastern Rif Mountains, Meknes has been called the Turntable of Morocco for its pivotal position between the Rif and Middle Atlas mountains and between the Atlantic Ocean and Sahara Desert. The Romans chose nearby Volubilis as their Moroccan headquarters for its central position, and this was probably Sultan Moulay Ismail's reasoning when he decided to govern from Meknes in 1673: a fiercely defensive military strategist, Ismail was probably unable to sleep a wink in the Fez River basin that his father, Er-Rachidia, had inherited from the Merenid dynasty. Reigning from 1672 to 1727, this ambitious and tyrannical sultan built 40 km (25 mi) of walls around the medina, the Imperial City (a stronghold within the medina), and, within that, the Royal Palace. Seemingly obsessive about more than just building, he is said to have owned 60,000 slaves, 12,000 horses, and 500 concubines; but it was his defensive genius that inspired him to construct behind his walls immense granaries, a reservoir, and elaborate palaces and mosques that earned Meknes comparisons to Versailles.

Meknes occupies a plateau overlooking the Boufekrane River, which divides the medina from the Ville Nouvelle. Most travelers stay in the Ville Nouvelle and approach the medina either on foot or by car.

Somewhat less inundated with tourists and more provincial than its traditionally potent neighbor to the northeast, Meknes offers a low-key initiation into the Moroccan processes of shopping and bargaining. A trip to Meknes is like a theater company performing on a shakedown cruise in New Haven before taking on Manhattan: the souks, the Imperial City, and even the Bou Inania Medersa are just as impressive as their Fez counterparts, but the pace is slower and the pressure lighter. Meknes's three sets of walls, Royal Granaries, Haras Regional, purebred Arabian and Berber horses, and Bab Mansour are as beautiful as anything in Morocco, even if you lose a bit of the electricity of Fez and Marrakesh. Whether it was post–Moulay Ismail exhaustion or the 1755 earthquake that quieted Meknes down, the result is a pleasant middle ground between Fez-style chaos and ho-hum sanity.

The Imperial City

A sweeping tour of Moulay Ismail's 40 km (25 mi) of walls (in three concentric rings), the granaries, the reservoir, the Haras Régional (equestrian stud farm), and the walled corridor between the Royal Palace and the Imperial City is best accomplished by car. Driving will give you the most effective sense of the scale of Ismail's vision. You can easily hire a taxi and a good guide through the tourist office.

A Good Tour

Begin your stroll on Rue El Meriniyne, across from the gardens of the Hôtel Transatlantique. From here, overlooking the Boufekrane River and medina, you can see the extent and sweep of the walls. Cross the river on the downstream bridge via Rue Andalous; then turn right and drive around the Boulevard Circulaire. The first major religious structure on your left is the **zaouia of Sidi Mohammed ben Aïssa** ①, focal point of the famous Aïssaoua cult known for its trance rituals. Continuing around the walls, go through **Bab el Khemis** (Gate of the Fifth Day), so named for the wool markets held here every Thursday. Each section of this double wall is more than 12 ft thick. Continue between the old and new Mellahs (Jewish quarters), then turn right and then left through **Bab el Qari.** Turn left again and go around the **Bassin de l'Agdal,** the reservoir Moulay built inside his defensive walls in case of siege. Your next stop is **Heri as Souani** ②, the Royal Granaries, one of the most beautiful structures in Meknes and a marvel of engineering. After exploring the granary, visit the **Haras Régional** ③ to see some drop-dead-beautiful purebred Arabian and Berber stallions. A drive around **Dar el Makhzen,** the Royal Palace (still used occasionally by the Alaouites) and through the corridor between the second and third sets of walls known as **Assaragh** (Corridor of the Open Sky, in Berber) and the **Bab er Rih** (Gate of the Wind) brings you to a narrow street off to the right, just short of the zaouia of Moulay Ismail. Take this street and park in the little parking lot at **Dar el Kebira** (the Main Palace). From here you can find your way to Moulay Ismail's great-great-grandson Raouf's restaurant **Riad** for lunch in what was once part of the Royal Palace.

TIMING
This tour takes three or four hours by car, a full day on foot. Note that the Haras Régional closes at noon; if you want to see it, set out by nine.

Sights to See

❸ Haras Régional. Purebred Arabian and Berber horses and fine hybrids are the star performers at this equestrian breeding and training farm. Under the supervision of Berber horseman Ben Salm, a dead ringer for Nikolai Gogol's character Taras Bulba (and perhaps further evidence that the Berbers have roots in Central Asia), these beautiful stallions receive hundreds of visitors daily during high season in Morocco. The horses, all of which are registered with Lloyds of London, are identified by plaques on their stable walls: red for Arabians, green for Berber stallions and mares, and red and green for hybrids, with the ratio of the two colors indicating their exact percentages in the horse's bloodline. Guided horseback outings can be arranged for about 250 DH.

❷ Heri as Souani (Royal Granaries). Also known as Dar el Ma (the Water Palace) for the reservoir beneath, the granaries were one of Moulay Ismail's greatest achievements, and the first place any Meknessi will take you to give you an idea of the second Alaouite sultan's exaggeratedly grandiose vision. The Royal Granaries were designed to store grain as feed for the 12,000 horses in the royal stables—not just for a few days or weeks, but over a 20-year siege if necessary. Ismail and his engineers counted on three things to keep the granaries cool enough that the grain would never rot: thick walls (12 ft), suspended gardens (a cedar forest was planted on the roof), and an underground reservoir with water ducts under the floors. The room on the far right as you enter has a 30-ft well in its center and a towpath around it—donkeys circulated constantly, activating the waterwheel in the well, which forced water through the ducts and maintained a stable temperature in the granaries. Out behind the granaries are the remains of the royal stables (the roofs were lost in the 1755 Lisbon earthquake). Some 1,200 purebreds, just one-tenth of Moulay Ismail's cavalry, were kept here. At a point just left of the door out to the stables, you can see the stunning symmetry of the stable's pillars from three different perspectives. The granaries have such elegance and grace that they were once called the Cathedral of Grain by a group of Franciscan priests, who were so moved that they requested permission to sing plainsong here. Acoustically perfect, the granaries are now often used for summer concerts and receptions. ⊠ *Heri as Souani.* 🔁 *10DH.* ☉ *Daily 9–1, 3–6:30.*

❶ Zaouia of Sidi Mohammed ben Aïssa. Built in 1776 by Sultan Sidi Mohammed ben Abdellah, this shrine is the focal point of the legendary Aissaoua cult, known for such voluntary rituals as swallowing scorpions, broken glass, and poison; eating live sheep; and cutting themselves with knives in prayer-induced trances. Ben Aïssa was one of Morocco's most famous and singular saints, said to have made a pact with the animal world and to possess magical powers, such as the ability to transform the leaves of trees into coins of gold and silver. Every year, during his moussem on the eve of Mouloud (the birth of the prophet Mohammed, a moveable feast celebrated in early and mid-June in 2000 and 2001), members of the Aissaoua fraternity gather from all over North Africa. Processions form and parade through Meknes, snakes are charmed, and the saint's followers perform ecstatic dances, often imitating the behavior of certain animals. Although some of the Aissaoua's more brutal practices have been outlawed, this moussem remains one of Morocco's most astonishing and mysterious events.

Bab Mansour and the Medina

A walk around Bab Mansour and Place El Hedim takes in nearly all the major sights in Meknes, including Moulay Ismail's mausoleum and the Prison of the Christian Slaves.

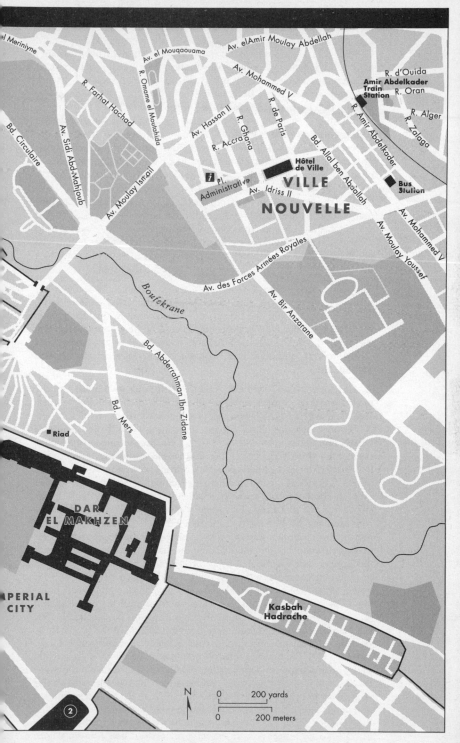

R. Meriniyne

Av. el Mouqaouama

Av. elAmir Moulay Abdellah

Av. Mohammed V

R. d'Ouida

Amir Abdelkader Train Station

R. Oran

R. Farhat Hachad

R. Omane el Moutahida

R. Alger

R. de Paris

R. Amir Abdelkader

R. Zalaga

Bd. Circulaire

Av. Sidi Abd-Mahjoub

Av. Hassan II

R. Ghana

R. Accra

Bd. Allal ben Abaailah

Av. Moulay Ismail

Hôtel de Ville

VILLE

Bus Station

Pl. Administrative

Av. Idriss II

NOUVELLE

Av. Mohammed V

Av. des Forces Armées Royales

Av. Moulay Youssef

Boufekrane

Av. Bir Anzarane

Bd. Abderrahman Ibn Zidane

Bd. Mers

Riad

DAR EL MAKHZEN

PERIAL CITY

Kasbah Hadrache

N

0   200 yards

0   200 meters

2

A Good Walk

Beginning at **Place El Hedim,** take a look around the square before launching into the food market and the souks. A smaller version of Marrakesh's Djemâa el Fna, Place El Hedim (meaning, essentially, Rubble Square, as Moulay Ismail used to pile construction debris here) gets active in the evenings. You might even browse through the impressive Museum of Moroccan Arts in the **Dar Jamai** ④ before starting. **Bab Mansour** ⑤ and the Bab Djemâa en Nouar (Gate of the Flowers), just to the right, are worth a close look, especially when the afternoon sun illuminates their colors and ornamentation. Facing away from Bab Mansour, the ceramics stalls on the left side of Place Hedim sell some good-size tagine pots for as little as 10 or 20 dirhams. Just past the ceramics stands, a narrow corridor leads into the **food souk,** a riotous display of everything from spices to great pyramids of fruit or multicolor olives. Work through the souk and emerge from the far-right corner; through the bird market outside and back to your right, in a corner, you'll find the fish market, usually packed with colorful treasures from the Atlantic coast. Continue right around the building, pass to the left of Dar Jamai, and you'll enter the Meknes souk. Continue straight in until you come to a T—on the left is a usually boisterous public auction area.

The street crossing the T is the main artery through the souk. A left turn will take you through the **Souk Nejjarin,** the woodworkers' souk, and then into the rug and carpet souk. Farther on in this direction is the **Souk Bezzarin,** a general flea market along the medina walls. Farther up to the right are basket makers, irosmiths, leather workers, and saddle makers, and, near **Bab el Djedid,** makers of tents and musical instruments.

A right turn at the T will take you through **Souk es Sabbat** and the more formal part of the souk, beginning with the *babouche* (leather-slipper) market. At the first right, take a quick look at an ancient fondouk, now in ruins. Back on the main street you'll pass **Fondouk Oueda** on the left, now endowed with a pharmacy, café, and teleboutique; and, shortly thereafter, the **Bou Inania Medersa** ⑥, one of the loveliest medersas in Morocco. Back out in the street you'll pass one of the 12 doors of the mosque before reaching the **camel-meat vendor** on a left-hand corner at stall No. 15, identifiable by the toy camel hanging in front of the stand. This meat is generally dark and rich in appearance, and the butcher is more than willing to open his refrigerator and haul out a camel head in case you have any doubts. Turn left here, leaving the main street, and take an immediate right. On the left you'll see a brass door surrounded by colorful ornamentation; this is an old fondouk, now used as a theater, library, and lodging house. Just 50 ft down, at the next corner on the right, is a tiny, old-fashioned **café** dominated by a large brass tank, a good place for a mint tea prepared and served in the traditional manner. Farther down on the left, at No. 91, is a **beignet,** a maker of fritters, or doughnuts, one of the few of these traditional artisans remaining. (For a single dirham you get two beignets; 8DH buys you a kilo.) You will now be hit by a powerfully milky aroma from the *laiterie* (dairy shop) on the right-hand corner; this is a signal to turn right and proceed down into the **Place du Murier** (named for its mulberry tree), where a 1,000-year-old mulberry, gnarled and about 3 ft in diameter, stands in the middle of what was once the salt vendors' souk. On the right, where he's seated in a bucket car seat at stall No. 27, meet celebrated zellij-tile artisan **Ben Adada,** whose father was also a well-known zellij maker and whose grandfather was one of the master craftsmen of Moulay Ismail's Royal Palace. Turn right just past Ben Adada's place (taking a look left into the ancient wood-burning public bakery as you leave the square) and follow signs to the

Palais des Idrissides ⑦, a 14th-century palace and carpet emporium and a gem of a visit whether you buy a rug or not. The proprietors will, in excellent English, French, Spanish, German, or just about any language you prefer, deliver a memorable discourse on the architecture and craftsmanship of the house before moving on to an eloquent and entertaining history and ethnographical portrait of Berber kilim and carpet creation.

Back out in Place El Hedim, cut across to Bab Mansour and go straight through it to the large rectangular Place Lalla Aouda. Pass through the next gate, Bab Filala, slightly to the right, and the building with the pyramidal dome on your right will be the **Koubt al Khayatine** (also known as Koubt Essoufara), once a reception hall for ambassadors to Moulay Ismail's imperial court. Just past the door into the pavilion are stairs leading down to the **Habs Kara (Prison of the Christian Slaves)** ⑧, where Moulay Ismail is said to have kept his 60,000 captives, 40,000 of whom were Christian prisoners of war. After a tour of the underground chambers, continue past the splendid wooden gate into the Royal Golf Gardens, stopping to inquire, if you wish, about playing on this unique nine-hole course enclosed entirely by 17th-century walls. Out to the right as you leave the gardens is the **Moulay Ismail Mausoleum** ⑨.

TIMING

This walk covers considerable distance, possibly 3 km (2 mi) in all, and is rich in things to study. Allow about four hours, plus a possible return trip to, say, purchase spices or move slowly through the Museum of Moroccan Art at Dar Jamai. The affable carpet salesmen at the Palais des Idrissides are unlikely to let you leave in less than an hour.

Sights to See

⑤ **Bab Mansour.** Widely considered the most beautiful gate in North Africa, this mammoth, horseshoe-shape arch of triumph was completed in 1732 by a Christian convert to Islam named Mansour Laalej (whose name means "victorious renegade"). The famous and much-repeated story of the gate's construction—the sultan asked, "Can you do better?" to which Mansour replied in the affirmative and was immediately executed—is surely a legend, as the gate was finished five years after Ismail's death. The smaller marble columns supporting the two bastions on either side of the main entry were taken from the Roman ruins at Volubilis, while the taller Corinthian columns came from Marrakesh's El Badi Palace, part of Moulay Ismail's campaign to erase any vestige of the Saadian dynasty that preceded the Alaouites. Ismail's last important construction project, the gate was conceived as an elaborate homage to himself rather than (for once) a defensive stronghold, thus its intensely decorative character. French novelist Pierre Loti (1850–1923) penned the definitive description: " . . . rose-hued, starshaped, endless sets of broken lines, unimaginable geometric combinations that confuse the eye like a labyrinthine puzzle, always in the most original and masterly taste, have been gathered here in thousands of bits of varnished earth, in relief or recessed, so that from a distance it creates the illusion of a buffed and textured fabric, glimmering, glinting, a priceless tapestry placed over these ancient stones to relieve the monotony of these towering walls."

⑥ **Bou Inania Medersa.** Begun by the Merenid sultan Abou el Hassan and finished by his son Abou Inan between 1350 and 1358, the Meknes version of Fez's residential college of the same name is arguably more beautiful and better preserved than its better-known twin. Starting with the cupola and the enormous doors on the street, virtually every inch of this building is covered with decorative carving or calligraphy. The central fountain is for ablutions before prayer; behind the small windows over the courtyard are rooms for some of the 60 theology students who lodged here. The rooftop terrace has the city's single best view of the Meknes medina. ⊠ *Souk es Sebbat.* 🖃 *10DH.* ⊗ *Daily 9–1, 3–6:30.*

❹ Dar Jamai. This 19th-century palace was built by the same family of viziers (high government officials) responsible for the Palais Jamai hotel in Fez. The building itself is exquisite, especially the carved-cedar ceilings on the second floor; and it now houses the **Museum of Moroccan Art,** which has superb collections of carpets, jewelry, and needlework. ⊠ *Place El Hedim.* 🖃 *10DH.* ⊗ *Daily 9–1, 3–6:30.*

❽ Habs Kara (Prison of the Christian Slaves). After you pass through Place Lalla Aouda and Bab Filala, on the right, the pyramid-shape dome on the right side of the next square is the Koubt al Khayatine (Tailors' Pavilion), named for the seamsters who once worked here. Also known as the Koubt Essoufara (Ambassadors' Pavilion), this was where Moulay Ismail received ambassadors from abroad. The stairs to the right of the pavilion entrance lead down to the grain silos originally built as a prison by the Portuguese architect Cara, himself a prisoner who earned his freedom by constructing these immense subterranean slave quarters. The caretaker and guide will show you how the 60,000 slaves (of which 40,000 were reportedly Christian prisoners of war) were shackled to the wall, forced to sleep in a standing position. Ambassadors visiting Meknes to plead for the release of their captive countrymen were received in the pavilion above, never suspecting that the prisoners were directly under their feet. ⊠ *Bab Filala.* 🖃 *10DH.* ⊗ *Daily 9–1, 3–6:30.*

★ **❾ Moulay Ismail Mausoleum.** One of four sacred sites in Morocco open to non-Muslims (the others are Casablanca's Hassan II, Rabat's Mohammed V Mausoleum, and Rissani's zaouia of Moulay Ali Sherif), Moulay Ismail's mausoleum was opened to non-Muslims by King Mohammed V (grandfather of Mohammed VI) in honor of Ismail's manifestly ecumenical instincts. Always an admirer of France's King Louis XIV—who, in turn, considered the sultan an important ally—Moulay Ismail maintained close ties with Europe even as he battled to eject the Portuguese from their coastal strongholds at Asilah, Essaouira, and Larache. A proponent of trade with Europe, he signed a commercial treaty with France in 1682. The mausoleum's site once held Meknes's Palais de Justice (Courthouse), and Moulay Ismail deliberately chose it as his resting place in the stated hope that he would be judged in his own court by his own people. The lovely ocher-hue walls inside (pale yellow on their sun-bleached upper parts) lead to the sultan's private sanctuary, on the left, heavily decorated with zellij tiles bearing colorful geometrical patterns. To the right is Moulay Ismail's tomb, surrounded with hand-carved cedar and stucco walls and more zellij. The large grandfather clocks were gifts of Louis XIV, allegedly bestowed on the sultan to ease Ismail's chagrin at the refusal of Louis's daughter, Princesse de Conti, to marry him. 🖃 *10DH.* ⊗ *Daily 9–1, 3–6:30.*

❼ Palais des Idrissides. Much more than a carpet emporium, this magnificent 14th-century palace built by the cult of the Idrissid dynasty is a treasury of art, artisanship, and architecture not to be missed (even at the risk of purchasing a rug). The unusual carved and inlaid ceilings of olive, rather than the customary cedar, wood are extraordinarily rich and ornate. The sloped floor, built for drainage, is made of Carrara marble, in exchange for which Morocco used to trade sugar. This carpet and kilim cooperative displays work from the 45 Berber tribes that have traditionally lived near Meknes, each with its own symbols and techniques. Kilims have long been woven specially for marriages, babies, high society, tents, or medicine; the marriage kilim, for example, served as a sort of ID card in which a bride's character, tastes, and life story were spelled out for a husband who would not see her face until they were wed. Baby kilims were fashioned in bright colors to entertain and educate; society kilims were decorative, designed to impress; tent carpets and kilims were heavy and functional, built to provide a floor in the desert; and medical kilims were made of camel hair, which was thought to cure rheumatism. ⊠ *11, Rue Kermouni,* ☎ *05/ 55-78-92.* ⊘ *Daily 8-7.*

Dining and Lodging

$$$-$$$$ ✕ **Le Dauphin.** Meknes's enclave par excellence for French and international cuisine, Le Dauphin is well respected for the quality of its food, its refined yet active (bistrolike) ambience, and service. Fish specialties, duck, and foie gras are standards on the menu, as are wines from beyond North Africa. ⊠ *5, Avenue Mohamed V,* ☎ *05/52-34-23. AE, DC, MC, V.*

$$$ ✕ **Collier de la Colombe.** A five-minute walk to the left inside Bab Mansour, this graceful medina space has giant picture windows and terraces overlooking the Boufrekane River and Ville Nouvelle. The menu is a classic range of Moroccan specialties, with the addition of grilled lamb and beef. ⊠ *Rue Driba (access via Bab Mansour),* ☎ *05/55-50-41. AE, DC, MC, V.*

$$$ ✕ **Palais Terrab.** This family-run restaurant in a residential part of the Ville Nouvelle is well known in Meknes for its serious cuisine, folkloric spectacles, and the ability to serve 600 people at once. The downside is that you may find yourself either dining in a vast empty space or surrounded by 598 tourists; the reliable upside is that the food is excellent and the family warm and generous. Try the *brique Tetuan,* a kind of briouate. The *tagine de kabab maghdour*—chunks of meat stewed in onions and spices—is a Meknes specialty. ⊠ *18, Avenue Zerktouni,* ☎ *05/52-61-00. AE, DC, MC, V.*

$$$ ✕ **Riad.** Hidden inside the ramparts of the Royal Palace, this stately yet intimate garden restaurant is so jarringly lovely that you almost rub your eyes upon arrival. The owner, Raouf Alaoui Ismail—a direct descendant of Moulay Ismail—speaks excellent English and serves fine Moroccan cuisine. Tables are arranged in and around the central patio on the second floor. ⊠ *79, Ksar Chaacha–Dar Lakbira,* ☎ *05/ 53-05-42. AE, DC, MC, V.*

$$-$$$ ✕ **Annexe Restaurant Metropole II.** This tiny, friendly family place on the Tangier road is just a five-minute walk from the Hôtel Transatlantique. Don't be put off by the less-than-grand aesthetics; this is real Moroccan cooking on a personal scale. *Mechoui* (roast lamb) is available without a day's advance notice and at a very reasonable price; try to order in advance anyway, just to be certain. ⊠ *4, Boulevard Yougoslavie (Route de Tanger),* ☎ *05/51-35-11. AE, DC, MC, V.*

$$-$$$ ✕ **Le Tangerois.** An intimate hideaway near the Hotel Akouass and El Amir Abdelkader train station, this combination Moroccan, Vietnamese, and international restaurant in the Ville Nouvelle is good at everything it does. The wine list is first-rate, and you're guaranteed never to find a busload of tourists in this local favorite. ⊠ *2, Rue de Beyrout,* ☎ *05/51-50-91. AE, DC, MC, V.*

$$$$ ✕⌂ **Hôtel Rif.** This modern Ville Nouvelle lodging may be the most comfortable, best-equipped place in Meknes. The Moroccan restaurant usually has a belly dancer and live Gnaoua music, especially when tour groups are in residence. The rooms are spacious and comfortable, and some have views across the river to the medina. ⊠ *Rue d'Accra,* ☎ *05/52-25-92,* FAX *05/52-44-28. 110 rooms. 2 restaurants, bar, free parking. AE, DC, MC, V.*

$$$–$$$$ ✕🏨 **Hôtel Transatlantique.** Overlooking Meknes from across the river, the Transatlantique offers poolside comfort, a good Moroccan restaurant, elegant bathrooms, and comfortable beds. The rooms themselves are not luxurious, but the ones with balconies over the pool and orange trees have a traditional old-world charm. ✉ *El-Meriniyine,* ☎ *05/52–50–52,* 🅵🅰🅇 *05/52–00–57. 118 rooms. 2 restaurants, bar, 2 pools, tennis court. AE, DC, MC, V.*

$$ ✕🏨 **Hotel Akouass.** The rooms here are merely adequate, but the helpful staff, the ample, tasty breakfast (including all the fresh-squeezed orange juice you can drink), and the glass-walled breakfast room perched over a busy street corner manage to compensate. Across the street from one of North Africa's better newspaper kiosks (with everything from *Time* to the *International Herald Tribune* and *Paris Match*), the Akouass also hosts an unbelievable downstairs disco scene (get a room as high up as you can), where men and women in Old Testament *djellabas* boogie with women in leather thongs and men in leather jeans. ✉ *27, Rue Emir Abdelkader,* ☎ *05/51–59–67,* 🅵🅰🅇 *05/51–59–94. 52 rooms. Restaurant, bar, breakfast room, dance club. AE, DC, MC, V.*

Nightlife and the Arts

A torrid, if somewhat tawdry, disco scene thrives in the hotels around the Ville Nouvelle's El Amir Abdelkader train station. The Akouass and the Royal Mansour have underground clubs that pound away until four in the morning. More interesting are the bar and live-music scenes in the better hotels, especially the Transatlantique and the Rif; sometimes you'll hear traditional Gnaoua, sometimes Western folk.

Shopping

The craftsmen and souks of Meknes are very much the equals of those of Fez, and what's more, they're easier to negotiate with. Just be prepared, if you try to tell a rug salesmen that you're pressed for time, to hear, "Ah, but a person without time is a dead person." **Ben Moussa** (✉ Food market, Place El Hedim, ☎ 05/55–73–21) is the place to stock up on Morocco's fragrant spices. Just inside the Place El Hadim entrance across from Bab Mansour, it's in the first aisle to the right, last stall on the left; follow your nose. At **Carreaux Traditionnels** (✉ 27, Rahbat Zrâa el Kadima, ☎ 05/53–04–96) you can watch a zellij (ceramic-tile) artisan in action. **El Ouadghiri El Edrissi** (✉ 77, Kourat Souk el Attarin, ☎ 05/53–34–41) makes doors and other wooden items. **L'Art Traditionnel** (✉ 7, Rahbat Zrâa Lakdimia Zaouia Tijania, ☎ 05/53–10–05) creates wooden sculpture and decorative objects of all kinds, including leather, ceramics, and copper. The **Palais des Idrissides** (✉ 11, Rue Kermouni, ☎ 05/55–78–92), in the souk near Dar Jamai, is the best place to look for Berber kilims, rugs, and carpets. **Palais de l'Artisan** (✉ 11, Koubt Souk Kissariat Lahrir, ☎ 05/53–35–02) is a specialist in damascene (watered steel or silver inlay work). **Produits Artisanaux Bennani Saâd** (✉ 21, Rue El Kissaria, ☎ 05/55–78–90) is another top damascene artisan.

SIDE TRIPS

Volubilis

28 km (17 mi) northwest of Meknes, 88 km (53 mi) northwest of Fez, 3 km (2 mi) west of Moulay Idriss. Marked as OUALILI *(Berber for "oleander"), Volubilis is beyond Moulay Idriss on Route P28, which leaves P6 to head northeast 15 km (9 mi) northwest of Meknes.*

One of the greatest of Morocco's many marvels, Volubilis was capital of the Roman province of Mauritania (Land of the Moors), Rome's southwesternmost incursion into North Africa. Forming a nearly perfect cross section of a Roman city, Volubilis's municipal street plan and distribution of public buildings are remarkably clear and coherent examples of Roman urban planning. The floor plans of the individual houses, and especially their well-preserved mosaic floors depicting mythological scenes, provide a rare connection to the sense and sensibilities of the Roman colonists who lived here 2,000 years ago.

Favored by the confluence of the rivers Khoumane and Fertasse and surrounded by some of the most fertile plains in Morocco, this site has probably been inhabited since the Neolithic era. The Roman epoch began in about 40 BC. Juba I, king of Numidia (present-day Algeria) sided with Pompey in his internecine Roman rivalry with Caesar and lost, committing suicide after Caesar's victory at Thapsus. His son Juba II, educated in Rome, was nevertheless favored by Caesar and reinstated as king, first of Numidia and later, in 25 BC, of Mauritania. Highly learned, the young prince lived in Volubilis with his wife, Cleopatra Selene (daughter of Antony and Cleopatra), writing lengthy historical and geographical works. The bronze bust of Juba II that was found in Volubilis and is now displayed in Rabat's Archaeological Museum portrays a brooding young aristocrat, who might well have preferred life in Rome to virtual exile at the edge of the empire. In any case, it was probably the influence of Juba II that made Volubilis such an opulent outpost. Juba and his son Ptolemy did a great deal for Mauritania, fostering trade, commerce with Rome, the arts, and diplomacy with the Berbers, until the emperor Caligula had Ptolemy murdered in 40 BC and the province rose up against Rome. After quelling the revolt, Emperor Claudius divided the province into the eastern Mauretania Caesarea and western Mauretania Tingitana, with Tingis (Tangier) as capital. Volubilis prospered, exporting to Rome olive oil, wheat, and wild animals for slaughter in the Colosseum. The latter resulted in the swift decimation of Volubilis's lion, bear, and elephant population over a period of 200 years.

Rome's ambitions to extend its empire beyond the Atlas mountains were never realized, and the Roman garrison withdrew in AD 285 after three centuries in North Africa. Volubilis, inhabited by a mixture of Berbers, Jews, and peoples from the eastern Mediterranean survived largely intact and still functioned in Latin when Moulay Idriss arrived in 786. With the construction of nearby Meknes, the decline of Volubilis accelerated, and by the late 17th century Moulay Ismail was using parts of the Roman ruins to build his lavish imperial capital.

A Good Walk

If you can possibly hire El Hadi (guide No. 171) at the tourist office, don't hesitate: it's like walking through Volubilis with a savvy Berber version of Jay Leno. Example: Finding a senior gardener taking a postprandial snooze, El Hadi dubs him "the last Roman." If you prefer to see Volubilis on your own (less informative, more contemplative), proceed through the entrance and make a clockwise sweep. After crossing the little bridge over the Fertassa River, climb up to the left edge of the plateau, and you'll soon come across a Berber skeleton lying beside the path with his head pointed east, a deliberate placement suggesting early Islamization of the Berber populace here. Remains of **Roman olive presses** are visible to the left, two of some 55 such presses identifiable at Volubilis, proof of the importance of the olive-oil industry that supported the 20,000 inhabitants of this 28-acre metropolis. The first important mosaics are to the right in the imposing **House of Or-**

pheus: a dolphin mosaic and a mosaic depicting the Orpheus myth in the *tablinum,* a back room used as a library and receiving room. Past the public **Baths of Gallienus** in a room to the right are a dozen sets of footprints raised slightly above the level of the floor. If you find this strangely redolent of European water-closet engineering, well, that's what this was: a communal bathroom. The wide paved street leading up to the **capitol,** the **basilica,** and the **forum** is the **Cardus Maximus,** the main east–west thoroughfare of any Roman town. Across the forum from the basilica were the market stalls. The **triumphal arch**— originally built in AD 217, knocked down by the 1755 Lisbon earthquake, and restored in 1932—is down to the left at the end of **Decumanus Maxiumus,** the main north–south street. The eroded medallions on the arch represent the emperor Caracalla and his mother, Julia Donna. Looking south through the arch, the first building to the left is known as the **House of the Dog** since a bronze sculpture of a dog, now on display in Rabat, was discovered here. The next building is the **House of the Athlete,** with a mosaic depicting an acrobat performing an equestrian trick. Just south is the entrance to the town brothel, or **Lupanar,** identifiable by an impressive phallus carved out of a block of stone.

The town's greatest mansions and mosaics line Decumanus Maximus from here north to the Tangier Gate, which leads out of the enclosure on the uphill end. Some of the most famous include the **House of Ephebus,** just west of the triumphal arch, named for the nude ivy-crowned bronze sculpture discovered here (now on display in Rabat). The *cenacula,* or banquet hall, has colorful mosaics with Bacchic themes. Continuing up Decumanus Maximus, the small spaces near the edge of the street held shop stalls, while mansions—10 on the left and eight on the right—lined either side. The House of **Dionysus and the Four Seasons** is about halfway down; its scene depicting Dionysus discovering Ariadne asleep is one of the most spectacular mosaics in town. The next house is known as the house of the **Bathing Nymphs** for the superb floor mosaics portraying a bevy of frolicking nymphs in a surprisingly contemporary, all but animated, artistic fashion. On the right side of the street, the penultimate house has a marble bas-relief medallion of Bacchus. Moving back south along the next street below and parallel to Decumanus Maximus, there is a smaller, shorter row of six houses. The fourth one down contains the best set of mosaics in Volubilis and should not be missed. This is the **House of Venus,** with mosaics portraying a chariot race, a bathing Diana surprised by the hunter Actaeon, and the abduction of Hylas by nymphs. The path back down to the entrance passes the site of the Temple of Saturn, across the riverbed on the left.

Dining and Lodging

$$$$ ✕🏨 **Volubilis Inn.** Surrounded by olive trees high on a hillside, this comfortable modern hotel has wonderful views from its pool and terrace over the Roman city and the fertile valley to the southwest. With two Moroccan restaurants, an international restaurant, and two more terrace dining areas overlooking the ruins, it also presents plenty of culinary options. Guest rooms are modern and, though not state-of-the-art, more than adequate. The inn is useful if you either accidentally run out of daylight or deliberately decide to watch the sunset from Volubilis. To get here from Meknes, take P6 north to Km 15 and turn right onto P28; pass the right turn for Moulay Idriss and follow signs for Oualili. Leaving Volubilis, turn left at the exit and look for the quick turn up to the right. ✉ *Route de Volubilis (P28),* ☎ *05/54–44–06,* 🆁🆇 *05/54–43–69. 54 rooms. 3 restaurants, bar, pool. AE, DC, MC, V.*

Moulay Idriss

23 km (14 mi) north of Meknes, 3 km (2 mi) southeast of Volubilis, 83 km (50 mi) west of Fez.

Moulay Idriss is the most sacred town in Morocco, the final resting place of the nation's religious and secular founder Moulay Idriss I. It is said that five pilgrimages to Moulay Idriss are the spiritual equivalent of one to Mecca; thus the town's nickname: the poor man's Mecca. A view over the town is interesting, but it must be said that Moulay Idriss is routine compared to other Moroccan sights and scenes. Non-Muslims are not allowed inside the tomb at all and until recently were not allowed to spend the night in town. If you must choose between trips to Volubilis and Moulay Idriss, go with the former; but the one-hour climb to the vantage point overlooking the **zaouia of Moulay Idriss I** is a nice hike and a symbolic bow to Morocco's secular and spiritual history.

Before your walk, it's helpful to accept the services of two of the trustworthy boys working the parking lot, thus ensuring, for a small price, both car security and some help navigating this hillside enclave. Your objective is the **Sidi Abdellah el Hajjam Terrace,** above the Khiber quarter on the left. The adjoining quarter across the gorge is called Tasga. Descending through the steep and twisting streets, find the **Moulay Idriss Medersa,** which boasts the only cylindrical minaret in Morocco: originally built with materials from Volubilis, the minaret is intensely decorated with green ceramic tiles bearing some of the 114 *suras* (chapters) of the Koran.

A splash of white against Djebel (Mt.) Zerhoun, Moulay Idriss attracts thousands of pilgrims from all over Morocco to its moussem in late August or early September. *Fantasias* (Berber cavalry charges with blazing muskets), acrobats, dancers, and storytellers fill the town, while hundreds of tents cover the hillsides.

Dining

The main street through Moulay Idriss (up to the parking area just in front of the zaouia) is lined with a series of small, indistinguishable stands and restaurants serving everything from brochettes of spicy meat to harira to mint tea.

FEZ AND MEKNES A TO Z

Arriving and Departing

By Bus

Bus stations: **Fez** (✉ Avenue Mohammed V, ☎ 05/62–20–41). **Meknes** (✉ 45, Avenue Mohammed V, ☎ 05/52–25–83).

By Plane

Fès-Saïss Airport (✉ Route P24, Km 13, ☎ 05/62–47–12 or 05/65–21–61) serves both Fez and Meknes. The taxi or bus ride to Fez itself takes about 15 minutes; to Meknes, half an hour.

By Train

O.N.C.F. has one station in **Fez** (✉ Avenue des Almohades, ☎ 05/62–50–01) and two in **Meknes:** one central (✉ Avenue El Amir Abdelkader, ☎ 05/52–06–89) and the other less so (✉ Avenue de la Gare, ☎ 05/50–26–17).

Getting Around

By Car

You can easily see Fez, Meknes, Volubilis, and Moulay Idriss without renting a car, but the latter two might warrant a day rental, as much for the surrounding countryside as for the destinations themselves.

Contacts and Resources

Car Rental

Avis (⊠ 50, Boulevard Chefchaouen, Fez, ☎ 05/62–67–46; ⊠ Airport Fès–Saïss, ☎ 05/62–67–46). **Budget** (⊠ Bureau Grand Hôtel, Avenue Chefchaouen, Fez, ☎ 05/62–09–19). **Hertz** (⊠ Hôtel de Fès, Avenue des FAR, Fez, ☎ 05/62–28–12; ⊠ Airport Fès–Saïss, ☎ 05/65–18–23). **Stop Car** (⊠ 3, Rue Essaouira, Meknes, ☎ 05/52–50–61). **Zeit Wagen** (⊠ 4, Rue Antsirabe, Meknes, ☎ 05/52–59–18).

Emergencies

For an **ambulance** call 05/52–11–34.

Guided Tours

Hire an official guide from the tourist office for 300DH a day.

Visitor Information

Tourist offices: **Fez** (⊠ Place de la Résistance–Immeuble Bennani, ☎ 05/62–34–60). **Meknes** (⊠ Place Administrative, ☎ 05/52–44–26). **Volubilis** (⊠ City entrance, ☎ 05/54–41–03).

4 THE MIDDLE ATLAS

Snowy cedar forests, ski slopes, and trout streams are not images normally associated with Morocco, yet the Middle Atlas unfolds like an alpine mirage less than an hour from the medieval alleys of Fez. To remind you that this is still North Africa, Barbary apes scurry around the roadsides, and the occasional *djellaba* (hooded gown) and veil appear in ski areas. Almost connecting Fez and Marrakesh, the Middle Atlas is a surprising series of forests, rivers, and peaks inhabited by what were once fiercely independent Berber tribes.

THE PRIVILEGED MIDDLE ATLAS, protected from the hot and dry Saharan wind (the *shergui*) by the loftier High Atlas to the south, is a North African Arcadia, where rivers, forests, and grasslands abound and the Berber villagers' worst physical hardship is the winter snow.

By George
Semler

The Middle Atlas is actually a bridge between the High Atlas and the Rif Mountains, which continue north—interrupted only by the Strait of Gibraltar—into Spain's Sierra Nevada. With the Azrou Cedar Forest at its heart, the range extends from 100 km (60 mi) northeast of Marrakesh to just northeast of Fez. Reaching its highest heights at Bou Iblane (10,463 ft), east of Fez, the Middle and High Atlas form part of the climatic barrier separating the Mediterranean basin from the Sahara Desert. Geologically similar in origin and composition to the alpine *cordilleras* of Europe, the Atlas mountains are predominantly sedimentary rock.

The Berber tribes that inhabited the Middle Atlas when the Phoenicians arrived in 1100 BC were aboriginal Caucasoid peoples who occupied the lands between the Sahara and the Mediterranean throughout North Africa, from Egypt to the Atlantic. The Berbers are thought to have originated in Central Asia, but various theories have also connected them to the Celts, Basques, and Canaanites. Prior to Roman annexation and imperial rule in AD 24, the Berber kingdom of Mauritania was a loose federation of Berber tribes centered around Volubilis. Juba II (25 BC–AD 23), one of the first romanized Berber rulers, was educated in Rome and married the daughter of Antony and Cleopatra. The 7th-century Arab invasion began the Islamization of the Berbers, who up to that point had been a mixture of pagans, Christians, and Jews. The modern history of Morocco has been a series of more or less successful attempts to subjugate the staunchly independent Berber tribes, who even today remain largely aloof to Morocco's government and state religion.

Most travelers to Morocco are content to glance at the Middle Atlas as they whiz between Fez and Marrakesh, or between Meknes and points south. Depending on how much time they have, this is only logical, considering that the High Atlas, the desert, the great oasis valleys, the Imperial Cities, and the Atlantic coast are all more emblematically Moroccan and more exotic to the Westerner than this alpine redoubt in between. Perhaps for this reason, some of the secret valleys and villages in this central highland are doubly rewarding discoveries for their integrity and authenticity.

Azrou and Ifrane are the central mountain resorts and winter-sports stations, with the towns of Imouzzer and Sefrou even closer to Fez. Farther afield, the Djebel Tazzeka circuit, the difficult mountain tracks through the Djebel Bou Iblane Massif and, farther south, the Massif de Tichchoukt are great for adventurers with four-wheel-drive vehicles and loose schedules. Midelt is on the southern edge of the range, with splendid views of the often snowcapped High Atlas, while Khénifra, Kasba Tadla, and Beni-Mellal are primarily base camps for exploring upland objectives like the source of the River Oum-er-Rbia, El-Ksiba, and (for the intrepid and well equipped) Imilchil. The loop south from Beni-Mellal on the S508 road makes a good final leg on a north–south (Fez to Marrakesh) tour of one of Morocco's least explored regions.

Pleasures and Pastimes

Dining

Most of the Middle Atlas hotels we recommend have excellent restaurants, but don't hesitate to stop at a small-town crossroads for the odd bowl of *harira* (chickpea, lentil, and meat soup) for 5DH or less in any souk. Brochettes (beef or lamb kebabs) may cost as much as 10DH, still under a U.S. dollar. You can also order a few lamb chops and some fresh countryside Moroccan bread at truck stops like the one at Itzer. Nearby Meknes produces Morocco's best wines, including such labels as the red Medaillon, Cuvée du Président, and Ksar and the white Coquillage. You may want to carry a few bottles with you, as wine is not often served in the mountains. Note that some Islamic villagers frown upon alcohol of any kind.

CATEGORY	COST*
$$$$	over 200DH
$$$	150–200DH
$$	100–150DH
$	under 100DH

per person for a three-course meal, including tax, house wine, and service

Festivals and Moussems

The increasingly famous September marriage *moussem* (pilgrimage festival) in Imilchil, to which Berber families bring brides to meet and marry their husbands in mass ceremonies, is the best-known moussem in the Atlas. Beni-Mellal's mid-March cotton festival, Sefrou's May cherry festival, and Imouzzer du Kandar's August apple festival are some other local revels.

Lodging

With the notable exceptions of Ifrane's Hôtel Mischliffen and Beni-Mellal's Hôtel Ouzoud, there are no luxury hotels in the Middle Atlas. Though perfectly survivable, lodging tends to be undistinguished. Some of the inns and auberges off the beaten path should be thought of as shelter rather than full-service hotels.

CATEGORY	COST*
$$$$	over 400DH
$$$	300–400DH
$$	200–300DH
$	under 200DH

All prices are for a standard double room, including service and tax.

Shopping

Buying Berber artisanry off the beaten consumer path is a good idea. Look carefully through Middle Atlas cooperatives and Maisons Berbères for authentic craftsmanship at reasonable prices. The souks are filled with handmade ceramics, handwoven kilims, knotted rugs, marquetry, leather goods, and jewelry. Beware, however: just because you're out in the country doesn't mean that some nine-year-old won't quote you an opening price five times higher than he's been instructed to accept.

Trekking and Skiing

Major treks beckon from the Djebel Ayachi Massif, south of Midelt, as well as above Beni-Mellal, Azilal, and Demnate. The Tessaout gorges above Lac des Aït-Aadel, west of Demnate, have some of the best and most spectacular long-distance trekking in Morocco. Michliffen and Djebel Hebri are the two ski resorts nearest Ifrane and within day-trip range of Fez. Don't expect too much of these snow bowls—the trails are few and relatively simple—but if your ambitions are modest, a day on the slopes is a pleasant option here.

Exploring the Middle Atlas

The ideal way to get to know the Middle Atlas, if you have a week or 10 days to devote to it, is to imagine four roughly circular routes and navigate them one at a time. The northeasternmost loop lies east of Fez, centering around Djebel Bou Iblane, and relies almost completely on tertiary roadways and tracks best covered in four-wheel-drive vehicles. Moving southwest, the next route is a circle connecting Azrou, Khénifra, Midelt, and Boulemane, easily navigable by a standard car on primary, secondary, and good tertiary roads. The third circuit includes Kasba Tadla, Beni-Mellal, and El-Ksiba. The fourth and southeasternmost circuit is bisected by the S508 secondary route through Afourer, Bin-el-Ouidane, Azilal, Khemis-Majden, and Demnate.

The main points of interest are well connected with surfaced routes, either main roads marked in red or secondary routes marked in yellow on the Michelin 959 road map. The routes marked in white may vary wildly from well-paved and passable thoroughfares to tracks only fit for four-wheel-drive vehicles with plenty of clearance. Generally speaking, the farther away from the red roads you get in Morocco, the more interesting and rewarding the terrain—and this is particularly true of the Middle Atlas. Avoid the main Fez-to-Marrakesh route, the P24, whenever possible (though you'll need it to reach Kasba Tadla and Beni-Mellal). You should usually believe the most pessimistic advice you hear on road conditions; optimists tend to be either misinformed or overeager to give you good news.

Great Itineraries

The routes we recommended are roughly lineal, north–south drives through the mountains from Fez to Marrakesh. The more time you have, the farther off these paths you can wander. The road you *must* see on any trip through the Middle Atlas is the S309 loop through Mischliffen, the Azrou Cedar Forest, and Ifrane, which takes very little time but sends you through some of Morocco's most surprising scenery, including giant cedars, banks of snow (in season), and riotous communities of Barbary apes.

IF YOU HAVE 3 DAYS

Leaving Fez, head south across the Saiss plain and drive up through **Imouzzer du Kandar** ③ to 🏨 **Ifrane** ④ for a night at the formidable Hôtel Mischliffen. Tour the cedar forests around Ifrane and **Azrou** ⑤, taking care not to miss the S309 route from Ifrane south through Mischliffen and past Djebel Hebri. On day two take either the 3398 or 3390 through the cedar forest to Aïn Leuh. Turn left (south) on the S303 to reach the **Sources de l'Oum-er-Rbia** ⑥, where you can dine at the edge of a roaring volume of clear water. Continue through **Khénifra** ⑦ and **Kasba Tadla** ⑩ to 🏨 **Beni-Mellal** ⑪. On day three take the S508 through Afourer, Bin-el-Ouidane, **Azilal** ⑫, and 🏨 **Demnate** ⑭.

IF YOU HAVE 5 DAYS

Leaving Fez, explore **Imouzzer du Kandar** ③ and the nearby freshwater lake Dayet Aoua on your way to a night in 🏨 **Ifrane** ④. The next day, investigate the **Azrou** ⑤ Cedar Forest, passing the Mischliffen snow bowl and following the 3390 through the forest to Aïn Leuh. Turn south on the S303 to reach the **Sources de l'Oum-er-Rbia** ⑥, where you can stop for an excellent tagine at one of the restaurants installed on the edge of a raging stream of crystalline water. Continue on through **Khénifra** ⑦ to the turn for the Berber village of 🏨 **El-Ksiba** ⑨. On day three explore the valley around El-Ksiba, and consider driving to Imilchil and the Plateau des Lacs (Plateau of the Lakes), depending on road conditions and your vehicle. From El-Ksiba continue through **Kasba**

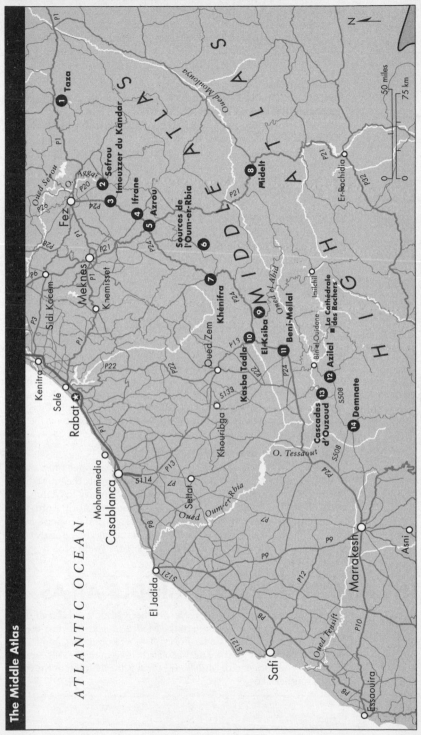

The Middle Atlas

Tadla ⑩, stopping to admire the crumbling fortress before going on to ⚅ **Beni-Mellal** ⑪. The next day, continue west, taking the C508 to **Azilal** ⑫ and the **Cascades d'Ouzoud** ⑬ before going on to ⚅ **Demnate** ⑭. On your last day, explore the area near Demnate and the Tessaout gorges, above the Aït-Aadel Lake, before moving on to Marrakesh.

IF YOU HAVE 10 DAYS

With 10 days you can start northeast of Fez with the **Djebel Tazzeka circuit** and the town of ⚅ **Taza** ①. The next day, heading south, have a look through **Sefrou** ② and Bahlil before driving up through **Imouzzer du Kandar** ③ to ⚅ **Ifrane** ④ for the night. On day three explore the town of **Azrou** ⑤ and the Azrou Cedar Forest, seeking out the Mischliffen snow bowl (if you want to ski) and the 3390 route through the cedar forest to Aïn Leuh. Turn south on the S303 to the **Sources de l'Oum-er-Rbia** ⑥ for lunch in one of the restaurants on the rocky terraces by the river's headwaters. Continue on through **Khénifra** ⑦ to the turn for ⚅ **El-Ksiba** ⑨, a Berber village and valley with stunning views over the Tadla Plain. Devote day four to Imilchil and the Plateau of the Lakes if you have the vehicle and the valor to make this 100-km (60-mi) trek over tracks that, even in a four-wheel drive, are slow and torturous but rewarding. As an alternative, you can backtrack to ⚅ **Midelt** ⑧ for a tour of the Cirque de Jaffar. From Midelt, on day five (or six if you've done Imilchil) head back up to through Itzer and the Col du Zad—where the Mediterranean and Atlantic watersheds divide—for a visit to Lake Aguelmame de Sidi Ali before turning west onto the picturesque 3485 back through Khénifra and **Kasba Tadla** ⑩ to ⚅ **Beni-Mellal** ⑪. The next day explore the highlands above ⚅ **Azilal** ⑫; the day after that, visit the **Cascades d'Ouzoud** ⑬ before stopping in ⚅ **Demnate** ⑭ for the night. On the penultimate day explore the natural bridge **Imi-n-Ifri** and the valley above, up to the Kasbah at Tizi-n-Oubadou, before returning to Demnate. On your last day explore the area around Demnate and the **Tessaout gorges** above the Aït-Aadel Lake before heading for Marrakesh.

When to Tour the Middle Atlas

This part of Morocco is relatively cool year-round, though often snowbound in midwinter. For skiing or a drive through the snow-filled Azrou Cedar Forest (often snow covered from January to March, but normally well plowed), come between December and April. April–June is the best time to hike and explore the headwaters of the region's many rivers. The high tourist season in the mountains (mid-March through summer) can draw the occasional crowd to sites you'd probably prefer to see *au naturel*.

THE MEDITERRANEAN MIDDLE ATLAS

Spreading south and east of Fez, the northern Middle Atlas is drained by the Moulouya River en route to the Mediterranean Sea near the Algerian border. The Azrou Cedar Forest, Djebel Bou Iblane, and Djebel Tazzeka massif above Taza are the main attractions in this heavily forested northern zone, along with Midelt and the Cirque de Jaffar at the more barren southern edge.

Taza

❶ *120 km (72 mi) east of Fez.*

An important capital during the Almohad, Merenid, and early Alaouite dynasties (11th–16th centuries), Taza was used as a passage into Morocco by the first Moroccan Arabs—the Idrissids—and nearly all successive invaders en route to Fez. The Taza Gap separates the Rif from the Middle Atlas mountains. Fortified and refortified, Taza was never easy to defend, and Berber tribes as well as succeeding dynasties managed to move through it like hot knives through butter. Taza's medina, both of its mosques (especially the **Grande Mosquée,** or Great Mosque, with a perforated cupola), the **city walls,** and the **Bab er Rih** (Gate of the Wind) are lovely and largely untouched.

Dining and Lodging

$$ ✕⌨ **Grand Hôtel du Dauphiné.** An Art Nouveau building that was once, like Taza, an elegant and grandiose affair, this hotel has seen better days but retains some charm for this very reason. The rooms are ample in size and basic (no superfluous extras like TVs or minibars), and the service is at best desultory, but the old-world feel of the place—its sense of time—gives the hotel a novelistic allure. ⊠ *Place de l'Indépendance,* ☎ *05/67–35–67. 26 rooms, 9 with bath. Restaurant, parking (fee). No credit cards.*

En Route The 123-km (74-mi) loop around the **Cirque du Djebel Tazzeka** is one of the most varied and spectacular circuits in the Middle Atlas. Packing a range of diversions from spelunking in the Gouffre du Friouato (Friouato Cave) to cresting the 6,494-ft Djebel Tazzeka to navigating the gorges of the Oued Zireg, this tour is a topographer's fantasy. The Friouato Cave complex is well marked; a guard will show you through the caverns, which are said to be the deepest in North Africa, extending down 590 ft. Note that the 7-km (4-mi) track to the crest is a dangerous drive in bad weather. The entire multisurface drive takes some five hours without stops.

Sefrou

❷ *33 km (20 mi) southeast of Fez, 136 km (82 mi) southwest of Taza.*

A miniature Fez at an altitude of 2,900 ft, Sefrou lies in the fertile valley of the notoriously flood-prone Agdal River, at the foot of the first heights of the Middle Atlas. A first stop on the caravan routes between the Sahara Desert and the Mediterranean coast, it was originally populated by Berber converts to Judaism, who came north from the Tafilalt date palmery and from Algeria in the 13th century. The town remained a nucleus of Jewish life until the (virtually entire) Jewish community left Morocco when the country declared independence from France in 1956.

Sefrou's **medina** would be considered one of Morocco's great treasures were it not overshadowed by that of Fez, probably the largest and densest medina in the world. The **Thursday souk** is a nice opportunity for some relatively unharried shopping, and the walls, *babs* (gates into the medina), and Jewish **Mellah** are all worth poking around. The word *mellah* essentially means "quarter," but it originally came from the Arabic word for salt. Morocco's Jewish quarters allegedly got this name from the Arab rulers' onetime habit of draining and salting the heads of decapitated rebels before they were impaled on the city gates (Jews were hired to assist in the salting). Separated from the medina by the River Aggai, the Mellah is now inhabited almost entirely by Muslims, with only a few Jewish families remaining.

The *zaouia* (sanctuary) of **Sidi Lahcen Ben Ahmed** contains the remains of this 17th-century saint. From the dark and narrow streets of the Mellah, stone bridges cross the Aggai into the souks north of the mosque. During the town's Cherry Festival, in June, a procession files out to the **Kef el-Mumen** cave, said to contain the tomb of the prophet Daniel; legend holds that seven believers and their dog slept here for centuries before miraculously resuscitating. West of Sefrou is the miraculous fountain of **Lalla Rekia,** believed to cure mental illness and the site of animal sacrifices during the annual moussem.

Dining and Lodging

$$$ ✗⟨⟩ **Hôtel Sidi Lahcen Lyoussi.** Named for the local saint, this mountain chalet is blessed with a fine restaurant and a distinctly alpine ambience that is startling and welcome in North Africa. The fresh wood decor and the pastoral surroundings combine to make this a favorite country getaway for Fassis (residents of Fez). ✉ *Rue Sidi Bou Serghine,* ☎ *05/68–34–28,* ☏ *05/60–10–78. 20 rooms, 4 bungalows. Restaurant, pool. MC, V.*

Imouzzer du Kandar

❸ *38 km (23 mi) south of Fez, 43 km (26 mi) southwest of Sefrou.*

Imouzzer du Kandar is virtually a suburb of Fez, but it's considered the first real stop in the Middle Atlas, a mountain retreat for stressed-out Fassis. A small town with little more than a central square and a Kasbah in ruins, Imouzzer holds a Monday souk where Berber artisans bring natural and homemade products and are even more eager to close sales than the hardened negotiators in the big cities. The town's apple festival, held in June, is the event of the year and is well worth a stop for its music, dancing, and general ambience. The nearby **Dayet Aoua,** a lovely freshwater lake just 9 km (5 mi) south of town, is a pretty place to camp or rent a boat and tool around.

Dining and Lodging

$$ ✗⟨⟩ **Hôtel des Truites.** This little mountain enclave—the Trout Hotel—is a welcome break after the intensity of Fez or Marrakesh, a pastoral sanctuary with excellent vistas over the Massif de Kandar and the Plaine du Saiss. The rooms are small and spartan but cozy and clean. ✉ *Rte. P24 from Fez entering Imouzzer,* ☎ *05/66–30–02. 18 rooms. Restaurant, free parking. MC, V.*

Ifrane

❹ *25 km (15 mi) south of Imouzzer du Kandar, 63 km (37 mi) south of Fez.*

Built in 1929 during the French Protectorate to form a deliberate "*poche de France*" (pocket of France), Ifrane's neat, faux-alpine chalets and clean well-lighted boulevards seem almost like some kind of officially organized sight gag if you've just come from Fez or Marrakesh, and particularly if you've come from Merzouga and the desert. But if you feel you could use a short break from Morocco, this is the place to find it. The ruling Alaouite dynasty has a royal palace in Ifrane, identifiable by its green-tile roof (an exclusive royal privilege), so you may encounter extraordinary security measures. With an altitude of 5,412 ft, Ifrane is known for its cold-water trout fishery, its excellent hiking trails up to the **Cascades des Vierges** (Cascade of the Virgins), and—in Zaouia de Ifrane, the village to the north—its artisans.

Dining and Lodging

$$$$ ✗⟨⟩ **Hôtel Mischliffen.** Pricey but supremely comfortable, this magnificent
★ hotel overlooks the cedar forest and alpine countryside of Morocco's most Europeanized mountain retreat. At the height of ski season, the place fills with the elite from Fez and government officials from Rabat, and all staffers speaks French, English, and Spanish. Service is impeccable and the restaurant, excellent; despite the cosmopolitanism, this is a good place to get away from it all. ✉ *Ifrane,* ☎ *05/56–66–07,* ☏ *05/56–66–23. 106 rooms. 2 restaurants, piano bar, pool, nightclub, shops. AE, DC, MC, V.*

Azrou

⑤ *17 km (10 mi) southwest of Ifrane, 67 km (40 mi) southeast of Meknes, 78 km (47 mi) south of Fez.*

Occupying an important junction of routes between the desert and Meknes and between Fez and Marrakesh, Azrou—from the Berber word for "rock"—is an ancient Berber capital of great significance. It was one of Sultan Moulay Ismail's strongholds after he built an imposing fortress here (now largely in ruins) in 1684; but Azrou was for centuries unknown, a secret mountain town that invading forces never fully located, thanks in part to a cave system designed for concealment and protection. Seeing a Berber nucleus, the French established the **Collège Berbère** here in an attempt to train an elite Berber opposition to the urban Arab ruling class; both Arabic and Islam were prohibited. After independence, Berber College became an Arabic school, and the movement faded. Azrou's artisanal center, the **Maison de l'Artisanat,** just off the P24 to Khénifra (and a mere five-minute walk from Place Mohammed V), is one of the town's main attractions—it's a trading post for the Beni M'Guild tribes, known for their fine carpets, kilims, and cedar carvings. Place Mohammed V, a square lined with numerous cafés, holds an important Tuesday souk where prices start significantly lower than in the major cities.

★ The **Azrou Cedar Forest** is a unique habitat in Morocco, as much a state of mind as a woodland. Even in the Fez medina, you can sense a breath of fresh air when the forest is mentioned, usually as the source of some intricate cedar carving. Moroccans are proud of their cedar forest, always one of the crown jewels of the national geography. Moroccan cedars grow to heights of close to 200 ft and cover some 320,000 acres on the slopes of the Middle Atlas, the High Atlas, and the Rif at altitudes between 3,940 and 9,200 ft; the forest's senior members are more than 400 years old. Cedar is much coveted by woodworkers, particularly makers of stringed musical instruments. Living among the enormous cedars to the south of Azrou are troupes of Barbary apes, the last panthers and leopards on earth (very rare though not yet extinct), and bird life ranging from the redheaded Moroccan woodpecker to the smallest bird in the forest, the kinglet or goldcrest, a sparrowlike bird with a yellow-gold crown. Owls, eagles, and weasels complete the local fauna, while flora include the large-leafed peony, the scarlet dianthus, and the blue germander, all of which house butterflies, including the cardinal and the colorful sulphur cleopatra.

Dining and Lodging

$$–$$$ ✕☒ **Hôtel Panorama.** This handy place near the center of Azrou has good views over the forest and town as well as an excellent restaurant and reliable heating—more than welcome during Azrou's long, snowy winters. The rooms have no particular charm, but they're clean and equipped with TVs. The owners are conscientious and pleasant. ✉ *Rue El Hansali, Azrou Centre,* ☎ *05/56–20–10,* FAX *05/56–18–04. 36 rooms. Restaurant, bar, free parking. MC, V.*

$$ ✕☒ **Auberge Amros.** Outside town on the road to Meknes, this little inn is popular among Azrou natives for its restaurant, which serves excellent French cuisine. Surrounded by oak and cedar forest, the auberge is a good place to use as a base camp for hiking or fly-fishing in the Middle Atlas. Rooms are small but adequate, and management is friendly and attentive. ✉ *Rte. P21, Km 3,* ☎ *05/56–36–63,* FAX *05/56–36–80. 74 rooms. Restaurant, bar, pool. MC, V.*

Sources de l'Oum-er-Rbia

⑥ *57 km (35 mi) south of Azrou.*

The 40 or more springs that form the source of the River Oum-er-Rbia are best approached from Azrou and Aïn Leuh through the cedar forest. Flowing across nearly the entire Moroccan heartland from the Middle Atlas to the Atlantic Ocean (at Azemmour, south of Casablanca), the great Oum-er-Rbia has been diverted, dammed, and largely destroyed over the years in favor of irrigation and hydroelectric projects. Spawning shad used to swim upriver from the Atlantic until the proliferation of dams interrupted their life cycle. The source is now impressive for the great volume of crystal-clear water exploding from the side of the adjoining mountain, part of the Djebel Hebri Massif and the Mischliffen ski area (thus the snow runoff). Several cafés and restaurants are built into the rock terraces around the flow, and as long as they're open (they're deserted when not overflowing with busloads of tourists), they'll fix you anything from mint tea to tagine. You will be greeted here by a mob of youths racing each other across the parking lot to divvy you up: you'll want at least one boy to guard your car, as well as a guide or two for the 10-minute walk uphill. Although it can be tempting to flee, it's more rewarding to play along; hand out a few five-dirham pieces and avoid having to battle with these kids the whole time you're here.

Trout are said to "swarm" in the headwaters of the Oum-er-Rbia, though this report is unconfirmed. Some of the upper springs are fresh and drinkable (in theory; don't try this), whereas the lower ones are known to be salty. Khénifra is a mere 10 hours by kayak, so if you happen to have brought a kayak to Morocco (many do: you can actually kayak in the Sahara, at the seasonal salt lake Dyet Sjri, near Merzouga), this is the place to start. There are no dams until after the Oued Tessaout River junction, 100 km (60 mi) north of Marrakesh. The Aguelmane (lake) Azigza, another 20 km (12 mi) south of the Sources de l'Oum-er-Rbia on the 3211 road, is another impressive Middle Atlas site, with red cliffs surrounding the blue waters.

Khénifra

⑦ *82 km (49 mi) southwest of Azrou, 45 km (27 mi) southwest of Sources de l'Oum-er-Rbia, 327 km (197 mi) northeast of Marrakesh.*

This dusty, red-clay city on the banks of the Oum-er-Rbia is no paradise, but it does offer a good look at life in a Moroccan market town. Khénifra is known locally as Red City for its pisé (rammed earth) houses and relentless red dust. The town holds a carpet auction on Saturday and souks on Wednesday and Sunday; look for the *taraza,* the typical equestrian headgear made of straw and decorated with colorful wool tassels and pendants. Berber Zaiane tribesmen have long been known for their horsemanship, and still compete on the local racetrack.

Dining and Lodging

$$ ✕⌂ **Hôtel Hamou Azzayani.** Named for the 19th-century *caid* (chief) Hamou Azzayani, leader of Khénifra's legendary resistance to centralized power, this modern building in the Ville Nouvelle (New Town) is surprisingly comfortable considering its rudimentary surroundings. The restaurant serves fine Moroccan cuisine and has a good wine list. Rooms are plain and unmemorable but perfectly serviceable. ✉ *Cité Anal, B.P. 94,* ☎ *05/58–60–20,* FAX *05/58–65–32. 58 rooms and 2 suites. Restaurant, bar, pool, nightclub, parking (fee). MC, V.*

Midelt and the Cirque de Jaffar

❽ *206 km (124 mi) east of Khénifra, 232 km (139 mi) south of Fez, 126 km (76 mi) north of Er-Rachidia.*

Midelt itself is nothing to go out of your way for, but the Cirque de Jaffar and Djebel Ayachi definitely are, and Midelt is the logical base camp for these excursions. The town has an interesting carpet souk—particularly active on Sunday—with rugs in original geometric designs and kilims made by Middle Atlas Berber tribes.

The **Atelier de Tissage–Kasbah Miryem,** a convent and workshop off the road to the Cirque de Jaffar, is a good place to buy carpets, blankets, and textiles of all kinds as well as to chat with the French Franciscan nuns, all of whom are experts on matters Moroccan. Another digression from Midelt takes you to the silver and lead mines at the **Gorges d'Aouli,** a 24-km (14-mi) round trip negotiable by a standard car. Formed by the Oued Moulouya—Morocco's longest river, flowing all the way to the Mediterranean—the gorges are sheer rock walls cut through the steppe.

You'll need four-wheel drive to tackle the notoriously rough but spectacular 80-km (48-mi) loop through the **Cirque de Jaffar,** a verdant cedar forest running around the lower slopes of the Ayachi peak. (Be wary of some of the advice you might get here about roads and routes. For example, the Rich–Assoul–Aït Hani road is *not* navigable by a standard car.) The 12,257-ft **Djebel Ayachi,** the dominant terrain feature in the Atlas mountains south of Midelt, was long thought to be Morocco's highest peak before Djebel Toubkal, south of Marrakesh, was found to be 13,668 ft. The view of this snowcapped (from December to March) behemoth from the roof of the eponymous hotel is inspiring: Djebel Ayachi is very much *there*. It calls you. If you have time for serious exploration, the 130-km (78-mi) loop around through Boumia and Tounfite will take you across the immense Plateau de l'Arid, through the gorges of the upper Moulouya River valley, and into the Cirque de Jaffar on your way back into Midelt. Overland adventurers with four-wheel drive might be tempted to bivouac in the Cirque de Jaffar and climb Djebel Ayachi. After that, the route over to Tounfite on the right fork of Route 3424 is another adventure, and even more rugged still is the left fork, Route 3425 over the 10,749-ft Djebel Masker to Imilchil.

Again, don't let anyone convince you that the overland trip through the Cirque de Jaffar to Imilchil and El-Ksiba, or south to the Todra gorges, is feasible in a standard car. You need a four-wheel-drive to have even a fighting chance, and even then you should expect excitement. It's wise to pack food, water, supplies, warm clothing, and camping gear for these pistes (tracks; marked in white on the Michelin 959 map), as the going is slow, and the freedom to stop and spend the night is key to peace of mind.

Dining and Lodging

$$–$$$ ✕▥ **Hôtel Ayachi.** Both the dining room and the service are pleasant surprises this far from a major city. Dinner jackets, a terrace near the bar, and excellent food go a long way toward making up for mediocre but perfectly adequate rooms. You're surrounded by the High Atlas to the south and the Middle Atlas to the north and west, so the rooms do have nice views; scale the roof first thing to admire the 12,257-ft Djebel Ayachi and the snow-covered High Atlas in the morning sun. ✉ *Avenue Mohammed V,* ☎ *05/58–21–61,* ℻ *05/58–33–07. 22 rooms. Restaurant, bar, parking (fee). AE, DC, MC, V.*

THE ATLANTIC MIDDLE ATLAS

Heading toward Marrakesh, the southern Middle Atlas is drained by the River Oum-er-Rbia, which flows across the Tadla Plain to the Atlantic Ocean south of Casablanca. Forested with olive groves and live oaks on their lower slopes, the rugged mountains to the south of El-Ksiba and Beni-Mellal offer memorable trek and jeep excursions and form a striking contrast to Azilal's lush Cascades d'Ouzoud and Demnate's natural bridge at Imi-n-Ifri.

El-Ksiba

⑨ *74 km (44 mi) southwest of Khénifra, 209 km (125 mi) west of Midelt.*

Just south of the P24 is the village of El-Ksiba, a busy Berber enclave surrounded by apricot, olive, and orange groves. It's most notable as a gateway for the back country to the south. The road into town is steep and can be dangerous in bad weather, but if you can get up into the highlands behind it, some of Morocco's least spoiled wilderness will unfold before you. Wide expanses of sparsely vegetated Middle Atlas countryside and mountains spread out in impossibly grandiose and sweeping panoramas that prove surprisingly difficult to capture on film. With the occasional pocket of cedar, live oak, or olive trees, the Middle Atlas gives way to the High Atlas and the peak of the 10,604-ft Djebel Mourik to the south.

The 113-km (70-mi) trip from the P24 to **Imilchil** is an unforgettable adventure best enjoyed in a four-wheel-drive vehicle. The surrounding **Plateau des Lacs** (Plateau of the Lakes) includes the lakes of Isli and Tisli (His and Hers), impossible lovers doomed to long for each other across the unbridgeable gap of dry land that separates them. The September marriage moussem brings the Aït Addidou tribe together to marry off eligible young people, an event that over time has become more of a tourist attraction than a marriage mart.

Lodging

$ 🏨 **Hostellerie Henri IV.** This place has seen better days, and rents only modest rooms with shared baths at equally modest prices. If the restaurant reopens, things could improve, but for the moment, consider it a place to sleep if you get stuck—and not much more. ⊠ *Cité Anal, B.P. 94,* ☎ *03/41–50–02. 20 rooms. Pool, free parking. MC, V.*

Kasba Tadla

⑩ *22 km (13 mi) west of El-Ksiba, 99 km (59 mi) southwest of Khénifra, 206 km (124 mi) west of Midelt.*

Occupying a strategic position at the junction of the P24 to Marrakesh and the P13 to Casablanca, this town takes its name from the Kasbah built here by Moulay Ismail in the late 17th century as an advance post against the local Berbers. The Kasbah and the two mosques inside it are the only buildings of note, forming a little walk of an hour or so. The massive walls are in full decay as the palace crumbles around the smaller farms and the reddish-clay pisé structures that have gone up in and around the fortress and mosques over the centuries. The best place to look down on the building is from the left bank of the River Oum-er-Rbia, just off the P24 toward Beni-Mellal. West of town, the Tadla plain stretches out along the river.

Beni-Mellal

⑪ *30 km (18 mi) south of Kasba Tadla, 211 km (127 mi) southwest of Azrou, 198 km (148 mi) northeast of Marrakesh.*

Ringed with fortifications built by Moulay Ismail in 1688, this rapidly growing country town nestles in the shadow of the 7,373-ft Djebel Tassemit, surrounded by verdant orchards that are well irrigated by the Bin-el-Ouidane reservoir, 59 km (35 mi) to the southwest. Beni-Mellal is largely modern and of little architectural interest, but its Tuesday souk is an event to catch, known especially for its Berber blankets with colorful geometric designs. The 10-km (6-mi) walk up to the Aïn Asserdoun spring and the Kasbah de Ras el Aïn is well worth the haul for the gardens and waterfalls along the way, and the views over the olive groves and the Tadla Plain.

Dining and Lodging

$$$–$$$$
★
✕⊞ **Hôtel Ouzoud.** Generally acclaimed as the best hotel in Beni-Mellal and one of the best in the Middle Atlas, this modern building nonetheless lacks character. The rooms are well equipped with good beds, hot showers—the kinds of minor amenities for which you may find yourself thirsting if you've just come from the wild country to the south. The restaurant serves fine Moroccan and international cuisine. ⊠ *Route de Marrakesh,* ☎ *03/48–37–52,* 🖷 *03/48–85–30. 60 rooms. Restaurant, bar, pool, 2 tennis courts. AE, DC, MC, V.*

Azilal

⑫ *86 km (52 mi) southwest of Beni-Mellal on the S508, off the P24; 171 km (103 mi) northeast of Marrakesh.*

The road south to Azilal passes the immense **Bin-el-Ouidane** (Between the Rivers) **reservoir,** one of Morocco's first modern hydraulic projects. Built between 1948 and 1955, the reservoir provides electricity for the entire region and irrigates the cereal-producing Tadla Plain. Azilal is a small garrison town used as a jumping-off point for routes into the southern highlands, especially toward the M'Goun Massif in the High Atlas, north of Ouarzazate. The pistes south of here become a maze of loops and tracks, great for exploring, but the main route forks 28 km (17 mi) after Aït Mhammed. To the right (southwest), the 1809 road descends into the valley of the Aït Bou Guemés, passing *ksour* (villages or tribal enclaves) at El Had and Agouti and looping eventually back to Aït Mhammed after a tough, tremendous 120-km (72-mi) trek that's much more effectively absorbed on foot than from a car. The left (northeast) fork takes the 1807 road through the Tizi-n-Ilissi Pass to the Zaouia Ahanesal shrine and eventually reaches the 260-ft rock formations known and marked on the Michelin 959 as **La Cathédrale des Rochers** (the Cathedral of Rocks) for its resemblance to the spiky spires of a Gothic cathedral. The road eventually becomes 1803 and passes through a live-oak forest to reach the Bin-el-Ouidane reservoir after 113 km (68 mi) of backbreakingly slow and tedious, though wildly scenic, driving.

Dining and Lodging

$$
✕⊞ **Hôtel Tanout.** This little hotel on the Beni-Mellal road into Azilal is the only viable lodging in Azilal. The rooms are generally clean and adequately equipped, and the restaurant will serve a passable lamb-and-fig tagine *sur commande* (upon advance request). ⊠ *Rte. Beni-Mellal (S508),* ☎ *04/45–87–78. 8 rooms. Restaurant. No credit cards.*

Cascades d'Ouzoud

★ ⓭ *22 km (14 mi) northwest of Azilal.*

The waterfalls of Ouzoud, approachable from the S508 via the 1811, form one of the most stunning sights in the Middle Atlas. Rarely will you see this spectacular waterfall without a rainbow hovering over the twin falls—which crash into a basin from which the water again falls, this time in a single white torrent to the riverbed below. A path through a grove of olive trees leads to the pools carved out of the rock at the base of the falls; here you can swim. At dusk families of Barbary apes come out to drink and to feed on the pomegranates along the banks.

Downstream, past the falls, on the 1811 road is the village of **Tanagh-melt,** a web of narrow alleyways. Continue up the 1811 (toward the P24) to see the **river gorges** of the Oued-el-Abid.

Demnate

⓮ *72 km (43 mi) southwest of Azilal, 158 km (95 mi) southwest of Beni-Mellal, 99 km (59 mi) east of Marrakesh.*

This walled town is a market center to which Berbers from the neighboring hills and plains bring multifarious produce, especially for the Sunday souk held outside the walls. Once famed for its ceramics artisans, Demnate still has some traditional kilns. The rectangular ramparts are made of an unusual ocher-color pisé and pierced by two monumental portals; within is a Kasbah built by T'hami el-Glaoui. Up a 6-km (4-mi) piste above town is the natural stone bridge **Imi-n-Ifri,** where the diminutive River Mahseur has carved out a tunnel inhabited by hundreds of crows. A path twists down through the boulders and under the "bridge," where stalactites and sculpted hollows dramatize the natural rock formations. Women come to bathe in the stream because it is said to bring them good luck, but the crows are considered harbingers of doom. The legend associated with these birds—a St. George and the Dragon–type saga in which a lovely maiden is saved from a monster who dematerializes into crows—is told in several variations by imaginative guides.

Lodging

$$ ✕▦ **Hôtel Iminifri.** Demnate's one hotel is rudimentary, but if you want to spend the night under a roof, this is your best option. The owners are friendly and are thrilled to see visitors, as this place is well off the standard tourist trail. The rooms are small but clean and moderately comfortable, and lunch and dinner are served upon request. ✉ *Rue Principale,* ☎ *04/45–60–03. 8 rooms. No credit cards.*

THE MIDDLE ATLAS A TO Z

Arriving and Departing

By Bus

Azrou, Ifrane, Sefrou, Imouzzer du Kandar, Beni-Mellal, Azilal, Midelt, Kasba Tadla, and Khénifra are all served by **C.T.M.** buses, if somewhat sporadically. The bus from Casablanca to Ifrane to Azrou (via Meknes) takes six hours from beginning to end; the one from Meknes to Azrou to Midelt takes four to five hours total. Try to avoid the marathon bus from Marrakesh to Fez (via Beni-Mellal, Kasba Tadla, Khénifra, Azrou, Ifrane, and Imouzzer du Kandar), a trip totaling 10 hours, unless you really have no other way to get around. For schedules and fares to the Middle Atlas, contact C.T.M. or the bus station in your city of origin.

Getting Around

The only reasonable way to explore the Middle Atlas is by car and preferably by four-wheel-drive jeep. Most rental-car agreements for standard cars stipulate in fine print that traveling on unpaved roads violates the terms of the rental agreement—i.e., if you run into trouble on some mountain track, you're on your own. This can be expensive. Buses can get you to the main towns in the Middle Atlas if you're planning a hiking excursion, but you'll need a taxi to get you to trailheads like the Cirque de Jaffar. Trucks serving remote markets can be used to explore the backcountry between the Middle and High Atlas, but these are often several days apart, and fares can approach extortion.

By Bus

Buses run from Beni-Mellal up to Azilal, a common departure point for excursions into the Middle and High Atlas; they depart approximately every three hours between 7 AM and 4 PM.

By Car

Even in the dead of winter, from December through February, the snow-removal system in the Azrou Cedar Forest is excellent. Ten-foot banks of snow may flank the road, but the driving surface will be clear unless you're in the middle of the snowstorm. The more remote roads (marked in white on the Michelin 959 Morocco map) will be completely closed in snowy conditions and are often difficult even at the best of times. Beware particularly the C1811 to the Cascades d'Ouzoud. The 63 km (37 mi) from the S508 to the P24 is also very rough going and should not be attempted in a car with low clearance. A general rule of thumb is to consider all roads marked in white on the Michelin 959 map to be suitable mainly for vehicles with four-wheel drive.

Contacts and Resources

Emergencies

Highway assistance: ☏ 177. **Police:** ☏ 19. **Fire:** ☏ 15.

Accidents and medical emergencies in the Middle and High Atlas should be reported to the nearest Gendarmerie Royale and/or Protection Civile. As helicopter assistance may be long in coming, it's best to pack as complete a first aid kit as possible.

Hiking, Skiing, and Trekking

Azourki Randonnées (✉ 81, Avenue Mohamed V, Azilal, ☏ 03/45–83–32) organizes hiking and skiing excursions. The **Délégation Provincial du Tourisme** (✉ Avenue Hassan II, Azilal, ☏ 03/45–83–34) recommends guides for hikes, treks, mule trips, ski outings, and fishing trips. **Imilchil Voyages** (✉ 416, Boulevard Mohamed V, Beni-Mellal, ☏ 03/48–90–60) organizes treks and trout-fishing trips.

Horseback Riding

A few outfits organize mountain outings on horseback. **Centre Equestre et de Randonnée** (✉ Aïn Amyer, Route d'Immouzzer, Km 2, Fez, ☏ FAX 05/60–64–21). **Club Omnisport** (✉ Route de Marrakesh, Km 4, Beni-Mellal, ☏ FAX 03/48–22–02). **Royal Club Equestre de Randonnée** (✉ Dayet Aoua, Ifrane, ☏ FAX 07/64–28–86).

Personal Guides

The Bureau des Guides et Accompagnateurs in the following towns can arrange sightseeing guides. **Azilal** (✉ B.P. 50, Avenue Mohamed V, Azilal). **Aït Mhammed** (✉ B.P. 2, Aït Mhammed Centre, Azilal, ☏ FAX 03/45–94–30). **Demnate** (✉ Café Restaurant d'Agadir, 12, Avenue Mohammed V, ☏ FAX 03/45–60–90). **Zaouia Ahanesal** (✉ Zaouia

Ahanesal Centre, ☎ FAX 03/45–93–78). **Rich** (✉ Hotel Al Massira–Rich, near Midelt, ☎ FAX 05/58–92–05).

Visitor Information

Tourist offices in Fez, Meknes, and Marrakesh all have information on the Middle Atlas. There are three offices in the mountains themselves: **Azilal** (✉ Avenue Mohamed V, ☎ 03/45–83–34). **Beni-Mellal** (✉ Avenue Hassan II, Immeuble Chichaoua, ☎ 03/48–39–81). **Ifrane** (✉ Avenue Mohamed V, ☎ 05/56–68–22).

5 RABAT, CASABLANCA, AND THE NORTHERN ATLANTIC COAST

Anchored by Morocco's two most international cities, this coastal stretch bears the marks of civilizations ranging from the prehistoric to the colonial to the entirely contemporary. Coastal roads and long beaches invite you to venture beyond the country's political and commercial capitals to explore seaside medinas and bask in the breezy sunshine.

By Jonathan G.
Bell

FROM ASILAH TO SAFI the Atlantic breakers roll in, contrasting markedly with the placid waters of Morocco's Mediterranean coast. From here the ocean stretches due west to the Carolinas. Much of this coast is lined with sandy beaches, and if you fly south to Morocco from Europe, you'll see them interspersed with rocky headlands, a pattern that continues as far as Dakar (Senegal) and beyond. The whole coastline, in both urban and rural areas, is dotted with simple white *koubba*s, the buildings that house a Muslim saint's tomb. In spring the tops of the cliffs bloom with irises, calendula, poppies, and mustard, and in summer, as Moroccans fill the beaches, the waterfront blooms with sunglasses. With fall come breathtaking sunsets over the Atlantic, and at the beginning of winter, if the rain falls on time, Morocco sees its first brilliant green. Winter also brings exceptionally high tides, which wash the coastline clean: huge waves breaking on jagged rocks shoot spray to the tops of the cliffs.

This region contains Rabat, the political capital of the kingdom, and, less than 100 km (62 mi) to the southwest, Casablanca, the undisputed commercial capital. Morocco's main industrial and commercial axis stretches from Casablanca to Kenitra, just northeast of Rabat. Yet Rabat and its twin city, Salé, just across the River Bou Regreg, have some of the most important historical sights in the country. Northeast of Kenitra is the region known as the Loukous, a low-lying coastal area that gets some of the heaviest rainfall in the country and is known for its profusion of migrating birds. Southwest of Casablanca is the region known as Doukkala, which contains the city of El Jadida, once a Portuguese stronghold. Apart from a few industrial developments, the area beyond El Jadida consists of beautiful coastline with pristine beaches. The climate is moderate throughout: when it's cold inland, the coast enjoys relative warmth; and when the landlocked regions bake in the summer sun, the sea breeze cools the coast.

Rich strata of history are piled here. A simple unmarked cave on the coast near Rabat is thought to be one of the first sites ever inhabited by man. At Lixus, near Larache, are the ruins of what was originally a Phoenician settlement. Rabat has monuments from successive Arab dynasties. Spanish occupation is reflected in the architecture of the city of Larache; and the modern city of Casablanca was founded by the French.

Yet Rabat, Casablanca, and indeed the rest of this region are removed from the pressures of the larger tourist centers—Marrakesh, Fez, and Agadir. If possible, come here at the beginning of your trip to relax and grow acclimatized to the ways of the kingdom. Quite apart from the gentle climate, you'll generally find yourself—unlike in, say, Fez—free to wander around unmolested. This part of Morocco treats travelers gently.

Pleasures and Pastimes

Dining

Morocco's northern Atlantic coast is its center of seafood par excellence. From Asilah to Safi the menus are remarkably similar: *salades*, *crevettes* (prawns), *friture de poisson* (fried fish and octopus), *calamar* (squid), and various kinds of fish. *Fruits de mer* are shellfish and prawns, not fish. If you haven't just come from Spain, you might also enjoy kicking back with a paella in one of Asilah's Spanish restaurants.

In addition to seafood, Casablanca and Rabat offer more international cuisine—lots of pizzerias and Chinese and Vietnamese restaurants—and, of course, traditional Moroccan fare and abundant French cuisine. Although it's tempting to think you can find Moroccan food anywhere, the best Moroccan restaurants are really limited to Casablanca and Rabat. (Moroccans eat Moroccan cuisine in the home; so when they dine out, they tend to want something more exotic.) In Casablanca and Rabat the more expensive French restaurants serve truly excellent French cuisine, so this is a good time to dip into it if your travels aren't taking you to France. Casablanca's best restaurants tend to be considerably pricier than those elsewhere in the region. A number of the restaurants we recommend in Casablanca and Rabat are some distance from the main centers of hotels and attractions, but it's never a problem to get a *petit taxi* (blue in Rabat, red in Casablanca) at low cost, and the taxi can actually be a big help in locating the place.

CATEGORY	COST*
$$$$	over 300DH
$$$	200–300DH
$$	100–200DH
$	under 100DH

per person for a three-course meal, excluding drinks, service, and tax.

Lodging

Both Casablanca and Rabat have hotels for every budget. Casablanca has branches of the familiar international business hotels, and most business hotels in both Casablanca and Rabat will discount their published rates by applying corporate rates at the drop of a company's name. In the smaller coastal resorts, you'll typically find mid-range sea-view hotels with a pool.

CATEGORY	COST*
$$$$	over 900DH
$$$	500–900DH
$$	300–500DH
$	under 300DH

All prices are for a standard double room, excluding tax.

When to Go

Avoid this region in July, August, and the first half of September unless you only plan to visit Rabat, Salé, and Casablanca. Corresponding to Morocco's school vacation, the coastal resorts are extremely crowded in summer, hotels are full, and prices are much higher. Moreover, huge numbers of Moroccans working in Europe return in July and August, driving down the coast from Tangier. In April, May, June, and October, the weather is delightful—easily warm enough to enjoy the beaches—and most resorts are pleasantly empty. If you don't need to swim or sunbathe, you can sightsee from November through March (and even then the weather can be quite warm). The relatively cold period (the *liali*) lasts from around Christmas through the end of January; temperatures on the coast can plunge to 39–43°F (4–6°C).

Exploring Rabat, Casablanca, and the Northern Atlantic Coast

This chapter divides the northern portion of Morocco's Atlantic coast in half. One suggested itinerary (Asilah to Rabat) works well if you you're coming from Tangier or Tetouan; the other (Casablanca to Safi) leads nicely into a trip farther south, to Essaouira, Marrakesh, or the Atlas mountains. Either way you'll absorb plenty of coastal scenery.

If you're flying into Casablanca but can't spend much time in this region, you may want to go straight to Rabat, as it's only an hour and a half from the airport by car or train and is richer in traditional sights than Casa.

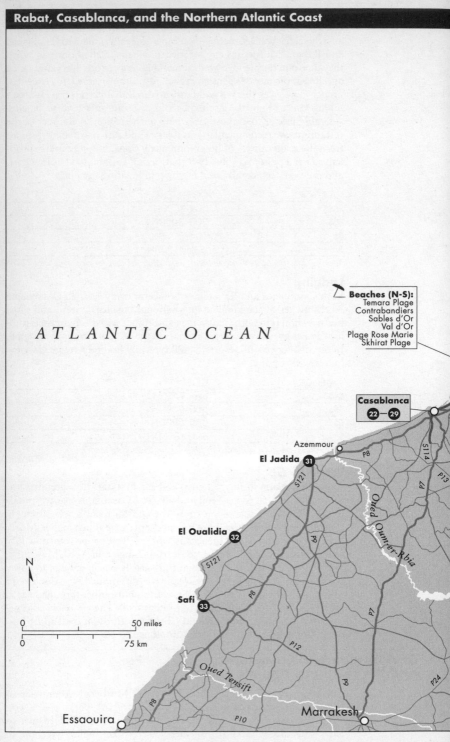

ATLANTIC OCEAN

Beaches (N–S):
Temara Plage
Contrabandiers
Sables d'Or
Val d'Or
Plage Rose Marie
Skhirat Plage

Casablanca
22 — 29

Azemmour

El Jadida 31

El Oualidia 32

Safi 33

Oued Oum-er-Rbia

P8

S114

P13

P7

S121

P9

S121

P8

P12

P9

P24

P7

Oued Tensif

P8

P10

Essaouira

Marrakesh

N

0 _____ 50 miles

0 _____ 75 km

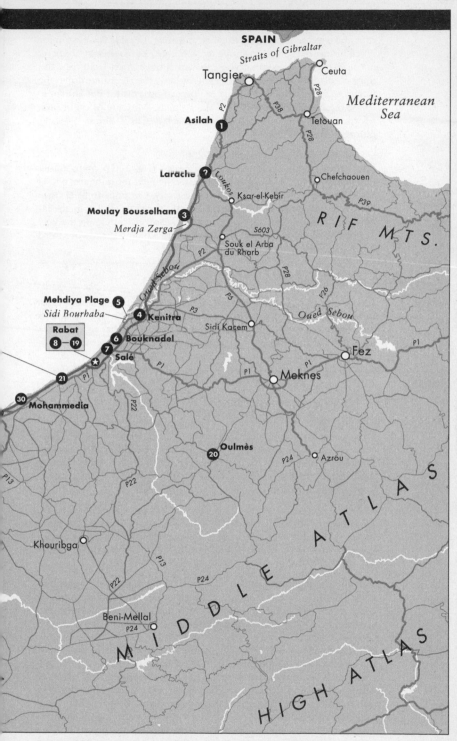

Spend your first night in 🏨 **Asilah** ①. Have dinner in a Spanish restaurant and explore the medina the next morning. Leaving town, stop for lunch in **Larache** ② and continue to 🏨 **Moulay Bousselham** ③, where, if you like a simple setting, you can watch the sun set from the sand dune across the lagoon. Spend the night here; then continue down the freeway as far as **Kenitra** ④, where you can turn off for **Bouknadel** ⑥ to see the Plage des Nations and the Belghazi Museum of traditional Moroccan art. Spend the rest of your time based in 🏨 **Rabat** ⑧–⑲, exploring Rabat and **Salé** ⑦.

Spend the first day exploring 🏨 **Casablanca** ㉒–㉙ and perhaps dining in a lavish French restaurant by the sea. The next morning drive to **El Jadida** ㉛ and explore the old Portuguese city. Continue to 🏨 **El Oualidia** ㉜ to have a seafood dinner and spend the night. Relax by the lagoon and beaches before continuing to 🏨 **Safi** ㉝, calling on the way at Plage Lalla Fatma. Visit the potters' hill in Safi and spend your third night there before moving on.

ASILAH TO SALÉ

The road along this northernmost stretch of the Atlantic coast passes through the western foothills of the Rif Mountains, several towns with Spanish accents, and a beach resort before it reaches Salé, Rabat's important next-door neighbor, with one of the most emblematic medinas in Morocco.

Asilah

❶ *46 km (29 mi) south of Tangier, 33 km (21 mi) north of Larache.*

The medina in this seaside town is photogenic and charming: it's laced with unusually clean and tidy cobbled streets, and windows on the whitewashed houses are decorated with *mashrabiya,* traditional wooden latticework. Asilah has a distinctly Spanish flavor, and it shares with its Andalusian counterparts from the Moorish caliphate a distinctly well-kept appearance. There is a beach to the north of town.

Asilah is exceptional for its robust selection of seafood restaurants. We recommend a few, but you're likely to have a delicious meal at any number of places. Between the food, the lodging, and the tidiness, Asilah is a nicer place to spend the night than Larache, its larger neighbor to the south.

If you're driving from Tangier, take the right-hand fork at the entrance to Asilah to reach the medina. Follow the coastal road south until you come to the restaurants opposite the medina's entrance. Walking into the medina, you'll pass the **Hassan II International Center** on your right: this incorporates an old Portuguese fort, the top of which was recently renovated and now looks rather like a Disneyland castle. In August the center hosts the annual Asilah Cultural Moussem, an artistic festival involving musicians, singers, writers, and painters. Just after the center, a number of attractive shops sell carpets and other handcrafted goods. Walk along the street nearest the sea, Rue Ibn Khaldoune, and you'll come to an impressive building with green doors and shutters: built at the beginning of the 20th century, this was the **palace of Raissouni,** who was a Rifi brigand before becoming governor of Asilah and the Rif. The building was restored in 1998 and is now part of the Hassan II International Center. The road goes through the palace, whose gates remain open, and continues through the small medina to an el-

In case you want to see the world.

At American Express, we're here to make your journey a smooth one. So we have over 1,700 travel service locations in over 130 countries ready to help. What else would you expect from the world's largest travel agency?

do more AMERICAN EXPRESS

Travel

Call 1 800 AXP-3429 or visit
www.americanexpress.com/travel

In case you want to be welcomed there.

We're here to see that you're always welcomed at establishments everywhere. That's why millions of people carry the American Express® Card — for peace of mind, confidence, and security, around the world or just around the corner.

do more   AMERICAN EXPRESS

Cards

To apply, call 1 800 THE-CARD
or visit www.americanexpress.com

In case you're running low.

We're here to help with more than 190,000 Express Cash locations around the world. In order to enroll, just call American Express at 1 800 CASH-NOW before you start your vacation.

do more AMERICAN EXPRESS

Express
Cash

And in case you'd rather be safe than sorry.

We're here with American Express® Travelers Cheques. They're the safe way to carry money on your vacation, because if they're ever lost or stolen you can get a refund, practically anywhere or anytime. To find the nearest place to buy Travelers Cheques, call 1 800 495-1153. Another way we help you do more.

do more **AMERICAN EXPRESS**

Travelers Cheques

©1999 American Express

evated **patio** overlooking the sea. From here you can look down to the north on a beautiful **koubba** (saint's tomb) and, if you want, clamber down to the rocky shoreline.

There is an old **Spanish church** in the new part of the town, near the Hotel Zelis.

Dining and Lodging

$$ ✕ **Casa Garcia.** Decorated with a fishing theme, Casa Garcia specializes in top-notch seafood. The fried octopus is out of this world: fresh, crisp, and tender. Avoid the paella; it seems a bit tired. ✉ *Rue Moulay Hassan Ben el Mehdi,* ☎ *09/41–74–65. No credit cards.*

$$ ✕ **Restaurante Oceano Casa Pepe.** This place has a very Spanish ambience and is very well kept. Pepe, the Spanish owner, is always here to greet customers and make sure they're happy and well fed. The menu is, needless to say, mostly Spanish, including lots of delicious tapas, superb paella, and scrumptious seafood. Service is excellent despite the constant crowds. ✉ *Place Zalaka,* ☎ *09/41–73–95. MC, V.*

$$ 🏨 **Hotel Al Khaima.** This well-managed hotel is just north of Asilah toward the train station, right across the road from the beach. It's an attractive environment, not far from a small stream; and the pool, unlike those at many hotels in this region, is open outside the summer season (a big draw, as it turns out, for foreigners). The rooms and the restaurant are nicely furnished. ✉ *B.P. 101,* ☎ *09/41–74–28,* ℻ *09/41–74–28. 90 rooms, 20 studios. Restaurant, bar, pool, billiards, dance club, playground. AE, MC, V.*

$$ 🏨 **Hotel Zelis.** Convenient to the medina, this hotel has a spacious and attractive lobby. The guest rooms are pretty and clean; their white walls are topped by a painted blue motif and accented with fresh blue-and-white bedspreads. There are two restaurants, one Moroccan and one international, but these only open when a large group is in residence. ✉ *10, Avenue Mansour Eddahabi, 90050,* ☎ *09/41–70–69,* ℻ *09/41–70–98. 55 rooms. 2 restaurants, bar. AE, MC, V.*

En Route   After the turnoff to Tetouan, the road from Asilah to Larache winds through the foothills of the Rif Mountains, which you can see in the distance on the left. There are large pottery stalls by the side of the road; if you want to buy some, bargain like mad. A little before the Loukos River, you'll see the ruins of the city of **Lixus** on a hilltop on the right. Excavations have revealed that this was originally a Phoenician settlement founded around the 7th century BC, and was subsequently occupied by the Carthaginians before finally becoming a Roman town around AD 40. Most of the visible ruins date from the Roman period—those you see by the road were salting factories, and the main extant ruins at the top of the hill are thought to have been temples. A little to the north are a semicircular structure and a circular pit lined with stones, thought to have been a theater and an amphitheater for fighting wild animals and staging games. Access is free at all times, and from the top of the hill you have a good view of Larache and the Loukos.

Larache

❷ *33 km (21 mi) south of Asilah, 117 km (73 mi) north of Kenitra.*

Like Asilah, Larache has a definite Spanish character, though it lacks its neighbor's cleanliness. Many people here speak Spanish, reflecting the Spanish occupation of the city from 1911 to 1956.

As you enter Larache from Tangier, turn left at the traffic circle at the bottom of the hill, go up the hill, and turn right at the top of the hill toward the city center. The old Portuguese walls, halfway toward the sea on the right, are a good place to start a tour. Walk behind the walls and you'll come to a little square with a view over the Loukos River. On the right is a small, square Spanish fort: this houses the **Musée Archéologique** (Archaeological Museum), a small museum devoted to archaeological finds from Lixus. Displays feature fragments of pottery from Phoenician, Carthaginian, and Roman times, and an ostrich egg and some Roman coins. Don't overlook the downstairs gallery. ⌸ *10DH.* ⊙ *Tues.–Thurs. and Sat. 9–noon and 2:30–6, Fri. 9–11:30 and 3–6.*

Opposite the museum are a mosque, with an unusual blue-and-white octagonal minaret, and an old Spanish colonial building. Enter the medina between these two buildings and go through a fruit-and-vegetable market to reach a wide street lined with shops, including one selling the traditional red-and-white–striped cloths worn by Rifi women. At the other end of the street you'll emerge at the Place de la Liberté, a circular area lined with small restaurants and cafés.

Dining and Lodging

$$ ✕ **Restaurant Al Khozama.** Omar Errais cooked for a large hotel in Riyadh, Saudi Arabia, for 10 years before coming home to Morocco to found this restaurant. His letters of recommendation are the main means of decoration on the walls; the rest of the color scheme is salmon pink. Fish is the specialty here, and the various fish entrées are rounded out by prawns, fish soup, and octopus. ⊠ *114, Avenue Mohammed V,* ☎ *09/91–44–54. AE, MC, V.*

$ ✕ **Restaurant Cara Bonita.** Right on the main square, the Cara Bonita (Pretty Face) serves a relatively inexpensive fixed-price menu consisting of soup, fried fish, and dessert. There is an English menu, which is not something you can normally count on. ⊠ *1, Place de la Liberté,* ☎ *09/91–16–68. No credit cards.*

$$ ⊡ **Hotel Riad.** This old hotel is spacious and has a quiet location, though carpets and curtains in the guest rooms are on the scruffy side. The pool is not open until June. ⊠ *Avenue Mohamed ben Abdellah,* ☎ *09/91–26–26,* ℻ *09/91–26–29. 23 rooms. Restaurant, bar, pool. No credit cards.*

$ ⊡ **Hotel España.** Overlooking the Place de la Liberté, the Hotel España offers clean rooms and a friendly welcome and may be the best all-around option for an overnight stay in Larache. General Franco once slept here. ⊠ *2, Avenue Hassan II,* ☎ *09/91–31–95. 45 rooms. No credit cards.*

Moulay Bousselham

❸ *46 km (29 mi) southwest of Larache, 82 km (51 mi) northeast of Kenitra.*

Moulay Bousselham is at the head of **Merdja Zerga** (Blue Lagoon), which gives its name to the 17,000-acre national park that contains it. This is a major stopover point for countless birds migrating from Norway, Sweden, and the United Kingdom to Africa: the birds fly south at the end of summer in the northern hemisphere and stop at Merdja Zerga in September, October, and November before continuing on to West Africa and even as far as Capetown. They stop off again on their way back to Europe in spring, so spring and fall are the times to bird-watch here. The pink flamingos on their way to and from Mauritania are particularly spectacular.

Saïd ben Saïd was a saint who immigrated to the Maghreb from Egypt in the 10th century, following a revelation instructing him to pray where the sun sets over the ocean. He had a disciple called Sidi Abdel Jalil, and according to legend Sidi Abdel Jalil saw Saïd ben Saïd fishing one day with a hook and asked him why a man with such great powers needed a hook. To show that he had needed no such aids himself, Sidi Abdel Jalil put his hands into the water and pulled out fish as numerous as the hairs on his hand. Provoked by this act, Saïd ben Saïd took off his *selham* (cloak), swept it along the ground, called out, "Sea, follow me," and proceeded to walk inland. He did not stop until he had walked 10 km (6 mi). The sea followed him, and so the lagoon was formed. After this, Saïd ben Saïd was called Moulay Bousselham—"Lord, Owner of the Cloak." Sidi Abdel Jalil begged his master to forgive him for his presumption, and Moulay Bousselham did so on the condition that he remain on the other side of the lagoon—and there **Sidi Abdel Jalil's tomb** remains to this day, on the large sand dune. **Moulay Bousselham's tomb** is at the foot of the village, near the sea. Both tombs are cubic white buildings capped with a dome; Sidi Abdel Jalil's is somewhat smaller.

Lodging

$$ ☒ **La Maison des Oiseaux.** The House of Birds is run by a French artist, ★ Gentiane (who speaks fluent English), and her Moroccan husband, Karim. Within the property is a guest house, Le Gîte Bleu, lighted only by candlelight. This is simple but charming accommodation: there is no electricity, and the house is not touched by the lights of the village, so on a moonless night you can see the stars as nature intended. Join Gentiane and Karim for supper *en famille*: delicious fish, salads, and strawberries served by the fire. If you want, Karim will take you across the lagoon in his boat to watch the sun set from the dune containing Sidi Abdel Jalil's tomb; he can also take you for a longer excursion to see the migrating birds. Reserve a room in advance if at all possible. To find the house, ask for Karim and Gentiane at the reception to the campground, signposted to the left as you enter Moulay Bousselham. ☎ *07/67–39–03 weekdays, 01/30–10–67 weekends. 6 rooms. No credit cards. Closed July–Aug.*

$$ ☒ **Villa Nora.** This hotel is run by a retired British actor, Gabriel Oliver, and his sister Jean and has been known to attract expats from the American embassy. The rooms recall an English bed-and-breakfast—except for the stunning view over the blue Atlantic. Gabriel and Jean also have on the premises a small art gallery with contemporary paintings. To get here, exit the autoroute and turn right (north) before the cafés in the village, then right again, and continue for about 1 km (½ mi) until you see the sign on the left. Reserve in advance if possible. ☒ *Villa Nora, Front de Mer, Moulay Bousselham, B.P. 74, ☎ 07/43–20–71. 6 rooms. No credit cards.*

Kenitra

❹ *40 km (25 mi) northeast of Rabat, 117 km (73 mi) southwest of Larache.*

Kenitra was only founded in 1913, so it has no monuments of great historical interest. If you find yourself longing, however, for a nice, juicy hamburger after your umpteenth plate of *friture de poisson,* stop in at Kenitra's El Dorado (☞ *below*). There was once an American air base nearby, so you can feel a slight American influence in the town; cafés have American names, and English is more widely spoken than elsewhere in Morocco.

Dining and Lodging

$ ✕ **El Dorado.** Think of this as a gold mine of such American delicacies as hamburgers and cheeseburgers. The food is appropriately tasty, and there's a menu in English. Near the Hôtel La Rotonde, this place is popular with the local business community. ☒ *64, Avenue Mohamed Diouri, ☎ 07/37–16–46. No credit cards.*

$$ 🏨 **Hotel Mamora.** Despite its modest rates, this family-run establishment has become the best hotel in Kenitra. It offers friendly service, attractive rooms decorated with pastels and blond wood, and continually changing cuisine in the restaurant. Views take in the verdant poolside terrace or the trees of the town square. To get here, follow signs for the Hôtel de Ville (which is not actually a hotel; it's more like a town hall). ✉ Avenue Hassan II, ☎ 07/37–17–75, ℻ 07/37–14–46. 69 rooms, 3 suites. Restaurant, bar, 2 snack bars, pool, meeting room. AE, DC, MC, V.

$ 🏨 **Hôtel La Rotonde.** Rooms at this inexpensive hotel are large, clean, and simply furnished in light colors. The restaurant is very popular with locals. ✉ 60, Avenue Mohamed Diouri, ☎ 07/37–14–01. 19 rooms. Restaurant. No credit cards.

Mehdiya Plage

⑤ 11 km (7 mi) west of Kenitra, 33 km (21 mi) northeast of Rabat.

A slight detour to the west of Kenitra will take you to this little seaside resort with a long sandy beach. Raw prawns are often sold cheaply at the fishing port. You'll pass **Lake Sidi Bourhaba** on the way back to the main road.

Dining

$$ ✕ **Restaurant Belle Vue.** Chef-owner Naima runs this seafood restaurant and the Chinese restaurant next door, both perched on a cliff on your left as you enter Mehdiya Plage from Kenitra. Try the friture de poisson. As the name suggests, there is a nice view of the sea. ☎ 07/38–80–06. No credit cards.

Bouknadel

⑥ 22 km (17 mi) southwest of Kenitra, 18 km (11 mi) northeast of Rabat.

Bouknadel itself (sometimes called Sidi Bouknadel) is not accessible from the autoroute, but its attractions lie to the north, halfway between Kenitra and Rabat and accessible via the coastal road from either of the two.

The **Plage des Nations** is a spectacular, long sandy beach with large Atlantic breakers. A heavy undertow makes it unsafe to swim here.

In 1991 an entrepreneurial craftsman named Abdelila Belghazi was contracted to carve cedar decorations for the huge sliding domes on the Prophet's Mosque in Medina, Saudi Arabia. Thanks to this windfall, he established a workshop in this building in Bouknadel and founded the **Belghazi Museum** to exhibit his collection of traditional Moroccan art. Patronized (that is, publicly supported) by Princess Lalla Meriam, it is the first and only private museum in the country and houses a far larger collection than any state museum. On display are pottery, wood carving, embroidery, manuscripts, musical instruments, agricultural tools, and weapons. One interesting room is full of Moroccan Jewish art, such as wedding clothes and temple furnishings. ✉ Route de Kenitra, Km 17, ☎ 07/82–21–78. 🎟 40DH. ☉ Sat.–Thurs. 8:30–6, Fri. 2:30–6.

South of Bouknadel are the **Jardins Exotiques** (Exotic Gardens), created in the mid-20th century by a Frenchman, named François, who used to play classical music to his plants. Since François's death the gardens have been maintained by the government, and although the landscaper's house has fallen into ruin, the leaves are still swept up daily. If anything, the gardens look even more beautiful than when François was alive. They were originally planned to represent different regions, such as Polynesia, China, and Japan, and in the tropical part you can almost imagine yourself in Malaysia. The gardens are a haven for birds and frogs, and the profusion of walkways and bridges makes them a wonderful playground for small children. A touching poem by François about his life forms an epitaph at the entrance. ⌨ *5DH.* ☺ *Daily 9–5.*

Dining and Lodging

$$$ ✗⌨ **Hotel Firdaous.** This hotel's spectacular location on the Plage des Nations makes it a worthy place to stay, and the rooms were recently redone. The restaurants serve good seafood. ⊠ *Plage des Nations, B.P. 4008, Bouknadel, Salé,* ☎ *07/82–21–31,* ℻ *07/82–21–43. 17 rooms. 2 restaurants, 2 bars, pool, beach. DC, MC, V.*

Salé

❼ *37 km (23 mi) southwest of Kenitra, just northeast of Rabat across river.*

Salé was probably founded around the 11th century. In medieval times it was the most important trading harbor on the Atlantic coast, and at the beginning of the 17th century it joined Rabat in welcoming Muslims expelled from Spain. Rabat and Salé were rival towns for more than 100 years after that, but Rabat eventually gained the upper hand, and today Salé is very much in its shadow. The medina, however, is well worth a trip even apart from its monuments, as it's particularly traditional; you're more likely to see people walking around in traditional dress or practicing traditional crafts than you are in most Moroccan medinas.

A good place to start a tour of Salé is at the entrance to the **medina,** near the Great Mosque, which you can access from the road along the southwest city wall. Enter on Zanqat Sidi Abdellah ben Hassoun—a street named after the patron saint of Salé, whose **tomb** you pass on the left. Every year on the eve of Mouloud (the Prophet Mohammed's birthday), in June, a colorful procession with elaborate candles makes its way to this tomb. On the right, before the tomb, is the **zaouia** (spiritual meeting place, or sanctuary) of the Tijani order. Just after the tomb you come to the **Djemâa Kabir** (Great Mosque) which dates from the 12th-century Almohad dynasty and is the third-largest mosque in Morocco after the Hassan II in Casablanca and the Kairaouine in Fez.

★ Turn left around the corner of the mosque, and you'll see on your right the **Abou el Hassan Medersa,** built by the Merenid sultan of that name in the 14th century and a fine example of the traditional Koranic school. Like the Bou Inania in Fez or the Ben Youssef in Marrakesh, this medersa has beautiful intricate plasterwork around its central courtyard, and a fine *mihrab* (prayer niche) with a ceiling carved in an interlocking geometrical pattern representing the cosmos. Upstairs, on the second and third floors, you can visit the little cells where the students used to sleep, and from the roof you can see the entire city. The medersa is open daily from 8:45 to noon and 2:30 to 6, and admission is 10DH.

When you come out of the medersa, turn right and take the first street on the right farther into the medina. Turn left at the end of the street and you'll come to a big triangular area on your right, the **Souk Alkabir,** or Great Market. (Don't worry if you lose track of where you are in the medina; many a shop will distract you, but you're never far from an entrance gate.) Turn right (southwest) to emerge at the city walls, which you can then follow back to your starting point. The low gate on this wall once served as an entrance to the city from the sea. Just as the road around the medina turns to the northeast, you have a spectacular view over the wall across the cemetery to the Kasbah des Oudayas, on the other side of the River Bou Regreg—particularly lovely in the late afternoon, when the tombstones cast clear shadows across the cemetery and seem to be fringed by a halo of light. Northwest of the medina, by the sea, is the tomb of **Sidi Ahmed ben Achir,** a much-venerated saint. Look through the windows in the wall by the sea for a fine view of the rocks and the ocean. Beyond the northern corner of the city is a big round fortress called **Borj Ar Roukni.** If you follow the road around the other two sides of Salé, you'll also pass the gates Bab Sebta, Bab Fez, and Bab El Mrisa.

Salé's other main attraction is its **pottery** complex, just off the road toward Fez (to the right after you cross the river from Rabat)—a whole series of pottery stores that sell their own wares. Each store has its own style, and you can walk around and see them all without any pressure to buy. Other crafts have recently been added to this complex, notably bamboo and straw work, and one large store carries a variety of handicrafts at rather high prices. A café stands ready to refresh you.

Dining and Lodging

$$$ ✕ **La Péniche du Bouregreg.** This restaurant is on a boat, a vessel brought from France and moored on the river. There are two decks outside—with wonderful views of Rabat's Hassan Tower and Mohammed V Mausoleum—and two inside. Down a carpeted stairway, you can hunker down at cozy little tables next to brass portholes; upstairs, the tables are lined up along the railings. The menu changes regularly, but it usually includes maritime specialties like oysters, snails, mussels, and, of course, fish, and some Moroccan food. Evenings bring live music, usually a keyboard-guitar duo singing French and American songs. This may be the most unusually situated restaurant in the region, and it lives up to its location by serving excellent food. ⊠ *Rive Droite du Bouregreg, Salé,* ☎ *07/78–56–59. DC, MC, V.*

$$$ 🏨 **Dawliz.** Set on a bank of the River Bou Regreg, this hotel has the same brilliant view across the river that the restaurant Péniche has. The rooms and bathrooms are unusually spacious and are decorated with wooden furniture and blue rugs. There are some popular cinemas in this complex, so if you want quiet evenings, ask for a room in the back, overlooking the river—particularly on weekends. ⊠ *Avenue Prince Heritier Sidi Mohamed, Rive Droite Bouregreg, Salé,* ☎ *07/88–32–77,* 𝔽𝔸𝕏 *07/88–32–79. 43 rooms. 4 restaurants, bar, tea shop, pool, bowling, 3 cinemas. MC, V.*

RABAT AND ENVIRONS

Rabat will keep you plenty busy for at least a day or two. If you have more time here, you may want to swim in the warm springs of inland Oulmès, collapse on the sand at any of various beaches, pay homage to a prehistoric cave dwelling, or treat the kids to Temara Zoo.

Rabat

❽ *Southwest of Salé across river, 40 km (25 mi) southwest of Kenitra, 91 km (57 mi) northeast of Casablanca.*

Rabat is an excellent place to get acquainted with Morocco, as it has a medina and an array of historical sites and museums, yet puts none of the pressure on foreign travelers that most experience in a place like Fez. As a diplomatic center, Rabat has a large community of foreign residents, so you'll generally find yourself free to wander and browse without being hassled to buy local wares or engage a guide. The city has grown considerably over the last 20 years, but it remains very reasonably proportioned for a capital, and most of the sights are clustered in a relatively small area. Attractive and well kept, with several gardens, it's a capital to be proud of.

Rabat gets its name from the Arabic word *ribat,* meaning "fortress." It was founded in the 12th century as a fortified town—now the Kasbah des Oudayas—on a rocky outcrop overlooking the River Bou Regreg by Abd al Mu'min of the Almohad dynasty. Abd al Mu'min's grandson, Yaqoub al Mansour, extended the city to encompass the present-day medina, surrounded it with ramparts (some of which still stand), and erected a mosque, from which the unfinished Hassan Tower protrudes as Rabat's principal landmark. Yaqoub al Mansour's ambitious city declined for a while, and after the Merenids took over from the Almohads in the 13th century, Chellah, a neighboring town now within Rabat, was developed as a necropolis. Chellah predated the original Ribat; it was probably founded by the Phoenicians, and was also a Roman town.

In the early 17th century Ribat itself was revived with the arrival of the Muslims, who populated the present-day medina upon their expulsion from Spain and whose descendents live here to this day. Over the course of the 17th century the Kasbah des Oudayas grew notorious for its pirates, and an independent republic of the Bou Regreg was established, based in the Kasbah; the piracy continued when the republic was integrated into the Alaouite kingdom and lasted until the 19th century.

Rabat was named the administrative capital of the country at the beginning of the French Protectorate in 1912, and it remained the capital of the Alaouite kingdom when independence was restored in 1956.

Today the city has many important districts outside the Kasbah, the medina, and the original French new town. These include L'Ocean, the seaside area that was once Spanish and Portuguese (during the French Protectorate); Hassan, the environs of the Hassan tower; Agdal, a fashionable residential and business district; and Souissi, an affluent enclave of wealthy folks and diplomats.

Numbers in the text correspond to numbers in the margin and on the Rabat map.

A Good Walk

Start at Bab Al Had, at the southwest corner of the **medina** ⑨. On the western flank of the medina you can see some of the original Almohad city walls. Enter the medina on Avenue Mohammed V, the continuation of the main avenue that runs through the new town and crosses Boulevard Hassan II. (Note that in the medina it's called Lugza, even though it's signposted AVENUE MOHAMED V.) Go through the **Marché Central,** a market at the edge of the medina. Immediately after entering the city walls, turn right along Souika, a busy street lined with shops. The first main street on the left, parallel to Lugza, is Sidi Fath: make an excursion up this street to see the interesting old **Sidi Fath mosque,** with an arch that bridges the street; the mosque has a lovely (albeit weathered) ceiling painted with a gray floral and arabesque design and a beautiful octagonal minaret of golden sandstone. Return to Souika and continue past the shops selling dates, herbs, spices, and all manner of foodstuffs. You'll pass two old mosques on the right, and after about 15 minutes (if it's crowded) you'll come to Souk Sabbat, a covered shoe market that also has some shops selling handicrafts. This is the place to buy traditional Moroccan *belgha* (slippers). Shortly be-

104

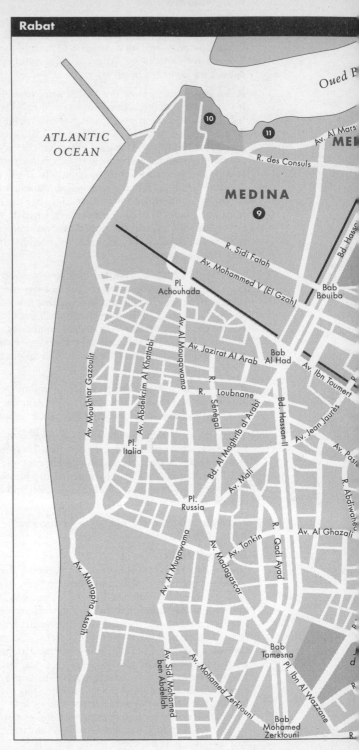

Rabat

Oued B

ATLANTIC
OCEAN

Av. Al Mars

ME

R. des Consuls

Bd. Hassc

MEDINA
9

R. Sidi Fatah

Pl.
Achouhada

Av. Mohammed V (El Gzah)

Bab
Bouiba

Av. Al Mouqawama

Av. Jazirat Al Arab

Bab
Al Had

Av. Ibn Toumert

Av. Maukhtar Gazoulit

Av. Abdelkrim Al Khattabi

R.
Loubnane

R. Sénégal

Bd. Al Maghrib al Arabi

Bd. Hassan II

Av. Jean Jaurès

Av. Pas

R. Abdiwahec

Pl.
Italia

Av. Mali

Pl.
Russia

R.
Qadi Ayad

Av. Al Ghazali

Av. Al Muqawama

Av. Madagascar

Av. Tonkin

Av. Mustapha Assaih

Bab
Tamesna

Pl. Ibn Al Wazzane

d

Av. Sidi Mohamed
ben Abdellah

Av. Mohamed Zerktouni

Bab
Mohamed
Zerktouni

R.

Marsa

MELLAH

d Bou Regreg

Av. Ar Rahba

12

13

Av. de la Tour Hassa

Av. Mohammed Lyazidi

R. Al Akbar

bd. Hassan II

Av. Chellah

Av. Moulay Ismail

R. Abdelmoumen

Av. Al Mouwahidine

Av. Alaouine

R. Al Marinhyine

R. Al Mourabatine

Mekka

Av. F. Oran

Av. Moulay Ismail

Av. d'Alger

Av. Fez

Av. Meknès

R. Tariq (A) Zaid

Parc du
Triangle
de Vue

R. Mansour Addahbi

R. Rachid

Av. N.Y. Patrice

R. Abou Inan

Av. Chellah

Lumumba

R. Annaba

Av. Ouarzazate

R. Roosevelt

R. Soekarno

Bd. Mohammed V

Av. Moulay Hassan

R. Moulay
Abdelaziz

15

R. Yousef Ibn Tachfine

Av. Mohammed V

18

Djemâa
Sunna

14

Bd. Yaqoub al Mansour

Bab
Zaërs

R. Descartes

Pasteur

R. Abou Chouaïb

Adoukkali

Bab
Rouah

16

Djemâa
al Fas

19

Av. John Kennedy

R. Abdlwahed
ali

Al Marrakchi

Av. de la Victoire)

Av. Ibn Batota

17

Bd. Amasr

R. Al Battani

Av. Ibn Khaldoune

Av. Ibn Hazm

R. Oqba

Jardin
d'Essais

R. Ibn Hajar

R. Al Achaari

Bab
Marrakech

Pl. Ibn
Zohr

R. Innaouen

Av. Al Oummam

Av. Al Mouttah'da

R. Bin Al Ouidane

0   250 yards

0   250 meters

N

yond the covered area, after some jewelry shops, the street opens up into a large street on the left, the **Rue des Consuls,** so called because it once housed diplomatic representatives. Turn left here and wander past the shops selling carpets and other handmade wares. This stretch is covered by a Far Eastern–style roof. At the top of the Rue des Consuls you'll come upon the Place des Oudayas on the left, which has a well-stocked pottery shop and another specializing in the manufacture and sale of antique wooden boxes.

Leaving the medina, take particular care as you cross the road to the **Kasbah des Oudayas** ⑩, as this is a busy intersection and the traffic pays you no heed. Leaving the Kasbah, turn left and walk down the road to the **Ensemble Artisanal** ⑪ on the left. From here you can rejoin the Rue des Consuls through a side street opposite, but, again, be careful crossing the road. Continue back along the Rue des Consuls, past Souk Sabbat this time, and you'll enter the **Mellah,** Rabat's Jewish quarter from 1808 to around the 1960s. Here the street narrows considerably. When you come out of the medina, cross Boulevard Hassan II and walk to the left; go around to the far side of the Hotel Safir, and you'll see the **Hassan Tower** ⑫ dominating the landscape. Walk alongside the gardens and enter the large rectangular site of the ruined mosque through any of the gates. On the far side from the Hassan Tower, the large, square, white building with steps is the **Mohammed V Mausoleum** ⑬.

Take a taxi to the **Sunna Mosque** ⑭—at the opposite end of Avenue Mohammed V from where you entered the medina. To get to the **Archaeological Museum** ⑮, go down the road on the left side of the Sunna Mosque with your back to Avenue Mohammed V, and take the first street on your left, near a house guarded by soldiers. The museum is on the right, near the Hotel Chellah. After you've seen it, go back past the Sunna Mosque and walk next to the wall, above the road, until you come to four modern arches in the city wall: to the left of these is **Bab Rouah** ⑯, the historic Almohad gate. Halfway between Bab Rouah and the Sunna Mosque is Bab Safara, the entrance to the immaculately kept Royal Palace complex. On the right as you enter are the barracks of the royal guard; then, on the left, you'll see the royal mosque; and finally you'll pass the **Royal Palace** ⑰ itself on the right. Leaving the palace complex, turn left and walk for about 1 km (½ mi; about 10 minutes) alongside the pleasant gardens opposite to arrive at Bab Zaer. Across the road, on the slope of the river valley, you'll see the unmistakable fortress of the **Chellah** ⑱. It's a fairly long walk from Bab Rouah to the Chellah, so if you're tired or it's very hot out, you may want to go by taxi; but don't miss the Chellah, as it's arguably the best attraction in Rabat. Finally, make a taxi excursion to the **Lalla Soukaina Mosque** ⑲.

TIMING

This walk takes a full day, but it can be tiring. If you have time, you may want to split it into two days so you can linger along the way.

Sights to See

⑮ **Archaeological Museum.** The Musée Archéologique holds items from around Morocco. The emphasis is on Roman pieces, included many inscribed tablets; the Chellah and Volubilis sites are particularly well represented, and there's an ample collection of Roman bronze items. Also on display is a plaster cast of the early human remains found at Harhoura, on the coast south of town (☞ Temara Plage *in* Rabat to Casablanca: The Beaches, *below*). ⊠ *23, Rue Al Brihi,* ☎ *07/70–22–24.* 🎫 *10DH.* ☺ *Wed.–Mon. 9–11:30 and 2:30–5:30.*

⑯ Bab Rouah (Gate of the Winds). This city gate was built by Yaqoub al Mansour in 1197. To see it, go outside the city walls and look to the left of the modern arches. Originally a fortification, the gate has an elaborately decorated arch topped by two carved shells. The entrance leads into a room with no gate behind it; you have to turn left into another room and then right into a third room to see the door that once led into Rabat. Bab Rouah is now used as an art gallery, but you don't need to go inside to appreciate the architecture. ▣ *Free.* ☉ *Gallery daily 8:30–noon and 2:30–7:30.*

★ **⑱ Chellah.** The Chellah was an independent city before Rabat ever existed. It dates from the 7th or 8th century BC, when it was probably Phoenician; and as you walk down the path, you'll see the Roman remains on your left. Sultan Abu Saïd and his son Abu al Hassan, of the Merenid dynasty, were responsible for the ramparts, the entrance gate, and the majestic portals. The Chellah was used by the Merenids as a spiritual retreat, and at quiet times the *baraka* (blessing) of the place is still tangible.

The entrance to the Merenid sanctuary is at the bottom of the path, just past some saints' tombs. To the right is a pool with eels in it. The ruins of the mosque are just inside the sanctuary: beautiful arches and the mihrab (prayer niche). Storks nest on the impressive minaret. On the far side of the mosque is a beautiful wall decorated with Kufi script, a type of Arabic calligraphy characterized by right angles. To the left of the mosque is the *zaouia* (sanctuary), where you can see the ruins of individual cells surrounding a basin and some ancient mosaic work. Beyond the mosque and the zaouia are some beautiful, well-maintained walled gardens. Spring water runs through the gardens at one point, and they give the Chellah a serenity that's quite extraordinary considering it's less than a mile from the center of a nation's capital. There is no place comparable in Morocco. From the walled gardens you can look out over the River Bou Regreg: you'll see cultivated fields below, and cliffs across the river. On the right is a hill with a small white koubba. Tour groups are elsewhere at lunchtime, so try to come then to experience the Chellah at its most serene. ▣ *10DH.* ☉ *Daily 8:30–6:30 (or until sunset if earlier).*

⑪ Ensemble Artisanal. Overlooking the River Bou Regreg is a series of small workshops where you can see artisans create Morocco's various handicrafts: everything from traditional mosaic tile work, embroidery, leatherwork, traditional shoes, and painted wood to brass, pottery, and carpets. You can buy the items at fixed prices, which are a little higher than well-negotiated prices in the nearby Rue des Consuls, but which save you the trouble of bargaining. The small café has a river view. ✉ *6, Tarik El Marsa, Espace les Oudayas,* ☎ *07/73–05–07.* ▣ *Free.* ☉ *Daily, approximately 9–12:30 and 2:30–6.*

⑫ Hassan Tower. At the end of the 12th century, Yaqoub al Mansour—fourth monarch of the Almohad dynasty and grandson of Abd al Mu'min, who founded Rabat—planned a great mosque. This tower is the only significant remnant of that dream. A few columns remain in the mosque's great rectangular courtyard, but the great tower was never even completed (which is why it looks too short for its base). Note the quality of the craftsmanship in the carved-stone and mosaic decorations at the top of the tower. From the base there is a fine view over the river. Locals come here at dawn to have their wedding photos taken. ▣ *Free.* ☉ *24 hrs.*

⑩ Kasbah des Oudayas. The history of the Kasbah is the early history of Rabat. Still inhabited, the Kasbah originally comprised the whole of the city, including the castle of Yaqoub al Mansour. You may be approached by a guide at the entrance, but you won't really need one.

Walk up the steps to the huge, imposing ornamental gate, built, like Bab Rouah, by the Almohads. The gate's interior is now used for art exhibits. Enter the Kasbah and turn right into Rue Jama (Mosque Street). The **mosque**, which dates from Almohad times (it was built in the mid-12th century), is on the left; it was supposedly reconstructed in the late 18th century by an English Muslim—Ahmed el Inglizi. Continue to the end of the road past a house called Dar Baraka, and you'll emerge onto a large platform overlooking the Bou Regreg estuary. Here you have a magnificent view across the river to the old quarter of Salé, and you can walk down to the water's edge. Go back along Rue Jama until you come to Rue Bazo on the left; this winds down the Kasbah past picturesque houses. Turn left, walk to the bottom of the street, and you'll be at the Oudayas café, an excellent place to pause for a drink or snack: the shady terrace is decorated with mosaic tile work and looks across the river to Salé. Once fortified, leave the café by the gate opposite the river to see the beautiful **Oudayas Garden** (Jardin des Oudayas), a walled Andalusian retreat that you can explore at your leisure. The garden was laid out in the early 20th century (and is now wheelchair accessible), but its enclosure dates from the beginning of the present Alaouite dynasty in the 17th century.

At the top of the garden, accessible by a bridge across a pool, is the **Oudayas Museum** (Musée des Oudayas), which holds various objects of traditional Moroccan art. The museum is set in a house built by Moulay Ismail in the traditional style, with rooms arranged around a courtyard. Thanks to fortuitous design, the rooms get sun in the winter but not in the summer. The two most valuable items are the 12th- or 13th-century Almohad Koran and the medieval astrolabe; other exhibits include Andalusian musical instruments, clothing, jewelry, and pottery from Fez.

Leave the garden by the wrought-iron gate at the top and turn left as you come out to exit the Kasbah by the lower gate. ⊠ *Museum: 1, Blvd. Al Marsa,* ☎ *07/73–15–12.* ▣ *Kasbah free, museum 10DH.* ☉ *Kasbah 24 hrs, museum daily 8:30–noon and 3–5:30.*

⑲ **Lalla Soukaina Mosque.** Just built in the 1980s by King Hassan II in honor of his granddaughter, this mosque is proof that the Moorish architecture that produced the Court of Lions in Granada's Alhambra is alive and well. Notice the exquisite sandstone work on the walkways surrounding the mosque, and look up at the colorfully painted geometrical designs on the ceilings. The mosque is surrounded by immaculately kept gardens. Non-Muslims may not enter, but there's plenty to admire from outside. ⊠ *Edge of Souissi, beyond Ibn Sina Hospital.*

⑨ **Medina.** Rabat's medina was first populated by the Muslims who fled from Spain after the Christian Reconquest. True to tradition, the houses face inward, with rooms opening onto central courtyards and only a door exposed to the narrow alleys of the medina. The more sumptuous houses were at the top end, toward Avenue Al Alou, but Rabat's wealthy have long since left for other parts of town, and the medina is now inhabited by poor families, often several to a house.

⑬ **Mohammed V Mausoleum.** Resting place of King Mohammed V, who died in 1961, the mausoleum is adjacent to the Hassan tower and, thanks to a commanding position above the river, is similarly visible to anyone approaching Rabat from Salé. The tomb itself is subterranean; the terrace that overlooks it is approached by steps on each side. Looking down, you're likely to see someone ritually reading the Koran. Designed by a Vietnamese architect and built between 1962 and 1966, the tomb is cubical, with a pyramidal green-tile roof, a richly decorated ceiling, and onyx exterior walls. A mosque, built at the same time, adjoins the tomb.

⑰ Royal Palace. Built in the early 20th century, Morocco's Royal Palace is a large, cream-color building set back behind lawns. Its large ornamental gate is accented by ceremonial guards dressed in white and red. Don't stray from the road down the middle of the complex; the palace is occupied by the royal family and closed to the public.

⑭ Sunna Mosque. Rabat's most important mosque was just built in the 1960s, but because it was designed in a traditional Maghrebi (Moroccan) style, it was sheltered from the architectural anarchy of the time and remains beautiful and dignified today. The French wanted, in their day, to extend Avenue Mohammed V through this site, but the Moroccans resisted, and thanks to the martyrs of that confrontation, the mosque stands here on the site of an earlier one. Non-Muslims may not enter.

Dining and Lodging

$$$$ ✕ **Le Goeland.** Located near the flower market on Place Petri, Le Goeland is one of Rabat's most expensive restaurants. The French cuisine and the service are excellent, and the atmosphere is warm yet dignified. Try the huge and elegantly presented turbot encrusted in salt, and for dessert a delicious café *liégeois* (iced coffee with ice cream and whipped cream). ⊠ *9, Rue Moulay Ali Cherif,* ☎ *07/76–88–85. AE, MC, V.*

$$$ ✕ **Dinarjat.** This is Moroccan food at its best. You'll start with a de-
★ licious spread of Moroccan salads, then savor classic dishes like pastilla, tagine, and couscous in the beautiful ambience of a traditional Rabat medina house. Live traditional Andalusian music forms an authentic background. The restaurant is not licensed for alcoholic drinks, so your likeliest accompaniment is Oulmès or Sidi Ali mineral water. You can get here from Boulevard Laalou, not far from the Kasbah des Oudayas; in the evening a man stands at the nearest entrance to the medina with a lantern, ready to guide you to the restaurant. ⊠ *6, Rue Belgnaoui, Medina,* ☎ *07/70–42–39. MC, V.*

$$$ ✕ **Entrecôte.** A traditional French restaurant, Entrecôte serves game and seafood in addition to the steaks implied by its name. The setting is provincial French, complete with wooden beams. ⊠ *74, Boulevard Fal Ould Oumeir, Agdal,* ☎ *07/67–11–08. AE, MC, V.*

$$$ ✕ **Fuji.** This Japanese eatery is one of the best restaurants in Rabat for both food and service, and the Japanese diplomatic community eats here—a nod to authenticity. The dining room has a pleasing Japanese ambience, with Japanese-style windows and a small rock pool with a fountain (not always operative). Adornments include little Japanese dolls and fans, and a tree made up of glass strips that change color. Entrées are mainly classics like sushi, teriyaki, and tempura (fried vegetables), all served with chopsticks in tasteful Japanese lacquer boxes. Even the Berber waiters are dressed up in passable imitations of Japanese style. ⊠ *2, Avenue Michlifen, Agdal,* ☎ *07/67–35–83. V.*

$$$ ✕ **Restaurant de la Plage.** Fish takes many forms here, like *sole meunière* or *filet St. Pierre* served with little boiled potatoes and rice. Wines include the likes of *les trois domaines* and claret. You dine right next to the Kasbah des Oudayas, overlooking the Atlantic Ocean. ⊠ *Plage Oudaya,* ☎ *07/70–75–86. AE, MC, V.*

$$ ✕ **L'Oasis.** Here you can sample Moroccan food at reasonable prices in simple surroundings and a central location. The couscous, served in a copious helping in the traditional earthenware dish, is especially good. ⊠ *7, Rue Al Osqofiah,* ☎ *07/72–05–57. No credit cards.*

$$ ✕ **La Pagode.** Take a sharp right coming out of the Rabat-Ville train station and you'll hit this Vietnamese restaurant on the left, just before the city walls. The restaurant is upstairs, where a Far Eastern look has been successfully re-created. The menu offers *nems*, spring rolls, Vietnamese salad (shredded vegetables with mint), ginger beef curry, and various other temptations. ⊠ *11, Rue Baghdad*, ☎ *07/70–93–81. MC, V.*

$$ ✕ **Pizzeria Roma.** Popular with the business crowd, this pizzeria serves a wide range of authentic Italian dishes and wines. The onion soup is delicious. ⊠ *1, Place Unité Africaine*, ☎ *07/72–02–68. AE, MC, V.*

$ ☷ **La Graille.** You can't beat La Graille for value: pizzas, hamburgers, and fries go for rock-bottom prices here. The *salade de chef* is almost a meal in itself: tuna fish, sweet corn, lettuce, tomatoes, olives, salad dressing, rice, potatoes, prawns, and bread. Ask for *jus de citron* and you'll get a tasty lemonade. ⊠ *66, Avenue Oqbah, Agdal*, ☎ *07/77–88–76. No credit cards.*

$$$$ ☷ **Hilton.** This is where visiting foreign dignitaries stay when breezing through Rabat. Near the Royal Palace, the Hilton is surrounded by parks and adjacent to the one most favored by Rabati joggers, Ibn Sina. The sumptuous lobby is neo-Roman, and there's a private Andalusian garden in back. The rooms have modern furnishings and tremendous views over the city. The luxury suites are very spacious and individually furnished, some with particularly fine carpets. ⊠ *Quartier Aviation, Souissi*, ☎ *07/67–56–56, FAX 07/67–14–92. 193 rooms, 28 suites. 3 restaurants, piano bar, air-conditioning, minibars, pool, barbershop, hammam, sauna, putting green, 4 tennis courts, exercise room, shops, meeting rooms, car rental. AE, DC, MC, V.*

$$$$ ☷ **Safir.** Near the medina and the Hassan Tower, the Safir has an attractively decorated Moroccan lobby. The ceiling on the plant-filled courtyard slides open in summer for stargazing, and there's a rooftop pool. Guest rooms are somewhat small, but they're traditionally furnished and comfortable. ⊠ *Place Sidi Makhlouf*, ☎ *07/73–47–47, FAX 07/72–21–55. 188 rooms, 6 suites. Restaurant, bar, pool. AE, DC, MC, V.*

$$$$ ☷ **Tour Hassan.** If you want a luxury hotel that still reflects traditional Moroccan architecture, stay at the Tour Hassan. Its traditional arches are beautifully decorated with carved plasterwork, and although it's in the center of town, it has a large interior garden in the Andalusian style, featuring walkways between flower gardens. Now part of the Meridien group, the hotel meets high international standards. Rooms are newly furnished with vividly hued bedspreads and net curtains, and each has a tasteful dark-wood table and chair, a mirror, and two armchairs. ⊠ *26, Rue Chellah*, ☎ *07/73–38–16, FAX 07/70–42–01. 118 rooms, 2 suites. 2 restaurants, bar, pool, air-conditioning, meeting rooms. AE, DC, MC, V.*

$$$ ☷ **Rabat Chellah.** The Chellah has been in business for some years and remains one of the best Rabat hotels in this price range. It's in the center of town, near the Sunna Mosque, but the area is relatively quiet. The building is fairly functional, but there is a pleasant courtyard near the breakfast area, with plants and cobblestones. ⊠ *2, Rue d'Ifni*, ☎ *07/70–10–51, FAX 07/70–63–54. 111 rooms, 4 suites. Restaurant, bar, air-conditioning. AE, DC, MC, V.*

$$ ☷ **Ibis Moussafir.** The Ibis Moussafir is adjacent to the Rabat-Agdal train station—that is, the first station you come to from Casablanca, not the downtown one near most tourist attractions. There's a private lawn out back, and the buffet breakfasts are much better than those usually served at hotels in this price range. ⊠ *32, Rue Abderrahmane Ghafiki, Agdal*, ☎ *07/77–49–19, FAX 07/77–49–03. 95 rooms. Restaurant, bar. AE, MC, V.*

$$ ⊞ **Rabat Yasmine.** This new hotel is not far from the Hassan Tower and offers a spacious lobby, a warm welcome, and well-kept rooms. The price–quality ratio is pleasingly high. ⊠ *Rue Marinyne at Rue Makka,* ☎ *07/72–20–18,* ℻ *07/72–21–00. 56 rooms. Restaurant, bar. DC, MC, V.*

$$ ⊞ **Sheherazade.** On a quiet street near the Hassan Tower, this hotel has what must be the most unusual ethnic eatery in Rabat: an Australian restaurant, specializing in grilled meat. Guest rooms are arranged so that the corners with windows jut out diagonally. Inside, furnishings are standard for the region: twin beds, curtains, and a rug on the floor. ⊠ *21, Rue Tunis,* ☎ *07/72–22–26,* ℻ *07/72–45–27. 75 rooms. Restaurant, bar. MC, V.*

$$ ⊞ **Terminus.** True to its name, this hotel is convenient for travelers arriving by train. It's on Rabat's main drag, closer to the Sunna Mosque than to the medina: as you come out of the Rabat-Ville station, turn right, cross the road, and you're there. The lobby is new and comfortable. Rooms are standard but satisfactory; those on the courtyard are quieter. ⊠ *384, Avenue Mohammed V,* ☎ *07/70–52–67,* ℻ *07/70–19–26. 130 rooms. Restaurant, bar. MC, V.*

$ ⊞ **Hotel Central.** If it's economy you want, come straight to this budget hotel. As the name suggests, it's centrally located, just off Avenue Mohammed V (next to the Hotel Balima). What you get—a big room with high ceiling and sink, in the center of town—is very reasonable for the price. ⊠ *Rue Al Basra,* ☎ *07/70–73–56. 37 rooms. No credit cards.*

Shopping

The medina's **Rue des Consuls** is a great place to shop for handicrafts and souvenirs: it's pedestrian-only, has a pleasant atmosphere, and imposes no real pressure to buy. Here you can find carpets, Berber jewelry, leather goods, wooden items, brass work, traditional clothing, slippers, and more. On Monday and Thursday mornings the entire street turns into a carpet market. For leather bags, wallets, and cases, go to the shop at Number 37; the affable owner, Abdelkader, speaks excellent English and can be trusted to bargain fairly. For carpets, try the shop with a birdcage outside, Number 200—it has a robust selection and will negotiate reasonable prices. You can peruse Zemour carpets (striped in white and burgundy) from Khémisset, near Meknes; deep-pile Rabati carpets, in predominantly blue-and-white designs; and orange, black, and white Glaoui carpets. Many of the larger shops take credit cards. In addition to the Rue des Consuls, the lower part of **Avenue Mohammed V** (Lugza), in the medina, is a good place to buy traditional Moroccan clothing.

For top-of-the-line leather jackets, try **Sedki** (⊠ 24, Avenue Mohammed V), on the right just after you leave the medina. Embroidered tablecloths and napkins are traditional Rabati crafts and make nice gifts; **Arts de Marrakech** (⊠ 387, Avenue Mohammed V), just beyond Sedki on the other side of the road, has a good selection.

Rabat is also a good place to get casual—if not necessarily high-fashion—Western clothes for men, women, and children at low prices, as this part of Morocco manufactures a good deal of clothing for export to Europe. **Casa Gallerie,** on Avenue Hassan II opposite Bab El Had, has a good selection at fixed prices.

Sports and Outdoor Activities

Royal Golf Dar es Salam. The most famous golf course in Morocco is on the road toward Romani, at the far edge of Souissi on the right. Designed by Robert Trent Jones, it's considered one of the 50 best courses in the world. There are two 18-hole courses and one nine-hole course in 162 verdant acres. ⊠ *Route de Zaers, Km 10,* ☎ *07/75–58–64.*

Oulmès

㉟ *136 km (85 mi) southeast of Rabat.*

Oulmès is about three hours' drive from Rabat and makes a pleasant excursion into the countryside, where, in contrast to the humid coast, the air is dry. If you're served a bottle of carbonated mineral water in any restaurant in Morocco, chances are it will have come from the **Lalla Haya spring** in Oulmès; Sidi Ali mineral water, one of the two major brands of still water, also originates here. From the hotel, walk down a winding track to see the warm springs—in which you can bathe—in their rocky gorge. Another walk from the hotel, a little farther to the left, brings you down to the river (the Oued Marrout) at a wider spot in the valley, from which you can ford to the beautiful hills opposite.

This countryside is particularly lovely in springtime, when the hills are green and wildflowers abound.

$$ ▥ **Hôtel Oulmès les Thermes.** This charming old-time hotel has held strong over the years. The high-ceilinged rooms are simple, with shower and sink but no toilet en suite. You look out on storks' nests or the rolling hills of Oulmès. The restaurant has a limited menu but prepares it very well; you'll typically have vegetable soup and roast beef or lamb, followed by crème caramel. Reservations are taken through Casablanca. To get here, turn right before the village of Oulmès. ✉ *Oulmès les Thermes,* ☎ *02/33–47–42,* ℻ *02/33–47–52. 42 rooms. Restaurant, bar. V.*

Rabat to Casablanca: The Beaches

㉑ *20 km (12 mi) southwest of Rabat, 71 km (44 mi) northeast of Casablanca.*

Just southwest of Rabat, toward Casablanca, is a series of attractive beaches. Temara also has the national zoo. If you're driving and happen to be here off season (from late September through June), this is a convenient and lovely place to spend the night.

The coastal road south from Rabat starts at the Kasbah des Oudayas. The first beach it passes is **Temara Plage,** a small, attractive bay beach. (A slightly faster and safer, but less scenic, way to get here is to take the autoroute toward Casablanca and exit at Temara.) Temara Plage is connected to the next beach, **Contrabandiers,** which is longer and has finer sand, by a walkway across the rocks. On the other side of the coastal road, roughly level with Contrabandiers but under some new, white, Spanish-style apartments is a **cave** with iron railings in front of it. There's no sign to identify the cave, but this site, known as Harhoura, is one of the earliest known sites of human habitation. A cast of the human skeletons found here is on display in Rabat's archaeological museum.

After Contrabandiers comes **Sables d'Or** (Sands of Gold), a bay with a picturesque harbor for fishing boats. Beyond this, after a private beach belonging to Morocco's royal family, is **Val d'Or** (Vale of Gold), the finest beach in this region. An island, which you can explore on foot at low tide, shelters the beach and forms a lagoon. Near the northern end of the beach, the lagoon's deep and sheltered water is perfect for swimming (except when the tide is lowest); at the other end is a sheltered bay with shallow water, ideal for small children. Beyond the hills—which sport a profusion of wildflowers in spring—is an open beach with dramatic breakers, intersected by the Ykem River. A dangerous undertow makes it unsafe to swim here. After this comes the **Plage Rose Marie,** which looks out on a rocky area in the sea; and finally, beyond the summer Royal Palace of Skhirat, the long, sandy **Skhirat Plage.** All beaches as far as Val d'Or are accessible by Bus 33 from Rabat, which departs from Bab El Had (except in summer, when—essentially to keep crowds away—it only goes as far as Sables d'Or). Rabat's petits taxis can't come out here, as the beaches are beyond the city limits.

Temara Zoo is just north of the town of Temara, slightly inland from Temara Plage. Originally formed around the royal collection of Atlas lions, the zoo has a commendable array of creatures, including panthers, giraffes, elephants, hippopotamuses, snakes, and gazelles. The bird collection, near the entrance, is particularly attractive, with golden pheasants, various parrots, and eagles, among other feathered specimens. Everything is laid out in pleasant gardens and costs almost nothing. Children will enjoy the boating lake and the bumper cars. If you're not driving, take Bus 17 from Rabat's Bab El Had to get here. ⊠ *R.P. 1, Km 8, Temara,* ☎ *07/74–12–59,* 🖾 *7DH.* ☉ *Mon.–Sat. 9:30– 6:30, Sun. and holidays 9–6:30; closing time earlier Oct.–Mar.*

Dining and Lodging

$$$$ ✕ **Le Provencal.** Before present-day Temara ever existed, this restaurant was a country inn; it's now surrounded by what is essentially a rather poor inland satellite town of Rabat. Still, Le Provencal succeeds in creating a rural French atmosphere, and although it's somewhat pricey compared to others of its kind, it serves excellent French cuisine, with an emphasis on fish dishes like *loup au fenouille* and *brochettes de lotte.* There's also a wide range of salads. If you like your prawns spicy, try *crevettes pil pil* (shrimp cooked slowly in oil so that a juice is created). ⊠ *Avenue Hassan II, Temara,* ☎ *07/74–11–11. AE, MC, V.*

$$$ ✕ **Le Miramar.** Sit outside on the terrace and let your eyes rest on the blue waters of the Atlantic; or in the winter, sit inside by a crackling fire. Either way you'll have fine seafood here; the *friture de poisson* is particularly good. ⊠ *Harhoura Plage, Temara,* ☎ *07/74–76–56. MC, V.*

$$ ✕ **San Francisco.** If you happen to come from northern California and are craving a fern bar, you might try this respectable replica, run by a man—Mr. Ziani—who has also established a Moroccan restaurant in California. The bar is downstairs, the restaurant upstairs; and the menu includes a range of international dishes, including paella, spaghetti, and, of all things, pancakes. The terrace has a sea view. ⊠ *Plages des Sables d'Or,* ☎ *07/74–45–60. No credit cards.*

$$$ 🏨 **Skhirat Beach.** With rooms opening directly onto the hotel's private sandy beach, this hotel is one of the finest in the area. The comfortable rooms have sliding glass doors and green bed covers. The gardens are pleasant, the pool is large, the food is good, and the whole place is well maintained. ⊠ *Route Rabat-Casablanca, Km 28, Skhirat Plage,* ☎ *07/ 74–27–27,* 🖾 *07/74–23–17. 220 rooms. Restaurant, pool. MC, V.*

$$$ 🏨 **Yasmine Club.** This new hotel is under the same ownership as the excellent Yasmine Hotel in Rabat. The rooms, arranged around a long, rectangular garden, are far more spacious than any in Rabat, and each even has a settee; the woodwork is finished in pink. Some rooms have a kitchenette (but no utensils). The bungalows, arranged around a pool, each have two rooms and a living room. The restaurant has a tremendous view over the rock pools and the ocean. ⊠ *Route Côtière de Rabat, Harhoura, Temara,* ☎ *07/64–13–52. 65 rooms, 40 bungalows, 4 suites. Restaurant, bar, snack bar, pool, tennis, bowling, nightclub, playground, 2 meeting rooms. MC, V.*

$$ 🏨 **Kasbah Club.** There's plenty of space here, both around the pool and on the seaside terrace, and plenty of scope in the surrounding area for horseback rides. The rooms are decorated with traditional handicrafts and vary in price according to view—those overlooking the sea are more expensive. ⊠ *Plage Rose Marie, Skhirat,* ☎ *07/74–91–16,*

FAX *07/74–91–35. 53 rooms, 2 suites. Restaurant, bar, snack bar, refrigerators, pool, hammam, massage, 2 tennis courts, horseback riding, nightclub. AE, DC, MC, V.*

$$ ⌐ **St Germain en Laye.** Overlooking the sea, the St Germain en Laye is an excellent buy in the fall, winter, or spring. The rooms, with white floor tiles, are furnished to a standard normally associated with much more expensive places. Try not to come here in July or August; it's unpleasantly crowded then and in any case is booked well in advance. ⊠ *Temara Plage, Temara,* ☎ *07/74–42–30,* FAX *07/74–48–50. 25 rooms. Restaurant, bar. DC, MC, V.*

CASABLANCA AND ENVIRONS

Morocco's French connection is most palpable in its most contemporary and, in many ways, most cosmopolitan city. Casablanca is by far the country's dominant commercial city, so if you're in Morocco on business you'll almost certainly be based here. If you have only a little time for excursions, head for the beach or the golf course at Mohammedia.

Casablanca

㉒ *91 km (57 mi) southwest of Rabat.*

True to its Spanish name—*casa blanca,* "white house," which, in turn, is Dar el Beida in Arabic—Casablanca is a conglomeration of white buildings. Known colloquially as Casa or El Beida, it moves at a faster pace than the rest of the kingdom. Since the present city was only founded in 1912, it's primarily modern and lacks the ancient monuments that resonate in Morocco's other major cities; but there are still some landmarks, including the famous Hassan II Mosque.

The earliest known settlement on this site was the port of Anfa, from which Berbers traded with Phoenicians and Carthaginians. Anfa started to grow in the 13th century, when the Berbers began trading with the Portuguese and Spanish, but in the 15th century the Portuguese destroyed the city in retaliation for Berber piracy, and in the 16th they named it Casa Branca. (Over the next century it became Dar el Beida, and finally Casablanca.) At the end of the 18th century the town was rebuilt under the Alaouite sultan Mohammed Ibn Abdellah and began trading with European ports once more. French General Hubert Lyautey's decision, at the beginning of the French Protectorate, to build the present-day harbor paved the way for a rapid urban expansion that continues to this day. In 1943 Casablanca hosted the famous Anfa conference of Franklin D. Roosevelt, Winston Churchill, and Charles de Gaulle, at which Morocco's Prince Moulay el Hassan was also present.

Casa is Morocco's most modern city, and various groups of people call it home: hardworking Berbers who came north from the Souss Valley to make their fortune; young bankers preparing to earn an MBA in the United States; older folks raised on French customs during the protectorate; pious Muslims who follow their religion closely; men and women of the world, living for the moment; wealthy businesspeople in the prestigious neighborhood called California; new and poor arrivals from the countryside, living in shanty towns; and thousands of others from all over the kingdom who have found jobs here. The city has its own stock exchange, and working hours tend to transcend the relaxed pace kept by the rest of Morocco. You'll find that dress is more or less indistinguishable from that of any European metropolis.

Numbers in the text correspond to numbers in the margin and on the Casablanca map.

A Good Walk

Starting from Place Nations Unis, the large open area in front of the Hyatt Regency, walk down Boulevard Houphouet Boigny toward the port. The street is lined with shops selling handicrafts. On the right you'll see the tomb of Sidi Belyout; just after this, turn right into the Boulevard des Almohades, which runs along the outside of the **old medina** ㉓. Entering the medina through the third entrance you pass, make a hairpin turn and walk back along the inside of the medina on Rue Al Bahriya, passing a typical medina mosque on your left. Farther along this street, you'll pass on your right a building that once housed the German consulate. A right turn after that will take you up to the shopping area that opens back out onto Place Nations Unis. Cross the road here, and keeping the Hyatt Regency on your right, continue along Avenue Hassan II until you reach the great **Place Mohammed V** ㉔. Farther along Avenue Hassan II on the right is the **Arab League Park** ㉕; pleasant shaded areas with cafés, where you can stop for a drink or an ice cream, are on either side of Boulevard Moulay Youssef, which intersects the park.

This is as far as you can reasonably go on foot. To continue, take a taxi to the **Hassan II Mosque** ㉖ on the coast. From here the coastal road leaves the port and passes the lighthouse, forming a strip known as the **Corniche** ㉗. From the Hassan II Mosque it's less than 1 km (½ mi) to the **Ensemble d'Artisanat** ㉘. Catch another taxi to finish your tour in the **Habbous** ㉙ neighborhood.

Sights to See

㉕ **Arab League Park.** This is the most substantial patch of green in the center of Casablanca. There are a children's amusement park on the far side of Boulevard Moulay Youssef (☞ 2DH) and, to the right of the amusement park, an avenue of tall palm trees. Casablanca's modern cathedral, built in 1930, is at the park's northwest corner.

㉗ **Corniche.** Get a feel for Casa's Atlantic setting by stopping at a Corniche café and basking in the sun and breeze. This is where the people of Casablanca go to relax—a seafront line of cafés, restaurants, and nightclubs, and a number of hotels. The Corniche goes on past a palace (home to resident Saudi Arabians) and a mosque to Aïn Diab, and finally to the tomb of Sidi Abderrahman, which is on a rock in the sea and accessible only at low tide.

㉘ **Ensemble d'Artisanat.** This handicrafts center is much like the Ensemble Artisanal in Rabat, albeit without the special setting. Here you can buy pottery, crafted wood, straw work, carpets, slippers, leatherwork, and handcrafted musical instruments in specialty shops, some of whose artisans create their wares in full view. ✉ 195, Boulevard de Bordeaux, Casablanca, ☎ 02/22–83–34. ☞ Free. ⊙ Daily, approximately 9–12:30 and 2:30–6.

㉙ **Habbous.** At the edge of the new medina, the Habbous is an attractive area built at the beginning of the 20th century in traditional style. Capped by traditional arches, its shops surround a pretty square with trees and flowers. As you enter the Habbous, you'll pass a building resembling a castle; this is the Pasha's Mahkama, or court. On the opposite side of the square is the Mohammed V Mosque—although not ancient, this and the Moulay Youssef Mosque, in the adjacent square, are among the finest examples of traditional Maghrebi (Moroccan) architecture in Casablanca. Look up at the minarets and you might recognize a style used in Marrakesh's Koutoubia Mosque and Seville's

Casablanca

Port

Bd. des Almohades

OLD MEDINA (23)

R. Zaïd ou Hmad

Pl. de Marrakesh

Pl. des Nations Unies

de l'Armée

C.T.M.

Bd. Moulay Abderrahmane

Bd. du Forbin

Bd. du Forbin

Av. de l'Ambassadeur

Bd. Mohammed V

Pl. Zellaga

Pl. Royale

Pl. Mirabeau

Av. Pasteur

Bd. Emile Zola

Bd. de Hassan II

Paris

Pl. Mohammed V (24)

Av. Lalla Yacout

R. Mohammed Smiha

R. Mohamed Diouri

Karatchi

Bd. Mohammed V

Rte. Guelta

Zemmour

Bd. Mohammed V

Bd. de la Résistance

Bd. Emile Zola

Bd. du 11 Janvier

Bd. de Khouribga

Pl. de la Victoire

R. Khattabi

Gare des Voyageurs

Av. de Mers Sultan

Bd. Rahal el Meskini

R. Hadi Amar Riffi

Bd. Ibn Tachfine

Rte. des Oulad

Bd. de la Gironde

Av. Hassan II

Mohamed Zerktouni

rond point d'Europe

Bd. de la

Pl. Dubreuil Lemalgre

Resistance

Rte. de Mediouna

Ziane

R. des Hôpitaux

R. de Ceuta

Av. du 2 Mars

R. de Rome

R. Ahmed el Figuigui

HABBOUS (29)

R. Tarik Ibnou Ziad

N

0   500 yards

0   500 meters

Giralda. Note also the fine wood carving over the door of the Mohammed V. The Habbous is well known as a center for Arabic books; most other shops are devoted to rich displays of traditional handicrafts. You can also buy traditional Moroccan clothes such as kaftans and *djellabas* (traditional long, hooded outer garments). Immediately north of the Habbous is Casablanca's Royal Palace. You can't go inside, but the outer walls are pleasing, their sandstone blocks fitted neatly together, and blend well with the little streets at the edge of the Habbous.

㉖ **Hassan II Mosque.** Casablanca's skyline is dominated by this massive edifice. No matter where you're staying, you're bound to see it from any upper floor thanks to its attention-grabbing green-tiled roof. Funded through public subscription, designed by a French architect, and built by a team of 35,000, the mosque went up between 1986 and 1993 and is now the third-largest mosque in the world, after the Haramain Mosque in Mecca and the Prophet's Mosque in Medina. Funded by public subscription, it was set in Casablanca primarily so that the largest city in the kingdom would have a monument worthy of its size. The building's foundations lie partly on land and partly in the sea, and at one point you can see the water through a glass floor. The main hall holds an astonishing 25,000 people and has a retractable roof so that it can be turned into a courtyard. The minaret is more than 650 ft high, and the mezzanine floor (which holds the women's section, about 6 ft above the main floor) seems dwarfed by the nearly 200-ft-high ceiling. Still, the ceiling's enormous painted decorations appear small and delicate from below. A eulogy to King Hassan II (written before he died, in July 1999, and was buried instead in Rabat's Mohammed V Mausoleum) is inscribed inside. If you fly out of Casablanca, try to get a window seat on the left for a good view of the mosque in relation to the city as a whole. ✉ *Boulevard de la Corniche,* ☎ *02/22–25–63.* 💴 *100DH.* ☉ *Guided tours Sat.–Thurs. 9, 10, 11, and 2 (all visits by guided tour only; times subject to change).*

㉓ **Old Medina.** The simple whitewashed houses of the medina, particularly those closest to the harbor, form an extraordinary contrast to Morocco's economic and commercial nerve center just a few hundred yards away. European consuls lived here in the 19th century, the early trading days, and there are still a youth hostel and a few very cheap hotels within. Near Place Nations Unis, a large conglomeration of shops sells watches, leather bags and jackets, shoes, crafted wood, and clothes, but the proximity of the Hyatt Regency makes negotiating a deal somewhat harder than usual.

㉔ **Place Mohammed V.** This is Casablanca's version of London's Trafalgar Square: It has an illuminated fountain, lots of pigeons, and a series of impressive buildings facing it. Coming from the port, you'll pass the main post office on your right, and on your left as you enter the square is its most impressive building, the courthouse. On the other side of Avenue Hassan II from the post office is the ornate Bank Al Maghrib; the structure opposite, with the clock tower, is the Wilaya, the governor's office. The more modest buildings on the right side of the square house the notorious directorate of the customs (where importers' appeals against punitive taxes stand little chance). To avoid confusion, note that Place Mohammed V was formerly called Place Nations Unis and vice versa, and the old names still appear on some maps.

Dining and Lodging

$$$$ ✕ **A Ma Bretagne.** This restaurant is quite far out of town, on the coast toward Sidi Abderrahman, but it's worth a trip for the finest French provincial cuisine. You can dine indoors or in a light and airy atrium overlooking the ocean. The menu centers around fish and shellfish—

the prawns make an excellent starter, and the grilled fish is particularly good. ⊠ *Blvd. Océan Atlantique, Sidi Abderrahman,* ☎ *02/39–79–79. DC, MC, V.*

$$$$ ✕ **Al-Mounia.** Come to this large Moroccan restaurant if you want to try the national dishes, such as couscous or tagine, in cosmopolitan Casablanca. You can dine in air-conditioned rooms with typically Moroccan decor or on the outdoor terrace under a hundred-year-old tree. ⊠ *95, Rue Prince Moulay Abdellah,* ☎ *02/22–26–69. AE, DC, MC, V. Closed Sun.*

$$$$ ✕ **Le Cabestan.** Look down from a window seat onto blue rock pools
★ as you savor a delicious fish dish like *sifflets de Saint-Pierre* (small John Dory), *choucroute crèmeuse au genièvre* (creamy pickled cabbage with juniper), or *pavé de saumon frais* (fillet of fresh salmon). To wind down, you might have *tarte fine caramélisée aux pommes d'oulmès* (caramelized apple tart). This is French cuisine at its best, with fabulous sauces, and it's served in a great location near the lighthouse on the Corniche. ⊠ *Phare d'El Hank, La Corniche,* ☎ *02/39–11–90. DC, MC, V. Closed Sun.*

$$$ ✕ **Don Camillo.** Run by an Italian in the Derb Omar area—Casa's Berber-dominated trading center—this authentic restaurant offers good value in a friendly ambience. The menu is ample; in addition to Italian specialties such as *escalopes Milanese* (i.e., thin slices of meat or fish in bread crumbs and Parmesan), ravioli, and other pastas, you can opt for prawns, fish, and *mechoui d'onions* (roast lamb with onions). ⊠ *15, Rue Abou Rakrak,* ☎ *02/31–16–44. MC, V.*

$$$ ✕ **Golden China.** Try this centrally located, award-winning restaurant for Chinese gastronomy in a typically Chinese setting. ⊠ *12, Rue El Oraibi Jilali,* ☎ *02/27–35–26. MC, V.*

$$$ ✕ **L'Entrecôte.** Reasonably close to the center of town, L'Entrecôte serves a good variety of traditional French cuisine. ⊠ *78, Avenue Mers Sultan,* ☎ *02/27–26–74. DC, MC, V.*

$$$ ✕ **Restaurant du Port.** Tucked inside the port, this is perhaps Casablanca's best-known fish restaurant and as such gets rather crowded at lunchtime. The fried fish is particularly good at any time of day. To get here, enter the fishing port by the gate near the train station and turn left toward the fishing port. ⊠ *Port de Pêche,* ☎ *02/31–85–61. MC, V.*

$$ ✕ **Le Dauphin.** Decorated in a marine style, the popular Dolphin is a good alternative to its pricier counterparts for all fish and seafood dishes. You'll find it on the left side of the boulevard leading to the port station; the entrance is around the back. ⊠ *115, Boulevard Félix Houphouet Boigny,* ☎ *02/22–12–00. DC, MC, V. Closed Sun.*

$$$$ ▥ **Hyatt Regency.** Casablanca's most conspicuous hotel occupies a large site next to Place Nations Unis and is popular with Americans. Waiters in the Casablanca bar are dressed as the characters in the movie of that name, and the one presently cast as Humphrey Bogart bears a striking resemblance to his namesake. The luxurious rooms are furnished in wine red, and some have four-poster beds. Dining options are plenty: Asian, Mediterranean, Moroccan, international, and poolside. ⊠ *Place Mohammed V,* ☎ *02/26–12–34,* ℻ *02/22–01–80. 214 rooms and 37 suites. 5 restaurants, bar, pool, hammam, massage, sauna, dance club, meeting rooms, business services. AE, DC, MC, V.*

$$$$ ▥ **Royal Mansour Meridien.** Overhauled by the architect and decorator Micheline Lefebvre, the Royal Mansour can now claim to be the best hotel in Casablanca. At the very least, its service and attention to guests have no equal here, and all rooms have double-glazed windows and overlook either the port or the Avenue des Forces Royales. Decor varies by floor—some rooms have blue walls and light-color bedspreads and curtains, others have pastel walls accented by deep blue.

The floors are thickly carpeted. The traditional Moroccan restaurant is decorated like a typical Moroccan house on one side, a Moroccan tent on the other; breakfast is served in an attractive indoor garden. The health and fitness center is one of the most comprehensive in the country. ⊠ 27, Avenue des Forces Armées Royales, ☎ 02/30–31–11, FAX 02/29–55–08. 159 rooms, 23 suites. 2 restaurants, 3 bars, air-conditioning, in-room safes, beauty salon, hammam, massage, 2 saunas, exercise room, business services, meeting rooms, airport shuttle, car rental, parking (fee). AE, DC, MC, V.

$$$$ 🏨 **Safir.** The Safir is considerably less expensive than the other hotels in this price range, and with a 50% discount for business travelers it drops into a different category altogether. It has a nicely tiled lobby, provides bathrobes in the guest rooms, and serves generous buffet breakfasts. ⊠ 160, Avenue des Forces Armées Royales, Casablanca, ☎ 02/31–12–12, FAX 02/31–65–14. 310 rooms, 12 suites. 3 restaurants, pool, massage, sauna, cabaret, nightclub, meeting room, parking (fee). AE, DC, MC, V.

$$$$ 🏨 **Sheraton.** Casablanca's Sheraton has an impressive lobby and a mezzanine bar area with a high ceiling dangling pendant lamps. It's entirely convenient to the business district, including most airline offices. Rooms are tastefully furnished in pink and gray. The restaurants include Japanese and French cuisines, and banquet service is sumptuous. ⊠ 100, Avenue des Forces Armées Royales, ☎ 02/31–78–78, FAX 02/31–51–36. 275 rooms, 31 suites. 4 restaurants, 2 bars, in-room safes, no-smoking rooms, pool, beauty salon, massage, squash, nightclub, meeting rooms. AE, DC, MC, V.

$$$ 🏨 **El Kandara.** Close to the Idou Anfa (☞ below), El Kandara offers a similar range of facilities and is a good alternative when its neighbor is fully booked. ⊠ 44, Boulevard Anfa, ☎ 02/26–29–37, FAX 02/22–06–17. 213 rooms. 4 restaurants, bar, sauna, nightclub, meeting rooms. AE, DC, MC, V.

$$$ 🏨 **Idou Anfa.** The Idou Anfa is known as an excellent business hotel and is often fully booked, so you need to reserve in advance. The food is very good and the meeting-room service impeccable. The small pool is slightly elevated, approached by a spiral staircase. ⊠ 85 Boulevard Anfa, ☎ 02/20–02–35, FAX 02/20–00–29. 207 rooms, 13 suites. 2 restaurants, bar, pool, meeting rooms. AE, DC, MC, V.

$$ 🏨 **Ibis Moussafir.** The Ibis is right next to the Casablanca Voyageurs train station, which makes it very convenient when you're arriving from the airport in the evening or going to the airport in the early morning (there are shuttle trains to and fro). Service is excellent, and, as at Morocco's other Ibis hotels, you get a particularly good breakfast for your money. Furnished in a pleasing blue-and-white style, the rooms are simple but pleasant. The hotel is often full, so reserve in advance. ⊠ Avenue Ba Hmad, Place de la Gare–Casa Voyageurs, ☎ 02/40–19–84, FAX 02/40–07–99. 97 rooms. Restaurant, bar. AE, MC, V.

$ 🏨 **Hôtel du Centre.** Opposite the entrance to the Royal Mansour is this budget option with clean rooms and a central location. You won't get the perks of the luxe lodging across the street, but at less than 10% of the price, who's complaining? ⊠ Avenue des Forces Armées Royales at Rue Sidi Balyout, ☎ 02/44–61–80, FAX 02/44–61–78. 34 rooms. No credit cards.

Shopping

Casa has three good places to shop for souvenirs and handicrafts: **Boulevard Houphouet Boigny** by the port, the **Ensemble d'Artisanat,** and the shops in the **Habbous.** Of these, the Habbous probably offers the best variety and prices, but you should still try to get an idea of the market prices before starting to bargain.

Casablanca also prides itself on fashionable Western clothing. The name of a small women's boutique in the Gautier district says it all: **AT751** (✉ 42, Avenue Hassan Souktani), the number of a daily flight from Paris to Casablanca. There are some other stores around the central port area, such as those in **Centre 2000,** next to the station, but the **Maarif** area, west of Boulevard Brahim Roudani, has a pedestrian street, two large shopping centers, and ultimately a greater selection.

Mohammedia

③⓪ *25 km (16 mi) northeast of Casablanca, 66 km (41 mi) southwest of Rabat.*

Mohammedia is basically a satellite town of Casablanca, housing many a commuter. It also happens to be Morocco's oil port. For the traveler its main attractions are an excellent golf course, a good restaurant, and a beach.

The **Royal Golf de Mohammedia** (☎ 03/32–46–56) is laid out between sea pines, eucalyptus trees, acacias, and oleanders. Par is 72 for 18 holes totaling 19,407 ft. To find it, take the Mohammedia exit from the autoroute and inquire when you get to the traffic circle (it's close by).

Dining and Lodging

$$$ ✕ **Restaurant du Port.** People come from outside Mohammedia to eat fish and other seafood here. Located right near the port, the restaurant is appropriately decorated in a nautical theme. The *crevettes au gratin* is particularly good. ✉ *1, Rue du Port,* ☎ *03/32–24–66. MC, V. Closed Mon.*

$$$ 🏨 **Sabah.** Mohammedia's only hotel in this class, the Sabah offers spacious, carpeted rooms and friendly service. The international restaurant looks out on the sea. ✉ *1, Rue du Port,* ☎ *03/32–14–51,* 𝐅𝐀𝐗 *03/ 32–14–54. 84 rooms. 2 restaurants, bar, hammam, meeting room. DC, MC, V.*

EL JADIDA TO SAFI

To drive from Casablanca to El Jadida, you can either take the coastal road (accessible by Boulevard d'Anfa) or the inland road (accessible by the autoroute from Rabat). The Cornice road also joins the coastal route eventually. Halfway between Casablanca and El Jadida, you can stop at Bir Jdid and grab a brochette from one of many little restaurants that line the road on both sides. Fifteen kilometers (9 miles) north of El Jadida, you'll cross the River Oum-er-Rbia and see on your right the white houses of the village of Azemmour atop the golden walls of the cliff. Just before entering El Jadida, you'll pass through an attractive forest of eucalyptus, fir, and pine trees.

El Jadida and Safi retain some Portuguese flavors from their 16th- and 17th-century occupations, and El Oualidia is a delightful natural distraction as you head south toward Morocco's finest resorts.

El Jadida

③① *99 km (62 mi) southwest of Casablanca.*

El Jadida's new town has a large, sandy bay and a promenade lined with palm trees and cafés. The name El Jadida actually means "the New" and has alternated more than once with the town's original Portuguese name, Mazagan. The Portuguese arrived here in 1502, built a fortress, and stayed until 1769, when they left to found Mazagão in Brazil after this Moroccan version was recaptured by the Sultan Sidi Mohammed ben Abdellah. In the interim, Mazagan was a thriving commercial center, busily exporting poultry to Portugal. (Doukkala, the province that contains El Jadida, is still known for its rural turkeys.) In the early 19th century, Moulay Abd er Rahman moved a large number of Jews here from Azzemour; he introduced the name El Jadida in 1815. The French reinstated the name Mazagan during the protectorate, and upon independence in 1956, El Jadida became current again.

To see El Jadida's attractions—about half a day's diversion—drive south along the coastal road until you see a sign pointing to the **Cité Portugaise,** where you can park opposite the entrance; or take a small white taxi there. The Portuguese city was originally a rectangular island with a bastion on each corner, connected to the mainland by a single causeway. Take the entrance on the right. You'll see that the original Portuguese street names have been retained, with the contemporary ones written underneath. Walk down Rua da Carreira (Rue Mohamed Al Achemi) and you'll see on the left the old **Portuguese church,** Our Lady of the Assumption, built in 1628 with a roof from the French period. At press time archaeological excavations had the church closed in preparation for its possible conversion to a festival hall; but you may be able to take a peek by inquiring at the Portuguese cistern (☞ *below*). Beyond the church, a small theater is under construction; behind it is a fine old **mosque** with a minaret dating from Portuguese times.

Farther along Rua da Carreira on the left is the old **Portuguese cistern,** where water was stored when El Jadida was the fortress of Mazagan (some say the cistern originally stored arms). A small amount of water remains to reflect the cistern's Gothic arches, a lovely effect. Parts of Orson Welles's famously low-budget *Othello* were filmed here. The cistern was not rediscovered until 1916, when a Moroccan Jew stumbled on it in the process of enlarging his shop—whereupon water started gushing in. ⊠ *Rua da Carreira.* 🎟 *10DH.* ⊙ *Daily 9–1 and 3–6:30.*

Continuing along the *rua,* you'll pass the simple, yellow-stone **Spanish church** (so called locally, despite having no real connection with Spain) on your left. At the end of the street you can walk up stairs to the walls of the **fortress.** Looking down, you'll see a gate that leads directly onto the sea and, to the right, El Jadida's **fishing harbor.** Walk around the walls to the other side of the fortress and you can look down on the **Jewish cemetery.**

Dining and Lodging

$$ ✕ **Ali Baba.** On the left side of the coastal road into El Jadida, Ali Baba overlooks the sea and has a bright, airy ambience. The chef is French, and the focus is seafood. ⊠ *Route Principale 8,* ☎ *03/34–16–22. MC, V.*

$$ ✕ **El Khaima.** Signposted on the left as you enter El Jadida from the north, this standard restaurant serves pizzas, seafood such as prawns and friture de poisson, and salads. ⊠ *Avenue des Nations Unis,* ☎ *03/34–16–03. No credit cards.*

$$ ✕ **Restaurant le Tit.** Commendable for its old-fashioned, thick-sauce French cuisine, Le Tit is the only restaurant of its kind in the city center. Turn off the coastal road on Avenue el Jaich el Malaki; the restaurant is on the first inland road parallel to the seafront, just before the square with the post office. ⊠ *2, Avenue Jamia Al Arabia,* ☎ *03/34–39–08. No credit cards.*

$$$$ 🏨 **Royal Golf.** The Royal Golf is a luxury hotel with large, well-appointed rooms. Views take in the lush green of the golf-course fairways, surrounded by trees; the Atlantic waves on the beach; or both. One of the restaurants serves traditional Moroccan cuisine, while the other two are international. The hotel is north of El Jadida, on the right as you

drive south, signposted GOLF from the Casablanca direction only. It's out of the range of El Jadida *petits taxis*, but you can charter a *grand taxi*. ✉ *Route de Casablanca, Km 7, B.P. 116,* ☎ *03/35–41–41,* FAX *03/35–34–75. 100 rooms, 7 suites. 3 restaurants, bar, refrigerators, 2 pools, beauty salon, hammam, massage, sauna, golf, tennis courts, exercise room, nightclub. AE, DC, MC, V.*

$$ 🏨 **Doukkala Abou Al Jadayel.** Rooms in this large hotel have balconies overlooking the beach, so the pleasing sound of breaking waves is constantly audible. They're furnished in novel designs incorporating *zellij*, traditional Moroccan tiling in patterns of blue, white, and green. On Saturday night the sounds of a highly amplified Moroccan band can imperil your sleep, so ask for a room away from the nightclub. The hotel is on the right as you enter El Jadida from the north. ✉ *Route Principal El Jadida,* ☎ *03/34–37–37,* FAX *03/34–05–01. 81 rooms. Restaurant, bar, nightclub. MC, V.*

$$ 🏨 **Palais Andalous.** The Palais Andalous is in fact a converted palace, and is remarkable for its elaborate decorations of intricately carved plaster. The rooms, which can seem rather somber (light only comes in through windows facing the courtyard) are reached by a long staircase ornamented with *zellij* and face the central courtyard, which centers around a fountain. ✉ *Boulevard Docteur de Lanouy,* ☎ *03/34–37–45,* FAX *03/35–16–90. 27 rooms. MC, V.*

En Route To leave El Jadida in the direction of El Oualidia, follow the sign to Jorf Laser. Jorf Laser itself is the site of a chemical plant responsible for serious pollution in this region. After this, the coastal road becomes more scenic, passing fertile fields and lagoons.

El Oualidia

㉜ *89 km (55 mi) southwest of El Jadida. From El Jadida, follow sign to Jorf Laser.*

As you enter El Oualidia you'll see salt pans at the end of a lagoon. This town is famous for its oysters, and if you visit the oyster parks, you can sit right down and eat them after learning how they're cultivated. (Oyster Park 7 is best.) Turn right in the center of town to reach the beach. El Oualidia's bay must be one of the most beautiful places on Morocco's entire Atlantic coast. The fine, whitish sand is gently lapped by the calm turquoise waters of the lagoon, and in the distance you can see the white breakers of the sea. The beach is surrounded by a promontory to the south, a gap where the sea enters the lagoon, an island, and another promontory to the north. Around the corner is a beach that seems wholly untouched: sandy bays and dunes bearing tufts of grass alternate with little rocky hills. Gentle waves make the lagoon a good place to learn surfing; experienced surfers will find waves to their liking on the straightforward Atlantic beaches south of town.

Dining and Lodging

$ ✕🏨 **Motel Restaurant à l'Araignée Gourmande.** This motel has sea views and is a good place to eat at reasonable prices even if you're not staying overnight. The lobster is, of course, more expensive than anything else on the menu, but it's superb here. The rooms are less exquisite, but they're perfectly adequate if you want to combine dining and lodging. ✉ *Oualidia Plage,* ☎ *03/36–61–44. 15 rooms. No credit cards.*

$$ 🏨 **L'hippocampe.** This family-run hotel overlooks the lagoon, offer-
★ ing direct access to the beach, and its rooms are arranged around a lovely garden. The staff can easily organize a boat trip on the lagoon, possibly combined with a bracing walk on the northern promontory from the tomb of Sidi Daoud. Two new and impressive suites overlook the sea (one on either side of the sea-view restaurant) and have

particularly spiffy bathrooms and private terraces with table and chairs. *Demi-pension* (half board) is compulsory—breakfast and one other meal are included in the room rate. ✉ *Oualidia Plage*, ☎ *03/36–61–08*, 𝔽𝔸𝕏 *03/36–64–61. 21 rooms, 2 suites. Restaurant, bar, pool in summer.*

En Route   The coastal road from El Oualidia to Safi has magnificent views, especially in spring, when the wildflowers are out. Just off the wild beach about 28 km (17 mi) south of El Oualidia, a **koubba** is built on a rock in such a way that it's only accessible at low tide. Some of the cliffs here are truly magnificent, reminiscent of the Atlantic coast of Ireland. **Plage Lalla Fatma,** 16 km (10 mi) before Safi, is a wonderful discovery, a pristine, empty patch of orange-gold sand beneath rocky cliffs.

Safi

③③ *69 km (43 mi) southwest of El Oualidia, 157 km (98 mi) southwest of El Jadida, 129 km (80 mi) north of Essaouira.*

Safi (Asfi, in Arabic) used to be a fishing port for sardines, but the sardines have since been killed off by pollution from the chemical factory in Jorf Laser, south of town. Despite the industrial presence, however, Safi's **old town** retains its charm. The Place de l'Indépendance is next to the medina, and the medina itself is bisected by a street lined with shops. On the ocean side of the square is the **Dar el Bahr** (House of the Sea), a 16th-century Portuguese castle.

A few kilometers inland, and best reached by car or taxi, is the **National Ceramic Museum,** housed in a large, old Portuguese fort. Displays present Morocco's various native pottery styles, such as refined blue pieces from Fez and Safi's own pottery (made of red clay and finished in white, black, and green or turquoise and black), including some fine pieces by the renowned master Ahmed Serghini. From the walls of the old fort you have an excellent view of the city, and to the north you can look down onto the **potters' hill,** its clay kilns an attractive pinkish color.

Walk down the hill to the north of the fortress until you come to the **shops** at the foot of the potters' hill. In shop Number 7 you can buy works from the school of Ahmed Serghini; ask to see the room with the most precious pieces. The pottery sold in all these shops is an excellent buy compared to what it would cost elsewhere in the kingdom; attractive turquoise bowls, for example, can be had for around 30DH. The clay kilns of the potters' hill surround a **koubba**; wander around and you'll see the different stages of a pot's creation, from throwing to firing to painting to glazing. 💰 *10DH.* ☉ *Daily 8:30–6.*

Dining and Lodging

$$ ✕ **La Trattoria.** North of Safi, just beyond the potters' hill, this Italian restaurant serves pizzas, fish, and other seafood in a pleasant Mediterranean atmosphere. ✉ *Rue Aouinate*, ☎ *04/62–09–59. DC, MC, V.*

$$ ✕ **Refuge Sidi Bouzid.** On the coast a little north of Safi, this is a reliable place for a seafood meal. ✉ *Sidi Bouzid*, ☎ *04/46–43–54. No credit cards.*

$$$ 🏨 **Hotel Safir.** This hotel has a pleasant terrace with a commanding view over the city of Safi. The rooms are spacious, pastel in hue, and furnished with a small settee in an alcove. Facilities are ample, including a playground for kids. ✉ *Avenue Zerktouni*, ☎ *04/46–42–99*, 𝔽𝔸𝕏 *04/ 46–45–73. 86 rooms, 4 suites. Restaurant, bar, snack bar, pool, nightclub, playground, meeting room. No credit cards.*

$$ 🛏 **Assif.** The Assif is nicely painted and quiet. The rooms are substantial, and the suite with a double bed and two child-size beds is ideal for a family. To get here, follow a series of yellow signs from the traffic circle by the ceramics museum. ✉ *Avenue de la Liberté, Plateau Safi, B.P. 151,* ☎ *04/62–29–40,* 🖷 *04/62–18–62. 62 rooms. Restaurant, tea shop, conference room. MC, V.*

$$ 🛏 **Atlantide.** Once a grande dame, the Atlantide is currently being restored to some of its former glory. The dining room is palatial, recalling perhaps a lodging on a Swiss lake; and the large rooms have high ceilings. A large swimming pool is in the works. ✉ *Rue Chawki, Safi,* ☎ *04/46–21–60,* 🖷 *04/46–45–95. 40 rooms, 2 suites. Restaurant, bar. AE, MC, V.*

RABAT, CASABLANCA, AND THE NORTHERN ATLANTIC COAST A TO Z

Arriving and Departing

By Bus

Buses are fine for trips from Larache to Rabat and from Casablanca to El Jadida or Safi. For Asilah and Larache to Rabat, make sure the bus will take the autoroute; the alternative route, via Souk el Arba, is much longer.

By Car

Much of the highway from Rabat to Fez is freeway now, and a freeway is under construction from Casablanca to Settat (en route to Marrakesh). The road from El Jadida to Marrakesh is pleasantly light on traffic.

By Plane

From overseas, Casablanca's Mohammed V Airport is the best gateway to Morocco itself: you're greeted by a beautifully decorated and well-maintained arrivals hall, efficient and courteous staff, and a trouble-free continuation of your journey by train or car. The banks here change money and traveler's checks at exactly the same exchange rate used everywhere else in the country, and the cash machine accepts Visa and MasterCard. Trains connect the airport to the national network from 7:35 AM to 10:30 PM, and taxis are available to the city of Casablanca at relatively expensive but fixed rates. **Royal Air Maroc** (☎ 02/31–41–41) flies daily between Casablanca and Fez, Marrakesh, Tangier, and Agadir, less frequently to Al Hoceima, Dakhla, Essaouira, Laayoune, Nador, Ouarzazate, and Tetouan. There are weekly flights from Rabat to Tetouan. **Regional Air Lines** (☎ 02/53–80–80) flies daily from Casablanca to Agadir, Laayoune, Oujda, and Tangier and from Rabat to Oujda and Agadir.

By Train

Rabat is three hours by train from Meknes (five trains daily), four hours from Fez (five trains daily), and four hours from Marrakesh (six trains daily). All of these trains also call at Casablanca. In addition, there are overnight trains from Casablanca and Rabat to Oujda, and two direct trains daily to Tangier, which also have bus connections from an intermediate stop (just before Asilah) to Tetouan.

Getting Around

By Bus

In Casablanca, the **C.T.M.** bus station (✉ 23, Rue Léon l'Africain, ☎ 02/45–80–80) is right next to the Sheraton and by far the most convenient, since the other stations are on the outskirts of town. In Larache, El Jadida, and Safi one station (Gare Routière) serves all the bus companies and the grands taxis. The bus station in Rabat is on the outskirts of the city en route to Casablanca, in a neighborhood known as Kamara; from there you can take a taxi or a city bus (Number 17 or 30) into town. Some of the buses coming from the north stop just after crossing the river from Salé; you may want to hop off here, as you're closer to Rabat than you will be in Kamara. You can then hail a cab the old-fashioned way.

By Car
If your stay in this region is limited to Casablanca and Rabat, you won't need a car at all. You're much better off taking the train between the two (or between either one and another major city) and using *petits taxis* within the cities. If, however, your aim is to relax in small coastal towns like Moulay Bousselham and El Oualidia, a car is far more useful than the slow and complicated public transportation to those places.

Within Casablanca, there's something to be said for using the red petits taxis even if you have a car. Traffic in this city is very hard to contend with, and the streets are hard for newcomers to navigate. A car is most useful here for cruising the Corniche road by the sea.

If you're driving, use the toll freeways from Larache to Rabat and Rabat to Casablanca whenever possible, as they're both quicker and safer than all other roads (note, however, that the new freeway from Larache to Rabat may not be marked on your Moroccan map yet). A freeway from Casablanca to El Jadida is in the works, but in the meantime take special care on the existing road, as it's one of the most dangerous—that is, one of the craziest—in the kingdom. Roads in this region are generally good, though signposting for places within cities can be inconsistent.

By Taxi
In Casablanca, Rabat, and most other cities in this region, the individual petits taxis (red in Casa, blue in Rabat) are plentiful, metered, and inexpensive. When a train arrives at the Casablanca Port and Rabat-Agdal train stations, taxi drivers tend to wait until they can fill the car with three people going to similar destinations.

Despite being cramped, the large, shared *grands taxis* are useful for short intercity journeys, such as Rabat to Salé, Temara, or Bouknadel or Casablanca to El Jadida.

By Train
The major train-accessible destinations in this region are Asilah, Kenitra, Salé, Rabat, and Casablanca. Casablanca has two stations: Casablanca Port, downtown, and Casablanca Voyageurs, for through trains between Marrakesh, Fez, and Rabat. The two are reasonably close together, and all trains from the airport call at both. Rabat also has two stations: Rabat-Agdal, on the outskirts of town toward Casablanca, and Rabat-Ville, closer to the majority of hotels and attractions. In Asilah the station is slightly out of town, so you'll need to take a petit taxi into the town proper. Although El Jadida and Safi have stations, trains arrive only once a day, at inconvenient times.

There is an excellent shuttle service almost hourly between Casablanca Port, Rabat, and Kenitra, and even more frequently at the beginning and end of the day. This is by far the best way to move between Rabat and Casablanca.

Contacts and Resources

Car Rental

Casablanca's airport is a good place to rent a car, as agencies are grouped together here (☞ Car Rental *in* Smart Travel Tips). There as also numerous agencies in downtown Casa and Rabat. Some recommendations: **First Car International** (✉ 157, Boulevard Hassan Seghir, Casablanca, ☎ 02/31–87–88, FAX 02/30–15–05). **Renaissance Car** (✉ 3, Rue El Bakri, Boulevard Mohammed V, Casablanca, ☎ 02/30–03–01, FAX 02/31–44–02). **Visacar** (✉ 9, Rue Bait Lahm, Rabat, ☎ 07/70–13–58, FAX 07/70–14–53).

Consulates

United Kingdom (✉ 43, Boulevard Anfa, Casablanca, ☎ 02/22–17–41, FAX 02/26–57–79). **United States** (✉ 8, Boulevard Moulay Youssef, Casablanca, ☎ 02/26–45–50, FAX 02/20–41–27). For embassies in Rabat, *see* Embassies *in* Smart Travel Tips.

Cybercafés

There are plenty of cybercafés in Rabat (mainly in Agdal) and Casablanca. Two of the most convenient for retrieving your E-mail: **Cyberplanete** (✉ 23, Rue d'Alger, next to Ennakhil Hotel, Rabat, ☎ 07/70–41–72). **Mondial Net** (✉ Centre Allal Ben Abdellah, 47, Rue Allal Ben Abdellah, behind Sheraton, Casablanca, ☎ 02/48–04–80).

Emergencies

Police: 19. Fire: 15. Physicians: **S.O.S. Médecins** (✉ Casablanca, ☎ 02/44–44–44; ✉ Rabat, ☎ 07/20–20–20). Clinics: **Clinique Badr** (✉ 35, Rue El Allousi, opposite Badr Mosque, Bourgoune, Casablanca, ☎ 02/49–28–00). **Clinique de la Tour Hassan** (✉ Rue Idriss Al Azhar, Rabat, ☎ 07/72–22–32).

Guided Tours

Guided tours of several cities in this region are best reserved in your home country. Generally speaking, you can't buy a place on a local guided tour upon arrival the way you can in many other countries. For customized tours, try **Afric Voyages** in Rabat (☞ Travel Agencies, *below*; ☎ 07/70–96–46). An individual guide for Rabat or Casablanca can easily be arranged through your hotel.

Houses of Worship

JEWISH

Beth-El Temple (✉ 67, Rue Verlet-Nanus, Casablanca). **Téhila le David Synagougue** (✉ Boulevard du Onze Janvier, Casablanca). **Bennarrosh and Em-Habanime synagogues** (✉ Rue Ibn Rochd, Casablanca). **Talmud Torah Synagogue** (✉ 9, Boulevard Moulay Ismael, Rabat, ☎ 07/72–45–04).

MUSLIM

Moulay Youssef Mosque (✉ Habbous, Casablanca). **Djemâa ech Chleuh Mosque** (✉ Medina, Casablanca). **Sunna Mosque** (✉ 1, Avenue Mohammed V, Rabat). There are numerous other mosques in Rabat's medina. With the exception of Casablanca's Hassan II, non-Muslims are not allowed to enter mosques in Morocco.

PROTESTANT

Anglican Church (✉ 24, Rue Guedj, Casablanca, ☎ 02/25–31–71). **Protestant Church** (✉ 33, Rue d'Azilal, Casablanca, ☎ 02/30–21–51). **Protestant Church** (✉ 44, Avenue Allal Ben Abdellah, Rabat, ☎ 07/72–38–48).

Anfa Church (✉ 13, Avenue Jeanne d'Arc, Casablanca, ☎ 02/36–19–
13). **Our Lady of Lourdes Church** (✉ Rond Point d'Europe, Casablanca,
☎ 02/26–57–98). **St. Francis of Assisi Church** (✉ 2, Rue Hsaine Ran-
dam, Casablanca). **St. Peter's Cathedral** (✉ Sahat Al Joulan, Rabat,
☎ 07/72–23–01).

Sports and Outdoor Activities

GOLF

The **Royal Golf Dar Es Salam** in Rabat is the best course in the country, and the royal golf courses at Mohammedia and El Jadida are also
good (☞ *above*).

SURFING

There are good beaches for surfing at Skhirat and around El Oualidia.
Surfland (✉ B.P. 40, Oualidia, El Jadida, ☎ FAX 03/36–61–10), a surfing school in El Oualidia, runs surfing holidays, including English-speaking instructors and camping accommodations for both adults and
children. Surfers staying elsewhere can join up without a reservation
if there's enough space.

Travel Agencies

There are numerous travel agencies in downtown Casablanca and
Rabat. **Menara Tours** (✉ 119, Rue Chenier, Casablanca, ☎ 02/22–52–
32, FAX 02/22–51–99), in Casablanca, is particularly good; it's on the
left on the street next to Wafabank, opposite the Hyatt Regency on
Place Nations Unis. **Afric Voyages** (✉ 28, Avenue Allal Ben Abdellah,
Rabat, ☎ 07/70–96–47, FAX 07/70–46–28) is a standout in Rabat; to
find it, go down Avenue Moulay Hassan past Royal Air Maroc (which
is opposite the train station) and turn left on Allal Ben Abdellah.

Visitor Information

Tourist offices: **Casablanca** (✉ 55, Rue Omar Slaoui, ☎ 02/27–11–
77 or 27–95–33; Syndicat d'Initiative et de Tourisme, ✉ 98, Boulevard Mohammed V, ☎ 02/22–15–24 or 27–05–38). **Rabat** (✉ 22, Avenue d'Alger, ☎ 07/73–05–62 or 72–79–17; Syndicat d'Initiative et de
Tourisme, ✉ Rue Patrice Lumumba, ☎ no phone). **Safi** (Rue Imam
Malek, ☎ 04/62–24–96).

6 MARRAKESH

Part Berber, part Arab, part African, Marrakesh is the heartbeat of Morocco. Marked by dramatic contrasts and infused with sensuality, it's a place where palaces and monuments of unrivaled refinement sit calmly alongside the snake charmers and Gnaouan drums pulsing constantly from Djemâa el Fna—the most exuberant marketplace in the world.

Pamela Windo

PEARL OF THE SOUTH, Jewel of the South, The Rose City—just a few of the nicknames this desert city has acquired over the years. The pearl and the jewel symbolize Marrakesh's importance as the center of Morocco ever since it was a trading and resting place on the crossroads of ancient caravan routes from Timbuktu. The rose attests to a city still painted entirely in salmon pink, in keeping with the red-clay earth below. Once called Morocco City by foreign travelers, Marrakesh eventually lent its name to the country itself.

Virtually unchanged since the Middle Ages, Marrakesh's solid salmon-pink ramparts encircle and protect its mysterious labyrinthine medina, which hides sultans' palaces, the ornate mansions of rich merchants, and some of the most colorful bazaars in the Arab world. Lying low and dominating the Haouz Plain at the foot of the snowcapped High Atlas mountains, the city was stubbornly defended against marauding tribes by successive Berber sultans, who surveyed their fertile lands and maintained their powerful dynasties from the tranquil olive groves and lagoon of the Menara Gardens and the vast orchards of the Agdal Gardens. The first Kasbah was built here around 1062, on the site of what is now the Koutoubia Mosque, by Abu Bakr, leader of the Almoravid tribe of black warriors from Mauritania. Abu Bakr was quickly overthrown by his cousin Youssef ben Tachfine, who became sultan of the first great Berber dynasty. Conquerors of Spain, the Almoravids essentially founded Marrakesh by adding a mosque to the Kasbah (of which no trace remains) in 1070. Thus, from its beginnings as a stronghold, Marrakesh became, together with Fez, the capital from which the sultan controlled the whole of Morocco and Andalusia. Tachfine's pious son, Ali ben Youssef, whose mother was a Christian slave, also kept his capital at Marrakesh, and an influx of craftsmen from Spain created the new city's buildings, including the ramparts, and an underground irrigation system.

Although conquered and sacked in 1147 by the Almohads, Marrakesh remained the dynastic capital and became even more significant under Yaqoub el Mansour, the third Almohad sultan. Perhaps the greatest of Marrakesh's sultans, el Mansour built extensively—palaces, mosques, and gardens—and introduced a more refined culture, importing materials from Italy and the Far East. The extraordinary Koutoubia Mosque, constructed on the site of an early Almoravid mosque, was begun by the Almohad sultan Abdel Moumen and finished (with extensive changes) by el Mansour. Peace did not last, however. By the early 13th century, after two centuries of strong control by the Almohads and Almoravids, Marrakesh relapsed into a long period of skirmishing between dissenting tribes that constantly attacked and ransacked each other's strongholds.

By the mid-13th century, the conquering Merenids had arrived and taken Marrakesh as their capital; but they soon moved it to Fez, which then became the center of Moroccan culture. In the 14th and 15th centuries, Marrakesh fell into decline, experienced famine, and was finally conquered in 1554 by the Saadians from the south, who restored Marrakesh as their capital. The rich and powerful Saadian sultan Ahmed el Mansour—the Golden One—was responsible for a period of prosperity in Marrakesh during the late 16th century, thanks to his raids of caravan routes from Timbuktu. This el Mansour was the creator of the El Badi Palace and the Saadian Tombs, his own final resting place.

The 17th century saw the beginning of the Alaouite dynasty, during which Marrakesh suffered another decline. The power-hungry sultan Moulay

Ismail turned north to Meknes for his capital, plundering every monument and palace in Marrakesh—especially El Badi—to build his version of Versailles there. The Alaouites have ruled Morocco ever since; today they reside in Rabat, administrative capital since the French Protectorate. In the 18th century, however, Moulay Ismail's successor, Sidi Mohammed ben Abdellah, restored many of Marrakesh's ruined palaces as well as the ramparts and mosques, and added to gardens like the Menara. This restoration did not last long, and although Marrakesh remained one of Morocco's Imperial Cities because of its strategic location, it declined again in the 19th century until Moulay el Hassan I, great-great-grandfather of the current King Mohammed VI, chose to be crowned and to build his palace here in 1873, giving Marrakesh renewed importance. When the French established a Moroccan protectorate in 1912, they built the Ville Nouvelle, which facilitated new trade. During the French period, Pasha T'hami el-Glaoui, famous governor of Marrakesh, ally of the French, and friend of Winston Churchill, kept the city (and all of southern Morocco) under his powerful control from a series of Kasbah strongholds, most notably Telouet.

Today Marrakesh is a traveler's Eden, vying only with Fez, its more introverted counterpart, for the honor of being Morocco's most intoxicating city. Marrakesh is for the eyes—a place where even the refined elements have a roughness to them, yet what is rough has its own refinement. Apart from the many things to see and do, one of the most refreshing things about Marrakesh is that time slows down here. The helter-skelter of mopeds, Mercedes, donkey carts, and pedestrians in the streets is really just a mirage; beneath it all, you can feel a languor in the way people walk, the way they take time to stop and talk to each other, conducting their daily affairs much as their ancestors did. Take advantage of this: think about nothing outside the moment, and say with the Marrakshis, *"Insh'Allah!"* ("God willing!")—what will be, will be. With its dramatic beauty and unhurried rhythm, the Jewel of the South can beckon even the most seasoned traveler to stop moving and stay forever.

Pleasures and Pastimes

Cafés

Sitting in a café watching life go by is one of the Marrakshis' most popular recreations in both Djemâa el Fna and Gueliz. Most of the cafés right on Djemâa el Fna have rooftop terraces with magnificent views of the whole square, the rooftops of Marrakesh, and the Atlas mountains in the distance. The best time of day to take in this panorama is the magic sunset hour, when the city earns yet another nickname, Marrakesh the Red—here the setting sun turns colors ranging from pale pink and orange to purple and red. Watch the sky glow while sipping mint tea or a glass (never a mug) of Moroccan-style coffee with steamed milk, and wait for the teeming world below to take on its nighttime aspect.

Calèche Rides

Calèches are green, canopied horse-drawn carriages used by the locals to get around Marrakesh and by travelers to see the sights on the perimeter. They hold four people and cost 60DH per hour. Board a calèche to take a tour of the ramparts or a trip out to the Palmery, or to see the Menara or Agdal gardens.

Cycling

Cycling around Marrakesh is fun and easy, as the city is relatively flat. Ride to the Menara or Agdal gardens or out on the Casablanca road to the Palmery oasis circuit and back, 25 km (16 mi) in all. You can rent bikes opposite the Hotel Imperial Borj, in Hivernage; or outside the Hotel Safir Siaha, on the Casablanca road; or inquire with the front desk at your hotel.

Dining

Paula Wolfert, author of several Moroccan cookbooks, has written that "Arab hospitality is legendary. It is an embarrassment of riches, total satisfaction, abundance as an end in itself and a point of pride with the host." Moroccan cuisine is widely recognized as one of the world's finest, and its colorful presentation makes it a feast for the eyes as well as for the palate. Outside (the much larger) Casablanca, Marrakesh has the best selection of restaurants in Morocco: as a group they serve equal parts Moroccan and international cuisine, including French, Italian, Spanish, Asian, and kosher options. You can also eat well at the popular sidewalk cafés in both the medina and Gueliz, which serve inexpensive grills: lamb cutlets, *kefta* (beef patties), *merguez* sausages, and beef brochettes with tomato salad, bread, olives, a hot sauce called *harissa*, and french fries.

A special treat is to spend a whole evening at one of Marrakesh's popular *riad* restaurants, mostly in the medina, which give you an idea (albeit a rather expensive one) of the sumptuousness of traditional Moroccan entertaining. Apart from a copious set menu that includes various cooked salads—featuring, say, eggplant, tomato confiture, spinach with preserved lemon, grilled green peppers, lentils, or fava beans—you're served small *briouates* (pastries akin to Indian *samosas*) filled with ground lamb or rice and almonds, and your choice of tagines. You can also try the famous local dish called *tangia*, made popular by workers who stew lamb or beef in an earthenware pot left in hot ashes all day; and the classic Moroccan pastilla. Couscous is de rigueur in these restaurants and comes in many varieties, including couscous *aux sept légumes* (with seven vegetables; for good luck) and a version covered with raisins, onions, and cinnamon. (Moroccans traditionally eat couscous mainly on Friday, their holy day, but you can choose it from a menu anytime.) All of these dishes are served with plenty of good local wines, such as Gerrouane *gris* and Boulaouane; mint tea; and almond-filled pastries like the horn-shape *cornes de gazelle* or *m'hensha*, curled up like a snake. While you dine, folk musicians and belly dancers entertain you, and courteous waiters in white *djellabas* (full-length hooded robes) satisfy your every whim.

CATEGORY	COST*
$$$$	over 450DH
$$$	300–450DH
$$	150–300DH
$	under 150DH

per person for a three-course meal, excluding drinks, service, and tax.

Evening Strolls

The souk is a hive of artisanal activity until 8 or 9 PM, so a leisurely stroll before dinner can be an exercise in pure discovery. Don't shop—just experience. You can't really get lost; if confusion threatens, just ask someone to point you back to the Djemâa el Fna. Stroll up or down Avenue Mohammed V with the rest of Marrakesh, always on its way to or from that magnetic square. In Gueliz take the elevator up to the Mirador rooftop terrace of the Renaissance Café, on Place Abdel Moumen, which overlooks the entire city including the illuminated Koutoubia. On very hot evenings, this is the coolest place in Marrakesh.

Festivals

Marrakesh's annual folklore festival of Moroccan music, theater, and dance—the Festival National des Arts Populaires de Marrakech—

draws performers from all over Morocco and may even include an equestrian event (☞ Fantasias *in* Nightlife and the Arts, *below*). Held in May or June on the grounds of El Badi Palace, the festival lasts about 10 days and usually offers an evening program at 8:30. Don't miss it if you're here; just check with the Moroccan Tourist Office, as the date is never confirmed until a month or so beforehand.

Aïd el Arch, or Throne Day, the commemoration of the king's coronation, is always on July 30. Parades and fireworks create a festive ruckus, and throngs of people fill the streets to listen and dance to live music. **Aïd el Seghrir** celebrates the end of Ramadan and is felt largely as a city-wide sigh of relief. **Aïd el Kebir,** the Day of Sacrifice, has a somber tone; on or around April 28 Muslims everywhere observe the last ritual of the pilgrimage to Mecca by slaughtering a sheep. The Youth Festival, **La Fête de Jeunesse,** held on July 9, celebrates children, who generally just run around the streets singing, dancing, and horsing around.

Lodging

Marrakesh draws travelers from all over the world and from all age groups. An array of international hotels offers good to excellent facilities, and an endless selection of small, inexpensive, clean, and aesthetically Moroccan hotels satisfies the young, adventurous, or budget-conscious. (These were popularized by Western hippies when Marrakesh was their haunt of choice). In the last few years the *maisons d'hôte* (pensions or bed-and-breakfasts) in mansions called *riads* have become increasingly en vogue; they're peaceful, stylishly Moroccan in flavor, brimming with plants and flowers, and often endowed with a pool for cooling off. Carefully hidden from view in the medina, the riads offer a privileged glimpse of the city's medieval aspects as well as easy access to the souk and bazaars. You can reserve by the night or rent the whole riad for a prolonged stay. There are also beautiful villas and complexes among the 150,000 date palms in the Palmery, available by the night or the week. The city's one campground is in the Hivernage district.

CATEGORY	COST*
$$$$	over 1600DH
$$$	750–1600DH
$$	500–750DH
$	under 500DH

All prices are for a standard double room, excluding tax.

EXPLORING MARRAKESH

Marrakesh has two distinct parts: the walled-in medina, or Old City, and the wide-open New City (Ville Nouvelle), Gueliz. When you can see the ramparts, you're either just inside or just outside the medina, a labyrinth of narrow alleys in which houses, souks, and bazaars form an interlocking honeycomb, specifically designed to confuse invaders and now serving much the same purpose for tourists. Walking among the twisting and turning alleys deep in the medina is a voyage in itself. If you are literally claustrophobic, ask for a guide at your hotel; if not, just follow your nose, keep walking, and you'll end up at one of the *babs,* or arched gates, that lead in and out of this ancient quarter. If that fails, ask a young Marrakshi to show you the way out, and give him a five-dirham piece for his trouble.

A street—usually no more than an alley—is called a *derb*. At the center of the medina is the famous Djemâa el Fna square, the heartbeat of Marrakesh, whose name translates roughly as "Meeting Place at the End of the World." Today it's a fun fair, but once upon a time the

Djemâa's purpose was more gruesome: it provided for public viewings of the severed heads of sinners, criminals, and Christians, hung on stakes around the square. Most of the monuments in the medina charge an entry fee of 10DH–15DH and have permanent on-site guides; if you use one, tip him about 30DH. Gueliz, in comparison, is flat and open, its wide streets lined with orange and jacaranda trees, office buildings, modern stores, and a plethora of sidewalk cafés.

Great Itineraries

IF YOU HAVE 2 DAYS

Start your first day with the **Koutoubia Mosque,** ①, **Saadian Tombs** ②, and **El Badi Palace** ③. Returning through the **Mellah** ④, you'll find the beautiful **El Bahia Palace** ⑤ and the **Dar Si Saïd** ⑥ museum in close proximity. North of **Djemâa el Fna** ⑦, the center of the medina, are the **souk** ⑧, the **Koubba Ba'adiyn** ⑨, the **Ali ben Youssef Mosque** ⑩, and the **Ali ben Youssef Medersa** ⑪. In the evening, watch the sun set from a café terrace overlooking Djemâa el Fna. Start your second day early, with a calèche ride to one or more of the gardens—the **Menara** ⑭, the **Agdal** ⑯ (via the **Méchouar** ⑮), or the **Majorelle** ⑲—then either shop quietly for gifts in Gueliz or return to the souk. At the end of the day, treat yourself to a *hammam* (Moroccan version of a Turkish bath) before dining at a Moroccan restaurant.

IF YOU HAVE 4 DAYS

With four days you have two options. The first is to follow the two-day itinerary above, then take half-day or day trips to the Ourika Valley, Asni, Moulay Ibrahim, Ouirgane, Amizmiz, or the Lalla Takerkoust Dam. The second is to spend your first day on leisurely visits to the monuments south of Djemâa el Fna, then spend your second day seeing the **Koubba Ba'adiyn** ⑨, **Ali ben Youssef Mosque** ⑩, and **Ali ben Youssef Medersa** ⑪ and shopping in the **souk** ⑧. On day three visit the **Menara** ⑭, **Agdal** ⑯, and **Majorelle** ⑲ gardens, and on day four venture out to the **High Atlas** mountains to see some Berber villages.

When to Tour Marrakesh

Morocco has been called "a cold country with a hot sun." Although the sun shines almost year-round here, the best time to visit Marrakesh is in the spring, from late March to late June, when the sky is generally blue and the temperature is still comfortable. The only exception in that period is the Christian Holy Week, which brings crowds of vacationers from France. If you like a hot sun, come in July, August, or early September. The months between late September and December are pleasant, with cool evenings. January, February, and March can be rainy, chilly, and changeable.

Numbers in the text correspond to numbers in the margin and on the Marrakesh map.

The Medina

Marrakesh's medina comprises everything within the 15 km (9 mi) of intact ramparts and 14 original babs. Until the French Protectorate, these gates were closed every night to ensure that only those who lived or had business in the city were inside it. In some respects, not much has changed here since the Middle Ages: the medina is still a labyrinth of narrow dirt streets lined with thick-walled interlocked houses; donkeys and mules still bear produce, wood, and wool to their destinations; and the workshops of age-old crafts still flourish as retail endeavors.

A Good Walk

Most of Marrakesh's monuments are in the southern part of the medina. Start with a walk around the **Koutoubia Mosque** ①, then head down to Bab Agnaou and the **Saadian Tombs** ②. After seeing the tombs, retrace your steps and turn right into the street just before the Bab Agnaou. Walk almost to the end of the wall, then turn right again and continue on this street to the Place des Ferblantiers. Go through the Bab Berrima and you'll be in a large, rectangular enclosure with the entrance to **El Badi Palace** ③ on the right. Return through the arch and walk a few minutes northeast through the **Mellah** ④ to **El Bahia Palace** ⑤ and **Dar Si Saïd** ⑥, two derbs north. From here it's a short walk north on Riad Zitoun el Jdid to **Djemâa el Fna** ⑦, where you can stop for lunch. Next, head across the square into the **souk** ⑧, where you can window-shop on your way to the **Koubba Ba'adiyn** ⑨, the **Ali ben Youssef Mosque** ⑩, and the **Ali ben Youssef Medersa** ⑪. You'll also pass some *fondouksd* ⑫, medieval warehouses and inns that are still in use. From here you could continue on Rue Bab Debbagh to the **tanneries** ⑬. At the end of the day, as the sun sets, take a calèche ride to some of the scenic spots on the city's perimeter—relax in the **Menara Garden** ⑭ or the **Agdal Garden** ⑯, via the **Méchouar** ⑮; or tour the **Ramparts** ⑰ or, just outside town, **La Palmeraie** ⑳.

TIMING

You can cover this territory in one day, if you don't stay too long in any one place.

Sights to See
Admission is free unless otherwise indicated.

⑯ **Agdal Garden.** Stretching a full 3 km (2 mi) south of the Royal Palace, the Jardin de l'Aguedal comprises vast orchards, a large lagoon, and other small pools, all once fed by ancient underground irrigation channels from the Ourika Valley in the High Atlas. Surrounded by high *pisé* (a mixture of mud and clay) walls, the olive, fig, citrus, pomegranate, and apricot orchards are still in their original form of raised plots. The largest lagoon, the grandiose Tank of Health, is said to be a 12th-century Almohad creation, but, as with most historic sites in Morocco, the Agdal was consecutively abandoned and rebuilt, the latest resurrection dating from the 19th century. Until the advent of the French Protectorate, it was the sultans' retreat of choice for lavish picnics and boating parties, equipped as it was with several pavilions. One unlucky sultan, Sidi Mohammed III, was actually fatally wounded at one of these fetes; his steam-powered launch sank in the lagoon. ✉ *Approach via Méchouar; or, outside ramparts, walk left on Rue Bab Irhil and the garden will be on your right.* ⊙ *Daily, usually 9–6.*

⑩ **Ali ben Youssef Mosque.** After the Koutoubia, this is the largest mosque in the medina and the oldest in Marrakesh. The building was first constructed in the second half of the 12th century by the Almoravid sultan Ali ben Youssef, around the time of the Koubba Ba'adiyn (☞ *below*). In succeeding centuries it was destroyed and rebuilt several times by the Almohads and the Saadians, who changed its size and architecture accordingly; it was last overhauled in the 19th century, in the then-popular Merenid style. Non-Muslims may not enter.

★ ⑪ **Ali ben Youssef Medersa.** The largest such institution in North Africa, the medersa is an extraordinarily well-preserved 14th-century Koranic school. As many as 900 students once lived in the tiny, upper-level rooms that look like monks' cells, arranged around inner courtyards. The building was originally built by the Merenids in a somewhat different style than that of other medersas; later, in the 16th century, Sultan Abdullah el Ghallib, of the famously refined Saadians, rebuilt it almost completely, adding the incredibly refined Andalusian details in the carved cedar, *gibs* (stucco plasterwork), and *zellij* (mosaic) so pronounced here.

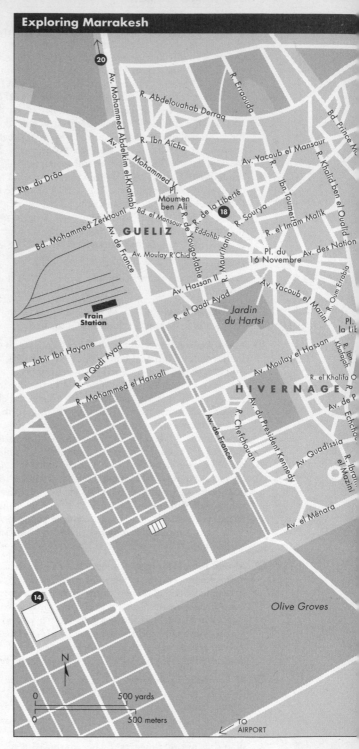

Exploring Marrakesh

Bd. Allal el Fassi

Rte. principale no. 24

Pl. des Ramparts

Oued Issil

19

13

17

Bus Station

Bab Doukkala

R. Gza

R. de Bab Tarizour

R. Assouel

11

R. de Bab Khemis

Bab Debbagh

R. Mohammed el Mellakh

ions Unis

12

10

Riad el Arous

R. de Baboul Doukkala

R. Fatima Zohra

R. Dar el Glaoui

R. Moussine

Pl. du Moukef

Pl. de Liberté

R.

9

Bab Larissa

Av. Mohammed V

R. Sidi el Yamani

8

MEDINA

R. Ibn

R. de Paris

Ottmane

R. Dabachi

Pl. Sidi Youb

R. de Bab Aïlen

Bd. el Yarmouk

R. Abou el Abbes Septi

Triq el Koutoubia

7

R. Ba Ahmad

R. Echchouada

R. Harroun Errachid

Bab el Djedid

Av. Houmman el

1

Djemâa el Fna

R. de Moulay Ismail

R. Beni Marine

Riad Zitoune el Kedim

R. Riad Zitoun Jdide

6

5

R. Ibrahim

R. Mazini

R. de Bab Agnaou

Ferouki

4

Pl. des Ferblantiers

MELLAH

Bab Agnaou

2

3

R. de la Kasbah

15

Rte. No. 501

Bab Ksiba

Agdal Garden

16

The large main courtyard, framed by two columned arcades, opens into an elaborately decorated prayer hall that features unusual palm motifs as well as the more customary calligraphy of Koranic texts. The medersa also contains a small mosque, whose beautiful carved cedar, gibs, and zellij remain in good condition. ✉ *Just off Rue Souk el Khemis.* 🎫 *10DH.* 🕐 *Daily 8:30–noon and 2:30–6.*

★ ➏ **Dar Si Saïd.** Built by Sidi Saïd, brother of Vizier (Minister) Bou Ahmed (☞ El Bahia Palace, *below*), this 19th-century palace is now an arts and crafts museum. The excellent collection of Moroccan antique crafts includes jewelry, local carpets and leatherwork, and pottery from the seaside town of Safi and from Tamegroute, near Zagora. One prize holding is a marble basin with an inscription indicating its 10th-century Córdoban origin; the basin was brought to Morocco by the Almoravid sultan Ali ben Youssef for his mosque—in spite of its decorative eagles and griffins, which defy the Koran's prohibition of artistic representations of living things. At some point during the Saadian dynasty, it found its way to the Ali ben Youssef Medersa, and was later moved here. The palace's courtyard is stunning, filled with flowers and cypress trees and furnished with a gazebo and fountain; and the adjacent salons burst with jewelry, daggers, and ornate kaftans. The most extraordinary salon is upstairs, a somber room in the most authentic style of the period: gibs cornices, zellij walls, and an amazing carved-cedar ceiling painted in the *zouak* style (bright colors in intricate patterns). Guides are available on site. ✉ *1st derb on right just up from El Bahia Palace.* 🎫 *Entry 10DH.* 🕐 *Wed.–Thurs. and Sat.–Mon. 9–noon and 4–7; Fri. 9–11:30 and 4–7; in winter, Wed.–Thurs. and Sat.–Mon. 9–noon and 2:30–6, Fri. 3–6.*

★ ➐ **Djemâa el Fna.** The endless, seething carnival that is the Djemâa el Fna encompasses just about every activity known to man. Centuries-old meeting place of regional farmers and tradesmen, the Djemâa stretches as far as the ground-level eye can see, flanked with mosques and a series of cafés, all with rooftop terraces that grant a panoramic bird's-eye view. From early morning, when Marrakesh is just waking up (and the first customer gets the cheapest price of the day for being the "early bird") until long past midnight, when most folks have gone to bed, the cacophony never ceases. Bazaars of bric-a-brac are accompanied by open-air entertainment, which includes elaborate sagas (sometimes with men dressed as women) that mesmerize the crowd; cobra charmers with raucous flutes; wild Gnaouan acrobats, dancers, and musicians with clashing cymbals; and a mélange of monkey tamers, fortune-tellers, henna ladies, tooth pullers, and astrologers. The crowd seems to swell in its quest for diversion. Roving water sellers in eye-popping costumes of red and green carry leather water pouches and polished-brass drinking bowls, and a semicircle of carts with orange-stripe awnings offers to squeeze orange, tangerine, or grapefruit juice while you wait, for 2DH a glass. The best time to behold the Djemâa is sunset, when the whole square turns purple, orange, or deep pink and takes on its smoky nighttime glow from the hundreds of gas lamps that light the still-sizzling food stalls. Then, as if on cue, most Marrakshis come out to meet, eat, and be entertained.

You can roam here for hours, but be armed with plenty of loose change for photo subjects. Beware, too, of the beguiling veiled ladies who appear from nowhere peddling bracelets for 100DH—these are made of tin and are worth less than 5DH.

➌ **El Badi Palace.** The vast pisé and sandstone ruins of this 16th-century palace are now a serene nesting ground for storks. Once the home of Sultan Ahmed el Mansour, and at the time often called the most beau-

tiful palace in the world—the name means, roughly, "The Marvel"—
El Badi was ransacked in the 17th century by Moulay Ismail for the
materials to complete his own palace at Meknes. The main hall was
called the Koubba el Khamsiniyya, a name that referred to its 50
columns. Along the palace's south wall are a series of underground dun-
geons and corridors, which you can freely explore. The vast, enclosed
grounds contain a sunken orange orchard, a lagoon, and several other
pools. Guides greet you at the gate. Once a year, in May or June, the
ruins come to life as the site of the Moroccan folklore festival. ⊠ *Enter
ramparts and enormous gateway near Place des Ferblantiers.* 🎫 *10DH.*
🕐 *Daily 8:30–noon and 2:30–6.*

★ ❺ **El Bahia Palace.** A jewel of a palace, with all the key elements of Moroccan architecture—light, symmetry, decoration, and water—El Bahia
was built as a harem's residence by the notorious Si Ahmed ben Musa,
Grand Vizier to Sultan Moulay el Hassan I and known popularly as
Bou Ahmed. The rooms vary in size according to the importance of
each wife or concubine, but each wife had her own quiet courtyard in
any case. Edith Wharton once stayed in the most-favored-wife's room
during the French Protectorate. Although the palace was ransacked upon
Bou Ahmed's death, you can still experience its layout and get a sense
of its former beauty. There are several cypress-filled courtyards, and
the entire building is filled with smooth arches, carved-cedar ceilings,
ceramic-tile lower walls and fountains, *tadlak* (shiny marbled) finishes,
gibs (stucco plasterwork) cornices, and *zouak* (brightly colored, intricately patterned) painted ceilings. Sadly, the rooftop tower that Wharton once climbed for its fabulous view of Marrakesh is closed to the
public; and when the royal family is in town the entire palace is closed,
as they stay here with their entourage. ⊠ *End of Avenue Houmane el
Fetouaki,* ☎ *04/38–54–65.* 🎫 *Free, but you are expected to use an
on-site guide, whom you should tip 30DH–50DH.* 🕐 *Daily 8:30–1
and 4–7; in winter, daily 8:30–11:45 and 2:30–6.*

⑫ **Fondouks.** Known as *caravanserai* in the Middle East, fondouks are
the original inns, storehouses, and trading places of merchants and artisans. Due to its onetime strategic position on the great caravan routes
of yore, Marrakesh's medina is full of them. There is one fondouk a
few minutes southwest of the Ali ben Youssef Mosque; another cluster north of the mosque, on Rue Amesfah via Rue Baroudienne; and,
farther north, on Rue Bab Taghzout, another by the fountain known
as Shrob ou Shouf ("Drink and Look"). Some fondouks are still in use
as wood or furniture workshops, and because they leave their doors
open to the derbs, you can easily enter and take a look at some of their
courtyards and upper galleries.

❾ **Koubba Ba'adiyn.** Perhaps because it's small and hidden behind high
walls, this *koubba* (saint's tomb) is not heavily visited. Having somehow escaped destruction by the Almohads, the koubba is the only intact example of Almoravid architecture in all of Morocco (the few ruins
include some walls here in Marrakesh and a minaret in El Jadida). Only
excavated from the rubble of the original Ali ben Youssef Mosque and
Medersa in 1952, the koubba is remarkable because it bears the origins of nearly all the motifs and forms of pure Moroccan architecture:
palms, pine cones, the classic shape of the windows, the dome with its
octagonal support. The tomb is in the middle of the northern part of
the souk, around the corner from the Ali ben Youssef Mosque. The
guardian acts as a guide. 🎫 *10DH.* 🕐 *Daily.*

❶ **Koutoubia Mosque.** Towering like a sentinel over Marrakesh, this Moorish mosque was begun in the early 12th century, at the start of the Almohad dynasty, by Sultan Abdel Moumen, who then used it as a model

for the Hassan Tower in Rabat and the Giralda in Seville. It was eventually completed toward the end of the 12th century by Yaqoub el Mansour, the third Almohad sultan. The mosque took its name from the Arabic word for book, *koutoub,* because there was once a book market nearby. With a square minaret that rises 230 ft, the mosque is visible from a great distance in every direction; and the minaret is topped by three golden orbs, which, according to local legend, were offered by the mother of the Saadian sultan Ahmed el Mansour Edhabi as a penance for fasting days she missed during Ramadan. Fresh from a late-1990s face-lift, the mosque now has floodlights to illuminate its curved windows, a band of ceramic inlay, pointed *merlons* (ornamental edgings), and various decorative arches. ⊠ *South end of Avenue Mohammed V.*

⑳ La Palmeraie. Marrakesh's famous date-palm oasis begins about 7 km (4 mi) north of town on the Casablanca road and forms a 25-km (16-mi) circuit that returns via the Fez road. Stretching for an immense 30,000 acres, the Palmery was once a great source of wealth to the reigning sultans, but, sadly, in recent years the date crop has been reduced by disease. Still more recently, the Palmery became the hideaway of choice for the rich and famous, who built within its sandy tracts Kasbah-style villas with palatial facilities—pools, terraces, gazebos, and hot tubs.

⑮ Méchouar. The huge, open Square of Allegiance, complete with formal garden, is the parade ground where Moroccan and foreign dignitaries congregate to show allegiance to the king on the yearly celebration of his coronation, Aïd el Arch (Throne Day), July 30. The square is in front of the Royal Palace, at the very southern end of the medina, near Bab Ksiba and the Agdal Garden; but the high, salmon-pink walls don't allow any peeks.

❹ Mellah. As in other Moroccan cities, the Mellah is the old Jewish quarter. Though now roughly synonymous with "ghetto," the term comes from the Arabic word for "salt," probably referring to the Jews' onetime relegation to the job of salting the heads of criminals before they were placed on public view on the city gates. Another possible etymology points out that, in medieval Fez, Jews were forced to live near a salty swamp.

⑭ Menara Garden. The Menara's peaceful lagoon and villa-style pavilion are ensconced in an immense olive grove, where pruners and pickers putter in the groves and local women fetch water from the nearby stream, said to give *baraka* (good luck). A popular rendezvous haunt for Marrakshis, the garden is a refreshing removal from the intense, inward-looking architecture of the city itself. The elegant pavilion— or *minzah,* meaning "beautiful view"—was created in the early 19th century by Sultan Abd er Rahman, but it is believed to occupy the site of a 16th-century Saadian structure. In winter and spring the backdrop is a seemingly endless stretch of snowcapped Atlas peaks that seem closer than they really are; and from October through January you can see the green, pink, and black olives being gathered from the trees. If you're pressed for time, you may want to take a taxi or calèche here rather than walk. ⊠ *From Bab el Djedid, garden is about 4 km (2 mi) down Avenue de la Menara.* ☉ *Daily 8–7.*

⑰ Ramparts. Marrakesh's amazingly well-preserved salmon-pink ramparts are an impressive sight and a constant reminder of the city's fascinating history. They measure about 33 ft high, 7 ft thick, and are 15 km (9 mi) in circumference, and an intermittent 8 of their 14 original babs (arches) are still in use, leading in and out of the medina. Even until the early 20th century, before the French Protectorate, the gates were closed at night to prevent anyone who did not live in Marrakesh from entering. A leisurely calèche drive around the perimeter takes about an hour; a taxi ride is faster.

★ ❷ **Saadian Tombs.** Edith Wharton once made reference to the Saadians' "barbarous customs but sensuous refinements." This beautiful necropolis was created by the Saadian sultan Ahmed el Mansour in the late 16th century as a burial ground for himself and his successors, for whom there are 66 indoor tombs decorated with colorful, intricate zellij. These are supplemented by hundreds more outside, amid palm trees and flowering shrubs, containing Saadian princes and members of the Royal House.

Unlike El Badi Palace and other artistic monuments, the Saadian tombs were not plundered by the infamous Moulay Ismail, probably for reasons of superstition; he simply sealed them up, leaving only a small section open for use. A few other luminaries were buried here after that, including the short-term 18th-century sultan Moulay Yazid, known as the Mad Sultan for his excessive cruelty.

The complex was discovered only in 1917 by General Hubert Lyautey during the French Protectorate. Passionate about every aspect of Morocco's history, the general undertook to restore the tombs for posterity. The central mausoleum, the **Hall of Twelve Columns,** which contains the tombs of Ahmed el Mansour and his family, is dark and lavishly ornate, with a huge vaulted roof, warm-toned doors of carved cedar and *moucharabia* (carved wooden screening traditionally used to separate the sexes), and columns of gray Italian marble. In a smaller inner mausoleum, built by Ahmed el Mansour on the site of an earlier structure containing the decapitated body of the founder of the Saadian dynasty, Mohammed esh Sheikh, lies the tomb of Ahmed el Mansour's mother. The serene garden of headstones also contains the tombs of several children. The guardian can show you around. ✉ *Rue de la Kasbah, across small square from mosque.* 🏷 *10DH.* ☉ *Sat.–Thurs. 8–noon and 2:30–7.*

❽ **Souk.** The souk is a vast and flourishing labyrinth of narrow derbs—some covered and dark, some open-air—containing the colorful, highly specialized handicrafts workshops and bazaars for which Marrakesh is so famous. The market stretches from the virtual heart of the medina to the northern ramparts. The easiest entry points from the Djemâa el Fna are: the street just to the left of the Djemâa's Café Argana, which leads into the Bab Ftouh area and up Rue Mouassine; Rue Souk Semarine, through the potters' market; and opposite Café de France, to the left of the mosque, through the olive market. You can also enter through any of the babs in the ramparts, like Bab Lakhsour, and simply walk toward Djemâa el Fna; you'll see handicrafts bazaars everywhere.

These days various goods are mixed throughout the souk, but most sections are still distinct. Souk Semarine has fabrics, various inexpensive souvenirs, and a *kissaria,* or covered miscellaneous market. Souk Rahba Qdima—also known as La Criée Berbére (roughly, the Auction Crier) for its proximity to the former slave market of that name—has rugs, carpets, and sheepskins as well as apothecaries; Souk el Attarine has perfumes; Souk des Bijoutiers has jewelry; Souk des Forgerons has copperware; Souk Larzal is wholesale wool market; Souk des Teinturiers is the wool dyers' market; Souk des Babouches sells the pointed slippers so beloved of Moroccans; Souk Chouari is where carpenters work in cedar; Souk Haddadine sells ironwork; and Souk Cherratin offers a variety of leather goods. *See* box: The Moroccan Zen of Bargaining.

⓭ **Tanneries.** Just inside Bab Debbagh, on the east side of the medina, Marrakesh's old tanneries are slowly diminishing in use. They're still interesting to visit, but they're in one of the city's poorest neighborhoods, so as soon as you pass through the arch, you'll be inundated with offers from would-be guides, making it all but unnecessary to find the

THE MOROCCAN ZEN OF BARGAINING

BY FAR the biggest challenge you'll face in Marrakesh is a shopping trip. Remember that making a deal is a way of life in Morocco—an art form, especially for Marrakshis. Everyone bargains, sometimes over tea, and it's considered serious business. A satisfactory purchase is contingent on a mutually satisfying bargain. Although anything goes among merchants, the usual practice with tourists is to ask roughly double or even triple an item's true value. To arrive at an agreeable price, halve the offer and then fine-tune the amount.

Moroccan bazaarists are great hustlers, and will find a way to pounce politely upon you as soon as you blink in their direction. Your best defense is the proper mind-set: the first time you go shopping, resolve firmly to browse rather than buy. Wander the stalls and get a sense of what's available; if you're considering big-ticket items, do some comparison shopping. Try not to make eye contact with or speak to any vendor, and do not enter a store. Almost everything sold in the bazaars is displayed on the outside anyway.

Next time you venture out, set your mind to buying. This is not simply a question of buying as cheaply as you can, but, since there are no fixed prices as we know them, buying something you love at a price you feel good about. Once you've found your quarry and asked the price, smile and, with deaf ears, leave the store. Finally, the moment arrives: you want to pay. Start by halving the lowest price you found for that item. Then keep a poker face until you arrive at the price that suits both you and the seller. If the vendor won't come down far enough, try walking away, but you'll have to convince *yourself* you can't live with that price if you want to convince him in turn. This game can be time-consuming, tiring, and just plain difficult; rest assured that you are not a wimp or a failure if you come home with a few overpriced items. Many travelers leave Morocco without buying things they really want simply because the bargaining process is too daunting. Think in terms of finding yourself a great souvenir rather than go home empty-handed, and things are bound to fall into place.

Some useful phrases for your arsenal:

Sh'hal hedi bil dirhams? How much is this?

Rali bezzef It costs too much.

N'bri I want . . .

Ma'britsh I don't want . . .

Iya Yes

La No

Biletti Wait

Arteni Give me . . .

Aufek Please

Chokran Thank you

M'andish floos I have no money [often helpful]

Ma'es salema Good-bye [literally, "Peace be with you"]

tanneries yourself. It's better to go with a guide—and a nosegay, as the tanning pits have an extremely pungent odor thanks to the pigeon excrement used in the tanning process.

Gueliz

The wide boulevards of Marrakesh's New City are bordered with orange, jacaranda, and ornamental fig trees, with the latter pruned to create shade on the sidewalks. Apart from office buildings and contemporary shops—none of which may exceed the height of the nearest mosque—Gueliz has plenty of sidewalk cafés, international restaurants, and upscale antiques stores.

A Good Walk

Start with a morning visit to the **Marché Central** ⑱. From there head north and turn right on Boulevard Zerktouni, then continue straight on to Avenue Yaqoub el Mansour and you'll arrive at the **Majorelle Garden** ⑲. Note that the garden closes at 12:30 PM.

Timing: 3½ hours.

Sights to See

⑲ **Majorelle Garden.** The Jardin Majorelle was created by the French painter Louis Majorelle, who lived in Marrakesh between 1922 and 1962, but it has since passed into the hands of another Marrakesh lover, Yves Saint Laurent. It's a sight for sore eyes, with thickets of green bamboo, little streams, and an electric blue gazebo and villa, now a small museum of Islamic art. ⊠ *Avenue Yaqoub el Mansour (main entrance on side street).* ☎ *Garden 15DH, museum 15DH additional.* ☉ *Wed.– Mon. 8–noon and 2–5 (in summer, 8–noon and 3–7).*

⑱ **Marché Central.** The vivid Central Market is the Western expatriate crowd's favorite place to shop for meat, fish, fruits, flowers, and vegetables. It also includes a handicrafts bazaar. The market is in the center of Gueliz, on Avenue Mohammed V near Rue de Liberté, which in turn has several sunny cafés ideal for breakfast.

NEED A BREAK?

A simple yet special way to experience an important aspect of daily Moroccan life—as well as refresh yourself after all that walking, eating, drinking, and contemplating—is to go to a **hammam,** the Moroccan version of a Turkish bath. Traditionally, upper-class Moroccan homes had their own hammams, but these have generally fallen into disrepair, so most Moroccans now use public hammams. If you want to try a public hammam, opt for the large and popular Hammam el Basha, near Djemâa el Fna, or ask your concierge for another recommendation. (Several hotels have their own, with fees ranging from 80DH to 200DH per person.) Bring everything you'd use in a regular bath, and buy in addition a *kiss* (scrubbing mitt) and *sabon bildi* (black olive-oil soap) from any small grocery store. At the hammam, ask for a *tayeba:* she (or he, in the men's hammam) will do everything for you, fetching buckets of hot water and scrubbing you until you feel not only the cleanest you've ever been but also quite decadent. Public hammams cost about 6DH, plus 30DH– 50DH for a *tayeba,* depending on how much he or she does.

DINING

Dinner in Marrakesh starts at 8, includes entertainment, and often lasts until around midnight. Unlike the international restaurants in Gueliz (which open around 7), those serving traditional Moroccan cuisine in the medina do not post menus outside and are often tucked inconspicuously into already out-of-the-way places. Try to make reservations for these places, as they're often booked solid. Make the call yourself if possible, as guides and hotel receptionists get commissions at certain restaurants and might be tempted to steer you away from your eatery of choice.

There is no set system for tipping. Occasionally your check will indicate that service has been included in the charge; if not, tip 10%, or 20% for excellent service.

CATEGORY	COST*
$$$$	over 450DH
$$$	300–450DH
$$	150–300DH
$	under 150DH

Per person for 3-course meal excluding drinks, service, and tax

If you're feeling adventurous and want to eat in the most popular Marrakshi style, sit at one of the sizzling food stalls in the nocturnal Djemâa el Fna and order what strikes your fancy from the wild array, which includes fried fish, meats, salads, and such Moroccan delicacies as sheep's head and brains and steamed snails. In cooler months or during Ramadan, try a bowl of hearty *harira* soup or country eggs in homemade bread. Watch the Moroccans: they know what to order, and they really get into their food. Everything is fresh, as the vendors give leftovers to the poor every night.

Early birds should make the most of morning life in Marrakesh by having breakfast at a café, where locals sit languorously with their newspapers and chat with friends. Although you can find good café au lait and croissants almost anywhere, a typical Moroccan breakfast is harder to find (outside the hotels that make special efforts to serve it). The meal consists of various hot pancakes called *bghrir* and *msaman*—with butter and honey, *argan* oil (a delicious nutty oil made only in the Moroccan southwest), or *amalo* (a mixture of ground almonds and argan oil)—or donuts called *sfinge*. **La Boule de Neige,** on Rue de Yougoslavie in Gueliz, serves most of the above, in addition to Continental breakfasts. You can get piping-hot sfinge with a glass of mint tea at a minuscule, unnamed café on Rue Mauritania, a side street that leaves Avenue Mohammed V at the Derby shoe store.

For dessert try **Oliveri's Café,** on Boulevard el Mansour Edhabi in Gueliz, around the corner from the Hotel Agdal. Young Marrakshis hang out here, savoring ice-cream concoctions. La Boule de Neige also has ice cream and milk shakes.

For a meal accompanied by folk entertainment from all over Morocco, consider an excursion to Chez Ali (☞ Fantasias *in* Nightlife and the Arts, *below*).

$$$$ ✕ **Dar Marjana.** The tiled courtyard of this charming authentic riad has a cedar minzah (salon overlooking the courtyard; the word means "beautiful view"), tall cypress trees, and a fountain. The proprietor was born within these very walls, and he continues to entertain, as his mother did, with typical Moroccan extravagance. Loll back on brocade divans at a table that has your name in sequins and contemplate the options, which include lamb tagine with tomatoes and onions, seven-vegetable couscous, and Moroccan wines (which come with free refills). The cocktail hour centers around the rose-filled fountain in the courtyard and is accompanied by the Andalusian strains of a lute; later, in the minzah, a lively troop of Gnaouans passes before you as you dine. The finale is a recorded Pavarotti aria, which you must savor with the fig eau-de-vie called *mahia*—guaranteed to bring a very mellow smile to

your face. The fixed price includes unlimited drinks. ⊠ *15, Derb Sidi Tair, opposite Dar El Basha,* ☎ *04/44–57–73 or 04/42–91–52. Reservations essential. AE, V. Closed Tues.*

$$$$ ✕ **Kasbah La Rotonda.** This sumptuously renovated 19th-century riad is filled to the brim with antiques from Morocco, India, and Italy. Legend has it there's a treasure trove underneath it all. The owners, Italian Roberto Tempo and his American wife, Michelle, maintain a dual menu: Moroccan and Italian. Entrées vary, but tagines have featured sea bass, lamb and pears, and chicken with walnuts and vermicelli. Roberto himself cooks the Italian dishes, specializing in tagliatelle with wild mushrooms and grilled swordfish *livornaise.* An Andalusian trio entertains while you dine, and a svelte belly dancer animates dessert. The fixed price includes unlimited drinks. Valet parking is available. ⊠ *Derb Lamnabha (tell driver "La Kasbah"),* ☎ *04/38–15–85 or 04/38–19–28. V. No lunch.*

$$$$ ✕ **Le Yacout.** It's not every day you're led to the door of your restaurant by a guardian with a lantern. Le Yacout is set in a palatial house ★ redesigned as a *Thousand and One Nights* restaurant by Marrakesh aficionado Bill Willis for owner Sidi Mohammed—who was recently appointed Honorary British Consul to Morocco. Its location deep in the medina only adds to its mystery. Aperitifs are proffered on the rooftop to the haunting chants of a Gnaouan musician. Dinner is served in several different settings: beside the turquoise pool, in a vaulted upstairs room, in an intimate glassed-in salon, or in the lush, cushion-filled main salon. The traditional Moroccan feast includes *djez makalli* (chicken with olives and preserved lemons) and yet more musical accompaniment. Courteous and efficient waiters in white djellabas and red Fez hats flurry inconspicuously under the paternal eye of Sidi Abdellah (Sidi Mohammed's brother) to fulfill your every need. The fixed price includes unlimited drinks. ⊠ *79, Sidi Ahmed Soussi, near Bab Doukkala,* ☎ *04/38–29–29 or 04/38–29–00. Reservations essential. AE, DC, MC, V. Closed Mon.*

$$$$ ✕ **Les Trois Palmiers.** If you're dying to see what La Mamounia is all about, the excellent lunchtime buffet at Les Trois Palmiers is one way to savor its ambience without savoring its room rates. You can take your meal in the shade under a *caidal* tent (made of thick white canvas; traditionally used to welcome *caids,* or local dignitaries), or eat beside the three palm trees that tower over the turquoise swimming pool and play at celebrity spotting. The varied buffet menu provides for all tastes. ⊠ *La Mamounia, Avenue Bab Jdid,* ☎ *04/44–89–81. AE, DC, MC, V.*

$$$$ ✕ **Tobsil.** Just inside Bab Lakhsour, an elegantly restored riad houses this charming little French-owned restaurant with 14 tables, spaciously placed in the plant-filled courtyard and in open salons on the upper level. The name means "dish" in Arabic, and the restaurant is known for its innovation; owner-hostess Christine's favorite entrées are lamb with quinces *agneau avec coings* and *poulet au miel* (chicken with honey). As with all Moroccan restaurants of this genre, candles, lanterns, and rose petals are strewn everywhere. The fixed price includes unlimited drinks. ⊠ *22, Derb Abdellah ben Hessaien, R'mila Bab Ksour,* ☎ *04/ 44–15–23, 04/44–45–35, or 04/44–40–52. AE, DC, MC, V.*

$$$ ✕ **El Baraka.** Once the home of a Marrakesh pasha, this grandiose, white-tile riad with an enormous tree-filled courtyard gives you some idea of the luxurious lifestyle of Morocco's 19th-century elite. As you dine beneath mulberry trees under a starry night sky or sit on brocade divans in the interior salon, it's easy to fancy yourself a pasha, too. The set menu features delicious cooked salads and *briouates* as well as the traditional tagines and couscous. ⊠ *Djemâa el Fna, next to Commissariat de Police,* ☎ *04/44–23–41. DC, MC.*

146

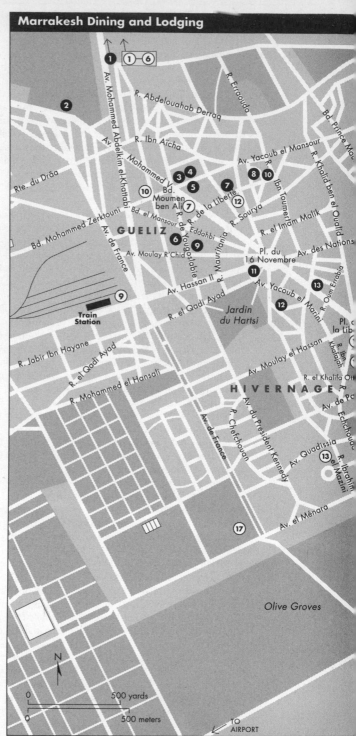

Marrakesh Dining and Lodging

$$$ ✕ **Le Pavillon.** Busy owner Philippe, who not only doubles as a waiter here but is co-owner of La Maison Arabe (☞ Lodging, *below*), has given this beautiful riad a chic, modern look. He serves excellent French cuisine in two settings: in the small courtyard—under fig trees beside a pond lighted with floating candles—and in cozy salon alcoves. The mouthwatering *feuillete de crevettes* (shrimp in flaky pastry) and *soufflé au citron* (lemon soufflé) are faultless. ✉ *47, Derb Zaouia, opposite Bab Doukkala Mosque,* ☏ *04/39–12–40. MC, V. Closed Tues. No lunch.*

$$$ ✕ **Stylia.** Renowned for its traditional Moroccan cuisine, this long-established restaurant is unusual for its immense, high-ceilinged Andalusian-style salon. The proprietor, Mr. Chami, fashioned the restaurant out of a 16th-century palace, keeping the refined decor of mosaic-tiled walls, ornate stucco cornices, red carpets, and a ceramic water fountain. An attendant in white djellaba waits inside Bab Lakhsour to lead you down the cobbled derb, and a trio of Andalusian musicians plays while you dine. Entrées include the local *tangia* (lamb cooked for hours in an earthenware jar) and chicken stuffed with lemon and rice. You can also order *mechoui* (lamb roasted in a great outdoor oven pit), *épaule d'orée* (braised shoulder of lamb), and, with advance notice, kosher dishes. ✉ *34, Rue Ksour,* ☏ *04/44–35–87. MC, V.*

$$ ✕ **La Bagatelle.** This well-established French-run place in the center of Gueliz has an attractive vine-covered courtyard as well as an indoor dining room with a log fire for cooler weather. The tried-and-tested menu is short, but its fare is consistently good, particularly the *truite à l'amande* (trout with almond sauce). ✉ *101, Rue Yougoslavie,* ☏ *04/43–02–74. V. Closed Wed.*

$$ ✕ **Le Jacaranda.** For a night out in the city center, try this pleasant restaurant overlooking the roundabout at the busy intersection of Avenue Mohammed V and Boulevard Zerktouni. Le Jacaranda is well known for its nouvelle French cuisine, particularly in the form of fish such as grilled swordfish and turbot. The menu also includes a few Moroccan dishes. ✉ *32, Boulevard Zerktouni, Gueliz,* ☏ *04/44–72–15. AE, DC, MC, V. Closed Tues.*

$$ ✕ **Le Sepharade.** This comfortable kosher restaurant is set in a large, salmon-pink villa on a quiet corner just opposite the Beth-El synagogue. The menu includes kosher versions of various Moroccan tagines and cooked salads. ✉ *Rue Ibn Aisha off Boulevard Zerktouni,* ☏ *04/43–98–09. MC, V.*

$ ✕ **Catanzaro.** One of the most popular restaurants in Marrakesh, this cozy Gueliz Italian has dining on two floors, brightened by red-chintz tablecloths. The menu is a good selection of basic Italian dishes and pizzas at prices that make them fabulous values. Pizza Royal—that is, with everything on it—is a favorite. ✉ *Rue Tariq Ibn Ziad, behind Marché Central,* ☏ *04/43–37–31. MC, V. Closed Sun.*

$ ✕ **El Fassia.** Unlike Marrakesh's more opulent restaurants, this relaxed and pleasant salon is run by women who cook and serve their food in kaftans tucked up at the arms. You feel like you've been invited into someone's home. The menu—cooked salads, lamb brochettes, kefta with eggs, tagines, couscous—is mostly basic, but everything is reliably delicious. ✉ *232, Avenue Mohammed V,* ☏ *04/43–40–60. DC, MC, V.*

$ ✕ **Kimson.** One of the few Asian eateries in town, Kimson has a creative menu of Vietnamese- and Chinese-style cuisine, including very good *nems* (spring rolls) and duck dishes. After several Moroccan meals, it can be a nice change to sit in this garden and pick on bamboo shoots with chopsticks. ✉ *Rue Ibn Toumert,* ☏ *04/43–01–59. MC, V. Closed Sun. No lunch.*

$ ╳ **L'Entrecôte.** It's run by a French couple, but Americans in particular will feel at home in this saloon-type restaurant. The spotlight is on great steaks and prime ribs—some with French sauces, some without—and there's an appealing variety of appetizers. ⊠ *55, Boulevard Zerktouni (in arcade next to Café Negociants),* ☎ *04/44–94–28. MC, V. Closed Sun.*

$ ╳ **La Taverne.** A simple set menu makes La Taverne a good place for a quick, basic, inexpensive lunch in Gueliz. Cool off a bit by dining in the back garden. ⊠ *Boulevard Zerktouni, opposite Cinéma Colisée, one block from Place El Moumen,* ☎ *no phone. No credit cards. Closed Sun.*

$ ╳ **Le Dragon D'Or.** This place has become a popular haunt with those Marrakshis who have acquired a taste for Chinese food. The decor is all red and gold, with embroidered lanterns, and the menu is varied, with good fried shrimp. ⊠ *10, Avenue Zerktouni,* ☎ *04/43–06–17. MC, V.*

$ ╳ **Niagara Pub.** Two sisters run this quasi-bistro. Their menu is large and varied, with fresh appetizers and salads as well as a good selection of pasta dishes and oven-baked pizzas. You dine on a shaded porch. ⊠ *31–32, Centre Commercial Ennakhil, Avenue Victor Hugo/Route de Targa,* ☎ *04/44–97–75. DC, MC, V. Closed Mon.*

$ ╳ **Puerto Banus.** This small, cozy eatery is Marrakesh's only Spanish restaurant. A table in the cool, white courtyard takes you far from the madding crowd; in the winter or on cool evenings, meals are taken indoors, near a log fire. The menu includes paella, tortillas (potato omelets), and *friture de soles.* A nice, fruity sangria and nightly guitar music enhance the ambience. ⊠ *Rue Ibn Hanbal (opposite police station),* ☎ *04/44–65–34. MC, V.*

$ ╳ **Rôtisserie Café la Paix.** If you feel like getting away from it all, drop into this much-frequented café and make the most of its lush tropical garden and relaxed atmosphere. The menu is part international, part Moroccan; the chicken and fish brochettes are good bets, as is the Berber tagine. ⊠ *68, Rue Yougoslavie,* ☎ *04/43–31–18. AE, DC, MC, V.*

Sidewalk Grills

Dining in a restaurant is a relatively new phenomenon for Moroccans, who see it as something of a shame on the household when people choose to eat out. They have, however, perfected the popular art of grills, traditionally the province of the working class. In Marrakesh, grills are scattered throughout both the medina and Gueliz, and a meal at one of these institutions costs next to nothing.

Two of the best-beloved grills (both nameless) are tucked beneath shady trees on Rue Ibn Aïsha, to the right of the top end of Avenue Mohammed V. They serve grilled beef and sausage, brochettes, Moroccan salads, and french fries, supplemented by bread, olives, and hot sauce, from midday to midnight.

$ ╳ **Bar L'Escale.** This small city-center bar is rather rowdy, but the smoky grill room in back serves the best grilled chicken in Marrakesh. Wash your meal down with a local wine or beer. ⊠ *Rue de Mauritania (off Mohammed V at Derby Shoes),* ☎ *no phone. Closed Sun.*

$ ╳ **Café Bahja.** This small, tiled medina café, two doors away from Marrakesh institution Chez Brek, is just as popular and has almost the same food at the same prices. Here, however, you can get beef and chicken tagines and *loubia* (bean stew) in addition to standard grill fare. ⊠ *Rue Bani Marine,* ☎ *04/44–03–43.*

$ ✕ **Chez Brek.** Hidden on a narrow side street off Djemâa el Fna, Chez Brek is one of the best grill-cafés in town. The menu focuses on grilled lamb chops, *merguez* sausages, kefta, and kidneys, each served with bread, olives, tomato salad, and hot sauce. It's a small selection, but everything is prepared so well that Chez Brek has been in business longer than most. Alcohol is not served. ✉ *41, Rue Bani Marine (walk through arch just left of post office in Djemâa el Fna).*

LODGING

Most hotels in Marrakesh are of a good to excellent standard. The high season lasts from March to May, with additional spikes at Christmas, the New Year, and Easter. Most of the finer hotels (classified as three, four, or five stars by the Moroccan government) are in Gueliz, with the exception of La Mamounia, which is just inside the ramparts of the medina. If you prefer to stay near the action and want something authentic and inexpensive, choose one of the endless small and clean hotels in the medina near Djemâa el Fna.

Most hotels provide their own free parking or oversee parking in the street nearby with a permanent guardian, who wears a badge. The guardian's fee for street parking is 2DH for a few hours, 5DH for a full day, or 10DH overnight.

CATEGORY	COST*
$$$$	over 1600DH
$$$	750–1600DH
$$	500–750DH
$	under 500DH

Prices are for a standard double room, including service and tax.

Medina

$$$$ 🏨 **La Mamounia.** Marrakesh's most prestigious hotel began with a vast garden just inside the ramparts—Arsat el Mamoun—offered to Prince Mamoun by his father, Sidi Mohammed ben Abdellah, as a wedding gift. Built in 1923 in a blend of ornate Moroccan and Art Deco styles, it took on legendary cachet in the late 1920s, when dignitaries flocked here. Sir Winston Churchill, for instance, liked to paint on the grounds. La Mamounia remains *the* place to stay if you want to be among the rich and famous, as celebrities generally won't stay anywhere else. (Hillary Clinton spent four days in one of the villas). Rooms that face south have balconies with fabulous views of the gardens and the Atlas mountains. You can see La Mamounia without paying its steep rates by taking a walk in the secluded olive gardens or by having lunch at Les Trois Palmiers (☞ Dining, *above*). ✉ *Avenue Bab el Djedid,* ☎ *04/44–89–91,* ℻ *04/44–49–40. 171 rooms, 57 suites, 3 villas. 5 restaurants, 5 bars, piano bar, air-conditioning, in-room safes, pool, beauty salon, hammam, massage, sauna, driving range, tennis court, casino, nightclub. AE, DC, MC, V.*

$$$–$$$$ 🏨 **Riad Enija.** This very large riad is known as the most authentic in
★   Marrakesh. The beautiful plant- and tree-filled garden courtyard is a haven of peace and elegance. Swiss owners Ursula and Bjorn have blended modern sculptures with the extraordinarily well-preserved Moroccan decor. The oversize guest rooms have fans and high ceilings, so they tend to stay cool, and the luxuriously spacious bathrooms are works of art in themselves, with sunken baths, tiles, and peach *tadlak* (shiny marbled) finishes. Meals are prepared on request. ✉ *9, Derb Mesfioui, Rahba Lakdima,* ☎ *04/44–09–26,* ℻ *04/44–27–00. 10 suites. Restaurant. MC, V.*

$$$ ⊞ **Dar les Zomorrodes.** Run by longtime Marrakesh resident Thierry Wauquiez, this jewel of a riad has all of its original fittings, including carved doors and *zouak* (bright, intricate) painted ceilings. You enter what feels like an oasis of tranquility from a narrow dusty derb near Dar Si Saïd. The bedrooms are quaint and comfortable, with wrought-iron bedposts, and the adjoining bathrooms are replete with ceramic and tadlak. A courtyard pool and a leafy terrace for sunning and reading complete the idyll. Note that the riad is rented as an entire unit, by the week only. ⊠ *36, Rue de la Bahia,* ☎ *04/44–10–19 or 04/43–15–60,* ᶠᴬˣ *04/43–15–59. 4 rooms, 3 with bath. No credit cards.*

$$$ ⊞ **La Maison Arabe.** This riad is an artful blend of Moorish and European design. Owners Fabrizio and Philippe have created peaceful courtyards and cool bedrooms that blend ceramics, mosaics, zouak painting, cedar, and stucco. In the medina near Bab Doukkala, the house was once a famous restaurant, the first to serve Moroccan cuisine to such European notables as Winston Churchill. Breakfast and afternoon tea are complimentary. Most rooms have air-conditioning, and the hotel offers free shuttle service to the nearby pool. ⊠ *1, Derb Assebhe, Bab Doukkala,* ☎ *04/38–70–10,* ᶠᴬˣ *04/44–37–10. 4 rooms, 6 suites. Restaurant, pool. MC, V.*

$$ ⊞ **Dar El Farah.** You enter this riad through a quiet garden near the El Bahia Palace. Owned by Thierry Wauquiez, who also runs the Dar les Zomorrodes (☞ *above*), the house has all of its original doors, ceilings, and tiles, and the charming guest rooms have painted wrought-iron window grilles and private bathrooms finished in tadlak. The courtyard has a small pool surrounded by jasmine, bougainvillea, and banana palms. The secluded terrace has great views of Marrakesh and the High Atlas, and meals are served there on request. ⊠ *Riad Zitoun el Djedid,* ☎ *04/44–10–19 or 04/43–15–60,* ᶠᴬˣ *04/43–15–59. 5 rooms. No credit cards.*

$ ⊞ **Hotel Ali.** Long frequented by young backpackers, this basic hotel just off Djemâa el Fna has expanded its clientele in recent years to a general crowd of travelers who prefer to spend their vacation money on commodities other than lodging. Guest rooms are small, sparse, and clean, but the hotel's pièce de résistance is a computer room with five modem-happy terminals. ⊠ *Rue Moulay Ismail,* ☎ *04/44–49–79,* ᶠᴬˣ *04/44–05–22. 45 rooms, 38 with bath. Restaurant. AE, DC, MC, V.*

$ ⊞ **Hotel Essaouira.** If you're on a tight budget and want to be close to Djemâa el Fna, this quaint riad follows Le Gallia as the best place to stay and is in fact often used by Peace Corps volunteers stationed in Morocco. It's all green plants and colorful ceramics, and the proprietor is charming and helpful. There's even a rooftop terrace. Bath facilities are shared. ⊠ *3, Sidi Bouloukate,* ☎ *04/44–38–05. 31 rooms. No credit cards.*

$ ⊞ **Hôtel Islane.** This hotel is a busy place, long popular for its prime location: just opposite the Koutoubia Mosque and around a corner from Djemâa el Fna. The rooms are simple and clean, and some have views of the mosque, which is dramatically illuminated at night. ⊠ *279, Avenue Mohammed V,* ☎ *04/44–00–81,* ᶠᴬˣ *04/44–00–85. 40 rooms. 2 restaurants, bar, pizzeria, air-conditioning. DC, MC, V.*

$ ⊞ **Le Gallia.** This small, spotless hotel is the nicest of its kind in the medina and is always full, so reserve in advance. Succulent plants trail from the upper floor in the courtyard, and green and yellow tiles add color throughout. The rooms are small, cool, clean, and nicely tiled. The building is near Djemâa el Fna, behind the post office. ⊠ *30, Rue de la Recette,* ☎ *04/44–59–13,* ᶠᴬˣ *04/44–48–53. 19 rooms. Air-conditioning. DC, MC, V.*

Hivernage

$$$$ ⊡ **Sheraton Marrakech.** Away from the bustle and a mere jog from the Menara Garden, the Sheraton has panoramic views of both olive groves and the High Atlas mountains. It's decorated à la Marrakesh, with a colorful zouak ceiling decoration in the lobby. Rooms are medium size; the best have sunny balconies with views of the pool and garden. A poolside grill adds a casual touch. ⊠ *Avenue de la Menara, B.P. 528,* ☎ *04/44–89–98,* FAX *04/43–78–43 or 04/43–81–28. 291 rooms, 9 suites. 2 restaurants, grill, ice-cream parlor, piano bar, pizzeria, air-conditioning, in-room safes, driving range, business services. AE, DC, MC, V.*

$$$ ⊡ **Es Saadi.** A quiet, green, residential part of Gueliz is home to this well-established 1950s-style hotel. The large guest rooms have a chic, airy look, and the spacious lobby is endowed with a high ceiling. A sizable secluded garden and popular public café adjoin the pool. Despite its calm location, Es Saadi is only a 10-minute walk from Djemâa el Fna and the souk. ⊠ *Rue Quadissia, Hivernage,* ☎ *04/44–88–11,* FAX *04/44–76–44. 150 rooms. 3 restaurants, café, piano bar, hammam, 2 tennis courts, casino, business services. AE, DC, MC, V.*

$$$ ⊡ **Imperial Borj.** The Imperial Borj has a rather formal entrance, but inside it's entirely relaxed, with a nice pool and quiet garden. Rooms are light and spacious, with good bathrooms, and all have balconies large enough for sunning and private dining. You're but a 10-minute walk from Djemâa el Fna and the souk. ⊠ *Avenue Echouhada, Hivernage,* ☎ *44–73–22,* FAX *44–62–06. 187 rooms, 20 suites. 3 restaurants, piano bar, business services. AE, DC, MC, V.*

The Palmery

$$$$ ⊡ **Hotel Amanjena.** Designed in traditional Moroccan style, this brand-new deluxe property near the Royal Golf club comprises 34 pavilions and seven villas around a large lagoon. The pavilions have specious bedrooms, living rooms with high domed ceilings, and private courtyards with soaking pools. ⊠ *B.P. 2405, Poste Principale de Gueliz,* ☎ *04/40–33–53,* FAX *04/40–34–77. 34 pavilions, 7 villas. 2 restaurants, bar, minibars, air-conditioning, pool, beauty salon, hammam, health club, 2 tennis courts, library. AE, DC, MC, V.*

$$$$ ⊡ **Les Deux Tours.** The Two Towers is actually a set of six exclusive villas hidden in the Palmery just outside Marrakesh, all designed by Charles Boccara. Every suite is decorated in a traditional style, with zellij, ceramic, and oleander-branch ceilings. In addition to quiet gardens of jasmine and bougainvillea, the villas have private courtyards and pools, as well as fireplaces for cooler evenings. Meals are served upon request. ⊠ *Douar Abiad, Circuit de la Palmeraie, B.P. 513, Marrakech Principale,* ☎ *04/32–95–27, 04/32–95–26, or 04/32–95–25,* FAX *04/32–95–23. 24 suites. Restaurant, air-conditioning, hammam. DC, MC, V.*

$$$$ ⊡ **Palais Rhoul.** This palatial horseshoe-shape mansion with classical columns half surrounds a luscious pool in the center of the Palmery. Everything is shaded by palm trees or covered with flowers. Each of the exceedingly large and ornate rooms, decorated in a mixture of Moroccan and Art Deco styles, opens onto the pool's verandah. The building was originally constructed for a French countess, who then decided to make it a luxury hotel. Everyone is at your beck and call, and meals are served upon request. ⊠ *Represented by Paris Office: 237, Boulevard Pereire, 75017 Paris,* ☎ *(33) 1/45–72–13–00, 04/32–94–95 in Marrakesh,* FAX *(33) 1/45–13–07. 7 rooms, 3 suites. Restaurant, air-conditioning, pool, hammam, tennis court. AE, MC, V.*

$$$$ ▦ **Palmeraie Golf Palace.** This deluxe complex greets you in its lobby with an impressive vaulted ceiling and a huge crystal candelabra. The entire hotel is furnished in ornate Moroccan style, and the guest rooms are at once bright, fresh, and luxurious, with plenty of gilt and marble. The biggest advantage here is a sense of space; the drawback is the 7-km (4-mi) distance from Marrakesh, which necessitates a car, a taxi, or use of the hotel shuttle. ⊠ *Jardins de la Palmeraie, B.P. 1488,* ☎ *04/30–10–10,* 𝕱𝕬𝕏 *04/30–50–50. 286 rooms, 28 suites. 3 restaurants, 3 bars, in-room safes, 2 pools, spa, 18-hole golf course, horseback riding. AE, DC, MC, V.*

$$$ ▦ **Iberotel Tikida Garden.** The main attraction of this hotel is its array of sports facilities. Serious swimmers and tennis players are particularly well accommodated. The entire place is open and spacious, and guest rooms are large, comfortable, and modern. Set in several acres of secluded gardens, the hotel is just 3 km (2 mi) from Marrakesh on the road toward Fez. Shuttle service into town is complimentary. ⊠ *B.P. 1585, Circuit de la Palmeraie, 40007,* ☎ *04/30–90–99 or 04/32–92–75,* 𝕱𝕬𝕏 *04/30–93–43 or 04/32–92–96. 206 rooms. 8 suites. 3 restaurants, 2 bars, air-conditioning, in-room safes, hammam, driving range, 8 tennis courts, archery, exercise room, jogging, bicycles, recreation room. DC, MC, V.*

Gueliz

$$$ ▦ **Melia Tichka Salam.** Designed by Marrakesh aficionado Charles Boccara, this upscale lodging illustrates his eye-catching, distinctively modern vision of Moroccan architecture. In a cobbled triangle off the main Casablanca road, the hotel offers quiet, medium-size rooms and a particularly elegant garden with poolside dining. The Moroccan and international restaurants are as beautiful aesthetically as gastronomically. ⊠ *Triangle d'Or, B.P. 894,* ☎ *04/44–87–10,* 𝕱𝕬𝕏 *04/44–86–91. 138 rooms, 8 suites. 2 restaurants, bar, air-conditioning, in-room safes, hammam. AE, MC, V.*

$$ ▦ **Nassim.** If you want to lodge in the city center, this small, charming, modern hotel is just right—it's near Place Abdel Moumen and all the surrounding cafés. The good-size guest rooms are nicely decorated, and the many facilities include a dipping pool, a quiet bar, and an exercise room, as well as a rooftop terrace. ⊠ *115, Boulevard Mohammed V,* ☎ *04/44–64–01,* 𝕱𝕬𝕏 *04/43–67–10. 50 rooms, 4 suites, 1 luxury apartment. Restaurant, bar, air-conditioning, pool, in-room safes, hammam, exercise room, piano bar. MC, V.*

$ ▦ **Hôtel de la Menara.** The heart of this hotel is its large, sunny lounge, which opens onto a pleasant, secluded garden and pool. Tucked behind Avenue Mohammed V, it has traditional Moroccan decor and an agreeable, relaxed atmosphere. Guest rooms are spacious, light, and well appointed. ⊠ *Avenue des Ramparts,* ☎ *04/43–64–78.* 𝕱𝕬𝕏 *04/44–73–86. 100 rooms. 2 restaurants, bar, air-conditioning. AE, MC, V.*

$ ▦ **Hôtel du Pacha.** This old, established hotel near the Central Market in Gueliz has a quiet, somber air. There's a small café inside and an airy courtyard for breakfast. Rooms have a slightly dated look, but they're comfortable. ⊠ *33, Rue de la Liberté,* ☎ *04/43–13–27,* 𝕱𝕬𝕏 *04/43–13–26. 37 rooms. Air-conditioning. MC, V.*

$ ▦ **Hotel Moussafir Ibis.** One of a chain of hotels that are always placed next to train stations, the Moussafir Ibis has an efficient and friendly atmosphere. The rooms are small but charming, decorated in blue and white with an uncluttered modern-Moroccan style, and have nice, ceramic-tile bathrooms. The pool is in a quiet garden. ⊠ *Avenue Hassan II, Place de la Gare,* ☎ *04/43–59–29,* 𝕱𝕬𝕏 *04/43–59–36. 98 rooms, 5 suites. Restaurant, bar, air-conditioning, pool. AE, MC, V.*

$ ⚇ **Hotel Oudaya.** The unpretentious Oudaya, on a quiet street in
Gueliz, is popular with young travelers. The aesthetic is modern Moroccan, and the rooms are small and cool, with well-appointed bathrooms. ✉ *147, Rue Mohammed el Bequal,* ☎ *04/44–85–12 or 04/44–
71–09,* ℻ *04/43–54–00. 77 rooms, 15 suites. Restaurant, air-conditioning, pool. MC, V.*

$ ⚇ **Le Toulousain.** Tucked behind the Central Market, Le Toulousain
is small and quiet, with two shady, tree-filled courtyards. Rooms are
good size, simply furnished, and cool. ✉ *44, Rue Tariq ben Ziad,* ☎
04/43–00–33, ℻ *04/43–14–46. 31 rooms, 13 with bath. Café, free parking. No credit cards.*

NIGHTLIFE AND THE ARTS

The Arts

Art Museums

Next to the Ali ben Youssef Medersa is the newly opened **Musée de
Marrakesh,** in which the association Les Amis de Marrakesh (Friends
of Marrakesh) displays paintings owned by local art collectors (☎ 04/
39–19–94).

Music

Performances of Western classical music are occasionally held at the
Ali ben Youssef Medersa. Western pop acts play El Bahia Palace. Details are announced on posters around town and in most hotels.

Fantasias

The fantasia is a significant part of several moussems throughout Morocco. This festivity has come to be most closely associated with its
horsemen, who are dressed in flowing white robes and turbans, their
horses in jewel-encrusted saddles. The climax of the fantasia comes when
the horsemen race at full tilt for some 300 ft, then come to a sudden
halt and simultaneously fire their rifles in a tumultuous finale.

CHEZ ALI

This *Arabian Nights* complex north of town might be best described
as a sort of Moroccan Disneyland (Aliwood?). It's actually well worth
a visit, because it presents a variety of folk music and folklore from
regions of Morocco that you might not otherwise see. Dinner, served
under caidal tents, includes the famous *mechoui* roast lamb and is followed by ringside entertainment: a staged camel caravan, a belly
dancer, a singer, bareback riding, and, finally, the horsemen. ✉ *Drive
7 km (4 mi) north of Marrakesh on the Casablanca road, then turn
left and continue for about 3 km (2 mi);* ☎ *04/30–77–30,* ℻ *04/30–
93–82.* ⚇ *400DH per person, including drinks. AE, MC, V.*

Nightlife

The most fascinating nocturnal scene in Marrakesh is, hands down, the
Djemâa el Fna. From sundown, when the gas lamps are lighted and the
cooking oil starts sizzling and smoking, through midnight, when the last
stalls are cleared away, the square hums with life in the form of acrobats, storytellers, musicians, jugglers, drummers, fortune-tellers, and even
tooth pullers. The Café de France, Café Argana, Café CTM, and Café
Glacier have roof space dedicated to viewing the ongoing festivities.

Bars

Bars are frowned upon by most Moroccans, so apart from a couple of
disreputable joints in Gueliz, they exist only in Gueliz hotels. (There are
no bars or liquor stores in the medina, with the sole exception of La

Mamounia.) All of the major hotels have their own bars, but the piano bars at **La Mamounia,** the **Hotel Atlas Asni** (⊠ Avenue de France, 04/44–82–26), **La Notte Gourmande** (⊠ Avenue de France, next to Sheraton, ☎ 04/43–85–95), and the **Hotel Pullman Mansour Edhabi** (⊠ Avenue de France, ☎ 04/44–82–22) are among the most popular, and they all stay open until around midnight. The American Bar in the **Hotel Kenzi Semiramis** (⊠ Triangle d'Or, ☎ 04/43–13–77) is also well attended.

Casinos
The casino at **La Mamounia** has a large room for roulette and a hall for one-arm bandits and is open until 4 AM. **Es Saadi** also has a casino annex. *See* Lodging, *above.*

Nightclubs
The city's best and most popular nightclub is **Paradise,** at the Hotel Pullman Mansour Edhabi (⊠ Avenue de France, ☎ 04/44–82–22). Other disco haunts are **New Feeling,** in the Palmeriae Golf Palace; **Le Diamant Noir,** at the Jets d'Eau roundabout; and the **Cotton Club,** in the Hotel Tropicana (⊠ Triangle d'Or, ☎ 04/44–74–50).

SPORTS AND OUTDOOR ACTIVITIES

Bowling
The game room in the **Palmeraie Golf Palace** (☞ Golf, *below*) includes a good bowling alley.

Fishing
The lakes and rivers surrounding Marrakesh contain pike, perch, roach, carp, and trout; contact the tourist office for details.

Golf
The 18-hole **Golf Amelkis** club (☎ 04/44–92–88) was built in 1995 on the road toward Ouarzazate. The greens fee is 350DH. The Hotel **La Mamounia** has a relatively new practice green (☎ 04/44–89–81). Robert Trent Jones designed the 18-hole course at the **Palmeraie Golf Palace** (☎ 04/30–10–10), 7 km (4 mi) north of Marrakesh in the Palmery; facilities include a clubhouse, pro shop, and equipment rental, and your cost is 350DH. The well-established **Royal Golf** club (☎ 04/44–43–41), founded in 1923, is a tree-filled 18-hole course 6 km (4 mi) south of Marrakesh on the Ouarzazate road. The greens fee is is 350DH.

Horseback Riding
The **Royal Club Equestre** (☎ 04/31–21–20) is 6 km (4 mi) southwest of Marrakesh on the Amizmiz road. Guided rides are 150DH per person, per hour. The **Palmeraie Golf Palace Riding Club** (☎ 04/30–10–10) charges 150DH per person per hour for guided rides.

Running
Serious runners have found that the strip running straight west from the Bab el Djedid past the Sheraton Hotel to the Menara Garden—about 4 km (3 mi) in all—is the best in Marrakesh. All but the skimpiest of shorts are usually acceptable.

Skiing
From December through March or April, Oukaimeden has good skiing; *see* Side Trips, *below.*

Swimming
All of Marrakesh's top hotels have nice, large pools. The **Palmeraie Golf Palace** complex (☞ Golf, *above*) has a public pool with a great restaurant and a garden to lose yourself in; admission is 100DH per person per day.

Tennis
The **Royal Tennis Club** (⊠ Rue Imam Shafii, Gueliz, ☎ 04/43–19–02) has eight courts and charges 100DH per person, per hour.

Trekking
Atlas Sahara Trekking (☞ Guided Tours *in* Marrakesh A to Z, below) can help you arrange a day or two of High Atlas trekking on foot or by mule. The **Hotel Ali** (☞ Lodging, *above*) can also set you up with a guide, as can many of the travel agencies on Boulevard Mohammed V in Gueliz. If you're planning a serious expedition, ☞ The High Atlas A to Z *in* Chapter 7 for contacts in the mountains.

SHOPPING

Marrakesh is a shopper's bonanza, full of the very rugs and handicrafts you may have seen in the pages of interior-design magazines back home. As a group, the bazaars in the souk sell everything imaginable and are highly competitive. Recently, boutiques have begun to spring up in Gueliz, part of a movement toward allowing buyers to browse at their leisure, free of the intense pressures of the souks. Most of these stores are happy to ship your purchases overseas. Some bazaars in the souk also ship merchandise, but it's worth sticking to recommended merchants only, as many travelers find that their shipments never arrive. The bazaars open between 8 AM and 9 AM and close between 8 PM and 9 PM; stores in Gueliz open a bit later and close a bit earlier.

As you wander through the souk, take note of landmarks so you can return to a particular bazaar without too much trouble. Once the bazaars' shutters are closed, they're often unrecognizable. Note that some bazaars are closed on Friday, the Muslim holy day.

Shopping Districts

Most bazaars are in the medina north of Djemâa el Fna, spread through a seemingly never-ending maze of alleys. In Gueliz there are a number of crafts and souvenir shops on Avenue Mohammed V, as well as some very good Moroccan antiques stores. The Central Market also has a bazaar section.

Specialty Stores

Medina
The following merchants are large and reputable, and most will ship your selections home. The large and well-established **La Porte d'Or** (⊠ Souk Semarine, ☎ 04/44–54–54) has two floors of good-quality Berber rugs and antique Moroccan furniture. Rugs range in price from 1,000DH to 100,000DH. The reputable **Khalid Art Gallery** (⊠ Rue Dar el Basha, ☎ 04/44–24–10) has become very popular with the international jet set for its collection of the most sought-after Moroccan items: lanterns, mirrors, jewelry, and antique furniture, including old doors and fountains from the riads. **Antique Jewelery Saharian** (⊠ 176, Rahba Lakdima, ☎ 04/44–23–73) specializes in handcrafted jewelry from southern Morocco. **Atelier Barkowski** (⊠ Souk des Potiers, ☎ 04/49–06–65) sells ceramic and terra-cotta pieces. **Bazaar Jouti** (⊠ 19, Souk des Tapis, Rahba Lakdima, ☎ 04/44–13–55) has rugs and carpets. **Boutique Musicien** (⊠ 63, Soukatt al Mouassine, ☎ no phone) sells all kinds of Moroccan musical instruments. **La Maison Berbère** (⊠ 23, Rue el Mouassine Fhal Chidmi, ☎ 04/39–08–48) has a variety of handicrafts. **La Maison du Kaftan Marocain** (⊠ 65, Rue Sidi Yamani, ☎ 04/44–10–51) sells kaftans and djellabas for women. **Le Trésor des Nomades** (⊠ 128, Rue Mouassine, ☎ 04/44–59–06) sells

antique doors and all kinds of lamps. **Palais Vizir** (✉ 29, Derb Essania, Rue el Khsour, opposite the restaurant Stylia, ☎ 04/44–15–91 or 04/39–03–30) carries a large selection of carpets, old and new.

Gueliz

La Porte d'Orient (✉ 9, Boulevard Mansour Edhabi, next to Glacier Oliveri, ☎ 04/43–89–67), a sibling of the medina's La Porte d'Or (☞ *above*) is a gallery with Moroccan and Asian antiques. It's geared toward those who prefer to browse before buying. **Al Badii** (✉ 54, Boulevard My Rachid, ☎ 04/43–16–93) sells artworks, crafts, and antiques in a quiet setting. **Atika** (✉ 212, Avenue Mohammed V, Residence Elite 4, ☎ 04/43–24–52) sells contemporary Western clothing, lingerie, and shoes as well as deluxe contemporary Moroccan shoes. The best place to buy Moroccan pastries to take home is **Chez Madame Alami Hakima** (✉ 11, Rue de la Liberté, ☎ no phone). The small store **Côte Sud** (✉ Rue de la Liberté) carries nice Moroccan artifacts with modern touches. **L'Orientaliste** (✉ 15, Rue de la Liberté, ☎ 04/43–40–74) features Oriental paintings and other antiques. **Marco Polo** (✉ Immeuble Taieb, 55, Boulevard Zerktouni, ☎ 04/43–53–55) has been in Gueliz for years, selling all kinds of antique Moroccan and Asian furniture as well as other artifacts. The **Matisse** gallery (✉ 61, Rue de Yougoslavie, 43, Passage Ghandouri, ☎ 04/44–83–26) has a nice collection of works by young Moroccan artists and the Orientalists. **T. M. Design** (✉ Rue el Arrak, Quartière Menara, ☎ 04/34–09–27) manufactures luxury articles and furniture based on Moroccan designs. The gallery **TinMel** (✉ 38, Rue Ibn Aisha, ☎ 04/43–22–71) sells artworks, antique carpets, and furniture.

SIDE TRIPS

Just south of Marrakesh, the High Atlas mountains are a fabulous world apart, an expanse of unspoiled mountain scenery and mud-roofed Berber villages. The possibilities for walking, hiking, camping, and skiing are endless.

The Ourika Valley

A popular excursion from Marrakesh is the Ourika Valley, which starts about 40 km (25 mi) southeast of the city. The drive offers not only a pleasant contrast from the city's hubbub but a chance to see the centuries-old rural lifestyle of the mountain Berbers. The Ourika River flows down from Djebel (Mt.) Toubkal to form this cool, green valley, a delight of walnut and fig trees as well as small vegetable and cereal gardens. The valley has been devastated by floods more than once, last in 1994, but it always manages to pull itself together again. You can stop in the mud-walled villages to buy pottery, have a country tagine, or just explore; it's not advisable to buy rugs here unless you already know how to judge their quality and prices. About 35 km (22 mi) south of Marrakesh, on the road toward Setti Fatma, you'll come to a left turn for **Tnine Ourika.** This Monday country market has a wonderful atmosphere, enhanced (for the curious traveler) by its riverside parking lot for donkeys. Continuing on toward Setti Fatma, after Arhbalou, the paved road ends at a small waterfall in **Oulmès,** where you can relax by the river or have lunch in one of the tiny riverside cafés. From here you can walk to **Setti Fatma,** a popular camping spot and the site of seven waterfalls in the cooler, wetter months. On the return trip to Marrakesh, take a sharp left toward **Oukaimeden.** The road climbs and twists through the mountains and villages to a small ski center perched at 9,840 ft. Berber ski instructors hang around at the base of the chairlift, eager to teach you or rent you equipment. The slopes don't get enough snow for skiing every winter, but when they do (usually in February, March, or early April), the skiing is excellent and the Alpine views are fabulous.

NEED A BREAK?
In Arhbalou you can have a good lunch and enjoy great valley views at the roadside **Auberge Ramuntcho** (✉ Route S513, ☎ 04/48–45–21).

A simple drive to Oulmès and back, with lunch on the way, takes about half a day. If you want to stop at the Tnine Ourika souk and Ouikameden, allow the better part of a day.

The Taroudant Road

The S501 south takes you through Tahanaoute to **Asni,** a small Berber market town (elevation: 3,805 ft) on a shaded tree-lined road. Its weekly event is the Saturday souk, but you can stop for refreshments anytime at one of several very basic roadside cafés. Just before Asni, a right turn leads to the hillside saint's village of **Moulay Ibrahim,** the site of a yearly pilgrimage to its mausoleum. Just after Asni, a rough road to the left leads up to Imlil, passing en route the fairy-tale **Kasbah Tamadot.** It takes a good half hour on a rough piste to reach the mountain village of **Imlil** itself, a place cast as a Tibetan village in Martin Scorsese's film *Kundun.* Returning to the Taroudant road—which from here on is a series of steep S curves through the wild holly-oak and pine forests of the Atlas slopes—you'll come to the village of **Ouirgane.** Suddenly the romantic rose-filled La Résidence de la Roseraie appears out of nowhere, sprawling surreally across an otherwise uninhabited landscape. Nearby is Au Sanglier Qui Fume (roughly, "The Smoking Boar"), an inn run by the same French family that opened it in the 1940s.

If you take a four-wheel-drive vehicle on these excursions, you can cross the Plateau du Kik by driving from Moulay Ibrahim to the **Lalla Takerkoust Dam.** Known for its unspoiled scenery, the dam is an ideal place for a long, quiet picnic—flanked by forested hills, the water has banks and beaches from which you can swim or fish for trout. Part of the film *Hideous Kinky* was shot here. A shanty café near the road, overlooking the dam, serves delicious country tagines.

The drive to Imlil and Ouirgane with a stop for lunch is a good day's outing. For a shorter drive, leave Marrakesh on the Taroudant road and veer right after 8 km (5 mi) to **Amizmiz.** En route you'll pass the hillside Kasbah of Oumnass, where parts of Scorsese's *The Last Temptation of Christ* and Gillies MacKinnon's *Hideous Kinky* were filmed. Amizmiz has a good, if rather boisterous, country market; practice saying "no" with conviction before you plunge in. On the way back to Marrakesh, stop at the Lalla Takerkoust Dam and soak up its tranquility before returning to Marrakesh.

NEED A BREAK?
Stop for lunch or tea at Ouirgane's exclusive **La Résidence de la Roseraie** (✉ Route Taroudannt, Box 769, 60 km [37 mi] south of Marrakesh, ☎ 04/43–91–28, FAX 04/43–91–30). In warm weather you can take your refreshments next to a turquoise pool; at cooler times, relax beside a log fire in the rustic dining room. The Résidence hides chalet rooms among its endless roses (doubles 850DH with half-board) and rents horses for rides in the hills.

A stone's throw from the Résidence, the restaurant-hotel **Au Sanglier qui Fume** (✉ Route Taroudannt, 61 km [38 mi] south of Marrakesh, ☎ 04/48–57–07 or 04/48–57–08) has a nice garden and good lunch and dinner menus.

The Ourika Valley and Taroudant Road A to Z

Transportation

If you don't have a rental car, you can still day-trip from Marrakesh in a variety of ways. One is to join a guided tour in a minibus for about 270DH per person (☞ Guided Tours *in* Marrakesh A to Z, *below*). Another is to hire a chauffeur-driven taxi, usually a Mercedes, through your hotel or outside the hotel for about 400DH per person for a morning drive. Be sure to negotiate the price before setting off. As an alternative, the adventurous can squeeze into a *grand taxi* with a group of up to six people for about 15DH one way. Be prepared to wait a bit for the return journey; the grand taxi only departs when it's full. Finally, for some serious local flavor, you can jump on a local bus: they're cheap, but they're uncomfortable, have vague timetables, and stop at every crossroad. For a grand taxi or a bus, go to Bab er Rob and ask for the buses or *grands taxis* going to Oulmès.

MARRAKESH A TO Z

Arriving and Departing

By Bus

Buses depart for Casablanca, Rabat, Fez, Agadir, and other cities from the Gare Routière bus terminal at Bab Doukkala. The blue-and-white buses of **C.T.M.** (✉ Gare Routière, ☎ 04/43–44–02 or 04/44-83–28; ✉ Boulevard Zerktouni, Gueliz, ☎ 04/44–65–69) are the best; they're air-conditioned and comfortable. **Supratours** (✉ Avenue Hassan II, ☎ 04/43-55–25) has bus routes all over Morocco, including Essaouira, which C.T.M. does not serve. There are many other, less expensive lines, but these are much less comfortable and tend to stop at every crossroads and outpost along the way.

By Car

Marrakesh is in the center of Morocco, so it connects well by road with Casablanca, Rabat, and Tangier to the north, Fez and Meknes to the northeast, Essaouira to the west, Agadir to the southwest, and Ouarzazate and Taroudant to the south over the High Atlas passes. Most of these roads are good, two-lane highways with hard, sandy shoulders for passing.

By Plane

Menara Airport is past the Menara Garden, about 5 km (3 mi) west of Marrakesh. It receives domestic flights as well as international connections from the United States, Europe, and the Middle East. **Royal Air Maroc** has an office in town (✉ Boulevard Mohammed V, ☎ 04/44–64–44 or 04/43–62–05).

By Train

Marrakesh is well served by train from Tangier, Rabat, Casablanca, and Fez. For schedule and fare information, call **ONCF** at the station on Avenue Hassan II (☎ 04/44–77–68).

From the Airport to the City

There are no buses from Marrakesh's airport. *Petits taxis* do not often wait here, either, and if you do find one, the driver will ask 50DH–60DH rather than use his meter. Your only option is bound to be a private **grand taxi,** which will charge 100DH to almost anywhere in Marrakesh.

Getting Around

The one good map of Marrakesh is available at all news agents, book-stores, and tobacco shops. If you don't hire a guide, keep the map with you at all times. Gueliz is easy to navigate, with wide streets and street names marked in French. The medina, while not quite so enclosed and intense as the one in Fez, takes some doing—street names are signposted only in Arabic.

By Car
Cars can pass through most of the medina's derbs, but not all, and un-less you know the lay of the land, you risk getting suddenly stuck and being hard pressed to perform a U-turn. Watch carefully for the directions of one-way streets.

By Public Bus
Public buses are frequent and run all over Marrakesh, with a fare of approximately 2DH. At rush hour this is not always a pleasant way to travel; the idea of forming a queue has yet to catch on in Morocco, so there's always a mad scramble to get on.

By Taxi
Petits taxis in Marrakesh are small, beige metered cabs. A petit-taxi ride from one end of Marrakesh to the other costs around 20DH. Note, however, that if you get into a petit taxi in the driveway of your hotel, the driver will ignore the meter and demand 50DH for just about any destination. **Grands taxis** are the ubiquitous old Mercedes and other large four-doors. Grands taxis have two uses. Most often they simply take a load of up to six passengers on short hauls to suburbs and nearby towns, forming a reliable, inexpensive network throughout each re-gion of Morocco. Fares for such trips are very cheap; a trip from the city to the airport entrance costs about 2DH, and although you'll get thoroughly squashed by your companions, you'll also get a real taste for the local ambience and the locals themselves. Alternately, if you want a car and driver to yourself, you can hire a grand taxi to ferry you around in style; just beware the driver might try to take you to in-ferior places where he receives a kickback. To avoid hard feelings at the end of the ride, negotiate the fare for such an excursion before you set off. An evening trip to a restaurant, with a pickup afterward, might cost 100DH.

Contacts and Resources

American Express
American Express has a representative in the **Voyages Schwarz** office (⊠ Immeuble Moutaoukil, 3rd floor, Rue Mauritania, ☎ 04/43–30–22). Note that services are available only from 9 to 12:30 and 3 to 4:30.

Banks
All banks are open from 8:30 to 11:30 and 2:30–4 from October to March and continuously from 8 to 2:30 from April to September and during Ramadan. There are cash machines at the BMCE bank oppo-site the tourist office in Gueliz and at the BMCE and WAFA banks in Djemâa el Fna.

Car Rental
Avis (⊠ 137, Avenue Mohammed V, ☎ 04/43–37–23 or 04/43–37–27). **Carole** (⊠ Rue de la Liberté, Immeuble Moulay Youssef, apt. A19, Gueliz, ☎ 04/43–21–67). **National** (⊠ 1, Rue de la Liberté, Gueliz, ☎ 04/43–06–83). **Europcar** (⊠ 63, Boulevard Zerktouni, ☎ 04/43–12–28). **Hertz** (⊠ 154, Avenue Mohammed V, Gueliz, ☎ 04/43–19–94).

Consulates

The only consulate in Marrakesh is the **French Consulate** (⊠ Rue Ibn Khaldoun, near Koutoubia Mosque, ☎ 04/44–00–06). The **Honorary British Consul** (⊠ 55, Boulevard Zerktouni, Gueliz. ☎ 04/43–60–78 or 04/43–78–74) is Mr. Mohammed Zkhiri.

Emergencies and Late-Night Pharmacies

Police: ☎ 19. **Ambulance:** ☎ 15. The **Clinique du Sud** (⊠ 2, Rue de Yougoslavie, ☎ 04/44–79–99) is open 24 hours.

Every hotel has a list of doctors, so you may want to inquire there first. **Dr. Ben Nahoud Mohammed Najib** (⊠ 5, Rue Soraya, Immeuble Rachadi, 2nd floor, Gueliz, ☎ 04/44–72–07) has treated American film crews. **Dr. Mekouar** (⊠ 39 Rue de Loubnane, Gueliz, ☎ 04/44–66–81) is a good dentist.

A list of the pharmacies open late at night is posted at the **Pharmacie du Progrès** (⊠ Djemâa el Fna, near C.T.M. hotel). A doctor is on continuous call at **Pharmacie du Nuit,** a late-night pharmacy in Gueliz (⊠ Rue Khalid ben Oualid, just off Place de la Liberté, next door to fire station, ☎ 04/43–04–15).

English-Language Bookstore

The **American Language Center** (⊠ 3, Impasse du Moulin, Gueliz, ☎ 04/44–72–59) has a small English-language bookstore.

Guided Tours

EXCURSIONS

Marrakesh lends itself to a great many side trips, including Asni, Ouirgane, Telouet, the Cascades d'Ouzoud, and the Ourika Valley. **Menara Tours** (⊠ 41, Avenue Yougoslavie, 40000, ☎ 04/44–66–54) leads excursions to all these regional destinations as well as farther afield. **Holidays Services** (⊠ 644, Complexe Kawkab, Rue Imam Shafii, Gueliz, ☎ 04/44–75–64 or 04/44–68–44) is one of Morocco's largest tour operators but can also arrange for custom tours of at least four people. **Diffa Tours** arranges all kinds of excursions for individuals (⊠ 2, Rue Ibn Aïcha, Gueliz, ☎ 04/43–48–79).

PERSONAL GUIDES

You can hire a personal guide through your hotel or at the tourist office, the **ONMT** (Office Nationale Marocaine de Tourisme; ⊠ Place Abd el Moumen, Avenue Mohammed V, ☎ 04/43–62–39 or 04/44–99–89).

TREKS

Atlas Sahara Trekking (⊠ 6 bis, Rue Houdhoud, Quartier Majorelle, Marrakesh, ☎ 04/31–39–01 or –03) draws on a wealth of experience to lead specialized treks in the High Atlas and bivouacs in the Sahara. The **National Association of Mountain Guides and Monitors (ANGM),** south of Marrakesh (⊠ B.P. 47, Asni, ☎ 04/44–49–79), is a loosely assembled group of trained mountain guides based in Asni, a popular High Atlas jumping-off point.

Houses of Worship

The Roman Catholic **Eglise des Saints Martyrs** (⊠ Rue el Imam Ali, opposite new mosque, Gueliz) was built in 1926. The **Beth-El Synagogue** (⊠ Impasse du Moulin, ☎ 04/44–87–54) is also in Gueliz. Entry to all **mosques** is strictly forbidden to non-Muslims.

Parking

Parking in Marrakesh is relatively easy; barring the red-and-white-striped gutters, you may park almost anywhere. Throughout the city, guardians (who usually wear blue overalls and a brass badge) watch cars for a few hours for 2DH, a day for 5DH, and 10 DH overnight.

Post Offices

The city has two main post offices. **Place du 16 Novembre** (on Avenue Mohammed V). **Djemâa el Fna** (one block from the Banque du Maghreb).

Travel Agencies

Most travel agencies are headquartered on the northern end of Avenue Mohammed V, in Gueliz, including **Royal Air Maroc, Menara Tours** (which has a sales office for British Airways), **Carlson Wagon-Lit,** and **Comanov Voyages** (✉ Complexe Kawkab, Rue Imam Shafii, next to Holidays Services, ☎ 04/43–02–65).

Visitor Information

The **Moroccan National Tourist Office** (✉ Place Abd el Moumen, on Avenue Mohammed V, ☎ 04/43–61–31 or 04/43–62–39) has brochures and can arrange for guides. The office is open weekdays and Saturday mornings.

7 THE HIGH ATLAS

Stretching from the ocean to the desert in a jumble of snowcapped peaks and plunging valleys, the High Atlas mountains were long considered inaccessible, even dangerous. Only in the 20th century did the region's resilient Berber farmers turn from guarding Morocco's southern caravan routes to maintaining the mountains' natural beauty. You still need to climb through one of three major passes to cross this range, but today you can get a good night's sleep along the way and take a quiet look at some intriguing aspects of Moroccan history.

By David
Crawford

THE HIGH ATLAS MOUNTAINS rise like a wall, a natural fortress between the fertile Haouz plain around Marrakesh and the deserts of the south. As recently as 1930 they were called the "forbidden Atlas," seen as a wild region of intransigent tribesmen and powerful local *caids* (feudal lords). Boasting a family of peaks over 13,000 ft, the Atlas defies our temptation to characterize North Africa as a dry, flat, and featureless expanse. Trapping much of the moisture that blows in from the Atlantic, the mountains return some of it to the farmers of the northern Moroccan plains and send some out in thin rivers that vanish into the desert. Such precipitation provides many farmers of this rugged area with an abundance of water, which their elaborate *targa* (canal) systems draw through intricately terraced hillsides.

There are limits to the number of people even this intensive agriculture can support, however, so the Ishelhin (Berbers) of this region can now be found in migrant communities all over Morocco and abroad. And although there is some local concern that the increasing penetration of roads allows livestock to be trucked up to summer pastures, potentially overgrazing and eroding the terrain, much of the High Atlas retains an unspoiled, often stark beauty. Largely undeveloped for tourism, they offer leisure in the simple form of walking, allowing you to breathe the cool air and experience the quietude of the high valleys. Many travelers pass through the High Atlas on the way to Ouarzazate, Taroudant, Agadir, and beyond, but even they are awed by the sheer peaks, the tumbling gorges, and the strikingly verdant fields etched into the folds of the mountains.

The human family has long occupied parts of the High Atlas—even before our ancestors became distinctly human. Although little is known of the prehistory of this region, Neanderthal man, *Homo erectus,* and even *Homo habilis* seem to have discovered its charms. As recently as 6,000 years ago the Sahara Desert was much more moist, and there was less geographic distinction between North Africa and the rest of the continent. Fossils of crocodiles, elephants, lions, and giraffes have all been discovered in Morocco along with early human remains.

The contemporary population of the High Atlas is marvelously heterogeneous. The genes of invading Vandals, Greek settlers, Roman bureaucrats, Phoenician sailors, and Arab scholars flow through the present population along with those of sub-Saharan soldiers, gold miners, and salt traders. The fact that none of these invading peoples were "pure" to begin with makes tracing the origins of the mountain Berbers a dubious business indeed. What we can say is still impressive: some of the ancestors of the current High Atlas population have been living here since the dawn of humanity. The language spoken in the western High Atlas, Tashelhit, seems to have arrived with migrants from somewhere in the East at least 3,000 years ago, perhaps in several waves. Closely related to Morocco's other Berber varieties, this language may be distantly related to other Semitic tongues like Arabic and Hebrew. There are still pockets of different Berber-language varieties across North Africa, from the Siwa Oasis in Egypt clear across to Mali, but the vast majority of today's Berber-speakers live in the mountains of Algeria and Morocco. Although the High Atlas had numerous Berber-speaking Jewish communities until the 20th century, the population is now almost entirely Muslim.

There is some disagreement over where the term *Berber* originated. One plausible theory is that it derives from the Greek word that essentially

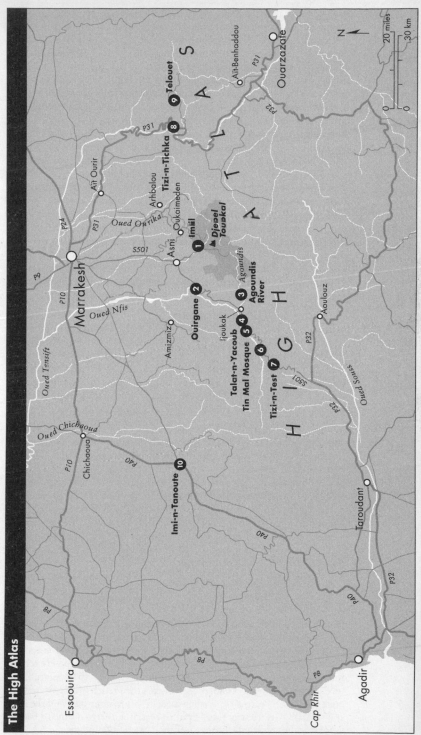

The High Atlas

means "barbarian" and was then used by the Romans to describe the people of the untamed hinterlands in their empire. These negative connotations have led some contemporary activists to argue that the word *Berber* should be replaced with the indigenous word *Imazighen,* which refers to all the people in North Africa who speak some variety of Berber. That most Tashelhit-speaking people in the High Atlas refer to themselves not as Imazighen but as Ishelhin confuses this issue; High Atlas farmers and shepherds know their language distinguishes them from Arabs and Arabic speakers, but they don't necessarily link themselves on this basis with other non-Arab Moroccans such as some Rifis of the north and the Berbers of the Middle Atlas. As devout Muslims and citizens of the Moroccan nation, most mountain Berbers do not trouble themselves about their ethnic identity, but this may be changing as more Berber speakers in the cities strive to retain their language and culture and as more monolingual Arabic teachers are introduced into rural, Tashelhit-speaking areas. Berbers now live in every part of Morocco and move in every social class, from the poorest rural farms to the wealthiest neighborhoods in Rabat. Those in the High Atlas still speak primarily Tashelhit, but many are now conversant in Arabic and some in French. Away from the few tourist areas and a few mines, most of mountain Ishelhin are poor farmers and shepherds; you'll find them notable for their friendliness, humor, business acumen, and hospitality.

Four periods stand out in High Atlas history. The first is the definitive arrival of Islam in the 12th century—exemplified by the mosque at Tin Mal, the crowning glory of the religious reformer Ibn Tumart. During this period the nominally Islamic tribesmen of the High Atlas were converted to the austere version of Islam he articulated, and transformed into the core of a far-flung empire. Some families in the valley of the Upper Nfis River, around Tin Mal, trace their arrival in the mountains to this time, pointing to their earlier origins in the Haouz plain, the southern desert regions, and the Anti-Atlas mountains.

The second significant period was that preceding the 1912 arrival of the French, when most of the High Atlas was dominated by local tribal caids. These overlords were often ruthless—even today a few locals can mesmerize you with tales of their power, of their arbitrary violence and brutal repression of dissent. In this period each of the three passes over the mountains was dominated by a different tribal confederation. The Tizi-n-Tichka was ruled by the Glaoui from the Kasbah at Telouet; the Glaoui became allies of the French and played a significant role in Moroccan politics during the French Protectorate, thus holding on to real power much longer than the other tribal leaders. To the west, the Tizi-n-Test was controlled by the Goundafa confederation from Tagoundaft and Talat-n-Yacoub. The most westerly route, heading south to Agadir, was ruled by the Mtougi.

French rule followed this tribal arrangement (or, in the case of the Glaoui, joined it). It was the French who began to build roads into the mountains and extend the reach of the central government. There is a small French fort along the P40 road to Agadir, but in general the French influence is more evident in a style of administration than in architecture. Many High Atlas residents remember the French Protectorate with great ambivalence: as a time when infrastructure improved and the constant tribal warfare was finally put to rest, but also as a time of forced labor and humiliating domination by Christian colonizers.

Independence from France in 1956 inaugurated the contemporary period in High Atlas history. The ascendance of King Mohammed V and the downfall of the French/Glaoui alliance are remembered fondly, especially by the traditional enemies of the Glaoui. Today, as roads are paved, schools are built, electricity arrives in ever more remote valleys, and national health care begins to serve local needs, mountain Ishelhin are becoming more integral parts of the Moroccan nation. If there is frustration at the pace of change and desire for more local control of resources, there is also resignation. Virtually all villages have access to radio broadcasts in Tashelhit and Arabic, and people are aware of the larger world. Shepherds and farmers whose villages lack even basic facilities sometimes hold strong opinions about the Gulf War with Iraq, the situation of the Palestinians in Israel, and the wars in the Balkans. Don't be surprised if illiterate villagers ask you incisive questions about, say, American politics. Concerning their own country, they might tell you that rural Morocco may not be as rich as France, but neither does it have the internal strife of neighboring countries like Algeria.

Pleasures and Pastimes

Dining

Beyond small cafés, there are no real restaurants in the High Atlas outside hotels (for price categories, ☞ *below*). If you're invited to a private home, eat with your right hand only (the left is traditionally employed when you use the toilet); and when sharing food with others, eat only the part of the tagine or couscous that's directly in front of you. Meat will be divided by your host—don't take it out of the dish yourself. Remember that the Ishelhin will continue to tell you to "*ish*" (eat) indefinitely, yet there are children and perhaps women who will be grateful for your leftovers. Once you decide to stop eating, you must be adamant in your assertions that you will perish if you have one more bite. Hold your stomach and groan; say, "*Shabagh*" ("I'm full"), or "*Safi*" ("That's enough"), or "*Sla ala nebi*" ("Prayers on the Prophet"), meaning the subject is no longer open for discussion.

Avoid alcohol. Beer and wine are available in upscale hotels, and consuming it there generally does not raise any eyebrows; but the practice of carrying wine and spirits with you wherever you go is not appreciated by villagers outside the main tourist areas. Alcohol is *haram*—forbidden by the Koran—but on a more earthly level it's simply not socially acceptable. Some villagers make no distinction between a beer after a long day's hike and full-blown alcoholism.

Hiking and Trekking

People come from all over the world to trek in Morocco's High Atlas. The combination of rugged scenery, bracing air, and distinct Berber culture makes any kind of walk here unforgettable. All High Atlas loops (as opposed to day hikes) are two-day affairs or more, and for these you'll need a bare minimum of a sleeping bag, hiking boots, water purifier, and food. Trips into the serious high country require even more elaborate preparations: maps, perhaps mules, and, for many people, a guide. These preparations should not be taken lightly. Casual walkers will find plenty to enjoy—and photograph—on day hikes and trips through the lower valleys.

Lodging

After Ouirgane's deluxe Résidence de la Roseraie—a sort of alpine extension of high-end Marrakesh—and the charming Au Sanglier Qui Fume, lodging in the High Atlas goes quickly down to backpackers' refuges. Most inns serve tagines and other basic meals. If you're traveling as a heterosexual couple, it will be assumed that you're married; for overnight stays in a home, do not disabuse your hosts of their matrimonial assumptions if these are incorrect. Wearing a ring helps.

CATEGORY	COST*
$$$$	over 400DH
$$$	300–400DH
$$	200–300DH
$	under 200DH

*All prices are for a standard double room, excluding tax.

Photography

It's hard to take a bad picture in these mountains, but ask permission before you photograph the Moroccans you meet here. Some villagers are happy to have their pictures taken, especially if you promise to send them a print; children tend to be especially keen to pose. (The sound of "*soora, soora*" means someone wants you to snap their picture.) Still, few men and even fewer women will agree without taking some time to put on their best clothes, primp a little, and strike a pose. Many seem fond of stiff, Victorian arrangements, and getting them to smile for a camera can take some doing. By all means get a name and address, and send prints to anyone you photograph; just remember that your subjects may need help writing their addresses, either from you or from a villager who has been to school.

Exploring the High Atlas

Tourism represents one of few opportunities for cash in the High Atlas, so most mountain people greet the arrival of visitors enthusiastically. This does not mean they necessarily approve of foreign behavior, however; attention to local standards is much appreciated, and often rewarded with the celebrated Berber hospitality. Most important to remember is that, although the Moroccan countryside varies tremendously, city dress and behavior are not widely accepted outside cities. Trust your instincts: even if you have a guide, he may be more interested in keeping you happy than in pleasing your mountain hosts. Many guides are Arabic-speakers with a limited ability to talk to the Berbers, and even Tashelhit-speaking guides may be urbanized and have little patience for "backward" mountain mores. *Rumiyin* (foreigners) who leave the confines of the hotels in Ouirgane and Imlil should keep these suggestions in mind:

1. Say hello. In all of Morocco, "*Salaam ou alaikum*" ("Peace unto you; hello") is infinitely preferable to the ubiquitous French "*Bonjour*"). In the High Atlas you can also try the Tashelhit "*Maneek a tgeet?*" ("How are you?") and "*Labass neet?*" ("Is everything all right?"). These are normally said rapid-fire, one after the other.

2. Say thank you. The Arabic "*Choukran*" works fine, or you might try "*Baraka Allahu fik*" ("God's blessings upon you").

3. Wear pants. Shorts are okay on the beach, but many country people are not used to them. Especially if you're female, you'll look as though you're walking around in your underwear. This causes more amusement and confusion than outrage.

4. Wear something on your head if you're female. In remote mountain villages, baring your hair is akin to walking around topless in the United States or Europe. Local women in particular will appreciate your covering up. Any scarf works fine, even a baseball cap.

5. Smoke discreetly. Smoking is typically an urban, male phenomenon. In the mountains women never smoke, and the men who do are gently disparaged by their neighbors (it's a little like California). If you must smoke, do so outside, away from public view.

6. Don't respond to children who beg. The sound of "*Bonjour—stylo*" ("Hello—pen") and "*Bonjour—dirham*" may follow you in areas where travelers have gone before. Say, "*Oor deri stylo/bon bon/serf*" ("I don't have a pen/candy/change"). Children are generally seen by Moroccans as lacking *'aql*, or sense, and some High Atlas villagers are outraged that their children behave as beggars; so giving money, candy, or pens to kids can get them into trouble with their parents. It's far better to accept an invitation to tea and discreetly present your host with tokens of your appreciation when you leave. If, on the other hand, children (or others) provide some small service, such as washing or watching your car, or guiding you back to a trail you've lost, a small gift is appropriate. Stock up on five- and 10-dirham coins before you come to the mountains. The polite way to refuse the legitimate requests of beggars all over Morocco is to say, "*Allah esahel*," ("God make it easy on you").

7. Smile. This goes farther than anything else in creating good will and in overcoming the inevitable misunderstandings. If you find that you've made a faux pas, say, "*Smahali*" ("Excuse me") and smile some more.

When to Tour the High Atlas
High Atlas scenery is at its peak in April, when the trees are flowering and the mountains are still cloaked in white. High-country hiking is safest and easiest in late summer. Winter can be cold but very peaceful, and on sunny days the lower passes just south and north of Imlil can make for pleasant day hikes.

IMLIL, OUIRGANE, AND ENVIRONS

Coming south from Marrakesh, the road to Imlil is a left turn off the S501 (the Tizi-n-Test road) just upriver from Asni. The stretch between Asni and Imlil is always spectacular, taking you from what are essentially arid foothills of scrub and cactus to the very foot of the Ouanoukrim Massif. Well into spring, the mountains just above Imlil retain their winter white, which can be stunning above the green, irrigated fields of the valley. In spring the trip is particularly beautiful: The fields overflow with flowering apple and quince trees, and the red poppies scattered among their trunks can be breathtaking. If you look left on the way up, across the Reghaia River, you'll see some of the trails that are far more common as transport routes in the high country than the road on which you're traveling. These are what you'll pick up if you decide to leave even the modest comforts of the road and village behind.

Imlil

❶ *17 km (11 mi) southeast of Asni.*

The village of Imlil is the preeminent jumping-off point for the high country and a quiet retreat in itself from the bustle of Marrakesh. Summertime finds the parking area in the village square crammed with the camper vans and cars of trek-minded travelers, and the cafés teem with guides (*accompagnateurs*), people offering you lodging in their homes, and mule owners selling the services of their essential means of mountain transport. As the base for exploring Djebel Toubkal—North Africa's highest peak, at 13,668 ft—and the point Moroccan tourists use to access the shrine of Sidi Chamrouch, Imlil and the valley leading up to it are well accustomed to visitors. In fact, tourism has made a strong impression on the local economy: There's little subsistence farming in the Reghaia Valley, barley and maize having been largely replaced by apples, quince, and other crops for market. Once you've spent some time in Morocco's more remote valleys, you'll notice Imlil's electric poles, cement construction, and glass-paned windows as signs of relative affluence. Still, accommodations here are relatively rough by most standards, and the road into town, although paved, has some questionable spots. Storms may occasionally make it impassable.

Dining and Lodging

Most of Imlil's hotels are right on the main square as you enter the village. Accommodations are relatively basic; you'll find hot water and sometimes a towel, but don't count on heat in the winter or anything to eat besides tagines, brochettes, and maybe a roasted piece of chicken. You can, if invited, always stay in a private home for about 50DH a night per person, and this can be a nice way to see something of everyday Moroccan life. If you go this route, pay special attention to the etiquette suggestions above and make sure you find out before nightfall what and where the bathroom facilities are.

$ ✕🖬 **Cafe Aksoual.** Run by Hassan, a local guide, the Aksoual has a more rustic look than the Etoile. Popular both with locals and with French hiking groups out to experience authentic Morocco, it's a reasonably busy place. Four of the rooms sleep four people, and several others sleep three. There are two bathrooms, one shower with hot water, and a pool table in the restaurant. Tagines are only 30DH here, and you can get breakfast for 12DH. Consider tea, as the only coffee available is instant. ⊠ *Downhill from main square,* ☎ *no phone. 7 rooms. Restaurant, billiards. No credit cards.*

$ ✕🖬 **Café Soleil.** The Café Soleil is a new stone building with a big deck. The newness of the place makes it feel something like a dormitory, but the premises are certainly clean, most notably the sheets. Each room has four beds. There is verifiably hot water, with two showers and three tidy bathrooms in both Western and Moroccan styles. Tagines are 30DH in the restaurant. Those (foolhardy?) trekkers bent on a winter ascent of Djebel Toubkal can rent equipment such as crampons and ice axes here. ⊠ *In front of parking area,* ☎ 🝙 *04/48–56–22. 5 rooms. Restaurant. No credit cards.*

$ ✕🖬 **Hôtel Etoile de Toubkal.** Slathered in brand-new tile, the Etoile (Star) is probably the chicest place around. Of the eight rooms, half sleep four people and face the street, while the other half sleep two and face the garden—a very nice view, particularly in winter. All rooms have small balconies. There is only one toilet for all, and it generally has no paper. There are three showers in a room next to the toilet, and the hot water often works. The bathrooms downstairs in the restaurant are *zwin* (nice) indeed but are a treacherous hike in the dark. Some lucky guests get sheets with little basketball players on them. The hotel can hook you up with a guide, mules, and whatever else you're likely to want for a trek, or you can simply peruse their maps and go it alone. The restaurant serves mainly tagines. This is the only place in town that accepts credit cards (Visa only). ⊠ *Slightly uphill from main square,* ☎ 04/43–56–63 (ask for Hussein), 🝙 04/48–56–18. 8 rooms. Restaurant. V.

$ 🖬 **Refuge de Club Alpin Français.** This is one of a series of refuges maintained by an association of French mountaineering buffs. (The others are at Oukaimeden, Djebel Toubkal, Tachdirt, and Tazaghart.) There is a kitchen for guests' use. If, after staying here, you decide to head up to the Nelter refuge below Djebel Toubkal, send word ahead! Many a trekker has arrived at this place to find every inch of space taken and no food to be had. If you send word, they may cook you dinner, but the days of just showing up and expecting to be taken in are over, at least during high season. First-aid equipment is available at all refuges. The Club Alpin has an office in Casablanca; call 02/27–00–90 for more information. ⊠ *Across square from Café Soleil,* ☎ *no phone. No credit cards.*

Hiking and Trekking near Imlil

Imlil is filled with guides, both official and unofficial. You can ask about guides at hotels or any of the town's small cafés (*see* The High Atlas A to Z, *below*). Typically, you can expect to pay guides 200DH day plus 80DH a day per mule. You may be able to talk a guide into taking you out for 160DH a day in the summer, but don't count on it. Be sure to establish who will pay for food before you leave. Note that finding an English-speaker is not terribly likely. If you're coming from Taroudant rather than Marrakesh, call **Abdelaziz** on his mobile phone (☎ 01/28–19–88). He'll work with you on a custom itinerary, anything from a series of short and easy walks to major excursions from one end of the Atlas to the other.

One-day outings northeast along the road to **Tizi-n-Tamatert,** south up to the Tizi Mzik toward Tizi Oussem, and up the Reghaia River past Aroumd are all pleasant, especially when the weather is reasonably cool. The intrepid (and the prepared) may elect to venture to Tachdirt, then north over the pass to Oukaimeden, or west-northwest to the Ourika Valley. This latter route is demanding, though there are good places in Ourika to recover (☞ Chapter 6). Another common route takes you up past Djebel Toubkal through the **Tizi-n-Ouanoums.** This leads down past Lac d'Ifni, then into the Tifnoute River valley. The Tifnoute is stunning but remote. Transportation is sometimes available down to Aoualouz in the Souss, but this is a long way from where you started. Another difficult but much less traveled route takes you from Tizi Oussem over Tizi Melloul and down into the **Agoundis River valley.** The Agoundis is another impressive valley, less isolated than Tifnoute, and even less often visited. An easier way out of Tizi Oussem to the Agoundis takes you south over the Tizi-n-Goudal. This is not too difficult a pass, and it's beautiful, worth a day hike if you're spending the night in Tizi Oussem. Simply walk up the river out of the village, then cross over; continue along the right bank through the fields and then through juniper forest up to the pass. For those continuing, once you're over the pass there's a steep descent; then the going is pretty easy for several hours. Stay to the left, hugging the base of the mountains, until you cross up and left through the Tizi-n-Forikht. From here you can go straight down past the *azibs* (shepherds' huts) to Tagharghist, where there is a licensed *gîte d'étape* (roughly, guest house; often just a room in someone's home) for tourists; or follow the crumbling old road to the left down to Aït Moussa, one village upriver from Tagharghist. The trail has some beautiful views but also some precipitous spots. You can make the trip from Tizi Oussem in one day, but it's a long day indeed.

Although the route is clear enough, the two-day ascent of **Djebel Toubkal** is not as easy as it's sometimes made to sound: the first day hike to the Nelter Refuge takes about six hours and leaves you about 4,000 ft higher than where you started. Waking up the next day, scaling another 5,000 ft, and then hiking all the way back to Imlil should be undertaken only by those reasonably fit and well prepared. Altitude sickness and dehydration are not uncommon.

Two-Day Loops: Imlil to Tachdirt to Asni

Walk upriver through Imlil, cross the river at the bridge, then continue northeast to Tizi-n-Tamatert. This is a dirt road, usually in good condition. (If you have a sturdy vehicle you can even drive this portion.) From the pass you can look down on the village of Ikkis, buy a soda, and watch colorful troops of Europeans puff by. A mule path leads straight down, and a dirt road winds to the right. The mule path leaves you downriver from the Tachdirt refuge; turn right at the bottom if that's where you're heading. If you want to drive down the road, note that it's sometimes washed out just before the Imenane River, and turning around is not necessarily easy. Conditions permitting, just after crossing the Imenane you'll find the refuge in the village to the left, past the school. Tachdirt itself is up to the right; from here you can follow the river back down to Asni, the better part of a day's walk.

Day Hikes or Two-Day Loops: Imlil to Tizi Oussem, then Asni or Ouirgane

Follow the road out of Imlil as it winds up the hill to the right. When it turns back toward the Reghaia, continue on and go straight up through the fields leading south to the pass. The path is not evident until you're a good ways up. The *tizi,* or pass, is more a general direction than a route, but there is a mule path along the right-hand side of the valley. Near the three *azib*s (shepherds' huts), cross the creek and go 25 yards uphill to join the mule path. Stay to the right all the way up to the pass; then take the left fork at the pass itself. The right fork goes straight down, while the left winds through a pleasant juniper forest. Some people lunch by a small waterfall a few hundred yards down on the left, after a field of scree. Day hikers might choose to eat here and head back to Imlil for the night.

After the waterfall, the trail climbs slightly, then drops precipitously. From here there are spectacular views all the way out to the Haouz plain. The trail forks several times, but virtually all trails hit something near the village of **Tizi Oussem** sooner or later. If you stay consistently to the right, you'll pass the **shrine of Sidi Oussem,** identifiable by its red-rock construction and white cupola. A moussem honors the saint here in June. Wind down the creek and stay to the right. The walk thus far has taken two hours to the pass, an hour and a half down.

If you're very lucky, you have chosen the path that leads directly to the local gîte (signposted on the left), where food and lodging await. If you find yourself on a different path, finding the **gîte of Si Lahcen** can be a little confusing, as Tizi Oussem is a rambling village with lots of paths. The gîte is not far from the mosque—just keep asking for the "gîte n'Si Lahcen." If you're staying the night, you'll be looked after by Hassan id Abdallah, Si Lahcen's son. Geared primarily toward large, guided groups, the gîte has a huge kitchen and dining area, several large rooms banked with narrow couches that serve as beds, and a few smaller rooms downstairs. Traditionally there have been two cold showers, but hot water is a possibility. There's also a *hammam,* which they'll heat up for 6DH a person. A night's stay costs about 35DH, as does a tagine. You can hike back to Imlil for the night, but it's a steep trip at this point.

There are two ways out of Tizi Oussem. The easiest is to walk down the paths toward the river until you see a trail up to the main mule track on the right, along the hill. If you miss one of these paths and wind up down by the river, you can take a trail up to Aït Aïssa, the red village just downriver from Tizi Oussem. (Ask for "piste Asni.") Here at Aït Aïssa the mule track becomes a recognizable road—narrow and unpaved, but distinguishable from the other trails. Follow this for about 2½ hours, winding ever higher above the river. The views are incredible for much of this way, especially if the **Ouanoukrim Massif** is still covered with snow and the barley is sprouting. You're on a south-facing slope here, so especially in warm weather take plenty of water, as none is available on the route. Transport runs by on Saturday (souk day in Asni), but otherwise you're unlikely to encounter anyone on the road. After about 2–2½ hours you'll pass north out of the Ouirgane River watershed. A few yards beyond the pass, a trail leads off the road to the right (staying on the left bank of the canyon as it goes down):

This will take you to virtually the same place as the road, but it's shady, a beautiful walk through a relatively dense forest of scrub oak. After about an hour and a half on this trail, you'll reach a village just above the paved road connecting Asni and Imlil, and you can just follow the stream down to the road. From here it's a long walk to either Asni or Imlil (especially up to Imlil), but plenty of trucks pass by, so if you give up, you can easily get a lift.

The second route from Tizi Oussem takes you straight down the Ouirgane River to Ouirgane. (Some people start this version of the route by leaving their cars at Au Sanglier Qui Fume or another Ouirgane hotel, hitching a ride to Asni and then Imlil, and walking back from there.) The walk from Tizi Oussem to Ouirgane makes for a long day, but it's relatively hard to get lost: Just stay by the river for a few hours, then move up to the path that parallels the river. Do not climb up, to your right, out of the watershed. Keep asking for Ouirgane; do not go to Asni. Once you pass the village of Tessaouirgane, notable for its electric poles and the possible presence of a few cars, you might need to employ local children to keep you on track. Basically, you're going to leave the dirt road a kilometer (½ mi) or so below the village and strike out through the series of villages clustered along the river. This part can be slightly confusing, but as long as you keep moving downhill, you'll eventually hit the paved road. Ouirgane's Résidence de la Roseraie and Au Sanglier Qui Fume are hard to miss, sitting on opposite banks where the Ouirgane River crosses the paved road.

Ouirgane

2 *60 km (37 mi) south of Marrakesh.*

Near the junction of the Ouirgane and Nfis rivers, the small village of Ouirgane pretty much hoards all available High Atlas luxury in a few great hotels. This is the place to plant yourself if you want to relax as well as explore. The main activities, should you require any, revolve around hiking, biking, or riding mules through the mountains; trout fishing is also an option. Close to both Imlil and the Kasbahs and to the sights of the Upper Nfis River, Ouirgane is the perfect base for an alpine vacation and can even work for those who want to explore Marrakesh by day and remove themselves from its noise, heat, and crowds by night.

The S501 road from Marrakesh to Ouirgane winds up and out of the Rheghaia watershed just after Asni, through eroding red hills of juniper trees. The road is in good shape, but narrow and twisting; and while you contemplate whether it's Europeans or Moroccans who drive most recklessly, remember that the combination of the two can be terrifying. Drive slowly. As the road begins to drop you into the Nfis Basin, you'll see the turnoff for the piste to the Hotel Adam on the right. After another kilometer (½ mi) on the S501 you'll come to the driveway for the Résidence de la Roseraie on the left; the road then crosses the Ouirgane River, and you'll see Au Sanglier Qui Fume on the left, at Km 61 from Marrakesh.

Your hotel is your best resource for information on local excursions. Many people like to check out the **Ouirgane Gorges,** half a day's walk down the Nfis River from the village itself. You might also find someone to drive you out to the Amizmiz road and drop you by the **salt mine** (you can try this yourself if you have four-wheel drive). Bring sturdy shoes: From the mine you can trek back up the river to Ouirgane, a pleasant walk with plenty of shade.

Another popular destination is the shrine of **Haïm ben Diourne.** Site of one of the few Jewish festivals still held in Morocco, this complex contains the tombs of Rabbi Mordekai ben Hamon, Rabbi Abraham ben Hamon, and others. About 4 km (2½ mi) from Ouirgane, the shrine is accessible by foot or mule in an hour or two, or you can drive right up to the gate on a dirt piste. Drive south from Au Sanglier and turn left after about 1 km (½ mi:) at Ouirgane's souk; follow the road as it winds through the village until you reach a pink cubic water tank. Turn right and go to the end of the road, about 3 km (2 mi). (If you're unsure, ask for the Tigimi n Yehudeen—House of the Jews—and locals will point the way.) The shrine is a big white structure on your left. Lahcen ben Hussein is the old caretaker; he claims to have been working here for 50 years. The moussem generally happens in May. On the way home for the night, you might stop for lunch in Ouirgane's Café Mouflon, which has inexpensive food and a wonderfully friendly staff.

Dining and Lodging

$$$$ ✕🏨 **Résidence de la Roseraie.** La Roseraie is the only truly sybaritic establishment in the High Atlas. Every room has a satellite TV and minibar, and each of the "junior" and "senior" suites has a fireplace and deck. The grounds are beautiful, with, as the name implies, swaths of roses. Certain spa facilities cost extra—sometimes quite a bit extra—so ask before you sign up for that massage. You can rent horses for local rides, or the Roseraie will set you up for full-blown treks and horse tours in the mountains, complete with food and lodging in Atlas villages. The restaurant is open to the public, with meals about 250DH per person and wine is served. The hotel offers daily minibus service to and from Marrakesh, and airport transfer as well. ⊠ *Route Taroudannt, Km 60, Box 769, Marrakesh 40000,* ☎ *04/43–91–28,* FAX *04/43–91–30. 35 rooms. Restaurant, minibars, pool, hammam, massage, spa, tennis courts, horseback riding. DC, MC, V.*

$–$$$ 🏨 **Au Sanglier Qui Fume.** The Sanglier, whose name means "The Smoking Boar," has been a favorite with the French for generations. Formerly upscale, it was hit hard by a flood in 1995 and is now something of a faded beauty, with plenty of charm. The staff is wonderful, if not especially proficient in English; they compensate with their enthusiasm to teach you Tashelhit. The terrific proprietors, Richard and Annich, can arrange all kinds of guided and unguided tours to local sights, and mules are easily available from locals just outside the main gates. Guest rooms, spread around the grounds in several buildings, range from small, viewless doubles to suites with private decks and fireplaces. A hammam is under construction. Plenty of families stay here, so kids will feel at home; and the TV in the main building offers video games and a movie selection that includes children's fare and French films. The restaurant—which serves wine—prepares incredible food. Moroccan favorites are always available, but the menu can be a blessed relief from tagines, with such occasional delicacies as duck *à l'orange,* frog's legs, and trout. Storks prowl the outdoor dining area, and the signature *sanglier* is kept in a cage beyond the pool. ⊠ *Reservations: Vallée d'Ouirgane, 61 km de Marrakech, C.P. 42150,* ☎ *04/48–57–07 or 04/48–57–08,* FAX *04/48–57–09. 15 rooms, 5 suites. Restaurant, bar, pool, Ping-Pong, bicycles, billiards, darts. V.*

$$ 🏨 **Hotel Adam.** Blessed with incredible views and bizarre art, the Hotel Adam is the newest hotel in Ouirgane. On a promontory above the Roseraie and Sanglier, it looks out over both the Ouirgane and Nfis rivers. The rooms are new, spotlessly clean, and comfortable, and their Western-style bathrooms have honest-to-gosh hot water. Try for a room on the south end, facing the Nfis. The proprietor, Mohammed, speaks good English, and for reasons that are not quite clear he likes to be called "John Barry." There are three spacious dining areas, and the tables on the shady part of the terrace are delightful in the afternoon heat. Wine is served. ⊠ *From S501 south, roughly Km 60, turn*

right onto a 1½-km (1-mi) dirt piste signposted HOTEL ADAM; ☎ 04/ 48–57–40. 10 rooms. Restaurant. No credit cards.

En Route After Ouirgane, the S501 climbs along the east bank of the Nfis River. Four dirt roads lead off to the left (at Km 10.5, 17.4, 24.4, and 27.6 from Ouirgane), each winding through valleys that spill down from the Ouanoukim Massif. Although road conditions are extremely uncertain, those with mules or four-wheel-drive transportation might enjoy exploring these valleys. Few travelers bother, however, so there are no facilities to speak of. A trail along the top of the valleys, essentially parallel to the paved road, runs from Tizi Oussem across to the Tizi-n-Forikht.

THE UPPER NFIS AND TIZI-N-TEST

The Upper Nfis Valley was the spiritual heart of the Almohad empire in the 12th century and the administrative center of the Goundafa caids up through the 20th century. It's best enjoyed as a day trip or as a series of day trips from Ouirgane, though there are a few rustic lodging options in the region itself. If you're just passing through, you'll find plenty to stop and do along the way, and scattered cafés will keep you fed and watered.

The Agoundis River

❸ *Ijoukak is 33 km (20 mi) south of Ouirgane.*

This is an easy place for a walk in the country, or even a drive if you don't mind taking your car over piste. From the paved road, turn left just before the bridge over the Agoundis River and simply follow the piste along the bank through a forested canyon. It meanders pleasantly and with little gain in altitude for about 8 km (5 mi) to an abandoned mine at Taghbart. There is little traffic except on Wednesday (souk day in nearby Talat-n-Yacoub). After the mine the road gets very narrow and begins to climb, at which point it's no longer recommended for standard cars. If you continue, you'll reach an open area with a government school after about 2 km (1 mi), and here the road forks. The right branch leads south down the hill to the Ounein Valley; the left continues uphill to the village of Maghzen. Just before Maghzen, there's another fork: here the right branch leads into the village proper while the left continues up and around the bend into the heart of the Agoundis Valley. There are two small stores in Maghzen on the main road, where you can buy warm Cokes and rest in the shade.

As you round the bend at Maghzen, the Ouanoukrim Massif heaves into view, dominating the twisting river far below. The road climbs through the villages of Tijrhist, Tazguart, and Ighir and after a steep climb arrives in **Tagharghist.** Very basic lodgings are available here in the home of Abderrahman Aït ben Oushen, the only licensed tourist facility in the Agoundis Valley. Abderrahman will be happy to show you around, his tour highlighted by a visit to his family's old *agadir* (fort)—built by his grandfather, the valley's former *amghar* (local potentate) under the Goundafi caid. You're now on the former border between Goundafi and Glaoui territory, so there is no shortage of stories about tribal warfare here.

On foot the trip from Ijoukak to Tagharghist will take you about four hours. If you drive, park your car in the olive grove just before the mine or in the open dirt area next to the mine itself, or at least park in Maghzen. Tagharghist is a two-and-a-half-hour walk from the mine. The tap water here is safe to drink.

Back on the paved road, cross the bridge over the Agoundis River, and you'll enter the town of **Ijoukak.** This is a generally avoidable little place, but you might stop here for a sandwich of liver kebabs from the stand halfway down the row of shops on the right. There's a dark little room in the back where you can enjoy your nominally priced snack away from the dust and bustle of the road. The last café on the right, Cafe Bidawi (☞ *below*), is somewhat better outfitted than the kebab stand. You can even get a decent haircut or shave a few doors down, or use the teleboutique across the street to make essential phone calls.

Dining and Lodging

$ ╳⊞ **Cafe Bidawi.** Guest rooms here are decorated in an urban Moroccan style, their walls lined with banquettes that serve as beds. The bathrooms also have a Moroccan look and are generally well maintained. There is a small private hammam. For the price, this place can hardly be beat. The restaurant serves good tagines. ⊠ *Ijoukak,* ☎ *no phone. 6 rooms. Restaurant. No credit cards.*

Talat-n-Yacoub

❹ *4 km (2 mi) southwest of Ijoukak.*

Talat-n-Yacoub is the district capital. Most of the time it has little to recommend it, though you might stop for tea on the terrace of the Café Bon Goût (Good Taste Café), just before the town proper. On Tuesday there is a low-key livestock souk, and on Wednesday a good-size general souk. The **Wednesday souk** is notable for its almost complete lack of touts, hustlers, and guides, making it an refreshing change for those jaded by their experience in Moroccan cities. Virtually none of the goods is aimed at tourists, but you might find a few nice gifts; quirky friends or relatives might be pleased with a candle holder made of sardine cans or a bright orange wooden suitcase lined with the labels of Moroccan Speciale beer bottles. This is also a good place to buy woven straw mats and cheap cassettes of wailing Soussi music. To find the souk, turn left at the sign for Talat-n-Yacoub and follow the line of olive trees. The post office (PTT) on your left is probably the easiest place to park. Enter the souk by walking through the vegetable market, or around the corner, past the fleet of waiting mules next to the minaret.

Dominating the hill above the souk is the Talat-n-Yacoub's old, massive **Goundafi Kasbah,** built by the Goundafi caids. Locals call it Aoregh-n-Gorj and say it was built in 1812. History books say it was not built until 1907, but in any case it's a tremendous, squat structure that testifies to the old caid's power. If you're driving, follow the sign into Talat-n-Yacoub, pass the post office on your lef, and continue 1 or 2 km (½ or 1 mi) past the red government building on your left. The second dirt road on your right heads up to the Kasbah itself, which is plainly visible from all over the area. On foot from Talat-n-Yacoub, head south from the minaret at the souk past the public rest rooms and the donkey parking lot to go through the first village, Talat-n-Yacoub Afila (Upper Talat-n-Yacoub). At the fork, take the shady path downhill to the right, wind through the village, then turn left at the new cement house. Go down through the dry stream and past the public fountain, then up and through another dry creek. Now there's nothing but dirt, rocks, and anemic scrub between you and the Kasbah. (The brush is said to have been trampled by a film crew that used this area as a set.)

As you near the fortress itself, you may be able to understand the fear in local songs that say, "Have pity on me, Aoregh-n-Gorj / Have pity on me, rifles of Aoregh-n-Gorj." Locals say the hands of slack workers were sealed into the Kasbah's walls during construction, though this would seem an odd way to speed things along. Today the scene is eerily peaceful, with hawks nesting among the scraps of ornately carved plaster and woodwork still clinging to the massive walls—and not a tourist in sight. From here you can see Tin Mal, to the south, across the juncture of the Nfis and Assif-n-Tiseft rivers; southeast are the mines of Tinseft. The Ouanoukrim Massif dominates the view to the north. The ruins near the river are all that remains of Talat-n-Yacoub Izdar (Lower Talat-n-Yacoub), which formerly housed the caid's family.

Tin Mal Mosque

⑤ *Turnoff for mosque is about 4 km (2½ mi) south of Talat-n-Yacoub.*

Moving south from Talat-n-Yacoub on the S501, you'll see the collapsing former **house of Bou Asri,** member of Morocco's parliament, on your right. One wall of the house has fallen away, revealing some spectacular Moroccan tile work. About 4 km (2½ mi) farther south, on the right, is the road to the venerable Tin Mal Mosque, birthplace and spiritual capital of the 12th-century Almohad empire. Locals call it the Timzguida Tomlilt, or White Mosque, though these days it's the ruddy color of the hills. Tin Mal was built by the great religious reformer Ibn Tumart, who, it is said, was a Tashelhit-speaker from the hills near the Souss Valley who traveled north to the great Kairaouine University in Fez and then east, perhaps as far as Baghdad. Studying with various scholars along the way, Ibn Tumart developed a particularly strict interpretation of the Koran, one that emphasized each believer's personal responsibility for the faith of his community. As he moved back west to Morocco, Ibn Tumart collected followers and proclaimed himself "Mahdi"—the rightly guided one, or the one chosen to purify the community of the faithful before the end of the world. This millennial vision was tolerated uneasily by the Almoravid authorities, who had themselves ridden to power on a wave of religious fervor a few centuries earlier. In Marrakesh the tension finally came to a head when the Mahdi threw the sultan's own sister from her horse for appearing in public without a veil. Ibn Tumart was forced to flee to the mountains, where he sought protection from the sultan's cavalry. Eventually he landed among the tribes settled around Tin Mal, and here he set about converting the locals to his version of Islam.

History books and local lore agree that Ibn Tumart's methods were ingenious, if sometimes brutal. One story has it that the Mahdi would teach the Koran to the mountain Ishelhin literally word by word. Supposedly men were lined up, taught their word, and then made to recite in turn; working together in this way, these Tashelhit-speakers could reproduce the resonant Arabic poetry of the Koran and quite literally embody the holy text. Another, less quaint story has it that the Mahdi had thousands of men killed in a four-day purge, with family members directed to put one another to the sword. True or not, what these stories illustrate is the ability of Ibn Tumart to reorganize the fractious mountain tribes into a new social, religious, and military order. Although their first assault on Marrakesh was brutally thwarted, Abd al-Mumin, the Mahdi's successor, eventually conquered all of the Moroccan mountains, followed by Fez and Marrakesh. The Almohads, as they came to be known, then replaced the Almoravids as rulers of the western Mediterranean, and the austere walls of Tin Mal turned out to be the cradle of a formidable empire. Although the mosque seems chronically closed for restoration, a 10-dirham token of appreciation for the guardian, Mohammed Filali, can usually get you inside.

Tagoundaft

❻ *18 km (11 mi) southwest of Tin Mal.*

Continuing south from Tin Mal, you'll see a hand-painted blue sign for Ighil after about 3 km (2 mi). A souk is held here on Sunday. The 9-km (6-mi) dirt road to Ighil is generally in good shape, but from there the road climbs precipitously through the villages known collectively as Ogdempt. After an additional 6 km (4 mi) and a sharp hairpin turn to the right, you're in the village of Tagoundaft, which has an awe-inspiring **Goundafi Kasbah** perched above it. Walking to this Kasbah is tougher than walking to the one at Talat-n-Yacoub (it takes about an hour), but the scenery is nice, and it's a great place to stretch your legs during the long trip over the mountains. If you want to avoid exercise, a piste leads back toward the Kasbah about 2 km (1 mi) above the village; you'll only have to walk the last stretch.

On foot, start with the steep path next to the cement house across from the small store with the Orange Crush sign. Follow this straight up, keeping the pines on your right and the old cemetery on your left. When you reach the dirt piste, turn left. Locals say the Kasbah was built in 1815, but the sprawling compound probably has bits and pieces from different epochs. Village boys will be thrilled to accompany you on your explorations, regaling you with tales of the caid's depredations: how he would steal the family cow, have his way with the women, seal his enemies into the walls of the Kasbah, and imprison anyone who dared to question him. They are particularly proud of the soccer field they built nearby but will also take you to three huge underground rooms that may have been prisons (*sijn* or *hibz*). There is also an enormous old water tank (*sherij*), now with almond and carob trees growing in it). The walls themselves are in an advanced state of disrepair. The huge prison rooms do not have doors, and the only way into them appears to be holes in the top through which the unfortunate might have been lowered . . . or dropped. Be very careful!

Back in the village, look for a telephone in the *hanut* (grocery store) with the Orange Crush sign—the nameless café next door makes nice tea. The people of Tagnoudaft are said to be descendants of various servants of the caid, including his private musicians. They are locally celebrated for their *ahouash,* drumming and dancing.

Tizi-n-Test

❼ *12 km (7 mi) south of Tagoundaft (past turnoff for Arg).*

From Tagoundaft the road begins to wind up to the Tizi-n-Test itself. As sunset approaches, the landscape deepens in color, with the soil turning blood-red, orange, and yellow; and as the air grows cooler, you might see wild boar as well as foxes and a variety of birds. The pass itself can be cold, rainy, and in the winter even snowbound. The twisting route down the mountains' southern face can be gut-wrenching—exercise great care.

At the summit of the Tizi-n-Test is a small café. From here you pass out of the Nfis watershed, out of the mountains that quench Marrakesh, and into the Souss Valley. A sign welcomes you to the province of Taroudant, and the earth seems to drop away to nothing. The Anti-Atlas mountains rise out of the haze in the distance, and beyond them lies the Sahara. On clear days you can see an astounding 6,000 ft straight down to the mud villages and barley fields crouched beside the Souss River. The road is very narrow, wide enough for only one vehicle in some places: honk as you round corners, and give way to traffic climbing uphill.

Dining and Lodging

$ ✕🏠 **Belle Vue.** This is a good place to collect your wits before finishing the descent from Tizi-n-Test—and a bizarre place to buy a rock. (Inquire at the orange van teetering over the abyss with NOT EXPENSIVE painted on the side.) The Belle Vue has three very modest rooms downstairs and a clean, Moroccan-style toilet; construction is underway on new, nicer rooms upstairs. Meals include simple tagines, salads, and desserts. ✉ *A few km (1 or 2 mi) down from Tizi-n-Test summit. Restaurant. No credit cards.*

En Route   Continuing down the pass, at Km 89 from Ouirgane you'll past the last hanut before the plains. At Km 103 is the turnoff to Tafingoulte, a nondescript little town that seems home to a surprising array of government buildings and little else. About 4 km (2½ mi) farther on is a roundabout: Veer left for Ouarzazate or continue straight for Oulad Berhil, Taroudant, and Agadir. Go slowly here, as the local police are not afraid to ticket you.

TIZI-N-TICHKA AND TELOUET

To relax and unwind from the rest of your Moroccan vacation, consider one of the few hotels on the Tichka pass for their peaceful, low-key atmosphere. If you're just passing through en route to the southern oases, the vista from the Tichka road itself is amazing—especially in spring—and the Glaoui Kasbah at Telouet is worth a lingering look.

Tizi-n-Tichka

❸ *57 km (35 mi) southeast of Marrakesh.*

The Tichka pass is the easiest way southeast into the desert, but that's not to say it's easy. Although the road is generally well maintained and wide enough for traffic to pass—and lacks the vertiginous, spine-tingling twists of the Tizi-n-Test—it still deserves respect. Especially in winter, take warm clothes with you, as the temperature at the pass itself can seem another latitude entirely from the balmy sun of Marrakesh. You should also carry water, and allow plenty of time to enjoy the views.

The road out of Marrakesh leads you abruptly into the countryside, to quiet olive groves and desultory villages consisting of little more than a hanut and a roadside mechanic. You'll pass the R'mat River and, after just a few kilometers, the Hotel Hardi (☞ *below*). Now the road begins to rise, winding through fields that are either green with barley and wheat or brown with their stalks. At Km 55 you'll encounter the brand-new Hotel Touama (☞ *below*). In spring magnificent red poppies blanket the surrounding fields.

From here the road begins to climb more noticeably, winding through forests and some of the region's lusher hillsides. A broad valley opens up to your left, revealing red earth and luminously green gardens. At Km 67 (Km 135 from Ouarzazate) stands Mohammad Noukrati's Auberge Touhfliht (☞ *below*).

From the Touhfliht there is little between you and the Tichka pass but a few dusty villages, shepherds, lots of rock, and a great deal of winding pavement. You might find a decent orange juice, trinket, or weather-beaten carpet in villages like Taddert, but you'll probably feel pulled toward the pass. The scenery can make it hard to keep your eyes on the road. Pines, oaks, olive trees, and prickly pear trees give way to the hardy shrubs of the higher altitudes; then the naked rock of the mountains begins to emerge from beneath the flora, and the walls of the canyon grow steeper, more enclosing. Oleander blooms beside the

road, while white poplar, walnut, barley, and maize form a narrow rib-
bon of green along the tangled river course. Approaching the pass itself, the slopes seem barely able to hold their moorings, and indeed
some have given up, tumbling into huge piles of scree. Around Km 105
you'll see several waterfalls across the canyon. The trail down is precipitous, but easy enough to follow; just park at the forlorn-looking
refuge and (former?) restaurant around Km 107. The trail winds to
the left of the big hill, then cuts to the right and drops down to the
falls after a short walk of half an hour or so. The Tichka pass is at 7,413
ft, high enough to be windy, wet, and cold on an otherwise sunny day,
but also high enough to be refreshing if the plains are enduring blis-
tering summer heat. Depending on the weather, the trip from to Marrakesh can take you from African heat to European gloom and back.

Dining and Lodging

$ ×🏨 **Auberge Touhfliht.** As the SPECIALE sign suggests, beer, wine, and
cocktails are available here, and—even more extraordinary—women
can have a drink without the ominous ambience of many Moroccan
watering holes. The main balcony has a wonderful view and is a delightful place to spend a warm afternoon. The rooms are basic and have
only twin beds, but at 100DH for two people, who's complaining? Showers have hot water but are down the hall from the rooms. Inquire about
towels before bathing. ⊠ *P31, Km 67 from Marrakesh (Km 135 from
Ouarzazate),* ☎ *04/48–48–61. Restaurant, bar. No credit cards.*

$ ×🏨 **Hotel Hardi.** The riverside Hardi makes a reasonable base for ex-
ploring Marrakesh from the relative peace of the countryside. Each room
has a private shower. Breakfast is a mere 15DH, and tagines can be
had for 40DH. ⊠ *South side of Rmat River,* ☎ *04/48–00–56. 18
rooms. Restaurant, bar. No credit cards.*

$ ×🏨 **Hotel Touama.** All rooms have two beds, and most have private
bathrooms with hot showers. There are two terraces, and the restaurant is well above average: if you time things right you'll be fed homemade cookies right out of the oven and what has to be the best lemon
cake in Morocco. The bread is fresh, the tablecloths are comforting
red gingham, and the staff is friendly. Tagines are sometimes joined by
more adventurous cuisine, like paella or fish. Alcohol is not served, but
good coffee and fresh juices are always on offer. The Touama makes
special arrangements for groups, evidently featuring folklore of the kind
performed in larger Moroccan hotels; if you're interested in this, or
interested in avoiding it, call ahead and ask for Mohammed Ladib, who
is always helpful. ☎ *04/48–47–74 or 01/34–01–91 mobile. 17 rooms.
Restaurant, coffee shop. No credit cards.*

Telouet

⑨ *Turnoff is about 60 km (37 mi) southeast of Marrakesh; Telouet is 21
km (13 mi) east of P31.*

About five minutes after Tizi-n-Tichka is the turnoff for the **Glaoui Kasbah** at Telouet. The road is paved but narrow, and winds from juniper-
studded slopes down through a lunar landscape of low eroding hills
and the Assif-n-Tissent (Salt River). In spring, barley fields soften the
effect, but for much of the year the scene is rather bleak. Just before
the Kasbah itself is the sleepy little town of Telouet, where you might
find a café open, especially if it's Thursday (souk day).

It was from Telouet that the powerful Glaoui tribe controlled the caravan route over the mountains into Marrakesh. Although the Goundafa
and Mtougi tribal confederations also held important High Atlas
passes, by 1901 the Glaoua were on the rise. Having secured some se-

rious artillery from a desperate Sultan Moulay el Hassan, the brothers Glaoui seized much of the area below the Tichka pass and were then positioned to bargain with the French when they arrived on the political scene. For their part, the French could not have been pleased with the prospect of subduing the vast wild regions of southern Morocco tribe by tribe, much less the fiercely intractable Berbers of the mountains; thus the French/Glaoui alliance benefited both parties, with Mandani el Glaoui ruling as grand vizier and his brother Tuhami ruling as Pasha of Marrakesh.

Parking for the Kasbah is down a short dirt road across from the nearby auberge Chez Ahmed. Entrance is free, though tips for the parking attendant and the guardian of the gate will be appreciated. Inside, walking through dusty courtyards that rise to towering mud walls, you'll pass through a series of gates and big doors, many threatening to fall from their hinges. Different parts are open at different times, perhaps according to the whims of the *guardien*; but most of the Kasbah has a sort of ravished feel, as though most of the useful or interesting bits were carried off when the Glaoui reign came to its abrupt end in 1956. This sense of decay is interrupted, however, when you get upstairs: Here, amid painted wood shutters and delicately carved plaster arabesques, exquisitely set tile, and broad marble floors, you get a taste of the sumptuousness the Kasbah once enjoyed. Because it was only built in the 20th century, ancient motifs are combined with kitschy contemporary elements, such as traditionally carved plaster shades for the electric lights. The roof has expansive views—villagers till their fields and busloads of tea-happy tourists lounge on carpets set out for them beneath the walls. The café next door to the Kasbah, **Chez Ahmed** (also known as Auberge Telouet), has one decent bathroom, but the meal prices are mutable in relation to how much you seem likely to pay. The nomad-camp atmosphere is pleasantly goofy.

South toward Ouarzazate

Back on the main road you begin the descent from scattered pine and juniper down through shrub toward the pre-desert. Locals sell fossils and minerals by the side of the road, hoping the glimmer of the rocks will catch your eye. On your left at Km 122 from Marrakesh you'll see the **Palais-n-Tichka,** a sort of Wal-Mart for these shiny minerals as well as other souvenirs. The villages on this road are mostly quiet clusters of mud-and-stone houses, their surroundings combining thin, rain-fed barley fields with the more intense green of irrigated plots, maize, and apple and almond trees. The snowy peaks form a magnificent background, especially on wash day (often Thursday, for Friday prayers), when the bright garments of different families festoon the trees of the villages.

At Km 134 from Marrakesh you'll pass through **Agouim,** which has a teleboutique and a gas station; then the road winds out of apple-blossom country along the Assif Imini. Lined with palms, figs, almonds, prickly pears, and poplars, this river forms a lush counterpart to the parched hills. A series of red villages hunker against the cliffs at bends in the river. At **Amerzgane** you hit the turnoff for the P32 to Taroudant. If you continue on toward Ouarzazate, you'll reach the turnoff to Aït-Benhaddou (☞ Chapter 8) after about 15 km (9 mi). It might be best to save this Kasbah for a day trip from Ouarzazate, as you've already had a long day if you've come through Tizi-n-Tichka.

MARRAKESH TO AGADIR: TIZI MÂACHOU

West of Marrakesh, the P40 road south from Chichaoua to Imi-n-Tanoute and over the Tizi Maachou is the express route through the High Atlas to Agadir and points beyond. Some of those heading to Taroudant might also prefer the P40 to the Tizi-n-Test, especially in stormy or snowy weather.

Several different roads lead west from Marrakesh to the P40, including the P10, the 6010, and the 6028, all of which lead eventually to Imi-n-Tanoute. The P10 is fastest, as long as you don't leave the city during the evening rush hour, when droves of trucks, buses, taxis, mopeds, bicycles, and donkey carts can turn the two-lane highway into a nerve-wracking four-lane road derby. Fortunately, traffic then thins quickly, and you're released into the wide-open Haouz plain. In winter and spring this bears soft shades of green, but in the hazy summer heat it can seem all but lifeless. There is little to distract you from the road.

After about 73 km (45 mi) you'll roll into the splendid roundabout at **Chichaoua,** whose new paint and well-tended flowers may deceive you into thinking you have arrived somewhere. Indeed, Chichaoua long had a reputation for carpet production, and you may still be able to ferret out some old craftsmanship here, but these days good rugs are easier to find in Marrakesh or Rabat. Just outside town heading south, a series of gas stations offer decent cafés. Back en route, the road starts to undulate through bleak hills, and after 6 km (4 mi) you'll pass through the village of **Sidi Bouzeid.** Another 21 km (13 mi) or so brings you to the turnoff for **Sept Mzouda.**

If you feel like a detour into some relatively unseen countryside, take a left toward Sept Mzouda. This small road has not been paved very long, and if you offer a ride to one of the old women hitching back from the souk at Chichaoua, you're almost sure to be invited to tea in one of the villages along the way. The road first passes through **Ras el Aïn**—literally, Head of the Well—and cross the Chichaoua River and stay to the right when the road forks—on your right is the **zaouia of Sidi Hmad.** This is followed by the hamlet of **Boukhart,** near which there is a three-day moussem in August. After passing the usually dry Bou Arfir River, you'll wind through gentle hills of barley and wheat occasionally peppered with mud and cinder-block houses, often set at odd angles to the new road. When you come upon an officious-looking government building on your left, on the opposite side will be the **Zaouia Saïdat,** a small religious school with about 40 students and a couple of *fqih* (religious teachers). After about 45 km (28 mi) you'll hit a junction with the 6403 road. A left turn takes you back to Marrakesh; turning right, it's 28 km (17 mi) to Imi-n-Tanoute.

A way to avoid Chichaoua altogether and see even more of the countryside is to turn left off the P10 just past Oudaya, about 27 km (16 mi) outside Marrakesh. This will connect you to the 6453 and then the 6403 into Imi-n-Tanoute (when you see the sign for a right turn to Chichaoua, just continue on). This road is narrow and somewhat winding, but it's safe enough if you drive relatively slowly. To the left you can see the northern foothills of the High Atlas, which seem brilliantly verdant in comparison with their counterparts on the southern slopes. The road begins to rise into some pretty country of broad fields and large olive groves. The mountains grow closer until you pass the Seksawa River and meander past the police station and an old Kasbah into the town of Imi-n-Tanoute.

Imi-n-Tanoute

⑩ *47 km (29 mi) south of Chichaoua.*

Arriving from either the P40 or the 6403, you'll find yourself in the main square, with a dead fountain and little shade. Imi-n-Tanoute is a bustling market town, but business is overwhelmingly focused on the needs of country people. Aluminum cookware, plastic washtubs, seed, pesticides, and agricultural implements dominate the available wares. There is, however, a female doctor available, as well as a pharmacy, hospital, and even a municipal pool. Just south from the main square (turn right across from the gas pumps) is a row of restaurant stalls; here, where the buses and *grands taxis* depart, you can dine on fried fish, brochettes of liver and other more exotic organs, and beef tagines. A huge, spicy tagine for two can be as cheap as 25DH. Continuing on this road through town, you'll pass a long row of car-repair shops, then join (or rejoin, if you've come from Chichaoua) the P40.

Lodging

$ 🏨 **Hotel Essalam.** Hot showers and a toilet are down the hall from these basic rooms, which are brightly painted and crammed with three sagging single beds apiece. The proprietors are very nice, and the clientele seems to be comprised mainly of villagers in town for the Monday souk rather than foreign tourists. ⊠ *Above main square,* ☎ *no phone. No credit cards.*

Leaving the Mountains

From Imi-n-Tanoute the P40 is the only way south, slipping over the western fringe of the High Atlas. This road is in wonderful shape and, except for the occasional rogue truck, quite safe (a portion of the road even has a passing lane, perhaps the only one in Morocco). The mountains are not as high or impressive as those of the Tichka or Test passes, but the rugged landscape is not without its charm. It's very hot here in the summer, and there are some long stretches without water or provisions, so stock up before leaving Marrakesh. Start early in the day, when the air is cool and the soft light brings out the texture of the dry riverbeds, forests of argan (an oil-producing nut), and wind-sculpted cliffs.

From Imi-n-Tanoute the road begins a gentle climb. About 6 km (4 mi) south, the hillside on your left holds a **Kasbah** that the locals call Taorirt, followed by almond fields and the occasional donkey-powered waterwheel. About 61 km (39 mi) south of Imi-n-Tanoute, past roadside argan-oil salesmen, is the turnoff to **Argana.** Most of the time this is a somnolent little village, but it does come alive for its Tuesday souk. The small **French fort** nearby makes a nice break if you want to stretch your legs; just turn toward Argana, cross a few creeks and then the river Assif-n-Aït Moussa, then turn left when the road forms a T. About 300 ft after the pavement ends, past the health center, turn right up a line of eucalyptus trees. Park here and walk up to the fort, which is behind the hill to your right. You'll notice cement in the fort's foundation. Berber fortifications are usually built using a *luh,* a wooden form into which mud and stones are packed; the luh gives these indigenous fortresses their characteristic lines of holes in the walls, which are patched up after the form is removed but become the first parts of the wall to deteriorate. Notice, too, the utilitarian nature of this French colonial outpost. Unlike the Glaoui Kasbah, at Telouet, this one has no grand gateway or imposing facade—it was not built to impress, merely to secure the surrounding territory. There is a cistern of brackish water in the middle. Some of the footing inside is suspect; be careful.

Back on the P40, heading south from the Argana turnoff, you'll continue through iron-red hills for roughly 11 km (7 mi), when you'll catch the first glimpse of the **lake** formed by the Abd al Moumen Dam. There's nothing particularly grand about the lake, but the sight of water here is so wildly improbable that many tour buses stop here for a photo-op. You can imagine baffled relatives and friends back home politely watching the vacation video, trying to figure out why this small splotch of blue was worth the film. Another 49 km (30 mi) through palm grottos and stunted juniper forests brings you to the **Amskroud** turnoff, your ticket to Taroudant. If your aim is Agadir, continue on—32 more km (20 mi) of argan savanna leads you to the forests of streetlights that mark Agadir's suburban perimeter.

THE HIGH ATLAS A TO Z

Arriving and Departing

If you don't have a car or are hiking around, you can catch frequent transport from Asni to **Imlil** in trucks, vans, and sometimes even a bus. There is no particular schedule; vehicles tend to depart only when it seems that adding one more person would probably suffocate somebody. The going rate for such a ride is 10DH–15DH. Asni holds a general souk every Saturday and a cattle souk each Thursday, so it's easier to catch transport then. For information on *grands taxis* from Marrakesh, ☞ Chapter 6.

Getting Around

It's best to rent a car in Marrakesh—at least to connect the dots between treks—unless you're up for serious adventure.

Contacts and Resources

Emergencies
Highway assistance: ☎ 177. **Police:** ☎ 19. **Fire:** ☎ 15. Pack as complete a first-aid kit as possible.

Sports and Outdoor Activities
FISHING
Arrange for a fishing guide at Ouirgane's hotel **Au Sanglier Qui Fume** (✉ Route de Taroudant, Km 60, ☎ 04/43–91–28).

HIKING AND TREKKING
Many travelers planning a longer excursion into the high country arrange guides through one of the (pricey) agencies along **Boulevard Mohammed V** in Gueliz, Marrakesh. These outfits take care of food, transport, equipment, and so forth, saving you the trouble of carting all your gear from home; normally you need to bring only boots and a sleeping bag. You can also inquire at the **Hotel Ali** (✉ Rue Moulay Ismail, Marrakesh, ☎ 04/44–49–79), historically a sort of matchmaker for mountain guides and the travelers in need of their services. **Atlas Sahara Trekking** (☎ 04/43–39–01 or 04/43–39–03) can arrange short High Atlas treks on foot or by mule.

In Imlil inquire at the Cafe Aksoual for **Abderrahim Bouinbaden,** who is licensed to lead both snow treks and mountain climbing as well as less ambitious adventures. His brother Hassan also guides. In both cases, if your French and Tashelhit are not strong you might start working on your pantomime. From outside town, the Bouinbadens can be reached at 04/48–56–12 or by mail at Imlil B.P. 15, Poste Asni, Marrakesh. Also in Imlil, the **Hôtel Etoile de Toubkal** is associated with a tour company that leads excursions lasting one to 15 days, including mountain climbing, mule tours, and more.

The **Fédération Royale Marocaine de Ski et de Montagne** (⊠ Parc de la Ligue Arabe, B.P. 15899, Casablanca, ☎ 02/20–37–98) has general advice on various outdoor pursuits.

8 THE GREAT OASIS VALLEYS

Morocco without the Sahara is like Switzerland without the Alps. The great oases on the desert's edge and the gorges leading toward them create some of Morocco's most dramatic landscapes. Sweeping expanses of bare and crevassed Atlas-mountain heights flatten into treeless plains in browns and buffs, cut by rocky canyons and punctuated by verdant date palmeries, before giving way to the tawny, wrinkled swirls of golden Saharan dunes.

By George
Semler

THE DESERT," WROTE COMPOSER AND NOVELIST Paul
Bowles, "will tweak your sense of time." Oft told in
the pre-Saharan oases is the story of French writer Antoine de Saint-Exupéry (1900–44), author of the beloved children's book
The Little Prince and celebrated for his mail flights across the Sahara.
Having landed his aircraft near a camel caravan somewhere in the desert
one day, he boasted to a nomad, "Look, my airplane made it here in
two hours, whereas it took your caravan two months . . ."—to which
the camel driver, unimpressed, responded, "And what did you do with
the rest of the time?"

A trip to the desert is fundamental to an understanding of Morocco.
Even the snow-filled Azrou Cedar Forest draws some of its aesthetic
power from its contrast with the Sahara, just as the Sahara seems to
reverberate with its prehistoric life as an ocean. Originally caravan routes
from the Sudan, Timbuktu, and Niger to Marrakesh and Fez, Morocco's
great oasis valleys have been of fundamental importance to its history.
From the Drâa Valley came the Saadian royal dynasty that ruled from
the mid-12th to the mid-17th centuries, and from the Ziz Valley and
the Tafilalt oasis rose the Alaouite dynasty, which relieved the Saadians in 1669 and which still rules (in the person of King Mohammed
VI) as Morocco enters the 21st century.

The oasis valleys form a geographical horseshoe, anchored logistically
and administratively by Er-Rachidia and Ouarzazate and terminating
at Merzouga and Mhamid, where the asphalt ends and the sand begins. In between are the Ziz, Dadès, Todra, and Drâa rivers and the
oases along them: the Tafilalt, Skoura, Todra, and Drâa. Flanking it
all are the High Atlas mountains and the Todra and Dadès gorges—
sister grand canyons separating the High Atlas from the Djebel Sarhro
Massif.

Over the course of Moroccan history, the edge of the Sahara Desert
has proven even more cosmopolitan than the Atlantic coast. Whereas
Roman, Portuguese, Spanish, and British invaders were sooner or later
repelled from the northern coastline, the federated Berber tribes Aït
Atta and Aït Yafelmane have received and accepted Arabs, Jews, and
Haratin (Sudanese) for centuries in the pre-Saharan trading posts of
the Tafilalt and Drâa oases. The Tafilalt, especially the city of Sijilmassa,
was long considered the *plaque giratoire* (turntable) between Africa
and the Maghreb, bringing Arabic and central and southern African
cultures into Morocco and North Africa while sending Islam south.

After you've seen the Atlas mountains, followed by gorges, oases,
palmeries, and Kasbahs, a trip down to the desert may seem a long
way to go to reach nothing, and some Moroccans and travelers will
warn you against it. Don't listen to naysayers. The void you encounter
in the Sahara will remind you why prophets and sages sought the
desert to purge and purify themselves.

Paul Bowles, author of *The Sheltering Sky,* saw (or heard) it this way:
"Immediately when you arrive in the Sahara, for the first or the tenth
time, you notice the stillness. An incredible, absolute silence prevails
outside the towns . . . even in busy places like the markets there is a
hushed quality in the air, as if the quiet were a constant force which,
resenting the intrusion of sound, minimizes and disperses it straight-
away. Then there is the sky, compared to which all other skies seem
faint-hearted efforts."

Pleasures and Pastimes

Dining

Far from the set-menu Moroccan cuisine of the urban palaces, the fare along the southern oasis routes tends to hearty *tagines* (stewed combinations of vegetables and meat (or fish) cooked in conical earthenware vessels) and couscous. *Harira* (hearty bean-based soup with vegetables and meat) is more than welcome as night sets in and temperatures plunge. *Mechoui* (roast lamb) is a standard feast, if you can order it far enough in advance. Some of the best lamb and vegetable tagines in Morocco are simmered over tiny camp stoves in random corners and campsites down here, so don't fear the free-range tagine. You may want to keep a decent bottle of wine handy, either in the car or even in a day pack, as many restaurants do not serve wine but have no problem with customers bringing their own. Always ask first, though, as some places do object.

CATEGORY	COST*
$$$$	over 200DH
$$$	150–200DH
$$	100–150DH
$	under 100DH

per person for a three-course meal, excluding drinks, service, and tax

Hiking and Walking

Hikes, treks, and even camel safaris can be the highlight of any trip through the southern oases, dunes, or gorges. Unless you have a four-wheel-drive vehicle, hiking is the only reasonable way to see the Todra Gorges, for instance, as the rocky *piste* (track) is lethal to most cars' oil pans and underpinnings. The Dadès Gorges, while paved, are still more spectacular on foot. North of Msemrir, a trekker with a fly rod in his backpack could easily dine on fresh trout every night. Serious trekking adventures through the M'Goun Massif (above the Dadès Valley) or around Djebel Sarhro, south of Tinerhir, are by far the best way to see this largely untouched Moroccan backcountry. Just beware of perambulating by camel travel if you have any tendency toward seasickness. Note, too, that driving in the desert can be tricky, as tracks spread out in all directions; it's wise to carry a compass.

Lodging

Hotels on the southern oasis routes generally range from mediocre to primitive, with several authentically charming spots and a few luxury establishments thrown in. Try to come here with the idea that running water and a warm place to sleep are all you really need, and accept anything above that as icing on the cake. Sleeping outdoors on hotel terraces is common (and cheap) in the summer, as are accommodations in *khaimas* (Berber nomad tents). Indeed, the stars and the sky in general are so stunning here that failing to sleep *à la belle étoile* (under the stars) seems criminal.

CATEGORY	COST*
$$$$	over 400DH
$$$	300–400DH
$$	200–300DH
$	under 200DH

All prices are for a standard double room, excluding service and tax.

Ksour and Kasbahs

Ksour (plural for *ksar*) and Kasbahs are fortified villages, houses, and granaries built of *pisé*, a sun-dried mixture of mud and clay. Ksour were originally tribal settlements or villages, while Kasbahs were single-family fortresses. The Erfoud–Ouarzazate road through the Dadès Valley is billed as the "Route of the Thousand Kasbahs," with village after village of fortified pisé structures, many decorated with intricate painted and carved geometrical patterns. The Drâa Valley is lined with Kasbahs and ksour throughout the length of the Agdz–Zagora road. Highlights are the Kasbah Amerhidil, at the Skoura oasis; the Tiffoultoute and Aït-Benhaddou Kasbahs, near Ouarzazate; the Tamnougalte and Timiderte Kasbahs, just south of Agdz; and the 11th-century Almoravid fortress at Zagora. In a different architectural category are the *babs* (gates) at Erfoud and Rissani and the door to the *medersa* (Koranic school) at Tamegroute, all very much worth seeking out.

Exploring the Great Oasis Valleys

Think of Morocco's complete southern oasis route as a rhomboid loop, with the northern Dadès Valley route (P32) carrying you east or west and the southern Agdz–Tazzarine–Rissani route (6956–3454) taking you back in the other direction. To miss either one would be to miss some of Morocco's most characteristic immensity—wide-open spaces and tundra-like scenery—as would missing the tangential Drâa Valley drive down to Zagora and Mhamid. Try to save three days for a trip through the Dadès Valley, starting from Erfoud (after sunrise at the Merzouga dunes), stopping at the Todra and Dadès gorges, and regrouping at Ouarzazate. (To explore the Dadès and Todra gorges alone could take a week.) The run out to Zagora, Tamegroute, and Mhamid is another two-day exploration, while the splendid drive back east across the excellent Agdz–Tazzarine–Rissani route can be done easily in a day unless you decide to trek into the Djebel Sarhro Massif.

Numbers in the text correspond to numbers in the margin and on the Great Oasis Valleys map.

Great Itineraries

Driving in Morocco is a thrilling and riveting adventure compared to your garden-variety freeway safari in a country with six-lane highways. In addition to the scenery, the obstacles presented by dromedaries and donkey-drawn carts make motoring more than interesting. Er-Rachidia and Ouarzazate make the best base camps for the oasis routes, with Fez and Marrakesh the respective connecting points farther north. The only possible drawback to covering a lot of territory is spending too much time in the car; keep your plan reasonable and aim to get out of the car, hike a few miles, and bond with the land a bit.

IF YOU HAVE 3 DAYS

Having traveled down the Ziz Gorges through **Er-Rachidia** ① the first day, spend the first night in 🏨 **Erfoud** ②. On day two, start before the first light of dawn to catch the gradual brightening and finally the sunrise at the **Merzouga** ③ dunes. Later that morning, explore **Rissani** ④ and the Tafilalt, then head west for the **Todra Gorges** ⑤ for lunch at the Hôtel Yasmine and a walk up into the gorges. After driving up into the **Dadès Gorges** ⑥ as far as you comfortably can (normally as far as Aït Oudinar), spend the second night in 🏨 **Ouarzazate** ⑨, including dinner with the stars (film stars, that is) at Chez Dimitri. On the third day drive south through the Drâa Valley through 🏨 **Zagora** ⑫ for lunch at the Rose des Sables. After stopping at **Tamegroute** ⑬ to see the medersa and the Naciri Sanctuary, catch sunset at the **Tinfou** ⑭ dunes or, farther south, at the Erg L'Houdi dune or **Mhamid** ⑮.

IF YOU HAVE 5 DAYS

After approaching through the Ziz Gorges and **Er-Rachidia** ① the first day, spend your first night in 🏨 **Erfoud** ② to see the sunrise at the **Mer-**

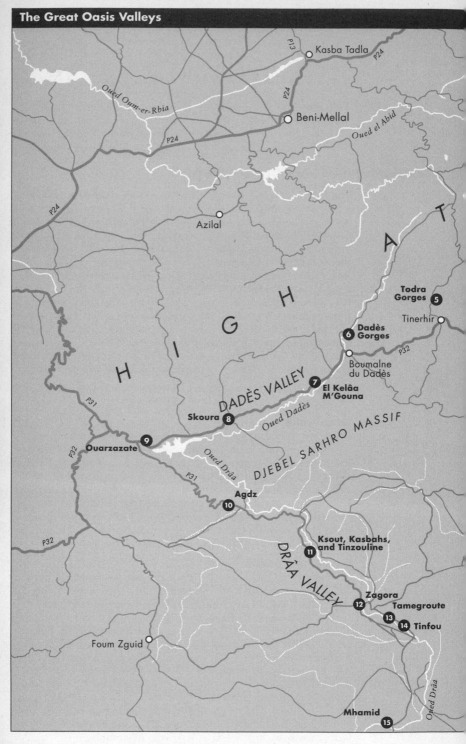

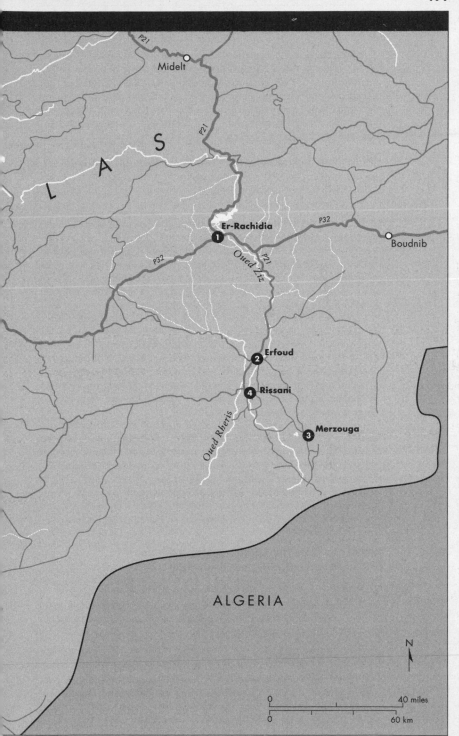

zouga ③ dunes. After exploring **Rissani** ④ and the Tafilalt that morning, head west for the **Todra Gorges** ⑤ and have lunch at the Hôtel Yasmine. Walk up into the gorges before continuing west and up into the ⌘ **Dadès Gorges** ⑥ for an afternoon and a night. On day three explore the **El Kelâa M'Gouna** ⑦ and **Skoura** ⑧ oases and Kasbahs before heading into ⌘ **Ouarzazate** ⑨ for dinner at Chez Dimitri and an overnight stay. The fourth day can take you through the **Drâa Valley** and **Agdz** ⑩ to **Zagora** ⑫ for lunch at the Rose des Sables, after which you can check out **Tamegroute** ⑬ and ⌘ **Tinfou** ⑭, another overnight option with its Auberge du Repos du Sable. On day five catch the desert sunrise at either the Tinfou dunes or, farther south, at the Erg Lihoudi (Dune of the Jew) or **Mhamid** ⑮ before starting back east to Erfoud, on the southern route through **Tazzarine,** or north to Ouarzazate and Marrakesh.

IF YOU HAVE 8 DAYS

With 8 or 10 days among the oasis valleys, you can really take the pulse of these places. On your way down through the Ziz Gorges and **Er-Rachidia** ① stop at Meski and the Source Bleue (Blue Springs). Spend a day exploring ⌘ **Erfoud** ② and a night at the Kasbah Derkouah. The next morning, drive and hike out to the top of the **Merzouga** ③ dunes in time to see the sun clear the eastern rim of the Sahara. After exploring **Rissani** ④ and the Tafilalt date palmery, head west in time to arrive at the ⌘ **Todra Gorges** ⑤ for the second night. On day three either drive (if you have a four-wheel-drive jeep) up to the head of the gorges for a night in the Auberge Baddou at ⌘ **Tamtattouchte,** or hike up the same 17½ km (11 mi) with a day pack and walk out the next day. In either case, spend day four getting over and through the ⌘ **Dadès Gorges** ⑥ and day five exploring them. On day six drive through the **El Kelâa M'Gouna** ⑦ and **Skoura** ⑧ oases and Kasbahs on the way into ⌘ **Ouarzazate** ⑨ for dinner at Chez Dimitri. The sixth day, after having a look at the Tifoultoutte Kasbah, drive through the Drâa Valley and **Agdz** ⑩ to ⌘ **Zagora** ⑫. On day seven explore **Tamegroute** ⑬ and the Zaouia Naciri before continuing out past the **Tinfou** ⑭ dunes through the town of Tagounite and the Tizi–Beni–Slimane pass to **Mhamid** ⑮. That night either stay in Mhamid or, better, turn back north and spend a night at ⌘ **Tinfou** at the Auberge Repos du Sable for a last desert sunrise before starting back east to Rissani, Erfoud, and Er-Rachidia, on the southern route through **Tazzarine,** or heading north to Ouarzazate and Marrakesh.

When to Tour the Great Oasis Valleys

For off-season rates, better temperatures, and fewer convoys of tourists, try to travel the oasis routes between October and April. The high season begins in early March but doesn't kick in properly until April. Summer is hot in the desert and can be crowded in the oases and gorges.

THE ZIZ VALLEY, ERFOUD, AND THE TAFILALT

This particular southeastern corner holds some of Morocco's greatest sights, principally the Sahara's Merzouga dunes and the Tafilalt date palmery. The trip south from Er-Rachidia to Erfoud through the Ziz palmery makes a good evening run, with reddish waves of desert encroaching from the east; at the other end of the day, a drive out to the Merzouga dunes as dawn's first light begins to brighten the rim of the Sahara is somehow even more rejuvenating than sunrise anywhere else. The town of Merzouga merits a visit just to see what the "end of the line" looks like, and the drive back north through Rissani and the Tafi-

Finally, a travel companion that doesn't snore on the plane or eat all your peanuts.

When traveling, your MCI WorldCom Card is the best way to keep in touch. Our operators speak your language, so they'll be able to connect you back home—no matter where your travels take you. Plus, your MCI WorldCom Card is easy to use, and even earns you frequent flyer miles every time you use it. When you add in our great rates, you get something even more valuable: peace-of-mind. So go ahead. Travel the world. MCI WorldCom just brought it a whole lot closer.

You can even sign up today at www.mci.com/worldphone or ask your operator to make a collect call to 1-410-314-2938.

EASY TO CALL WORLDWIDE

1 Just dial the WorldPhone access number of the country you're calling from.
2 Dial or give the operator your MCI WorldCom Card number.
3 Dial or give the number you're calling.

Argentina	
To call using Telefonica	0-800-222-6249
To call using Telecom	0-800-555-1002
Brazil	**000-8012**
Mexico	
Avantel	01-800-021-8000
Telmex ▲	001-800-674-7000
Collect access in Spanish	980-9-16-1000
Morocco	**00-211-0012**

For your complete WorldPhone calling guide, dial the WorldPhone access number for the country you're in and ask the operator for Customer Service. In the U.S. call 1-800-431-5402.

▲ When calling from public phones, use phones marked LADATEL.

EARN FREQUENT FLYER MILES

AmericanAirlines
AAdvantage

Continental Airlines
OnePass

Delta Air Lines
SkyMiles

MILEAGE PLUS.
United Airlines

U·S AIRWAYS
DIVIDEND MILES

MCI WorldCom, its logo and the names of the products referred to herein are proprietary marks of MCI WorldCom, Inc. All airline names and logos are proprietary marks of the respective airlines. All airline program rules and conditions apply.

MCI WORLDCOM

The first thing you need overseas is the one thing you forget to pack.

FOREIGN CURRENCY DELIVERED OVERNIGHT

Chase Currency To Go® delivers foreign currency to your home by the next business day*

It's easy—before you travel, call 1-888-CHASE84 for delivery of any of 75 currencies

Delivery is free with orders of $500 or more

Competitive rates—without exchange fees

You don't have to be a Chase customer—you can pay by Visa® or MasterCard®

◯ CHASE

THE RIGHT RELATIONSHIP IS EVERYTHING.®

1•888•CHASE84
www.chase.com

*Orders must be placed before 5 PM ET. $10 delivery fee for orders under $500.
©1999 The Chase Manhattan Corporation. All rights reserved. The Chase Manhattan Bank. Member FDIC.

lalt date palmery seems doubly miraculous once you've seen the desert. More than a million date palms grow in the Tafilalt oasis, a phenomenon created by the parallel Ziz and Rheris rivers, which flow within 3–5 km (2–3½ mi) of each other for 26 km (16 mi). Dubbed the Mesopotamia of the Maghreb (that is, of Morocco) for the confluence of the Rheris and Ziz rivers, as well as for its role as the cradle of the Alaouite dynasty, the Tafilalt date palmery and the town of Rissani have played key roles in Moroccan history.

Er-Rachidia

❶ *365 km (218 mi) south of Fez, 126 km (76 mi) south of Midelt, 81 km (49 mi) north of Erfoud.*

If you approach Er-Rachidia from Midelt, enjoy your view of the **Ziz Gorges,** immense and dramatic cuts through rock walls with views out into the brown-then-green expanses of the Middle and High Atlas. *Ziz* is a Berber word for "gazelle," and although the only gazelles you'll see today are the ones leaping across Ziz gasoline signs, the word pops up everywhere in Morocco, used for everything from crescent-shape cookies to sleek young women.

This French-built garrison town is now capital of the province of Er-Rachidia and the most important secondary-school enclave south of the Atlas mountains. Er-Rachidia is your base for everything from the regional hospital to the tourist office, and nearly any trip to the Merzouga dunes or north through the Ziz Gorges will pass through here. It's a good place to buy gasoline, make a phone call, or just stock up on supplies; beyond that, there's no real reason to pause here.

Dining and Lodging

$$$ ✕🏨 **Hôtel Rissani.** If you've come from Ouarzazate's Hôtel Le Zate, you'll think you've walked through the looking glass: they're identical twins. Although this hotel is no luxury destination, the service is invariably friendly and helpful, and the overall package is the best and most comfortable in town. The swimming pool is a town rendezvous point and a good place to have breakfast in the shade. ✉ *Avenue El Massira, Er-Rachidia,* ☎ *05/57–21–86,* 🖷 *05/57–25–85. 65 rooms. Restaurant, bar, pool. AE, DC, MC, V.*

En Route   South of Er-Rachidia, you'll be distracted by Meski, the Source Bleue (Blue Spring), and the Tafilalt date palmery as you reach the lower Ziz Valley. **Meski,** 18 km (11 mi) south of Er-Rachidia (well marked off the road to the east), is an oasis with spring-water swimming pools, a campground, and a restaurant. Named not for the water but for the legendary Sudanese "blue men" (traders tinged indigo from the running dye of their turbans) whose caravans used to stop here, the spring waters of the **Source Bleue** are said to cure sterility. The final descent of the green swath of the Ziz Valley through the ancient Arab villages of the **Tafilalt date palmery** is spectacular and surprising, with scalloping sand dunes cresting just beyond the oasis.

Erfoud

❷ *81 km (49 mi) south of Er-Rachidia, 300 km (180 mi) northeast of Ouarzazate.*

A French administrative outpost and Foreign Legion stronghold, this frontier town on the Algerian border has a definite Wild West (in this case, Wild South) feel to it. As the key urban presence in the Tafilalt, one of Morocco's most important oases, Erfoud comes into its own during its October date festival. The military fortress at Borj-Est, just across the Ziz to the east, provides the best possible view over the date palmery, the desert, and Erfoud from its altitude of 3,067 ft above sea level. Between Borj-Est and the Auberge Kasbah Derkaouah are marble quarries famous for their black marble, one of Erfoud's principal products; interestingly, this luxurious solid is rich in petrified marine fossils.

Erfoud is not without its peculiar charm, though this dusty, fly-bitten border post is best known as a traveler's jumping-off point for the Merzouga dunes. Its finest architectural feature is the main gate into the medina, designed in the typical Almohad style with flanking crenellated bastions and an intricately carved stucco portal.

Dining and Lodging

$$$ ✕🖼 **Hôtel Tafilalet.** Old colonial trappings and a hint of elegance lie behind this unimpressive street-side facade on the main drag through Erfoud. Neither luxurious nor especially charming, the Tafilalet is nonetheless clean, efficient, and perfectly adequate as a pit stop. The rooms are on the small and drab side, but the service is urbane and friendly, and the hotel runs a dawn shuttle out to the dunes. ⊠ *Avenue Moulay Ismail, Erfoud,* ☎ *05/57–65–35,* FAX *05/57–60–36. 65 rooms. 2 restaurants, bar, pool. AE, DC, MC, V.*

$$–$$$ ✕🖼 **Auberge Kasbah Derkaouah.** This extraordinary lodging is at the edge of the desert, half an hour's drive from the Merzouga dunes. Michel Auzat and his daughter, Bouchra, serve excellent Moroccan and French cuisine and offer cozy, well-designed accommodations of various kinds: there are nine doubles, two duplexes, two bungalows, one apartment, and two tents. To find Kasbah Derkaouah from Erfoud (it's 24 km, or 14 mi, southeast of town), cross the market square, Place des Far, and follow signs for DUNES SABLES D'OR straight out into the desert. Don't be surprised when you find yourself driving across the Ziz River—this is not a mirage but a dam and bridge *over* which, in early spring, the river flows at a depth of an inch or two. Once the pavement ends, follow the green-and-white markers that Michel has provided to guide you in. ⊠ *Write c/o Michel Auzat, Erfoud,* ☎ *05/57–71–40,* FAX *05/57–71–40. 11 rooms, 2 bungalows, 2 tents, 1 apartment. Restaurant. AE, DC, MC, V.*

Merzouga

★ ❸ *53 km (32 mi) southeast of Erfoud.*

A sunrise trip to the Merzouga **dunes** (Erg Chebbi) has become a classic Moroccan adventure. A series of some half a dozen café-restaurant-hotels overlook the dunes, and the Café du Sud runs camels (specifically, one-humped dromedaries) out to the top of the dunes, a 45-minute walk on foot. The nearby seasonal salt lake **Dayet Sjri** is a surprising sight, and is filled in early spring with pink flamingos. The town of Merzouga has little to recommend it other than a few not-too-compelling but survivable hotels. Between Erg Chebbi and the town, have a look at the underground aqueduct, Merzouga's main water supply and flowing (oozing) proof that sand dunes form as a result of moisture, which causes the sand to stick and agglomerate. The dune at Merzouga is thought to be the highest in Morocco, perhaps in the world, towering more than 815 ft over the surrounding desert. If you come this far south, complete the loop through Rissani and the Tafilalt oasis before heading west for the Dadès Valley or north for Fez.

The Auberge Dunes d'Or, distinguished by a small wooden airplane that appeared in Saint-Exupéry's film *Le Petit Prince,* has simple, slightly dusty rooms and running water. The Auberge Kasbah Derkaouah (☞ *above*) is 11 km (7 mi) from the dunes, 25 km (15 mi) from the town of Merzouga; follow the telephone poles to be sure you're on the right track.

Rissani

❹ *17 km (11 mi) south of Erfoud, 40 km (24 mi) northeast of Merzouga.*

Straddling the last visible (i.e., aboveground) flowing section of the Ziz River, Rissani once had a population of some 100,000 people, who lived by the trans-Saharan caravan trades in salt, gold, and slaves—all of which continued until the end of the 19th century. Rissani stands on the site of the ancient city of Sijilmassa, Morocco's first independent southern kingdom, which thrived here from the 8th to the 14th centuries. Founded in 757 by dissident Berbers, who had committed the heresy of translating the Koran to the Berber language (Islamic orthodoxy forbids translation from the Arabic of the direct revelations of God), Sijilmassa and the Filalis, as they were known, prospered from the natural wealth of the Tafilalt oasis and the Tafilalt's key role on the Salt Road to West Africa. Sijilmassa was almost completely destroyed in civil strife in 1393; archaeological excavations are now attempting to determine the city's size and configuration. All that remains of Sijilmassa today is the excellent 13th-century gate **Bab Errih**, notable for the green ceramic-tile frieze over its three horseshoe arches.

Modern Rissani is known as the cradle of the (still-ruling) Alaouite dynasty, of which King Mohammed VI is the 15th sultan. In the mid-13th century the Berber chiefs of the Tafilalt brought a descendent of the prophet Mohammed to end a severe drought. Hassan the Alaouite (the name means "family of Allah") was credited with bringing rains, and Moulay Ali Sherif, father of Er-Rachidia and brother of Moulay Ismail (of Meknes fame) officially founded the dynasty. The well-marked Circuit Touristique guides you through the main remnants of the Alaouite presence here. The **zaouia of Moulay Ali Sherif,** the mausoleum of the dynasty's founder, is 2 km (1 mi) southeast of the center of Rissani. Next to the zaouia is the **Ksar Akbar,** in which Alaouite sultans exiled rebellious family members and the wives of deceased sultans to the edge of the desert. Moulay Ismail had two of his sons sent here to put some distance between his heirs and his power base at Meknes. Another kilometer along the circuit is the **Ksar Oualad Abdelhalim,** the most voluminous and impressive of these Alaouite structures; it was built in 1900 for Sultan Moulay el Hassan's older brother, who had conveniently been named governor of Tafilalt. Loop around past the remaining ksour and climb the high ground at **Tinrheras,** correctly marked on the Michelin map as an excellent lookout point over the Tafilalt.

En Route　At this point, depending on your plans, you might head west on the southern oasis route (Routes 3454 and 6956 to Agdz and Zagora) or loop around on the northern route through Erfoud (Route 3451 to the P32) past the Todra and Dadès gorges to Ouarzazate. If you're headed back up to Fez and Meknes, either way works. If you're going on over the High Atlas to Marrakesh, take the northern route for its distinctive gorges.

THE TODRA GORGES AND DADÈS VALLEY

At sunset the drive through the Todra and Dadès gorges and Dadès Valley is so beautiful, with the descending sun casting shadows in every draw and wrinkle of the earth's crust, that it seems tragic to miss the scenery by driving west into the increasingly blinding sunlight. The only solution is to start early—in the morning, shadows shorten and disappear as the sun rises, but at least you'll be able to see them. The turnoff up into the Todra Gorges at Tinerhir is clearly marked. If you've already spent some time in the gorges and the High Atlas, Tinerhir will seem a metropolis; in reality, it's barely worth a stop, though the view up over the palmery into the Todra from the Hotel Sarhro (next to the ruins of the Kasbah) is spectacular. To get a decent look at the Todra and Dadès gorges, plan to spend at least a day—ideally, several—exploring Morocco's smaller versions of the Grand Canyon.

The Todra Gorges

⑤ *194 km (107 mi) northwest of Rissani, 184 (101 mi) northeast of Ouarzazate.*

The 15-km (9-mi) drive up from Tinerhir to the beginning of the Todra Gorges will take you through lush but slender palmeries, sometimes no wider than 100 ft from cliff to cliff. About halfway to the beginning of the gorges is La Source des Poissons Sacrés (the Spring of the Sacred Fish), so named for the miracle performed by a sage said to have struck a rock once to produce a gushing spring and twice to produce fish. An inn and a café await near the spring, but you're better off not stopping, as the site itself is only fair, not remarkable, and the concentration of hustlers and overhelpful children is dense.

The 66-ft-wide entrance to the Todra Gorges, with its roaring clear stream and its 1,000-ft-high rock walls stretching 325 ft back on either side, is the most stunning feature of the whole canyon, though the upper reaches aren't far behind. The farther off the beaten path you get, the more rewarding the scenery; a walk or drive up through the gorges to **Tamtattouchte** is particularly recommended, though only by four-wheel-drive vehicle if you're driving. (A standard rental hatchback might make it after hours of torturously slow driving, but it's risky, not at all amusing, and may break your rental agreement.)

From the thin palmery along the bottom, the walls of the Todra Gorges remain close and high for some 18 km (11 mi), dappled only with occasional families of nomads and their black *khaimas* (tents) tending sheep, goats, or camels (dromedaries) up on the rocks. Colorfully attired young Berber shepherdesses may appear from nowhere, willing to pose for a photo in exchange for a coin or two; sometimes you can hear them singing Berber melodies from high in the crags, their sounds echoed and amplified by the rock walls of the canyon. Eagles nest in the Todra, along with choughs (red-beaked rooks), rock doves, and blue rock thrushes.

Dining and Lodging

$$ ✕🏨 **Hôtel Yasmina.** This is as close as you can stay to the Todra Gorges, about 150 ft from the entrance next to a gushing spring of crystal-clear water that provides nonpareil sleeping music, especially for North Africa. Rooms 11 and 12 are among the best—they overlook the stream and the entrance to the gorges. The restaurant cooks excellent Moroccan fare. No wine is served, but you can bring your own. ✉ *Gorges du Todra, Tinerhir,* ☎ *04/83–30–13,* 📠 *04/83–33–95. 30 rooms. Restaurant, café. MC, V.*

$ ✕🏨 **Auberge Baddou–Chez Moha.** Mohammed "Moha" Abaz is your host at this clean and simple mountain inn with excellent food, hot water, showers, and cheerfully painted rooms. Mr. Abaz also organizes hiking and four-wheel-drive excursions and serves as a general outfitter and adviser to travelers in the upper Todra Gorges. Have breakfast or a gin and tonic on the roof, after being hauled up by Moha's ingenious dumbwaiter. ⊠ *Gorges du Todra, Km 18, Tamtattouchte, Aït Hani, Er-Rachidia,* ☎ *05/88–21–52. 7 rooms. MC, V.*

En Route   If you have a four-wheel-drive vehicle with good clearance, you can take the adventurous route from the top of the Todra Gorges: pop over into the Dadès Gorges by the difficult but passable Route 3444 from Aït Hani (first village after Tamtattouchte) to **Msemrir.** Hikers can do this as well, forming an ideal three- or four-day walk up the Todra and over to, down, and out the Dadès Gorges. Other four-wheel-drive options include continuing north to Agoudal and **Imilchil** (especially if it's September and you're looking to drop in on the annual marriage moussem), or heading east through Aït Hani, Tiidrine, and Assoul to Rich, a tortuous but stunningly beautiful route on which you ford several rivers and see no one except Berber villagers and the occasional nomad. Whatever you do, watch out for the children of Aït Hani, who have marked up their town with bogus road signs and will attempt to climb aboard your conveyance and "direct" you on your way. Roll up the windows and proceed straight through, staying true to your Michelin map. If necessary, try barking, "*Bah*-lek!" (roughly, "Clear out!").

The Dadès Gorges

❻   *Boumalne du Dadès is 53 km (31 mi) southwest of Tinerhir, 116 km (70 mi) northeast of Ouarzazate.*

The town of **Boumalne du Dadès** marks the southern entrance to the Dadès Gorges, which are even more beautiful—longer, wider, and more varied—than their sisters, the Todra Gorges. The first 25 km (15 mi) of the Dadès Gorges, from Boumalne to Aït Ali, are paved and approachable in any kind of vehicle; the next 38 km (23 mi), from Aït Ali to Msemrir, are comfortably navigated only in four-wheel-drive vehicles with good clearance. Boumalne itself is only of moderate interest, though the central market square and, overlooking it, the terrace café of the Hôtel Adrar are good vantage points for a perusal of local life. The shops Artisanale de Boumalne and Maison Aït Atta, on the way to the Hôtel Madayeq, merit a browse for their local products at local prices, particularly rosewood carvings and rose water.

The lower Dadès Gorges and the Dadès River, which flows through them, are lined with thick vegetation. Surprisingly, after the Todra palmery, palm trees are conspicuously absent in favor of *argán* (an olive-like nut), Atlas pistachio, and carob trees. A series of Kasbahs and ksour (groups of *ksar*, or fortified houses) give way to Berber villages such as Aït Youl, Aït Arbi, Aït Ali, Aït Oudinar, and Aït Toukhsine—*Aït* meaning "of the people" in the Tamazight Berber language. Two kilometers (1 mile) up the road from Boumalne is the **Glaoui Kasbah,** once part of the empire of the infamous Pasha of Marrakesh, T'hami el-Glaoui. The ksour at **Aït Arbi** are tucked neatly into the surrounding volcanic rock 3 km (2 mi) farther on. Ten kilometers (6 miles) farther is the **Tamnalt Valley,** the "Valley of the Human Bodies," where the eroded rock formations seem curiously organic, like soles of feet or elephant hides. Just as you enter the Tamnalt Valley, the Café-Restaurant Meguirne appears, offering panoramic views, good meals, and several rooms; a few minutes north is the Auberge Gorges du Dadès, another option for a temporary halt, an exploration of the river, or an overnight stay.

After **Aït Oudinar** the road crosses a bridge and gets substantially more difficult, and the valley narrows dramatically. If you have four-wheel drive, don't turn back: some of the most dramatic views in the Dadès are just around the corner. Six kilometers (4 miles) north of the bridge there are three little inns, the best of which is the Kasbah de la Vallée, offering different levels of comfort ranging from tent to terrace to rooms with bath.

Aït Hammou is the next village, 5 km (3 mi) past the Kasbah de la Vallée. It makes a good base camp for walking and climbing north to vantage points over the Dadès River or, to the east, to a well-known cave with stalactites (ask the Hotel Kasbah de la Vallée for directions). At the top of the gorges is **Msemrir,** a village of red-clay pisé ksour that has a café with guest rooms. From Msemrir the road leads north over the High Atlas through Tilmi, the Tizi-n-Ouano Pass, and Agoudal to Imilchil and eventually up to Route P24, the Marrakesh–Fez road. The road east climbs the difficult Route 3444, always bearing right, to another gorge-top town, Tamtattouchte.

Dining and Lodging

$$ ✕⊡ **Hôtel Madayeq.** This singular Kasbah, constructed of haphazardly strewn blocks of pisé, has nonpareil views up the valley and over the Boumalne palmery. The rooms are plain and a little threadbare, but the restaurant's lamb-stew tagines are excellent. ⊠ *Boumalne du Dadès,* ☎ *04/83–07–63,* ⅏ *04/83–07–67. 68 rooms. Restaurant, bar, pool. AE, DC, MC, V.*

$–$$ ✕⊡ **Auberge Gorges du Dadès.** Overlooking the Oudinar's bridge and an abruptly narrow point in the gorges, this little inn offers various accommodations: rooms for two, four, or six, with or without views. The aesthetics are not especially charming, but the helpful and cosmopolitan staff can help arrange hikes, treks, and safaris around the gorges. The road gets rougher north of here, so this is the end of the line for standard cars. ⊠ *Aït Oudinar,* ☎ *04/83–17–10,* ⅏ *04/83–01– 31. 22 rooms. Restaurant. MC, V.*

$–$$ ✕⊡ **Hôtel la Kasbah de la Vallée.** This tiny spot high in the Dadès Gorges is pretty much your last chance for dependable rooms and meals here. At the gorges' midpoint, halfway between Boumalne and Msemrir, the hotel overlooks one of the most dramatic parts of the canyon. Some rooms are superior, with views over some of the most dizzying reaches in the gorges; others are both viewless and hapless. Ask to see a few. Accommodations include terrace cots, tents, and rooms with private bath. ⊠ *Aït Oudinar, Gorges du Dadès, Boumalne du Dadès, Ouarzazate (6 km, or 4 mi, north of Aït Oudinar; 27 km, or 16 mi, north of Boumalne),* ☎ ⅏ *04/83–17–17. 25 rooms. Restaurant. MC, V.*

El Kelaâ M'Gouna

❼ *24 km (13 mi) southwest of Boumalne du Dadès, 92 km (57 mi) northeast of Ouarzazate.*

Known for its annual Rose Festival, held in May, this oasis town can send you on a tour of the Valley of the Roses as well as launch you on treks into the M'Goun Massif, farther north. For a springtime drive through fields of roses, head west from the P32 into Route 6904 toward Bou Thrarar, 8 km (5 mi) north. (At Bou Thrarar, Route 6903 leads back down the Asif M'Goun River to El Kelaâ M'Gouna and the Ouarzazate road.) In addition to enfolding you in a heady scent, this excursion takes you to an excellent Kasbah at Bou Thrarar.

Dining & Lodging

$$–$$$ ✕⊡ **Les Roses du Dadès.** One of Morocco's great southern colonial hotels, Les Roses du Dadès retains a sense of preterit elegance, a hint of nostalgia for times unknown. It's a good place for pre- or post-Dadès staging and regrouping; the pool in particular is refreshing and well maintained. The rooms are somewhat faded, but they're clean and acceptable. The inn runs equestrian tours to the local Kasbahs and into

the mountains. ⊠ *El Kelâa M'Gouna,* ☎ *04/83–60–07,* ℻ *04/83–63–36. 102 rooms. Restaurant, bar, pool. AE, DC, MC, V.*

Skoura

8 *50 km (30 mi) southwest of El Kelâa M'Gouna.*

Surprisingly lush and abrupt as it springs from the tawny landscape, the Skoura oasis deserves a lingering look for its Kasbahs and its rich concentration of date palms and olive, fig, and almond trees. Pathways tunnel through the vegetation from one Kasbah to another within this fertile island—a true oasis, perhaps the most intensely verdant in Morocco. The main Kasbah route through Skoura is approached from a point just over 2 km (1 mi) past the town center toward Ouarzazate. The 17th-century **Kasbah Ben Moro** is the first fortress on the right. The family next door is usually more than willing (for a small fee) to watch your car and guide you through the palmery, past the Sidi Aissa *marabout* (shrine to a learned holy man), to the Amerhidil River and the tremendous **Kasbah Amerhidil,** the largest Kasbah in Skoura and one of the largest in Morocco. Down the (usually bone-dry) river is another Kasbah, Dar Aït Sidi El Mati, while back near the Ouarzazate road is the Kasbah El Kabbaba, the last of the four fortresses on this loop. There are more Kasbahs north of Skoura, on Route 6829 through Aït-Souss: Dar Lahsoune, a former Glaoui residence, and, a few minutes' farther north, the **Kasbah Aït Ben Abou,** the second largest in Skoura after the Amerhidil.

Dining

$$ ✕ **Hôtel Nakhil.** Recommended for its food rather than its lodgings, the Hôtel Nakhil is Skoura's nerve center. If wandering through the oasis and Kasbahs has heightened your appetite, try the Nakhil's tagine of lamb, figs, and sesame seeds. ⊠ *Place Central, Skoura,* ☎ *04/88–38–89. Restaurant. MC, V.*

Ouarzazate

9 *42 km (25 mi) southwest of Skoura, 204 km (122 mi) southeast of Marrakesh, 300 km (180 mi) west of Erfoud.*

At first sight, Morocco's Hollywood and desert crossroads is disappointing—a line of modern buildings fronting a commercial main street. Still, aided by Chez Dimitri and the ubiquitous Western movie industry, Ouarzazate can go from dusty ghost town to desert tinsel town in a matter of hours. Royal Air Maroc and Air France both fly direct to Ouarzazate from Paris, so the town might be said to have one foot in the Sahara and another on the Champs-Elysées. Surrounded by some of Morocco's most dramatic terrain, from the snowcapped High Atlas to the Sahara, with tremendous canyons, gorges, and lunarlike steppes in between, Ouarzazate's combination of luminosity and landscapes has made it a mainstay for filmmakers. *Lawrence of Arabia, The Sheltering Sky, The Last Temptation of Christ,* and, last we heard, Spielberg's *The Gladiators* are just a few of the familiar titles shot in and around Ouarzazate.

At the junction of the Dadès, Drâa, and Souss valleys, Ouarzazate was settled and fortified by the French in the late 1920s for its obvious strategic value. Known for its fine artisan traditions in ceramics and carpet-making, the **Kasbah Taourirt,** once a Glaoui palace, is the oldest and finest building in town, a rambling pisé castle built by those so-called Lords of the Atlas in the late 19th century.

Interesting excursions from Ouarzazate into the High Atlas would begin with the Glaoui Kasbah at Telouet, 70 km (42 mi) north of town on

Route 6802–6803 (☞ Tizi-n-Tichka *in* Chapter 7). Returning from
★ Telouet, a detour to the village and Kasbah of **Aït-Benhaddou** makes
a superb four-wheel-drive outing. (From Ouarzazate you can drive to
Aït-Benhaddou in a standard car.) Strewn across the hillside and surrounded by flowering almond trees in early spring, the red-pisé towers of this village fortress resemble a melting sand castle. Crenellated
and topped with blocky towers, it's one of the most sumptuous sights
in the Atlas. Trust Orson Welles and David Lean for unforgettable
scenery: they filmed *Sodom and Gomorrah* and *Lawrence of Arabia*
here. The Auberge El Ouidane, with splendid views across the river, is
a good place to stop for lunch or an evening tagine. Another option
would be to walk from the P31 to Aït-Benhaddou and back in a loop,
a four- or five-day jaunt of 77 km (46 mi), to be executed only with
full camping and backpacking equipment (☞ Chapter 7 for more on
trekking in the High Atlas). The **Kasbah Tiffoultoute,** on the Zagora
road that branches off the Marrakesh road and passes west of Ouarzazate, is another good visit—a nice place to explore and have a rooftop
drink or dinner even if you don't stay overnight (☞ Dining and Lodging, *below*).

Dining and Lodging

$$–$$$ ✕ **Chez Dimitri.** Founded in 1928 as the first store, gas pump, post of-
★ fice, telephone booth, dance hall, and restaurant in Ouarzazate, Chez
Dimitri may look unimpressive on an initial sweep through the town's
banal main drag, but the food, whether international or Moroccan, is
carefully purchased and prepared and invariably excellent, from soups
to salads to lamb chops. The owners are friendly and helpful, and the
photographs of legendary movie stars on the walls are sometimes enhanced by real stars at the next table. If Ouarzazate is still the crossroads of the southern oasis routes, Chez Dimitri is still at the heart of
it. ⊠ *22, Avenue Mohammed V,* ☎ *04/88–26–53. MC, V.*

$$ ✕ **Ichbilia (Seville).** If Chez Dimitri is booked solid, which it may well
★ be if the movie crowd is around, this gourmet enclave out on the Mar-
rakesh road near the studios serves top Moroccan fare in an elegant
context. Combining Spanish, French, and Moroccan cuisine, this is one
of the finest dining spots south of Marrakesh. Call in advance for a
mechoui (shoulder of lamb with peas and fennel) or the steamed cous-
cous with quail. ⊠ *Route de Marrakech (P31), Tamassint,* ☎ *04/88–
67–21. AE, DC, MC, V.*

$$$$ ✕⌂ **Berbère Palace.** Movie stars and magnates tend to stay here. The
pool, public rooms, and indeed everything about this hotel is impec-
cable; the only drawback is that it has a rather empty feel when it's
not choked with throngs of tourists. Still, the quality of the rooms and
bungalows, all elegantly furnished and lavishly decorated, and the
level of poolside chic are tops in Ouarzazate. The international and
Moroccan cuisine is very much on a par with the hotel's high standards.
⊠ *Rue Mansour Eddahbi,* ☎ *04/88–31–05,* FAX *04/88–30–70. 222 rooms
and bungalows. 3 restaurants, 2 bars, pool. AE, DC, MC, V.*

$$–$$$ ✕⌂ **Kasbah Tiffoultoute.** Scenes from *Lawrence of Arabia* were shot
here, especially those including the beautiful cedar door to the dining
room. Accommodations are rustic and somewhat stark, and the bath-
rooms are outside on the corridor surrounding the courtyard, but this
onetime fortified palace of the T'Hami el-Glaoui—the formidable
pasha of Marrakesh evoked in Gavin Maxwell's *Lords of the Atlas*—
is the most romantic place in or around Ouarzazate. Overlooking the
Drâa River and its palmery, the Kasbah takes full advantage of its views
with a panoramic rooftop breakfast terrace. Berber dancing and mu-
sical spectacles enhance dinner. ⊠ *Avenue Mohammed V,* ☎ FAX *04/
88–58–99. 7 rooms without bath. Restaurant. AE, DC, MC, V.*

$$ ✗⬚ **Riad Salam.** This simple, friendly, unpretentious place is down toward the southern end of Ouarzazate, just short of the Kasbah Taourirt. The staff tries hard, the pool is in fine shape all year long, and Berber musicians perform until midnight, often in front of a roaring fire. The manager, Monsieur Benjeddin, is happy to advise you on excursions of all kinds. Rooms are adequate though imperfect: don't be shocked if your shower nozzle falls off the wall or the toilet runs continuously. ⊠ *Avenue Mohammed V,* ☎ *04/88–33–35,* 𝔽𝔸𝕏 *04/88–27–66. 62 rooms. Restaurant, bar, pool. AE, DC, MC, V.*

THE DRÂA VALLEY

Morocco's longest river, the Drâa once flowed all the way to the Atlantic Ocean just north of Tan-Tan, some 960 km (600 mi) from its source above Ouarzazate. With the sole exception of a fluke flood in 1989—the only time in recent memory that the Drâa completed its course—the river now disappears in the Sahara southwest of Mhamid, some 240 km (150 mi) from its headwaters above Ouarzazate. The Drâa Valley and its palmery continue nearly unbroken from Agdz through Zagora to Mhamid, one of Morocco's most memorable tours.

The road south from Ouarzazate through the Drâa Valley has a certain power, perhaps precisely because it's a dead end and, though remote, takes you nowhere even remotely useful (in the logistical sense of the word). As wild as you may have found certain parts of Morocco thus far, the trip down to the Sahara will seem more so, something like steady progress into a Biblical epic. The plains south of Ouarzazate give way to 120 km (75 mi) of date palmeries and oases along the Drâa River, and between Agdz and Zagora more than two dozen Kasbahs and ksour line both sides of the river. The occasional market town offers a chance to mingle with the diverse peoples you will otherwise see walking along the road in black, reflector-spangled Berber shawls. Though most of the inhabitants are in fact Berbers, the Drâa Valley also contains Arab villages, small communities of Jews or the Mellahs they once inhabited, and numerous Haratin, descendants of Sudanese slaves brought into Morocco along the caravan routes that facilitated salt, gold, and slave trading until late in the 19th century.

After Zagora and Tamegroute, the road narrows as the Tinfou dunes rise to the east and, farther south, a maze of jeep tracks leads out to Erg Lihoudi (Dune of the Jew). Finally, in Mhamid el Gouzlane (the Plain of the Gazelles), with sand drifting across the road and the Drâa long since gone underground, there is a definite sense of closure, the end of the road: you've left Western Europe in another universe.

En Route Coming south from Ouarzazate, look for the turnoff to the **Cascades du Drâa** on the left, 30 km (19 mi) south of Ouarzazate and 10 km (6 mi) before Agdz. The 10-km (6-mi) track down to the waterfalls is steep, rough, and all but impassable in bad weather, but the falls are magnificent. Natural pools invite swimming, and a falls-side café serves good tagines.

Agdz

⑩ *69 km (41 mi) southeast of Ouarzazate.*

Agdz, at the junction of the Drâa and Tamsift rivers, marks the beginning of the Drâa palmery. A sleepy market town and administrative center, Agdz (pronounced *ah*-ga-dez) has little to offer other than the 5,022-ft peak **Djebel Kissane,** the Kasbah **Dar El Glaoui,** and a surprisingly good hotel. From Agdz south to Mhamid, the P31 road follows the river closely except for a 30-km (18-mi) section between the Tinfou dunes and Tagounite, where the Drâa again draws close before temporarily looping east again.

Dining and Lodging

$$ ✕🏨 **Kissane Hotel Agdz.** Near the ceremonial arch welcoming you to Agdz, this little inn is bright, clean, and competent. The manager, Jabli El Houcine, can arrange anything from an overnight bivouac under the stars to visits to local Kasbahs or the waterfalls. ✉ *Avenue Mohammed V,* ☎ *04/84–30–44,* 🖷 *04/84–32–58. 47 rooms. Restaurant, bar, pool. AE, DC, MC, V.*

Ksour, Kasbahs, and Tinzouline

⓫ *Zagora is 95 km (57 mi) southeast of Agdz.*

Lining virtually the entire Drâa Valley from Agdz to Zagora are some two dozen ksour and Kasbahs on both sides of the river. Perhaps the most amazing ksour in this region are at **Tamnougalt,** 6 km (4 mi) south of Agdz—the second group of red-pisé fortifications on the left. The resident Berber tribe, the Mezguita, governed its own independent republic from here until the late 18th century; the crenellated battlements and bastions were a necessary defense against nomadic desert tribes. **Kasbah Timiderte,** 8 km (5 mi) farther south on the left side of the road, was built by Brahim, eldest son of the pasha of Marrakesh. The truncated pyramidal towers and bastions of the **Ksar Igdâoun** are visible 15 km (9 mi) past the turnoff onto Route 6956 to Tazzarine.

Tinzouline, 59 km (35 mi) southeast of Agdz, holds an important weekly souk. If you're here on a Monday, take this opportunity to shop and make contact with the many peoples of this southern Moroccan region, where communities of Berbers, Arabs, Jews, and Haratin (descendants of Sudanese slaves) have coexisted for centuries. The Tinzouline ksour are clustered around a majestic Kasbah in the middle of an oasis that includes several villages. Tinzouline is also one of the most important prehistoric sites in pre-Saharan North Africa: from the ksour a 7-km (4-mi) gravel path leads west of town to some cave engravings depicting mounted hunters. These drawings are attributed to Iron Age Libyo-Berbers, lending further substance to the theory that Morocco's first inhabitants, the Berbers, may have originally come from Central Asia via central and eastern Africa.

Zagora

⓬ *95 km (57 mi) southeast of Agdz, 170 km (102 mi) southeast of Ouarzazate.*

Zagora is—and does feel like—the boundary between the Sahara and what some writers have called "reality." After Zagora, time and distance are measured in camel days: a famous painted sign at the end of town features a camel and reads, TOMBOUCTU 52 DAYS—that is, "52 days by camel." The town of Mhamid, 98 km (65 mi) farther south, marks the actual end of the paved road and the beginning of the open desert, but Zagora is definitely where the sensation of being in the desert kicks in.

On your way into Zagora from Agdz, bear immediately left down to the Hôtel Ksar Tinsouline. You'll pass the Rose des Sables restaurant, complete with sidewalk tables, about halfway down on the left. Zagora's highlights include the much-photographed Tombouctu sign, in the square at the end of Boulevard Mohammed V; the town of Amazrou and, just across the river, **La Kasbah des Juifs** (Kasbah of the Jews);

and **Djebel Zagora** (Mt. Zagora), reached via the first left turn south of the Hôtel Kasbah Asmaa. (There is also a twisting footpath up the 3,195-ft mountain from the hotel itself.) The town's promontory, with its 11th-century Almoravid fortress, is an excellent sunset vantage point, overlooking the Drâa palmery and the distant Djebel Sarhro Massif to the north and the Tinfou dunes to the south. If you head south from Zagora, don't miss the panoramic view up the Drâa River when you cross it on the way to Tamegroute and Tinfou.

Dining and Lodging

$$ ✕ **La Rose des Sables.** This unpretentious little restaurant is always
★ recommended by the nearby Ksar Tinsouline—and with good reason. The Moroccan salads and tagines are first rate, the staff is quick and congenial, and the afternoon sun slants in nicely on the terrace overlooking the street. A *mechoui* (roast lamb) can be rustled up with two hours' notice, and the *tagine do poulet* (chicken stewed in lemon, onions, olives, potatoes, and spices) is excellent. ✉ *Avenue Allal ben Abdellah,* ☎ *04/84-72-74. No credit cards.*

$$$ ✕🛏 **Ksar Tinsouline.** With high ceilings and a general air of elegance, this old, colonial-style hotel is a Saharan version of Fez's Palais Jamai, albeit on a far more modest scale. The bar, Tombouctou, is comfortably paneled in wood, an invitation to bacchic truth and reflection. The rooms are a little disappointing compared to the elegance of the majestically chandeliered public spaces, but they overlook a garden of palms and bougainvillea that shelters what must be the largest and most musical community of desert sparrows in the Drâa Valley. ✉ *Avenue Hassan II,* ☎ *04/84-72-52,* 🖷 *04/84-70-42. 90 rooms. Restaurant, bar, pool. AE, MC, V.*

Tamegroute

⑬ *18 km (11 mi) south of Zagora.*

When you leave Zagora, follow signs carefully for Tamegroute; you should be turning left across the Drâa into Route 6958, not going straight on the old 6965 to Mhamid. Tamegroute (literally, "the last town before the border," an accurate name when the Algerian border was closer than it is now) is the home of the **zaouia of Sidi Mohammed Ben Naceur,** a sanctuary devoted to this *marabout* (sage). It's closed to non-Muslims, but you can admire the exterior—the door bears an intricately decorated archway of carved cedar and stucco. The surrounding courtyard is perennially filled with dozens of mental patients hoping for miraculous cures or just for charity from the Naciri brotherhood. Outside to the left are onetime slave quarters, still inhabited by descendants of Sudanese slaves.

Just north of the zaouia is Tamegroute's other claim to fame, a 17th-century **medersa** that still lodges 400 students preparing for university studies. The accompanying **Koranic library** was once the largest such collection in Morocco, with 40,000 volumes on everything from mathematics, philosophy, medicine, and astronomy to linguistics and Berber poetry. Following a loss of power and influence here, most of the books have been distributed to other libraries around the country, but the remaining volumes are plenty impressive: hand-illuminated manuscripts written in mint (green), saffron (yellow), and henna (red) on gazelle hide, a genealogy of the prophet Mohammed, manuscripts adorned with gold leaf, and a medical book with afflictions written in red and remedies in black. Ask for a look at the 13th-century algebra primer with Western Arabic numerals, which, though subsequently abandoned in the Arab world, provided the basis for Western numbers. They were introduced to Europe via the universities of Moorish Spain.

Don't miss Tamegroute's **ceramics cooperative,** at the south end of the library, medersa, and slave quarters. The characteristic green-glazed pottery sold here is all handmade.

Tinfou

⑭ *10 km (6 mi) south of Tamegroute.*

The hamlet of Tinfou is famous for the freak **sand dunes** that circling winds have deposited 2 km (1 mi) north of the Tamegroute–Mhamid road. Marked on the Michelin map with a black triangle and the word *dunes,* Tinfou is further identifiable by the Auberge Repos du Sable and Porte au Sahara inns. Beyond the dunes, the sheer cliffs of the Djebel Tadrart Massif loom darkly on the horizon, while to the south and west is the high surrounding plateau of the Djebel Bani Massif. The dunes are a result of the Drâa River's narrow slot in high ground, a gap that sucks wind and sand from the desert and sticks them onto the moist edge of the Drâa palmery here.

Dining and Lodging

$$$ ✕⌂ **Kasbah Hôtel Porte au Sahara.** Less charming than the Auberge Repos du Sable but better equipped with plumbing and infrastructure, this recent addition to the Tinfou landscape is the closest you can stay to the dunes. The staff can organize anything from three-week camel safaris across the desert to bivouacs—overnight stays in tents with dinner and belly dancing performed by *alharatin,* descendants of the Sudanese slaves who were traded until the late 19th century. The rooms are sizable and the most comfortable in town, if not especially captivating; and the place feels grand and even cavernous when not overrun by a tour group. ✉ *Tinfou Dunes, Tamegroute,* ☎ *04/84–85–62,* ℻ *04/84–70–02. 11 rooms. Restaurant, hammam. AE, DC, MC, V.*

$–$$ ✕⌂ **Auberge Repos du Sable.** For a strong taste of the desert, spend a night at this charming inn and walk out to the dunes at daybreak. Be warned: the plumbing is primitive, but the aesthetics more than compensate. Owners Hassan and Fatima El Farouj are also painters who have exhibited all over Europe, and everything from the paintings on the wall to the locks on the doors has an artistic touch here. The medieval wooden door-lock system was restored (essentially invented) by Hassan's father. ✉ *Chez El Farouj, Tinfou Dunes (29 km, or 18 mi, south of Tamegroute on Route 6958), Tamegroute,* ☎ ℻ *04/84–85–66. 18 rooms without bath. Restaurant, pool, hammam. MC, V.*

En Route Between Tinfou and Mhamid lies more dramatic scenery. A Monday souk is held at the junction of the P31 and the Drâa. The first pass through the Djebel Bani is the Anagam, after which the road leaves this dry steppe and enters a lush palmery. Note that at Tagounite you might be examined by police controls, as you are approaching the Algerian border. After Tagounite a second pass, Tizi-Beni-Selmane, descends to the turnoff for **Erg Lihoudi** (Dune of the Jew), a favorite dune for bivouacs. Dozens of sets of four-wheel-drive tracks mark the way to the dune, some 5 km (3 mi) from the P31.

Mhamid

⑮ *68 km (40 mi) south of Tinfou, 162 km (97 mi) south of Zagora, 260 km (157 mi) south of Ouarzazate, 395 km (237 mi) southwest of Rissani.*

Properly known as Mhamid el Gouzlane, or Plain of the Gazelles, Mhamid neatly marks the end of Morocco's great oasis valleys. Despite a distinct absence of attractions, however, it is definitely worth reaching. The sand drifting like snow across the road (despite the placement of palm-frond sand breaks or fences), the immensity of the horizon, and the patient gait of camels combine to produce a palpable change in the sense of time and space at this final Drâa oasis.

Mhamid, once an outpost for the camel corps of the French Foreign Legion, has a famous Monday souk notable for the occasional appearance of nomadic and trans-Saharan traders of the Saharan Reguibat tribe. Much chronicled by Paul Bowles, these ebony-skinned fellows habitually wear the indigo *sheish,* a linen cloth wrapped around the head and face for protection from the cold and from sandstorms. The dye from the fabric runs, tingeing the men's faces blue and leading to their nickname, the Blue Men. Don't expect too much in the way of merchandise; the souk has lost much of its exotic appeal in recent years.

The ocean of dunes 7 km (4 mi) beyond Mhamid will satisfy any craving for some real Saharan scenery, and the ruins of the ksour **Ksebt el-Allouj,** across the Drâa riverbed, are interesting to poke around.

Dining and Lodging

$–$$ ✕⍓ **Hôtel Restaurant Iriqui.** The first stop on the right as you enter Mhamid, this little spot is run by some very enterprising young men. Their father—pictured in the lobby with founder-of-the-nation Mohammed V in 1958—oversees operations. The rooms are modest but clean and surprisingly well equipped considering the remote location. Less expensive tent accommodations can also be arranged. The gang will be happy to help you plan a short desert excursion or bivouac. ✉ *B.P. 13, Mhamid,* ☎ *04/84–80–23,* ☏ *04/88–49–91. 8 rooms, 6 with bath. Restaurant, bar, travel services. MC, V.*

En Route For an extended encounter with desert life, continue on through the Hamada del Drâa, the high plateau beyond Mhamid where the desert becomes a 360-degree reality. Let Iriqui Excursions take you on their **Circuit Saint Exupéry** through the sacred oasis of Oum Lâalag, where water bubbles miraculously from a stone in the middle of the sand; the towering Lâabidlia dunes, 12 km (7 mi) farther out; and the Chegaga "ocean" of sand dunes. Walk the dry riverbed of the Drâa and wander the also-dry **Iriqui lakes;** a nature reserve with fish and flaming-pink flamingos until the 1960s, these are now completely desertified. Reconnect with terra firma at Foum-Zguid. Four-wheel-drive adventurers might contemplate a loop west from Mhamid to the pit stop Foum Zguid, then through the Anti-Atlas to Taroudant and the Atlantic Ocean, thus connecting Sahara and Atlantic. But the most obvious routes back north are the P31 or the good road east from Agdz to Tafilalt, which passes south of the Djebel Sarhro Massif.

Djebel Sarhro and Tazzarine

95 km (57 mi) east of Agdz, 68 km (41 mi) east of Route P31, 165 km (99 mi) southwest of Rissani.

The wonderfully panoramic oasis route 6956 (which becomes 3454 after Tazzarine) still appears as a desert piste on Moroccan tourist-office maps, but it has since been made a proper road. Indeed, it's one of the safest, fastest, and least crowded in all of Morocco, and it grants unparalleled views up into the **Djebel Sarhro** Massif and all way over to the Tafilalt date palmery. Count on three hours for the 233-km (140-mi) trip from Route P31 (the Ouarzazate–Zagora road) to Rissani, in the date palmery. **Tazzarine,** the first and last significant town on this route, is little more than a market and administrative center.

Dining and Lodging

$$ ✕🍴 **Hôtel Restaurant Bougafer.** This is the only game in town for both dining and lodging, but it's not a bad one. The rooms are clean, complete, adequate, and practical, if a little perfunctory; they serve as a perfectly good option if this is where nightfall finds you. Tent accommodations are also available. The staff can organize treks, bivouacs, and four-wheel-drive excursions into the Djebel Sarhro and Djebel Mrhorfi. ⊠ *Avenue Mohammed V, Tazzarine,* ☎ *04/83–80–10,* ℻ *04/ 83–80–86. 24 rooms. Restaurant, pool. MC, V.*

THE GREAT OASIS VALLEYS A TO Z

Arriving and Departing

By Plane

Ouarzazate's Taourirt International Airport, 1 km (½ mi) north of town, receives direct flights from Paris and domestic connections from Casablanca, Agadir, and Marrakesh. Er-Rachidia also has an airport for domestic flights. Call **Royal Air Maroc** for schedules and fares (⊠ 1, Avenue Mohammed V, Ouarzazate, ☎ 04/88–50–80; ⊠ Avenue Moulay Ali Cherif, Er-Rachidia, ☎ 04/88–50–80). *Petits taxis* are available for the short ride into town.

By Bus

There are no train connections south of the Atlas mountains. C.M.T. buses run to Ouarzazate, through the Dadès Valley, and down to Zagora, but busing around southern Morocco is not recommended unless you don't mind assuming a full-time study of transport logistics. Schedules are not convenient.

Getting Around

By Car

The only practical way to tour the great oasis valleys is to drive. Being surrounded by gorgeous and largely unexplored hinterlands like the Todra or Dadès gorges without being able to explore them safely and comfortably defeats the purpose of coming down here. Four-wheel-drive vehicles are available for rental in Ouarzazate and are highly recommended; standard rental cars with a doughnut-type spare are completely inadequate and should be outlawed. Because of the frequent need to drop two wheels off the right side of the road in an effort to avoid oncoming vehicles, the life expectancy of these temporary spares is about five minutes. Driving the oasis roads requires full attention and certain safety precautions: slow down when cresting hills, expect anything from camels to herds of sheep to appear in the road, expect oncoming traffic to come down the middle of the road, and be prepared to come to a full stop if forced to the right and faced with a pothole or other obstacle.

Ouarzazate is the regional center for car and jeep rentals.

Avis (⊠ Place 3 Mars, ☎ 04/88–48–70). **Budget** (⊠ Avenue Mohammed V, ☎ 04/88–42–02). **Desert Adventure** (⊠ Place 3 Mars, ☎ 04/88–49–43). **Europcar** (⊠ Place 3 Mars, ☎ 04/88–20–35). **France Car** (⊠ Avenue Mohammed V, ☎ 04/88–42–02). **Hertz** (⊠ Avenue Mohammed V, ☎ 04/88–20–84). **Iriqui** (⊠ Avenue Mohammed V, ☎ 04/ 88–57–99). **Mars Car** (⊠ Place 3 Mars, ☎ 04/88–69–82).

Contacts and Resources

Emergencies
Police: ☎ 19. **Fire brigade:** ☎ 15. **Highway SOS:** ☎ 177. **Directory assistance:** ☎ 16.

Guided Tours
In Erfoud, **Tafilalet Aventure & Découverte** (✉ Hotel Tafilalet, Avenue Moulay Ismail, ☎ 05/57–75–18) organizes bivouacs, guides, camels, and four-wheel-drive vehicles for treks to various desert points. **Iriqui Excursions** (☎ 04/88–57–99), based in Marrakesh and Mhamid, organizes treks in the desert beyond Mhamid or trips through the Atlas mountains and the Dadès and Todra gorges. The excellent Canadian outfit **Butterfield & Robinson** (✉ 70 Bond St., Toronto, Canada M5B 1X3, ☎ 416/864–1354 or 800/678–1147) leads treks and bike trips.

Sports and Outdoor Activities
GOLF

The only golfing possibility in the southern oasis region (aside from infinite opportunity to practice sand shots) is the nine-hole **Royal Golf** (✉ Route P32 east of Ouarzazate, Km 6, ☎ 04/88–47–90).

HIKING AND TREKKING

The Todra Gorges, the Dadès Gorges beyond Aït Oudinar, the M'Goun Massif, and Djebel Sarhro offer excellent hikes in or along the edges of the oasis region. **Club Alpin Français** (✉ B.P. 6178, Casablanca, ☎ 02/27–00–90) maintains a network of mountain huts. The **Fédération Royale Marocaine de Ski et de Montagne** (✉ Parc de la Ligue Arabe, B.P. 15899, Casablanca 01, ☎ 02/20–37–98) helps with expeditions ranging from mule trips in the High Atlas to hikes through the Djebel Sarhro Massif. The **Association Nationale des Guides et Accompagnateurs en Haute Montagne** (ANGAHM; ✉ B.P. 47, Asni, ☎ 04/44–49–79), headquartered near Marrakesh, is also a key source of information, expertise, and guides.

Visitor Information
There are two tourist offices in the oasis valleys: **Er-Rachidia** (✉ Avenue Moulay Ali Cherif, ☎ 05/57–09–44). **Ouarzazate** (✉ Avenue Mohammed V, B.P. 297, ☎ 04/88–24–85).

9 ESSAOUIRA, THE SOUSS VALLEY, AND THE ANTI-ATLAS

Southwestern Morocco is a scenic amalgam of palm oases, low-lying hills, deserted Kasbahs, verdant farmland, and some of the most fabulous beaches in Morocco. Berber culture and warm hospitality bring the landscape to life, and the towns and topography reveal a side of Moroccan history that you won't see in the Imperial Cities of the north.

THE MOROCCAN SOUTHWEST combines glorious stretches of beach and crashing waves, arid mountains flanked by palm groves, and lush olive and orange groves, all within a few hours' drive of each other. The region's character is strongly flavored by its Tashelhit-speaking Berbers, who inhabited these mountains and plains before Arabs ever set foot in Morocco: there are no Imperial Cities anywhere in the south, and the feel is distinctively not Arab. Primarily agricultural in nature, the region has industrialized and gained importance post-independence. Separated from the north by the Atlas mountains, the Souss Valley has retained its distinctive character yet remains internally heterogeneous.

Colonialism was less pervasive here than in other parts of Morocco, but although French is little used among the local population, schooling and tourism have ensured that you'll find someone who speaks some French (and, increasingly, English) just about anywhere you go. The Soussi (people of the Souss Valley) are socially conservative but friendly and curious about foreigners, offering details on local sights and customs to travelers who behave respectfully. Both women and men should cover their legs and upper arms in public, saving their shorts and sleeveless shirts for hotels. Local women, schoolchildren, and elderly people often hitchhike along the roads, so giving a few of them a lift to the next town is a sure way to make human contact. In fact, any mode of movement—driving, walking, or using shared public transportation—will give you a feel for life on the ground in rural and small-town Morocco, which is, after all, where most of the population resides. If you just need a few days of peace and quiet, head straight for the Souss coast.

Pleasures and Pastimes

Beaches
The coastline between Essaouira and Sidi Ifni presents some of the most spectacular waterside views and strolls anywhere in Morocco. The first half of the trip north from Agadir on the P8 road to Essaouira is particularly stunning. A drive is pleasant in itself, but you can stop and relax at several turnoffs from the main road both north and south of Agadir. Unspoiled beaches lie just 10 km (6 mi) north of Sidi Ifni; the only travelers who find the unmarked dirt road come in campers with their large dogs during the summer months. North of Agadir, the beach at Taghazoute is packed in summer with vacationing Moroccans, from the water right to the back of the beach, but in winter its clean, empty stretches are a welcome escape from urban hassles. The beaches around Essaouira and, a bit farther south, around Diabat and Sidi Kaouki are beautiful and clean, but they're more appropriate for walking and exploring the eucalyptus forests and ruins than for sunbathing, as the winds can be deafening and might bury a sleeping sunbather. Agadir offers a more touristy beach vacation, with year-round crowds and a range of water sports.

Dining
Along the coast, grilled fish is inexpensive and a logical choice for lunch, dinner, or snacking. The Swasa eat tagine at lunchtime, here a stew of meat and/or vegetables, preserved lemons, fresh coriander, and home-cured olives cooked in a clay pot over coals. Roadside restaurants and cafés in any town start a number of tagines simmering in individual pots late in the morning. When fresh fish is available, tagines include chunk-white fish stews and minced sardine balls with vegetables. For breakfast try *harira* (or, in Tashelhit Berber, *azzakif*), the barley-flour

Essaouira, the Souss Valley, and the Anti-Atlas

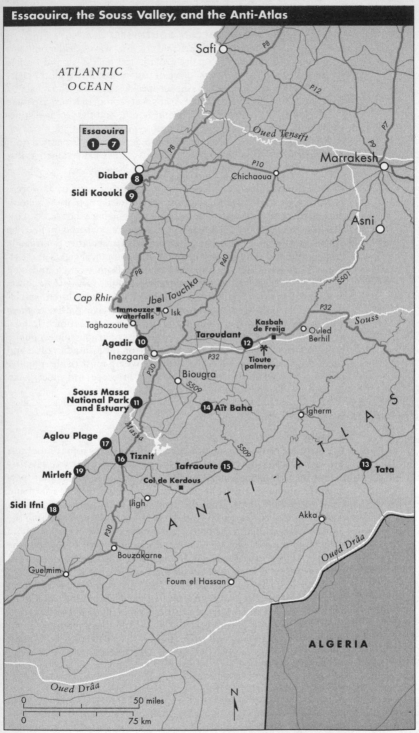

and olive-oil soup that serves as a regional staple for hardworking farmers. Depending on the time of year, local tastes, and each café's specialty, harira may be seasoned with pepper to warm the body or with dill to cool it down. Harira is also taken with a few dates and coffee on the side to satisfy the urge for a morning sweet. Southern couscous is mild, usually containing lamb or chicken and vegetables. Basic Moroccan fare can be had in any medium-size town or rest stop catering to travelers, including a selection of tagines, couscous, lamb kebabs, and salads of fresh vegetables.

CATEGORY	COST*
$$$$	over 200DH
$$$	150–200DH
$$	100–150DH
$	under 100DH

*per person for a three course meal, including tax, house wine, and service

Pick up locally grown supplies for the road in any town center or weekly market. Dates range from the firmer, drier varieties to the sticky, melt-in-your-mouth kind to small yellow dates, considered a delicacy here. Black olives are popularly served with lemon and garlic, spicy green olives with red pepper. Olive oil from the plains around Taroudant is known throughout Morocco, though it's not yet exported internationally. *Argan* oil is a delicacy, drawn from the nuts of a tree that grows only in southern Morocco and South America; extracting it is highly labor-intensive, requiring hours of manual grinding with a stone mill. Pure honey, which comes from bees feeding on regional herbs such as thyme and marijuana, is expensive by local standards but highly valued. You can buy it in stores or on the roadside.

Festivals

The southwest hosts a number of saints' festivals (*moussem* in Arabic, *almuggar* in Tashelhit), most of which are determined by the Islamic lunar calendar or the agricultural seasons. The Islamic calendar shifts back 11 days each year, so festival dates are approximate; moussem observances are scheduled by local authorities, often to accommodate school schedules. The majority of moussems fall in the spring (March and April) or late summer (July and August). A few have become national events, with Moroccans traveling from distant parts of the country and others sometimes arriving from abroad to experience several days of storytelling, lively buying and selling, and visits to the local saint's tomb.

Tazerwalt, south of the road between Tiznit and Tafraoute, hosts the weeklong moussem of **Sidi Hmed u Moussa** in July and/or August. Renowned as the patron saint of the acrobats, Sidi Hmed u Moussa inspires entire families of followers to entertain crowds with gymnastics, monkey tricks, and joke telling throughout the country. Musical entertainment also figures prominently, and local women cook meals in honor of the saint in the local *zaouia* (saint's tomb). The former Spanish colony of Sidi Ifni celebrates its independence every summer with a weeklong **Independence** almuggar. The festivities are much the same as those for Sidi Hmed u Moussa, and there's the added attraction of fine merchandise from Morocco's deep south: you'd be hard pressed to find higher-quality silver than the delicate beaded necklaces and chunky bracelets sold at this fair, or a better selection of colorful Mauritanian wraps (find out what local women pay before you buy). Aside from these large moussems, every local community hosts a small annual moussem for its local saint, but these tend to be more uniformly religious than festive or commercial affairs. Taroudant hosts the moussem of **Sidi Mbarek** for two days every March, when Arabs from the Houari plains (between Agadir and Taroudant) entertain the locals with energetic performances of *dqa* song and dance, which involves collective jumping to drums and a triangle.

In the secular realm, Essaouira hosts a weeklong festival of Gnaoua music in late June.

Hiking

Excellent day hikes can easily be extended into several-day excursions. A guide is recommended for female travelers and for all longer treks, and arrangements for overnight lodging should be made in advance whenever possible. The western High Atlas region north of Taroudant is among the most verdant in this area, and the shaded villages of Afensou and Had Imoulas have guest houses that can serve meals and find guides for local treks. Walks from the center of Tafraoute into the Ammeln Valley cover mostly flat terrain and require extended exposure to the sun, but they allow you to see village life up close. Copy a map from your hotel in Tafraoute and ask about trail conditions. Ifni and Mirleft are also good starting points for coastal Anti-Atlas hikes; and Immouzer, with its shaded river valleys, is a favorite destination for young athletic Moroccans. Modestly dressed hikers are entirely likely to be invited in by local villagers for a glass of tea or a light meal, hospitality that can be repaid with a trinket such as a visor, flashlight, T-shirt, or watch. Take care to avoid walking through garden plots or plowed fields and to be quiet when moving through villages that may appear deserted. Especially in areas where a large number of males have migrated to northern cities, the potential for a compromising encounter with an outsider sometimes drives women and girls indoors.

Lodging

The Souss has a few choice small hotels: restored palaces, *riad*-like houses decorated with an antique Moorish aesthetic, and small auberges (inns). Otherwise, hotels here are mostly modest affairs. In the summer it's best to reserve rooms in advance for Essaouira, Ifni, or Agadir, but during the rest of the year you can usually find a clean bed with little effort. An appealing alternative for travelers with time to spare is to set up house in one central location, like the full-service Environmental and Cultural Center in Taroudant or a rental apartment in Essaouira or Agadir, and make excursions from there.

CATEGORY	COST*
$$$$	over 1,500DH
$$$	500–1,500DH
$$	200–500DH
$	under 200DH

All prices are for a standard double room, excluding service and tax.

Exploring Essaouira, the Souss Valley, and the Anti-Atlas

This is not a place to go in search of medieval Islamic architectural wonders; leave those thoughts when you depart Fez or Marrakesh. Natural beauty, human warmth, and local color bring the southwest to life, and the towns and topography here will show you another side of the ancient history of Morocco as well as the pervasiveness of rapid social, economic, and material change. Palm oases give way to stretches of low-lying hills sprinkled with deserted Kasbahs and to ocean views from verdant farmland.

Great Itineraries

If you fly into Agadir or the new airport in Essaouira, you save not only a day of domestic travel but much of the traffic and hassle that delay an escape from Morocco's capital and major industrial zone. Roads are good, and most of the main attractions are accessible by bus and *grand taxi*.

IF YOU HAVE 3 DAYS

Fly into **Agadir** ⑩, enjoy an early lunch at one of the grilled-fish stands in the port, then head directly for ▦ **Tafraoute** ⑮. Spend the night in Tafraoute and leave early in the morning for the palm-grove circuit: make a day out of looping through the paved road that becomes a dirt road through Aït Mansour. Loop back to Tafraoute by late afternoon and swing by the immense, blue-painted rocks just south of town. Take in the sunset and wipe the dust off your car. On day three leave Tafraoute early for Tiznit—have breakfast at the Kerdous Hotel overlooking the spectacular mountain valley, then stop in Tiznit and do some silver shopping. Head north and stop off at the **Souss Massa National Park** ⑪, with its fantastic bird-watching, before looping back up to Agadir.

IF YOU HAVE 5 DAYS

Fly into **Agadir** ⑩ in the morning and go directly east to ▦ **Taroudant** ⑫. Relax over lunch, explore the market, and take a horse-drawn carriage ride around the city's salmon-color walls while the sun sets. On day two, head south through **Aït Baha** ⑭ into Tafraoute and then directly into the palm grove. Turn back when the paved road becomes dirt, and spend the night in ▦ **Tafraoute** ⑮. Continue south the next day, stopping briefly in **Tiznit** ⑯ but leaving the rest of the day to enjoy the cool ocean breezes and deserted coastline. Stop for sunset at the Al Jazira Beach, north of Ifni, and end the day in ▦ **Mirleft** ⑲ with a hearty Italian meal and a comfortable bed at Albergo de la Plage. On day four tour the Spanish Art Deco buildings of **Sidi Ifni** ⑱, heading north by midmorning to make it to ▦ **Essaouira** ①–⑦ before nightfall. Spend day five relaxing in ocean-side Essaouira after your dusty inland tour.

When to Tour Essaouira, the Souss, and the Anti-Atlas

Spring is the most spectacular time to visit this region, when almond trees and wildflowers are in bloom, the harvest is near, and the weather is sunny but not too hot. Fall temperatures are moderate, though landscapes are a bit more drab after the summer harvest. As long as rains don't wash out the roads, winter is pleasant as well—coastal areas are warm, though inland temperatures can be cold and heated rooms hard to find. Views of snowcapped mountains to the north, in the High Atlas, and south, in the Anti-Atlas, are eye candy during a winter visit. If you must come in summer, stick to the coast: even an hour inland, in Taroudant, the July and August heat is unbearable in all but the nighttime hours. Business hours change with the seasons; in summer, post offices and banks stay open straight through, from roughly 7:30 AM to 2 PM, in contrast to their usual morning and afternoon hours with a two- to three-hour lunch break in-between.

ESSAOUIRA TO AGADIR

This stretch of the central Atlantic coast offers a heady mixture of historic sights and beach culture. The resort town of Agadir has long been popular with Europeans; Essaouira is quieter and more emblematically Moroccan. Between the two are some excellent surfing spots.

Essaouira

❶ *171 km (102 mi) west of Marrakesh, 351 km (211 mi) southwest of Casablanca.*

The calm coastal port town of Essaouira—known in the local Tashelhit language as Tassort—is allegedly named for its walls, but it could just as aptly be named for the "picture" (*saouira* in Moroccan Arabic) it creates. Essaouira's cool breezes and relaxed atmosphere have made it a favorite return destination for European and American artists, expats, and independent travelers. The Phoenicians established a commercial center called Migdal here in the 7th century BC; the Romans came six centuries later in search of the prestigious purple dye murex, hence the name for the adjacent Îles Purpuraires. The Portuguese took over the port briefly, from 1506 to 1510, but left their distinctive ramparts when the populations of Chiadma Arabs and Ihihin Berbers joined to oust the Christians from what *they* called Mogador. More than a century later, the port became a city when Moroccan sultan Sidi Mohammed Ben Abdellah decided to punish coastal Agadir, then in revolt; he commissioned French fortification architect Theodore Cornut, student of the architect of contemporary sister city St. Malo, to design what is now the Essaouira medina. The sultan wooed a large Jewish population to develop commerce, and they remained a significant presence until the mid-20th century, when all but about 6,000 Moroccan Jews emigrated to Israel.

Brown volcanic stone is the characteristic building material of Moroccan Portuguese architecture, and its best examples (outside El Jadida) are Essaouira's medina and main portal. Unlike the more rust-color earth used for southern Moroccan buildings farther inland, this stone is a light brown. Like Fez, Essaouira is benefiting from UNESCO attention—its walls, ramparts, and Portuguese church are being carefully restored—so painted walls such as those around the main square and near the port have turned from their former light-pink hue to a natural beige that accents the subdued brown stone.

The opening of an airport in 1998 has increased the number of weekending Moroccans from Casablanca enjoying the pleasures Westerners have been hoarding for decades. It also means that more hotels are opening, and prices are rising. The town remains peaceful in its bustle, however—an enticing blend of Moroccan fishing port and European seaside haven. Essaouira is a logical first stop on your trip through the south and can even serve as a short break from the heat in Marrakesh, but it also makes a perfect place to unwind after more physically or socially demanding forays farther inland. Make Essaouira the very last stop on your Moroccan vacation and you'll leave the country relaxed and in good humor.

A Good Walk
A stroll around Essaouira's Portuguese ramparts, port, and medina could begin at the working **port** ②. The portal leading into the city is a good example of the doorways the Portuguese built of brown volcanic stone during their brief 16th-century stay here; the top of the arch was inscribed with elaborate Arabic calligraphy by Arabic workmen asking for *baraka* (divine protection). Facing Place Moulay Hassan, follow the wall into the medina and take your first left on the Rue de la Sqala, lined with dozens of woodworking shops. Rented out by the Moroccan Habbous (Ministry of Religious Affairs), these rooms used to hold maritime munitions. You can watch the craftsmen at work, then purchase their wares directly. Wind around this residential street until you come out to a wide passageway with rows of woodworking shops framed by arched doorways. Walk up the sloped entrance to the cannon-lined Kasbah of the **sqala** ③ and enjoy the water views from various angles along the fortified walls and the **North Bastion** ④. Go down the stairs and you'll be on Rue Laalouj, where you'll soon see the **Ethnological Museum** ⑤ on your right.

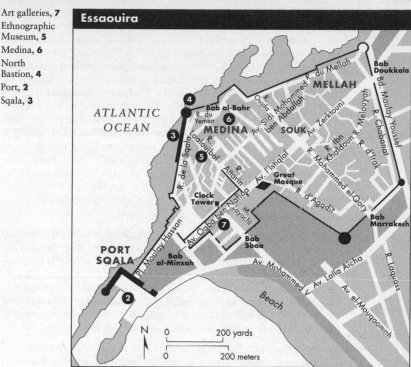

Begin your tour of residential **medina** ⑥ neighborhoods by walking from the museum back toward the sqala and turning right on the Rue du Yemen just before the city wall. Follow the rows of houses and local shops and turn right at the second large avenue you encounter, Rue Oujda. Walk straight as the street's name changes, noting the portals on your right and left when you reach Avenue de l'Istiqlal. When you see Bab Marrakesh in front of you, take the last left turn. Wind through the whitewashed streets, noting the colorful portals decorated with a single floral motif or a Star of David. When you reach Bab Doukkala, on your right, take a left back up Avenue Zerktouni, past the medina's active **souks.** After the first large arch is a vegetable, basket, and spice market in a narrow lane leading to a square on your right; a few yards down on your left is the entrance to the main silver- and gold-jewelry market. Walk straight up the avenue, back toward the port, until you pass the clock tower on your right, then another archway. On the opposite side of Avenue Oqba Ibn Nafiaa is an **archway** with insignia dating from shortly after the city's founding in 1765. The Arabic script is a Koranic verse, juxtaposed with the interlocked Rose of Mogador and Star of David, saluting the importance of the urban Jewish population. The archway's Portuguese design is understood locally to represent the Christian population, thus tying together the three components of Essaouira's population at that time.

End your tour of town by doing as the locals (and temporary locals) do: people-watching while sipping *café maharasa* (coffee with a splash of steamed milk) or *louisa* (warm milk with fresh vervain leaves) in one of the outdoor cafés on the **Place Moulay Hassan.**

TIMING

This walk is not long; allow about two hours.

Sights to See

❼ Art galleries. Essaouira has inspired a sizable expatriate art community in addition to numerous regional artists. Essaouira artists are best known for what has been termed "tribal," "naive," or "trance" (Gnaoua-inspired) art, but those who disagree with such characterizations may see a similarity with Caribbean-island-style painting in the colors and fluid designs. The **Gallerie d'Art Fréderic Damgaard** (⊠ Avenue Oqba Ibn Nafiaa), across from the clock tower, has well-curated displays, with artists' biographies, of work by Essaouira painters and sculptors; the gallery also sells books and pamphlets on regional art and culture. Half a dozen other spaces in the same quarter display contemporary Moroccan and expatriate mixed-media productions—one standout is the **Espace Othello Gallerie d'Art** (⊠ 9, Rue Mohamed Layachi, ☎ 04/47–50–95), where part of Orson Welles's *Othello* was shot. ⊘ *Fréderic Damgaard, daily 10–1 and 3–7; Espace Othello, daily 9–1 and 3–8.*

❺ Ethnological Museum. The stunning former French-colonial town hall holds this smartly arranged collection of items from everyday and ritual life in and around the Essaouira area. Ground-floor displays of musical instruments distinguish between Gnaoua and Sufi sects; upstairs, exhibits survey regional carpet styles, wood-carving techniques and motifs, and comparative kaftans, bridal costumes, and men's dress for the urban Muslim, Jewish, and rural Ishelhin Berber populations. ⊠ *Rue Laalouj.* ☎ *10DH.* ⊘ *Wed.–Mon. 8:30–6:30.*

❻ Medina. Essaouira's city walls contain three sections. The Kasbah used to house urban aristocrats and governing authorities and was thus double-secured with additional walls; the medina is primarily a residential and commercial center; and the Mellah, the old Jewish quarter, once housed merchants who benefited from preferential tax and commercial laws designed to establish Essaouira as a market center. (Some locals say there were more Jews in Essaouira in the 19th century than there were Muslims.) The medina today is a vital commercial center for local residents.

❹ North Bastion. The distinctive outlines of the bastion's corner tubular moldings frame the waves dramatically at sunset. The large circle of stones in the center of this round structure was a call point in earlier days, when the bastion held emergency supplies of fresh water below. If you stand in the middle of the circle and stomp your foot or yell, you'll hear the echo ring far.

❷ Port. Deep-fishing rigs and smaller, blue-and-green wooden sailboats share the marina with middlemen and independent sailors selling the daily catch of sardines, calamari, and skate from small dockside tables.

❸ Sqala. Essaouira has three sqala (bastions): the Kasbah sqala, the port sqala, and the sqala currently housing the Ensemble Artisanal, on the Rue Modhem el Qorry near Bab Marrakesh. Each was a strategic maritime defense point. Unlike the straight-edge Moorish constructions in other Moroccan cities, the ramparts in Essaouira are triangular, so that the insider looking out has a broader field of vision than the enemy peering in. Check the cannon engravings: the second and third to the right are signed CARLOS III, BARCELONA 1780, and a Dutch cannon dated 1743 is inscribed with a lion and the Latin phrase VIGILANTE DEO CONFIDENTES—"Those who trust in God are under his protection." ☎ *Kasbah sqala, 10DH.*

Dining and Lodging

Restaurants in Essaouira are among the best in Morocco, with fresh fish dishes headlining menus when the surf permits. Creative nonfish dishes are also available. Kill two birds with one stone by opting for lunch in one of the **seafood grills** along the port: feast on, say, charcoal-grilled sardines, calamari, red snapper, or shrimp that you've selected yourself (crab is usually too dry) from among the dozens of stalls, and experience the color and bustle of the port. You choose your fish, establish a price, and find a table; your meal is then served once it's cooked.

Beyond the luxurious Villa Maroc and Riad, there are plenty of housing options, including older, moderately priced standbys as well as more expensive, spanking-new *maisons d'hôtes* decorated in modern (as opposed to traditional) Moroccan style. Rooms are hard to find in the summer, so reserve in advance if possible.

$$$$ ✕ **Dar Louban.** One of the most accomplished restaurants in southern
★ Morocco, Dar Louban excels in culinary innovation and quirky ambience. The restaurant is set in an 18th-century *riad*-style home decorated with 1920s photos and Orientalist bric-a-brac collected from flea-market excursions during the 20-year Paris sojourn of your hosts, an Essaouira native and his French wife. You're treated to coconut-crusted skewered lotte (monkfish), sautéed fresh St. Pierre with mushroom sauce, or a tender tagine of lamb and artichoke hearts. As an appetizer, try the fried eggplant with a garlicky tomato coulis; wind down with rich, Calvados-laced chocolate mousse or English meringue. There's a full wine list, and local Gnaoua musicians entertain on Thursday and Sunday. Upstairs, three rooms are available for overnight lodging. ⊠ *24, Rue de Rif,* ☎ *04/47–62–96. No credit cards.*

$$$ ✕ **Chalet de la Plage.** In the red-checked-tablecloth atmosphere of a family restaurant, this one serves delicious conventional fish dishes. It's a better bet than the overrated Chez Sam's, at the port's edge. ⊠ *1, Boulevard Mohammed V,* ☎ *04/47–21–58. No credit cards.*

$$$ ✕ **Taros.** A newcomer to the Place Moulay Hassan, Taros has a relatively upscale menu and a terrific rooftop terrace with views of the port. For starters, try the shrimp and vegetable salad with argan oil; follow that with spicy stuffed sardines. The literary café downstairs was a creation of the restaurant's Breton owner, who is also a decorator and architect. Managed by the owner's son, the café offers drinks and snacks to an international crowd, which gathers to browse the eclectic multilingual library, sample the impressive CD collection of world music, and play Scrabble. ⊠ *Place Moulay Hassan,* ☎ *04/47–64–07. No credit cards.*

$$ ✕ **Dar Baba.** The specialties here are a luscious house lasagna and an improbable cheese plate—cheese of any kind is exceedingly rare in Morocco, much less entire plates full. ⊠ *Rue Marrakech,* ☎ *no phone. MC, V.*

$$ ✕ **La Petite Perle d'Essaouira.** The Little Pearl of Essaouira is crowded and cozy, with low tables and low lights. The menu features fish tagines and pastillas. ⊠ *2, Rue Hajalli (between Place Moulay Hassan and clock tower),* ☎ *04/47–61–23. No credit cards.*

$$ ✕ **Les Chandeliers.** Run by a French family, Les Chandeliers offers fresh pizzas and a salad buffet, as well as a few rooms for rent. ⊠ *14, Rue Laalouj,* ☎ *04/47–64–50. No credit cards.*

$ ✕ **Restaurant Essalam.** Situated on Essaouira's main square, this place serves delicious standard Moroccan fare, such as couscous and tagines, as well as fried fish. You're poised for prime people-watching. ⊠ *Place Moulay Hassan,* ☎ *no phone. No credit cards.*

$$$ ✕ Villa Maroc. Embodying much of what international travelers
★ seek in a Moroccan hotel, the Villa Maroc inspires interior designers
and photographers from all over the Western world. Tucked into a small
side street, with a complex layout that has you climbing, turning, and
ducking as though you're navigating a medina, the house is delight-
fully decorated to epitomize a "traditional" Moroccan style that never
really was. White is abundant, to keep the look fresh, but adornments
include the best of Moroccan textiles, metalwork, and ceramic tiles.
Upstairs rooms get good doses of natural light. The restaurant serves
a different sophisticated three-course dinner each day; one recent menu
featured liver *briouates* (pastries akin to Indian samosas) with spicy
tomato-and-olive dipping sauce, pigeon with toasted almond, corian-
der, garlic and olive oil, and a soft chocolate brownie. Dinner is served
in nooks around the second floor, and breakfast of assorted pancakes
in the sunny central terrace upstairs. Book well in advance. If you can't
get a room, enjoy a drink by the fireplace. Half board is required in
April, July, and August. ✉ *10, Rue Abdellah Ben Yacine,* ☎ *04/47–
61–47,* FAX *04/47–58–06. 22 rooms. Restaurant. MC, V.*

$$$ Hôtel des Iles. It's popular with tour groups, but this hotel remains
low-key and is conveniently near both the beach and the medina. Ask
for a room in the main building with an ocean view and a terrace; the
others, all on the ground floor, are arranged around an uninspiring pool.
✉ *Boulevard Mohammed V,* ☎ *04/78–46–20,* FAX *04/78–55–90. 70
rooms. Restaurant, bar, pool. MC, V.*

$$$ Hotel Riad Al Madina. Remodeled after the Villa Maroc in the *riad*
(courtyard) style that has grown so fashionable, this hotel must also
be reserved well in advance. The multilevel rooms with intricate tiled
bathrooms and large sleeping nooks get rave reviews for aesthetic ap-
peal and comfort; less acclaimed are those on the central courtyard,
where a stereo sometimes plays music late at night and where the
breakfast rush can be deafening. The standard rooms upstairs are
smaller but quieter, so it's a bit of a trade-off. ✉ *9, Rue Attarine,* ☎
04/47–57–27, FAX *04/47–66–96. 30 rooms. Restaurant, café. MC, V.*

$$$ Hotel Villa Quieta. At the south end of town, this house is archi-
tecturally beautiful and close to the beach, but its gaudy decorations
are joined (exacerbated?) by hit-or-miss service and somewhat inflated
prices. ✉ *86, Boulevard Mohammed V,* ☎ *04/78–32–81,* FAX *04/78–
50–06. 12 rooms, 2 suites. MC, V.*

$$ Essaouira Apartments. For longer-term stays, try one of these Mo-
roccan-style furnished apartments in the medina. ✉ *Inquire at Jack's
Kiosk, 1 Place Moulay Hassan,* ☎ *04/47–55–38,* FAX *04/47–69–01. 8
apartments. No credit cards.*

$$ Hotel Cap Sim. Set in a restored medina house, this family-run hotel
is friendly and low-key. Highlights are the great beds and superb
rooftop views over the medina. ✉ *11, Rue Ibn Rochd,* ☎ FAX *04/78–
58–34. 27 rooms. Café. MC, V.*

$$ Hôtel Le Méchouar. Outside the medina walls, Le Méchouar has a
restored lobby and an appealing restaurant menu. The rooms are
purely functional and look a bit worn, but they're quiet, and some have
balconies. ✉ *Avenue Oqba Ben Nafiâa,* ☎ FAX *04/47–58–28. 26 rooms.
Restaurant, café. No credit cards.*

$$ Hotel Souiri. If the Riad Al Madina (next door) is full, try this new-
comer. Both rooms and beds are small, but furnishings include nice tiled
floors and couches. The clientele sometimes includes student groups.
✉ *37, Rue Attarine,* ☎ FAX *04/47–53–39. 21 rooms, 1 apartment. Café.
MC, V.*

$$ Hotel Tafukt. This comfortable, if fading, full-service waterfront hotel
is within walking distance of the medina. Some rooms have large bath-
tubs and ocean-view balconies, and all are heated in winter. ✉ *58,*

Boulevard Mohammed V, ☎ *04/78–45–04 or 47–25–05,* FAX *04/78–45–05 or 78-44–16. 40 rooms. Restaurant, bar, bicycles, billiards, parking. MC, V.*

$$ 🏨 **Résidence El Mehdi.** Just off a small medina street, these comfortable rooms are arranged on three floors around a central garden courtyard. Take advantage of the *demi-pension* (half-board) specials to taste the restaurant's excellent food: rabbit with mustard sauce or seafood pastilla. ✉ *15, Rue Sidi Ebdessmih,* ☎ FAX *04/47–59–43. 16 rooms. Restaurant, bar. MC, V.*

$$ 🏨 **Résidence Le Poisson Volant.** The Flying Fish has six funky double rooms—hippie-style, with batik on the walls and such—and a pleasant-enough terrace. ✉ *34, Rue Labbana,* ☎ FAX *04/47–21–52. Restaurant.*

$$ 🏨 **Sahara Hotel.** Here you have a good location and a heated room, but you'll probably sleep on a lumpy bed. Traveler's checks are accepted—unusual in Morocco. ✉ *Avenue Okba Ibnou Nafiaa,* ☎ *04/47–52–92,* FAX *04/47–61–98. Café. AE, MC, V.*

$ 🏨 **Hotel Smara.** Tops among the cheap hotels, the Smara snuggles right up to the ramparts. The rooms surround a courtyard, and while they're basic inside, some have phenomenal ocean views. The staff is very enthusiastic. ✉ *26, Rue Skala,* ☎ *04/47–56–55. 17 rooms.*

Shopping

Essaouira is the best shopping destination south of Marrakesh, with a vast range of high-quality products and very few hustlers. Boxes, platters, and picture frames made of the local **thuya wood** make excellent gifts, and the woodcarvers' souk below the sqala is the place to purchase them. Scan a number of stores to see whether you prefer the even-toned thuya branch inlaid with mother-of-pearl or walnut or one with swirling root designs. To get a bulk price, buy a bunch of picture frames from a craftsman who specializes in them. If you've gotten used to haggling in Marrakesh or Fez, you can relax here, as starting prices are often reasonable. **Carpets, goatskin lamps,** and **metal candlesticks** are sold in the square next to the clock tower; compare their prices with those in the shops on side streets off Avenue de l'Istiqlal. The goatskin lamps are etched with henna and are highly fashionable at the moment. There's a veritable warehouse of carpets and **carpet-scrap pillow covers** down the Rue de Marrakech, off Avenue de l'Istiqlal; tell the store owners that you're looking for a bigger selection than they offer, and they'll lead you to the warehouse. Colorful, square **woven baskets** hang from herbalists' stores in the medina. New and old **silver jewelry** is sold in the extensive silver souk between the medina's inner gates or in the shops starting from the BMCE Bank, heading off Place Moulay Hassan down Avenue de l'Istiqlal. For tasteful used **pewter platters and goblets** and **ceramic teapots,** as well as new and used English and French books, check the Galérie Aida, whose owner, Jewish Essaouiran multimedia artist **Joseph Sebag,** and his staff are knowledgeable about remnants of the city's Jewish past (✉ 2, Rue de la Skala, ☎ 04/47–62–90). If you packed too light to brave the chilly Atlantic wind, buy a **handwoven sweater** in Place Moulay Hassan or the square off Rue Laalouj.

Sports and Outdoor Activities

Serious surfers can rent **windsurfers and surfboards** at the beachside shacks in season. A **sailing school** gives lessons. You can rent **bikes** at the Hotel Sheherazade or at the Gallery Kasbah on Rue Tangier.

Diabat

❽ *Turnoff is 7 km (4 mi) south of Essaouira, 3 km (2 mi) west of Agadir road.*

Essaouira's beach is fine for an early-morning jog or a late-afternoon game of soccer, but serious sunbathers, surfers, and beach walkers typically head south. A few miles south of town, nestled in eucalyptus fields, are some **ruins** that allegedly inspired Jimi Hendrix's "Castles in the Sand." Opinions differ on whether the ruins are of Portuguese or more recent French vintage. On a windy day, the only escape is a two-story rock that affords a nice resting spot at low tide. Loving the cold, rugged beauty of this coast, Hendrix tried to buy the entire (rather sterile) village of Diabat itself.

Dining and Lodging

$$$ ✕🏠 **Auberge Tengaro.** With only a eucalyptus forest dividing it from
★ the beach, this French-run establishment has tasteful, airy rooms and some duplex suites, many with fireplaces and terraces. Everything is lighted by tall brass candlesticks and lanterns. Campsites are also available. The mandatory half board is a gastronomic tour de force—country French meets Mediterranean—featuring baked whole fish with lemon and coriander, peeled spiced shrimp, or hearty rabbit stew with olives. Nonguests are welcome with advance notice. At press time the management was about to open a suite hotel across from Essaouira's clock tower. ✉ *7 km (4 mi) south of Diabat,* ☎ *04/78–47– 84 or, to leave message, 78–57–35. 18 rooms. Restaurant, parking.*

Sidi Kaouki

❾ *27 mi (17 mi) southwest of Diabat. Turnoff is 15 km (9 mi) south of Diabat on Agadir road. Bus 5 runs between beach and Essaouira.*

Tranquil Sidi Kaouki is a mellow surfing spot with a few café-restaurants. Numerous other paved roads jut off of the road to Agadir, including the fishing and camping site at Plage Tafadna, 37 km (23 mi) south of the Sidi Kaouki turnoff; however, 1999 floods washed away chunks of road. Accessibility to beaches and locals' enthusiasm for foreign visitors lessens until you leave Haha territory (the land of the Ihihin Berbers) behind and move into Cap Rhir (☞ Around Agadir, *below*).

Dining and Lodging

$$ ✕🏠 **Auberge de la Plage.** This rustic beachfront lodging has an Italian-Moroccan restaurant and can arrange for horseback rides. ✉ *Route d'Agadir, Km 20, Sidi Kaouki, Essaouira,* ☎ *04/47–66–00. 11 rooms. Restaurant, horseback riding.*

$ 🏠 **Résidence Le Kaouki.** This hotel is a favorite with return visitors to Essaouira. When you arrive, place your dinner order with Saïd in advance to enjoy the quaint, white- and bright-blue-painted fireside dining room. Guest rooms are sparse and clean. ✉ *Route d'Agadir, Km 20, B.P. 72, Sidi Kaouki, Essaouira,* ☎ *04/78–32–06,* 📠 *04/47–28– 06 (via Villa Maroc).*

Agadir

❿ *172 km (103 mi) south of Essaouira.*

Moroccans remark that Agadir is not really Morocco and not really Europe; it seems placeless. Razed by an earthquake in 1960, Agadir is today a modern city where even Moroccans feel fewer social restraints than in other towns. Europeans on package vacations fill the massive beachfront hotels and roam the wide streets in shorts year-round, lending the city a holiday feel despite its importance as a regional commercial and educational center. Agadir draws tourists year-round for its mild climate, not its charm; there are no sights per se, except the abandoned *agadir* (fortified granary) perched on a cliff north of town.

Yet this can be a surprisingly relaxing place to spend a few days en route to or from the airport: you can get oriented, withdraw cash from an ATM, rent a car, stock up on supplies, or just unwind with a good dinner. You can also use Agadir as a base for sampling regional beaches and the Souss Massa bird estuary, or for a day trip to Taroudant.

Agadir's **Musée Municipale** (Municipal Museum), open only when an exhibition is mounted, features photography and local handicrafts. Check with the tourist office in the Hôtel de Ville (town hall) for details on other exhibits.

In Aghroud, a few miles south of Agadir on the Inezgane road, **La Medina d'Agadir** is a 13-acre project-in-progress orchestrated by a Moroccan-born Italian decorator-architect who dreamed of crafting a living medina on his own land. A combination living ethnological museum and high-quality bazaar, it's being constructed by Moroccan craftsmen following centuries-old techniques. The buildings are made of earth, rock from the Souss, slate from the High Atlas, and local woods such as thuya and eucalyptus, and each stone is laid by hand. Decorations follow both Berber and Saharan motifs. Mosaic craftsmen, painters, jewelers, a henna artist, metalworkers, and carpenters welcome spectators as they practice their crafts (and welcome customers for the results) in workshop nooks throughout the medina. ⊠ *Aghroud Ben Sergao, B.P. 526 Inezgane,* ☎ *08/22–49–09.*

Dining and Lodging

For lunch and dinner in Agadir, choose from the open-air seafood restaurants along the Corniche beachfront or the town-center restaurants listed below. In addition, all major hotels have both Moroccan and Continental restaurants, and some even have Mexican or Lebanese options. For breakfast have a buttery *pain au chocolat* (chocolate croissant) and strong coffee at the **Pâtisserie Louban** (Avenue du Prince Heritier Sidi Mohamed, next to Hôtel Les Palmiers). For a light meal or coffee at any time of day, go straight to the open-air **Pâtisserie La Fontaine** (Place de L'Esperance, off Avenue Hassan II), which serves outstanding individual pastillas and spicy shrimp rolls as an alternative to plain old toast.

Select a hotel in Agadir according to whether you simply need a bed while passing through or you want to dig in and enjoy the beach. The less expensive hotels are in the center of town. Luxury hotels come in the form of tourist complexes along Avenue 20 Août, each of which has enough amenities and restaurants that you'll feel no need to leave the complex. Breakfast is accordingly expensive. If you have beach aspirations, you may as well get a room with beach access right off the property, as they're not much more expensive. The complexes cater primarily to European package tours. All hotels can arrange full-day biking, trekking, golf, and windsurfing excursions.

$$$$ ✕ **Le Miramar.** Sumptuous fish dishes and pastas are served here in an elegant setting, albeit on a heavily trafficked street. Sit indoors to avoid street noise. The restaurant is particularly popular with Western expats. ⊠ *Hotel Miramar, Boulevard Mohammed V (toward the port),* ☎ *08/86–26–73.*

$$$ ✕ **Le Tonkinoise.** Come here for an unusual Vietnamese or Chinese break from brochettes and tagines. ⊠ *Avenue du Prince Heritier Sidi Mohamed (next to Hôtel Les Palmiers),* ☎ *08/82–27–25.*

$$$ ✕ **Restaurant Chahoua.** In this Korean eatery, the authentic Bibimbop rice dishes and marinated spinach are tasty, the beer is cold, and many of the diners are soccer-watching Korean seamen. ⊠ *Between Av-*

enues Hassan II and Mohammed V (behind Monoprix store), ☎ *no phone.*

$$ ✕ **La Siciliana.** Entirely unassuming, La Siciliana is recommended for wood-oven pizzas. ✉ *Avenue Hassan II,* ☎ *08/82–09–73.*

$$ ✕ **Le Veneto.** Amid international kitsch, this Italian-flavored restaurant serves good pizzas, fish, and baked potatoes. ✉ *Avenue Hassan II,* ☎ *no phone.*

$$$ ⊞ **Agadir Beach Club.** This attractive open complex of sprawling terraces, cafés, and guest rooms has a large central pool and a private beach area whose padded lounge chairs have their own parasols. The club is popular with families, and ironically, it's so big that it doesn't retain a package-tour flavor. There's something for everyone, especially those who like having a selection of sunbathing spots. Rooms with ocean views cost extra. ✉ *Route de l'Oued Souss, B.P. 310,* ☎ *08/84–43–43,* ℻ *08/84–08–63. 340 rooms, 26 suites, 36 apartments, 14 duplexes. 7 restaurants, 3 bars, hot tub, beauty salon, massage, sauna, tennis court, exercise room, nightclub, meeting room.*

$$$ ⊞ **Hotel Tafukt.** Well situated between the Atlantic and the town center, the Tafukt has spacious grounds and extensive facilities. Rooms have balconies and phones, but they're somewhat sterile, and the staff is generally dour. ✉ *Boulevard 20 Août,* ☎ *08/84–01–23,* ℻ *08/84–09–71. 116 rooms, 44 suites. 2 restaurants, air-conditioning, in-room safes, minibars, pool, beauty salon, hammam, massage, Ping-Pong, billiards, nightclub.*

$$$ ⊞ **Melia Al Madina Salam.** Under new Spanish management, the Melia offers tasteful rooms, most with single beds, and attractive rustic-style tiled bathrooms within a full tourist complex. All rooms have phones and hair dryers. The focus is on amenities rather than flavor; you'll be entirely comfortable here. ✉ *Boulevard du 20 Août,* ☎ *08/84–53–53,* ℻ *08/84–53–08. 180 rooms, 26 suites. 6 restaurants, 2 bars, ice-cream parlor, air-conditioning, in-room safes, minibars, beauty salon, exercise room, dance club, recreation room, baby-sitting, laundry service, business services, meeting room, travel services. DC, MC, V.*

$$ ⊞ **Hotel Aferni.** Conveniently located in town, this character-free hotel is perfectly comfortable if you're just passing through. The clientele is mostly Moroccan. ✉ *Avenue General Kettani,* ☎ *08/84–07–30,* ℻ *08/84–03–30. 45 rooms. Restaurant, in-room safes.*

$$ ⊞ **Hôtel Les Palmiers.** This hotel is a good mid-range choice in town, and it has a good restaurant. It's open only in summer; call ahead. ✉ *Avenue du Prince Heritier Sidi Mohamed,* ☎ *08/84–37–19.*

$$ ⊞ **Hotel Petite Suède.** Complete with a central location, this is one of the best inexpensive hotels in Agadir, albeit open only in summer. ✉ *Avenues Hassan II and General Kittani,* ☎ *08/84–07–79 or 84–00–57,* ℻ *08/84–00–57.*

$$ ⊞ **Hotel Solman.** Well situated in town, the comfortable Solman has particularly large beds. ✉ *Avenue Hassan II,* ☎ *08/84–45–65,* ℻ *08/84–34–47. Restaurant, café, pool.*

$$ ⊞ **Hôtel Transatlantique.** This luxury lodging offers tasteful, sunny rooms in a no-fuss full-service atmosphere. Some rooms overlook the pool and the Atlantic, and all rooms have phones and heat. Curtains and bedspreads in bright, geometric patterns enliven the look. ✉ *Avenue Mohammed V,* ☎ *08/84–21–10,* ℻ *08/84–20–76. 200 rooms. 3 restaurants, 2 bars, in-room safes, minibars, pool, massage, sauna, tennis court, exercise room, billiards, travel services AE, DC, MC, V.*

$$ ⊞ **Résidence Sacha.** In this French-run apartment building, all units are heated, and some have balconies, private gardens, or Moorish-style decor. The minimum stay is two nights. ✉ *Place de la Jeunesse,* ☎ *08/82–55–68. 48 studios. Pool.*

Around Agadir

In late summer the beaches north of Agadir on the Essaouira road are crammed with camping Moroccan families, especially those in the rapidly expanding **Taghazoute.** The rest of the year, a few stray Western surfers seek out waves around the bend from the lighthouse at **Cap Rhir,** but otherwise the neighboring village of Aghrod is, like Taghazoute, quiet—a pretty detour, with empty sands and calm waters. You may come across a bald ibis, as their preserve is nearby (☞ Souss Massa National Park and Estuary, *below*).

From Aourir (12 km, or 7 mi, north of Agadir), take the paved road 50 km (31 mi) up the Ida Outanane Mountains to the (occasional) waterfalls at **Immouzer,** near Isk. Dry hills nearer the coast give way to the palm gorge of **Paradise Valley,** where the rocky riverbank hosts picnicking Moroccan families and foreigners alike.

Lodging

$$–$$$ 🏨 **Hôtel des Cascades.** Five kilometers (3 miles) up the paved road from Aourir, these lush grounds of cow lilies, daisies, and olive trees sprawl above a natural spring, momentarily distracting the eye from the ocean in the distance. Between tour groups, this hotel makes an excellent base for quiet walks or horseback meanderings; English-speaking local Mbarek Aneflous organizes weeklong excursions that alternate hotel stays with overnights in alpine Berber homes. Tennis rackets are handily available, and donkey rides can be arranged. ⊠ *Immouzer des Ida Outanane, Agadir,* ☎ *08/82–60–16, 82–60–23, or 82–60–24,* 𝔽𝔸𝕏 *08/ 82–16–71. Restaurant, bar, pool, 2 tennis courts. No credit cards.*

$$ 🏨 **Auberge du Littoral.** This cheery new inn is well positioned for foot or bicycle access to the surrounding beaches. The colorful wooden furniture in the bedrooms is locally crafted, and the bathrooms sparkle. Apartments with kitchens are available for longer stays. All rooms have telephones. ⊠ *Route d'Essouira (accessible via Agadir Buses 12 and 14), B.P. 80, Aourir, Agadir,* ☎ *08/31–47–26 or 31–43–54,* 𝔽𝔸𝕏 *08/31– 43–57. 28 rooms, 4 suites, 4 apartments. Restaurant, café, bicycles. No credit cards.*

$$ 🏨 **Hôtel Tifrit–Chez Zenid.** Make this hotel, nestled in a bend in the road through the shady gorge, your base for short walking excursions, then enjoy a copious tagine for dinner before settling down to sleep near croaking frogs in the adjacent river. Awaken to homemade bread and *amalou,* a Soussi specialty of crushed almonds in argan oil and honey base. Son Rachid will sell you a jar of thyme-tinged honey; his family tends the small hotel, riverside pool, and café and can offer hiking suggestions as well as local lore. ⊠ *Route d'Immouzer, Ida Outanane,* ☎ *08/82–60–44. 10 rooms. Restaurant, pool. No credit cards.*

Souss Massa National Park and Estuary

⓫ *Entrance is 51 km (32 mi) south of Agadir.*

Midway between Agadir and Tiznit, at the intersection of the Souss and Massa estuaries, is the world's last remaining colony of the endangered bald ibis. Stretching 64 km (40 mi) down the coast, the park provides refuge for a total of 257 bird species, 46 mammal species, 40 reptile species, and numerous butterflies. A gorgeous vantage point, where you might spot cranes, a great gray shrike, cuckoos, and tufted ducks, is near the town of Sidi Rbat. Here you're surrounded by contrasting landscapes—mountains on one side, mimosa-lined sand dunes on another, and verdant fields flanking the river on a third. A place of natural beauty and true calm, Souss Massa is well worth the detour.

Recognizing the park's potential for ecotourism, government has built an entrance to the grounds and plans to open a park-side environmental museum on an overlooking hill. To get here from the main road, follow the signs to Sidi Rbat (if you miss it, take the turn for Massa, farther south, and just follow the paved road to the right until it reaches Sidi Rbat). After 10 km (6 mi) of unspectacular scenery, you'll arrive at Massa village, and when the road forks, turn right (north). After about 5 km (3 mi) more, the road becomes a piste; keep going until you reach the park gates. Park your car under the trees and pack your bag with binoculars and plenty of water for the two-hour walk to the beach. Try to arrange for English-speaking scientist Saïd Ahmoume, of Taroudant's Environmental and Cultural Centre, to meet you here; he knows where the most unusual birds and reptiles hide and can tell you all about their habitats (✉ 422, Derb Afferdou, Taroudant, ☎ 08/85–47–61). If you're a bird-watcher, it's best to visit between November and March, but the nature trail is carpeted with wildflowers in March and April.

THE SOUSS VALLEY AND ANTI-ATLAS

East and south of Agadir, you leave the world of beach vacations and enter Berber country. Scenic drives take you past hills covered with barley and almond trees, palm groves, Kasbahs, and the Anti-Atlas mountains themselves. In town, poke around the monuments and souks of Taroudant or shop for Morocco's finest silver in Tiznit.

Taroudant

⑫   *85 km (51 mi) east of Agadir, 223 km (134 mi) southwest of Marrakesh.*

Taroudant is a bustling market town where people, customs, and the Arabic and Tashelhit Berber languages mix according to the ebb and flow of local agricultural and commercial dynamics. After a few glory days in the 16th century as a center of the Saadian empire, Taroudant retained allegiance to the sultan even when the Souss Valley plains and Anti-Atlas mountains revolted. Its population seems to have held steady between 5,000 and 10,000 until the 1970s, when rural emigrants to Europe returned to the region, built houses, opened businesses, and otherwise attempted to facilitate their children's access to schooling and the expanding middle class. The place retains a small-town feel, with narrow streets and active markets, despite almost 60,000 residents whose lives are unaffected by travelers passing through.

In many respects Taroudant epitomizes the environment of growing numbers of rural-to-urban migrants, sustaining aspects of country life in the midst of modern conveniences. It feels thoroughly southern Moroccan, distinct even from Marrakesh. The salmon-color walls encircling the town are the object of a French-government restoration project. Few *pisé* (sun-dried mud) buildings in the Souss Valley architectural style remain, as rains have worn them down in recent years, and they tend to be quickly replaced by charmless cinder-block structures. Taroudant's ramparts and markets can easily be explored in a day, but the town's relaxed feel, the easy interaction with locals, and inexpensive dining make Taroudant an ideal base for exploring the Souss Valley and the western High Atlas.

There is no medina–Nouvelle Ville division in Taroudant; rather, the markets are inside the walls, and the modern administrative and residential quarters are outside. A good place to begin a walk is outside the newly restored double-arched **Bab El Kasbah** along Avenue Moulay Rachid, one of half a dozen major doors that locked residents in every

WITHOUT KODAK MAX
photos taken on 100 speed film

TAKE PICTURES. FURTHER.™

© Eastman Kodak Company, 1999. Kodak, Max and Take Pictures. Further. are trademarks.

Ever see someone waiting for the sun to come out while trying to photograph a charging rhino?

New!
Kodak Max film:

Now with better color, Kodak's maximum versatility film gives you great pictures in sunlight, low light, action or still.

WITH KODAK MAX
photos taken on Kodak Max 400 film

It's all you need
to know about film.

www.kodak.com

Fodor's

Distinctive guides packed with up-to-date expert advice
and smart choices for every type of traveler.

Fodor's. For the world of ways you travel.

night during the French Protectorate. Facing the Kasbah door, you'll
see the hospital on your left, across from which is the **Dar Baroud,** the
French ammunition-storage facility. This building is closed to the public—and is locally rumored to be haunted—but you can admire its delicate carved-stone walls from the exterior. Continue along this street
and take the first right, following the signs toward the Hôtel Saadiens. The mosque on your right marks **Farq Lhbab,** the "loved ones' part-
ing place." In the 16th century, it is said, five holy men reached this
spot after years of religious study in Baghdad; each threw a stone, and
each settled where his rock landed. The best-loved of these saints are
Sidi Beni Yaqoub, of the province of Tata; Sidi u Sidi, who stayed in
Taroudant; and Sidi Hmed u Moussa, who went on to Tazerwalt (in
the province of Tiznit) and whose House of Iligh held important political power until the 19th century. Keep following signs to the Hôtel
Saadiens, passing **Sidi bu Sbaa's** tomb on your right and a French church
with magnificent gardens on your left. Just past the hotel, on your left,
is the French lookout post **Talborjst.** Head straight into the residential
area here, emerging on a narrow street lined with fish vendors, produce carts, and men selling cilantro from their bike baskets. A short
jog right lets you peek into the **tomb of Sidi u Sidi,** patron saint of
Taroudant. From the fish vendors walk straight into the **kisaria,** or covered market (inexplicably termed the "Arab market" by some). Veer
left to emerge on **Place Assareg** (literally, "the Place of the Square" or
"Square Square"). With yor back to the C.T.M. bus station, go straight
past food vendors to the **koubba of Sidi Beni Yaqoub.** Back out on Place
Assareg, turn right and follow the main street through a commercial
thoroughfare to the other main square, **Place Tamoklate** (Frying Pan
Square), on your right. Down a slight incline next to the parking lot
is the main entrance to **Jnane Edjemâa** (the "Mosque's Gardens";
called the "Berber market" by some), which formerly housed the
weekly regional market. Weave past the vendors of spices, kitchenware,
and mountain thyme and lavender to turn left and come out on the
carpenters' street. These handmade tables and cabinets—as well as such
domestic items such as lanterns made from sardine cans—furnish rural
Moroccan homes.

Turn back into the market, exit where you entered, and take another
right until you come out in front of the **Grande Mosquée** (Djemâa Lkbir,
or Great Mosque), with its yellow minaret dappled in blue-green
houndstooth tiles. Hug the salmon-color walls of the mosque as you
move past the Koranic school, around the corner, and past the high
school; on a clear day you'll now have a view of the snowy peaks of
Djebel Toubkal until you reach the Kasbah in front of you. Walk
through the Kasbah's gates, and if it's Sunday, keep going toward the
weekly vegetable market. If you're up and out before around 10 AM
on Sunday, you can catch the livestock market, behind the vegetables,
an instant view of the varieties of cows, goats, and sheep in local demand. Follow the Kasbah wall out around the corner to see the Hôtel
Palais Salaam, elegantly housed in the courts of Haïda Mouis, former
pasha of Taroudant.

To see Taroudant and the olive groves encircling town in their finest
light, go back to the circle outside Bab El Kasbah at sunset and hire a
calèche (horse-drawn carriage) in front of the playground for a ride
around the ramparts. Whatever you do in the late afternoon, don't miss
the sight of colorfully dressed Roudani (Taroudant native) women
lined up against the ramparts near the hospital like birds on a ledge,
socializing in the cool hours before sunset.

Dining and Lodging

$$ ✕ **Restaurant Jnane Soussia.** Situated between olive groves and the ramparts just outside Bab Zorgan, this restaurant has the best view in town. Traditional Moroccan cuisine is served under a *caidal* (white canvas) tent around two small swimming pools; use of the pools is free with a full meal. If the summer heat is overbearing, just order a banana shake and pay the admission fee to swim (40DH). Gnaoua music can be arranged for large groups. ☎ *08/85–49–80. No credit cards.*

$$$$ ✕🖬 **La Gazelle d'Or.** One of the most exclusive hotels in Morocco, the Gazelle d'Or offers secluded bungalows with airy, exquisitely tasteful rooms and terraces. These are arranged around (improbable) watered lawns and an excellent pool—beside which is served possibly the finest luncheon buffet in the country, open to non-guests if they reserve ahead. The staff is gracious, the clientele is largely British, and the atmosphere tends to be somber and private. Rates are negotiable in low season. ✉ *Taroudant 83000 (2 km, or 1 mi, outside Taroudant on the Amskroud–Agadir road),* ☎ *08/85–20–39,* FAX *08/85–27–37. 28 rooms, 2 suites. 2 restaurants, bar, café, pool, 2 tennis courts, horseback riding, parking.*

$$$ 🖬 **Hôtel Palais Salaam.** This friendly full-service hotel is built into the ramparts in the former pasha's courts. The newer, riad-style rooms upstairs are elegantly decorated, and some have balconies, but the older, less expensive rooms are still peaceful, set around a series of courtyards shaded with lush banana palms. Details like fly screens and bathrobes are a nice touch, as are amenities like telephones and heat. Bike trips and treks can be arranged. The restaurant serves delicious Moroccan and Continental food: try the salad sampler and order a pastilla in advance. *Enter outside ramparts,* ☎ *08/85–21–30,* FAX *08/85–26–54. 2 restaurants, bar, air-conditioning, 2 pools, bicycles, travel services, parking. No credit cards.*

$$ 🖬 **Environmental and Cultural Centre.** This facility is unique in combining affordable, fully furnished, Moroccan-style apartments with extensive staff services for those who really want to learn about Moroccan geography, culture, and society. Make the center your base for a short or extended Souss sojourn and let the English-speaking staff scientist accompany you on a flora/fauna/geography/geology tour while the resident linguist tutors you in the Arabic, Tashelhit Berber, or French language. Nestled in a residential neighborhood, the town house is ideal for couples, families, and groups up to 25, and a well-edited library and personable, knowledgeable staff cater to a curious, thoughtful clientele. Cooking facilities are available, but you might opt instead for home-cooked meals or Moroccan-cooking lessons. ✉ *42, Derb Afferdou, Jnane Remman, 83000; reserve through Naturally Morocco Limited, Wales,* ☎ FAX *(44) 01267/241999; in Taroudant,* ☎ FAX *08/55–16–28. two 3-bedroom apartments. Business services, meeting room, travel services, airport shuttle, car rental.*

$$ 🖬 **Hôtel Saadiens.** Simple rooms, no-fuss management, and a rooftop terrace restaurant make this hotel a good choice in the moderate range. There's an excellent pastry shop downstairs. To avoid noise, ask for a room overlooking the pool. ✉ *Bordj Oumansour,* ☎ *08/85–25–89,* FAX *08/85–21–18. 50 rooms. Restaurant, café, pool, parking. No credit cards.*

$$ 🖬 **Hotel Tiout.** Accommodations here are almost too cheery: the rooms are busily stenciled with brightly colored paints, and the hallways have murals. You can even opt for two-bedroom suites. The prices don't seem justified, but the premises are clean, and the staff is friendly. ✉ *Avenue Prince Heritier, B.P. 228,* ☎ *08/85–03–41,* FAX *08/85–44–80. 37 rooms, 6 suites. Restaurant, café, parking. No credit cards.*

$ ◫ **Le Soleil.** Owned and managed by a local family, Le Soleil pleases guests with its peaceful courtyard, rooftop terrace, and Roudani tagines. The rooms are simple, but they have private bathrooms—not a given in this price range—making this a great value compared to the competition. ⊠ *Outside Bab Targhount, near circle for Amskroud road,* ☏ *08/55–17–07. 8 rooms. No credit cards.*

Shopping

A little of everything is for sale in Taroudant. Local products include **saffron** and **lavender,** sold by the ounce in Jnane Edjemâa herbal stores. The locally pressed **olive oil** is nationally renowned; ask the herbalists if they can get you a liter. Moroccan handicrafts fill the kisaria; the jewelry stores in the small square as you enter the kisaria from Avenue Bir Zaran (to the right of the café that's to the right of the BMCI) have quality **silver** at good prices. Colorful round-toe **Berber slippers,** some with sequins and fanciful pompons, are another favorite with both locals and travelers. Some of the tourist bazaars in the kisaria have unusual pieces bought from rural homes, such as wooden doors and old books; store owners usually ask high prices, for few tourists buy much in Taroudant. The kisaria also has reasonable selections of **carpets, pottery,** and **wooden boxes;** just keep in mind that such items are generally brought in from Marrakesh or Essaouira, so prices are not rock-bottom.

East of Taroudant: The Souss Plains

A looped drive east of Taroudant will take you through the agriculturally rich Souss Valley plains and a tour of colonial-era *caids'* (local dignitaries') former homes. From the main circle outside Taroudant's Bab Kasbah, take the road toward Tata/Ouarzazate to Aït Iazza; then turn right toward Igherm/Tata, crossing the Souss River (provided it's not flooded, as it sometimes is in winter) into Freija. Back on pavement, look on your right for a decorated mud house, the **Kasbah de Freija.** It's now largely deserted, but you can usually find someone to show you around. Continue on until a sign marks the turnoff to Tioute. The **Tioute palmery,** about a 45-minute drive from Taroudant, was the base used by the merciless colonial caid El Tiouti, whose French-armed forces broke some of the last pockets of mountain resistance to French rule. Recently restored, El Tiouti's Kasbah now houses a restaurant (☏ 08/55–05–75). From the Kasbah or a short hike up the hillside, you have superb views over the palmery and verdant fields of mint.

From here you can continue the scenic loop northeast to Aouluz, then turn back west toward the Tizi-n-Test pass until argan trees give way to olive groves and you reach **Ouled Berhil,** whose long-standing café-restaurant is now the unique and delightful hotel Riad Hida (☞ Lodging, *below*). As an alternative, if you're pressed for time, simply return to Aït Iazza and take the Ouarzazate road straight to Ouled Berhil.

Lodging

$$$ ◫ **Complex Touristique Arganier d'Or.** Twenty-two kilometers (14 miles) east of Taroudant, these clean, albeit pricey, rooms are arranged around a lovely central courtyard. Meals are served in a tasteful tented restaurant, and folklore shows provide evening diversion. The real treat is the 10-acre orange farm directly behind the hotel. ⊠ *Zaouiat Ifergane, Aït Igass,* ☏ *08/55–02–11,* FAX *08/55–16–95. 10 rooms. Restaurant, hammam, bicycles. No credit cards.*

$$$ ◫ **Riad Hida.** Along the 1-km (½-mi) piste approach to this palace, you'll
★ first pass the mud walls of the original. Former home of the caid Haïda Mouis, notorious for the blood he ordered shed before meeting his own death near Tiznit, the riad recently turned another page in its bizarre

book: The building's French owner sold it to a Scandinavian, who, locals recount, arrived at Ouled Berhil in a wheelchair and suddenly recovered the use of his legs. Inspired, the man lived out his life here (another 25 years), distributing medicine to locals. When he died, he willed the palace, then a café and restaurant, to one of his Moroccan employees, who now comes to work as hotel manager. Surrounding a large courtyard crowded with grapefruit trees, oleander, bougainvillea, and olive and palm trees, the guest rooms are exquisitely decorated, each in a different style. Colorful *zellij* tiles make the bathrooms almost as lovely as the sleeping quarters, most of which have double beds and some of which have silk duvets. High ceilings and correspondingly tall windows lure the fresh breeze from outside. The pasha's bedroom is the best value, with two private terraces granting superb views over fields of olive and orange trees. This is one of those choice few Moroccan lodgings worth a special trip, especially considering the price. ⊠ *Ouled Berhil,* ☎ ⅂AX *08/53–10–44. 8 rooms. Restaurant, bar. No credit cards.*

Tata

⑬ *200 km (124 mi) southeast of Taroudant.*

From Taroudant follow signs to reach Tata, a four-hour drive on a frequently narrow road. The contrast between Anti-Atlas hills of barley and almond trees and the pre-Saharan plain farther south makes this a rewarding drive. En route you'll pass through **Igherm,** with a Wednesday market and a Wild West feel; women should cover their heads and dress modestly, as this is very conservative territory. Farther along is the verdant town of Issafen. Tata itself is an uninteresting military and administrative post, but nearby villages, abandoned Kasbahs, and saints' tombs make interesting exploring for those who can bear the heat. **Coppersmiths** have been crafting mugs and buckets in the Tata region for at least 1,000 years, and small shops dotted around commercial parts of town sell their wares at fair prices. You can make good time on the wide road through the flat desert-scape to **Bouzakarne,** stopping during the two-hour drive only at a few police checkpoints.

Lodging

$$ ⅋ **Le Relais des Sables.** This is your priciest and most comfortable option in Tata, with rooms arranged around pools and dinner served poolside. The suites are air-conditioned and have telephones. ⊠ *Avenue des FAR,* ☎ *08/80–23–01,* ⅂AX *08/80–23–00. 55 rooms, 10 suites. Restaurant, bar, pool. No credit cards.*

$–$$ ⅋ **Hôtel de la Renaissance.** The rooms are merely functional, but the suites are affordable (the price of a room at Le Relais des Sables), and the location is convenient. ⊠ *9, Avenue des FAR,* ☎ *08/80–22–25,* ⅂AX *08/80–20–42. 28 rooms, 4 suites. Restaurant, bar, pool. No credit cards.*

Toward Tafraoute: Aït Baha

⑭ *60 km (37 mi) southeast of Agadir.*

To reach Tafraoute from Agadir, take the Tiznit/Laayoune road 32 km (19 mi) south and turn left (east) at the sign for Biougra. On its way past commercial agriculture, the road occasionally narrows, and you sense you're playing a perennial game of chicken with the oncoming traffic. The scenic landscape begins around 20 km (12 mi) north of Biougra and remains hilly, with panoramic views, as you move through Ida ou Gnidif territory. Early in the 20th century men from the Ida ou Gnidif tribe fled a drought to join the Casablanca grocery trade, and they eventually replaced their Jewish managers as the latter migrated to the new state of Israel. The Ida ou Gnidif opened the floodgates for an Anti-Atlas-wide male migration: few Soussi villages now maintain significant adult male populations year-round. Young men generally move to the city as adolescents, return to marry and have children, and migrate once more. Before reaching Aït Baha, the road whisks by hilltop stone villages, some deserted, and rolling fields of barley with scattered argan trees.

Aït Baha is a lively market town whose stores outfit rural dwellers. The surrounding mountains are stunning, and the general atmosphere is relaxed. With the opening of the Hotel Al Adarissa, Aït Baha is now used by geographers and adventurers as a base for exploring the mountains and numerous rocky caves. For a great natural vantage point, gather picnicking supplies in town and stop farther down the Tafraoute road at a wide clearing overlooking the valley below. Solitary hilltop Kasbahs on this road hint at the quest for security in earlier eras of tribal warfare. Periodic signs in Arabic mark turnoffs to *medersas* (Koranic schools) such as the Medersa Beni Yaqoub, around 80 km (50 mi) north of Tafraoute up a piste to the left. Before independence, schooling in the Souss took place exclusively in such religious institutions, and the region continues to prepare young men from all over Morocco to serve as local *fqihs* (religious experts). Soussis actually comprise the majority of students at the prestigious Kairaouine University in Fez. About 21 km (13 mi) north of Tafraoute, take the right at the fork, marked only in Arabic (*not* the road to Aït Abdallah). On your right is the large saint's compound of **Sidi Abd e Jabar,** the only building illuminated at sunset. Here believers tormented by *jnun* (spirits) are cared for by the local community until the saint's *baraka* (blessing) heals them.

Lodging

$$$ ▣ **Hotel Al Adarissa.** All these bright, comfortable rooms have telephones. The hotel organizes a 70-km (43-mi) combined trek and jeep circuit southward for groups of five or more; smaller groups can wander on foot through the hilly landscape visible from the spacious terrace snack bar. ✉ *Avenue Mohammed V,* ☏ *08/25–44–61 or 25–44–64,* ﬁﹲ *08/25–44–65. 32 rooms. Restaurant, snack bar. No credit cards.*

Tafraoute

⑭ *152 km (94 mi) southeast of Agadir, 92 km (57 mi) southeast of Aït Baha.*

Tafraoute is a regional market and administrative center nestled in a valley that can serve as a base for exploring the area. The town itself holds little interest, aside from the stacks of massive boulders that encircle it. Market day is Wednesday. As in most Moroccan towns, there is nothing here to keep you up after dinner; turn this to your advantage by making an early-morning departure for the outskirts before the midday sun hits. Although the dizzying mountains around Tafraoute may prove forbidding to cyclists or light hikers, half-day excursions can take you to prehistoric rock carvings, the Ammeln Valley, or the villages off the main road to Tiznit. To rent a bike, find Rent-a-Cycle, which has seven; from the traffic circle the shop is a few steps past the river on the left, across from the new, popular Café-Restaurant Amanouz.

★ The **palm groves** southeast of Tafraoute deserve a full day's excursion, and the former piste circuit through them is increasingly paved. From the roundabout take the road in the opposite direction from the Agadir sign. Follow the signs toward Tiznit, and after 2 km (1 mi) you'll see the so-called "Napoleon's cap" of massive boulders on your right. Follow signs toward Agard Oudad. When the road forks, with the right going to the Painted Rocks, take the left branch. A winding paved road takes you higher into the Anti-Atlas mountains, with views over the Ammeln Valley below; 20 km (12 mi) out of Tafraoute, turn right toward Aït Mansour, which you'll reach after another 14 km (9 mi) of wending down into the palm groves. Five kilometers (3 miles) farther on is the village of Zawia; another 5 km (3 mi) brings you to Afella-n-Ighir. Along the paved road you'll pass shrouded women, either transporting on their backs palm-frond baskets of dates supported by ropes around their foreheads or walking to Timguilcht to visit its important saint's shrine. Continue on the piste to Souk Lhad, whose busy market is held on Sunday. From there the piste loops back to Tafraoute.

The whole drive can easily be done in less than a day, and the palm grove calls out to be explored on foot. Massive cement villas are under construction in the grove as vacation and retirement homes for migrant shopkeepers. Note that construction (such as the installations that led to the valley's 1998 electrification) and uneven piste conditions may require occasional delays on an otherwise purely scenic tour. Changes to the infrastructure in this area provide food for thought on the effects that rural development and migration are having on the Moroccan countryside, and a sense of how locals with cash earned elsewhere are integrating modern conveniences into their traditional homelands.

Walks in the **Ammeln Valley** offer another glimpse of contemporary rural life in Morocco. You might start at the village of Oumesmat, where the ubiquitous **Maison Berbère** is, for once, worth a trip. Here the gentle, blind Si Abdessalem will take you through his traditional Anti-Atlas home, introducing you to domestic implements, and with agility will wrap women visitors up in the local gold-laminated black wrap, the *tamelheft*. This visit is unique in southern Morocco for its clear look at local material culture and domestic life. Express your appreciation for the tour by tipping generously. From Oumesmat you can follow paths to the neighboring villages. **Taghdicte** makes a good base for ambitious Anti-Atlas climbers; Mohammed, in Souq Al Had Afella (☎ 08/80–05–47), can help with arrangements.

A trip to the **Painted Rocks** outside Tafraoute (follow signs) is most dramatically experienced in late afternoon, when the hillsides stacked with massive round boulders turn a rich mustard hue before sunset. Belgian artist Jean Veran painted a cluster of these natural curiosities in varying shades of blue in 1984; more fun than admiring the originals is checking out amateur attempts to copy the idea and judging which ones are most convincing.

The prehistoric **gazelle rock carving** just 2 km (1 mi) south of Tafraoute is an easy walk or bike ride from town. The sparse etching has been retouched, but it's still interesting. To get here, follow signs to Tazka from behind Hotel Les Amadiers; go through the village to the palm and argan fields beyond, taking along a local child to point out the way. (Be sure to thank kids for such services with a small gift, such as a few dates, a pen, or an elastic ponytail holder.)

Dining and Lodging

Two cheap hotels, the **Hotel Tanger** (☎ 08/80–00–33) and the **Hotel Redouane** (☎ 08/80–00–66) have simple, roughly 30DH rooms overlooking the putrid-smelling river that runs through town. Both have shared showers; the Redouane's are better.

$$ ✕ **Restaurant L'Etoile du Sud.** The "Star of the South" serves delicious couscous and tagines in a red-velvet dining room or under a huge red-and-green velvet tent of the kind used for Moroccan rooftop weddings. The solicitous staff will scarcely distract you from the good food and colossally kitschy decor. ✉ *Avenue Hassan II*, ☎ *no phone.*

$ ✕ **L'Etoile d'Agadir.** Standard Moroccan dishes are prepared with inventive flair here. The beef tagine simmers with prunes, caramelized onions, and tomatoes in a rich sauce with toasted almonds and a sesame garnish. Local administrators bide their free time in this somewhat smoky café, but don't let that discourage you from enjoying the fine cooking. ✉ *Avenue Hassan II*, ☎ *no phone. No credit cards.*

$$$ 🏨 **Hôtel Les Amandiers.** Designed in a mock-Kasbah style, this luxury hotel is set on a hill behind town, up a path well marked by signs. Arranged around two courtyards, all of the clean, bright guest rooms have spacious bathrooms, phones, and heat, and many have mountain views. Apartments are also available. The lovely pool is a welcome anomaly in these parts. ✉ *B.P. 10, Tafraoute*, ☎ *08/80–00–88*, FAX *08/80–03–43. 58 rooms, 7 apartments. Restaurant, bar, air-conditioning.*

$ 🏨 **Hotel Salama.** Staffed by a helpful team of English-speakers, the Salama offers quiet, cool rooms with excellent showers and heat. Rooms overlook the market, where old men sell dates and local women bring their homemade argan oil. The public lounge has panoramic views of the town and rocky mountains beyond. ✉ *Centre Tafraoute*, ☎ *08/80–00–26*, FAX *08/80–04–48. 28 rooms. Café. No credit cards.*

$ 🏨 **Hôtel Tafraout.** Basic rooms share toilets and showers here, and a public lounge invites mingling. The staff is happy to help plan day trips, but the hotel's good value makes it a favorite with partying off-duty policemen, whom the hotel staff do nothing to quiet. ✉ *Place Moulay Rachid*, ☎ *08/80–00–61 or 80–01–21. No credit cards.*

Shopping

Tafraoute's central market has a good selection of woven palm-frond baskets, Berber slippers, argan oil, and *amalou* (almond and argan paste).

Tafraoute to Tiznit

The newer road from Tafraoute to Tiznit (follow signs out the back of Tafraoute, beyond the post office) is flat and bike-accessible for about the first 15 km (9 mi), after which it begins an incline into the mountains. As the road winds over the Anti-Atlas peaks and through the valleys, you'll see many sights, of which the former Kasbah site **Col du Kerdous** is a highlight. The moderately priced Hotel Kerdous offers lofty panoramic views; a flavorful tagine in its restaurant is worth a stop (☎ *08/86–20–53*, FAX *08/86–28–35*). At night, if you're lucky, you may hear music from wedding festivities in one of the villages below echoing off the mountain walls under the clear, starry sky.

Continuing toward Tiznit, follow the signs and take the short, paved detour southwest to Iligh, former capital of the regional Tazeroualt kingdom and site of the **tomb of Sidi Hmed ou Moussa.** The tower of the now-deserted empire of Iligh is still visible. Although the family of this 16th-century saint is no longer a political force, the saint is still revered by the Swasa, and the moussems held in his honor each March and August draw thousands of followers. The tomb is marked by a green-tile dome within a white-fenced yard; local men might show you around while visiting groups of women prepare commemorative meals at the neighboring zaouia.

⑯ *100 km (62 mi) west of Tafraoute.*

If the number of hotels under construction is any indication, Tiznit seems to see itself as an alternative to Agadir; but for the traveler's purposes, it's primarily a market town. The markets can be either calm and friendly or hostile, depending on the heat, the time of day, and the particular streets you take. Take a short walk and have lunch here, saving extra time for the silver markets—Tiznit has Morocco's widest selection of silver jewelry both old and new. Some shops buy cream-color throws of light wool, characteristic of traditional regional dress, from local women in exchange for a few pieces of newer silver or gold jewelry.

Park your car in the main square, the Méchouar, and walk or rent a bike from the bike shop just inside the square's southern entrance. From the Méchouar, take the Rue Bain Maure, to the left of the C.T.M. bus station. Follow it as it winds through neighborhood markets, and you'll emerge on a main medina street at a slim minaret (visible from the Méchouar). Cross the street and turn right along the arcade; then follow the cemetery walls around to the **Grande Mosquée** (Great Mosque)—unusual in Morocco for its sub-Saharan–style minaret, with sticks poking out from all sides. Next to the mosque is a saint's tomb. Facing the pisé wall of the prison housed in the old Kasbah, continue left around the prison walls until you reach the **Lalla Zeina spring** on your left, which honors the saint after whom Tiznit is named. Legend has it that this shepherd girl brought her flocks to this spot and smelled the then-undiscovered spring below; her sheep dug until they found the water, and the town was born. To catch a glimpse of her tomb on afternoons when devotees visit, follow the prison wall and turn left on the first narrow neighborhood street; the tomb is behind a green-painted door on your left.

Return to the main square and cross it to head into a small square lined with orange trees, where locals buy from the mint, date, and dried-thyme vendors whose carts are parked between the rows of clothing and housewares. The square gives way to a silver souk and a larger concentration of tourists (and hasslers).

Banks with ATMs and currency-exchange service are clustered around the Avenue du 20 Août and Avenue Hassan II. You can confirm flights at a travel agency here, too.

Dining and Lodging
Classified hotels are clustered around the main circle heading out of town. Unclassified hotels are in the medina.

$$ ✕🏨 **Tiznit Hôtel.** Here spacious rooms surround a lovely central pool and garden removed from highway noise. Poolside billiards and an impressively well-stocked bar add to the full Moroccan restaurant menu to make this a more attractive destination than its neighbors. ✉ *Rue Bir Inzaran, B.P. 57,* ☎ *08/86–24–11 or 86–38–86,* ℻ *08/86–21–19. 40 rooms. Restaurant, bar, billiards, parking.*

$ 🏨 **Hôtel de France.** These simple rooms have deep bathtubs, phones, and heat, and there's a nice patio café. ✉ *Avenue Hassan II,* ☎ *08/86–28–65 or 60–13–95. 20 rooms. Restaurant, café.*

$ 🏨 **Hôtel de Soleil.** This relatively new hotel offers clean rooms decorated with burgundy-velveteen bedspreads and curtains, which lend the place either a Renaissance or a brothel character, depending on your perspective. Unfortunately, the rooms overlook cinder-block construction next door, and the management can be inappropriately friendly to women traveling without men. ✉ *B.P. 467,* ☎ *08/60–02–89,* ℻ *08/86–22–59. 11 rooms, 3 suites. Restaurant, patisserie.*

Shopping

Tiznit has earned a reputation as *the* place to buy silver jewelry in Morocco, and the local market has responded accordingly. Merchants cater increasingly to Western tastes and wallets. Many shops around the main square are owned by profiteers who ask outrageous prices; to find unusual pieces for reasonable amounts, scour the backstreets for older men haggling with local women. An exception to the racket is the low-pressure **bijouterie** run by Mohamed Chakour, who sells Saharan and Berber silver jewelry and tasteful, handwoven cream-color blankets traded in by local women (✉ 6, Souk Joutia, ☎ 08/86–40–93).

Aglou Plage

🔟 *17 km (10 mi) west of Tiznit.*

Despite rapidly expanding housing developments, the beach at Aglou has no tourist infrastructure, such as cafés or lodging. Signs warning beachgoers to remain 1,640 ft from the rough waters confirm that despite the stretches of clean sand, this is more an ocean-watching than a swimming site. Built into the cliffs are troglodyte dwellings, which you can reach on foot.

Sidi Ifni

🔟 *60 km (37 mi) south of Tiznit.*

The word on the street in Sidi Ifni (also known simply as Ifni) is that a European committee concerned with Art Deco restoration worldwide is trying to get UNESCO funding for the preservation of both Ifni and Asmara, Eritrea. Attempts to get Ifni's 25,000 coastal and inland residents their own province, independent from Tiznit, are also under way. Built in the 1930s, this town, many of whose residents recall their Spanish rule with nostalgia and retain Spanish citizenship, is on the move—but not too fast. For the moment it remains an architectural quirk of yellow, Moorish-style Art Deco buildings, welcoming those seeking low-hassle ocean-side beauty and a moderate climate. Ifni has a relaxed feel; its young men would rather play soccer on the beach than bother the few Western travelers drawn to its rust-red boulder-framed beaches and fresh fish. If you visit in late June, before the crowds arrive, you can attend the weeklong almuggar (moussem) in the former airfield, a lively mix of Saharan market activity, musical performances, and cultural exhibitions. In February the Al Badil Cultural Association sponsors a weeklong exposition of Ifni. At any time of year half a day's walk will cover the town's architectural highlights, but Ifni's pace and climate might tempt you to relax here for much longer.

The most exemplary **Moorish Art Deco** buildings are clustered around Place Hassan II (locally called the Plaza de España), near the coastal hillside, but small architectural gems are sprinkled about; along with an attractive sequence of residential doors, they make a walk around Ifni rewarding. The Place Hassan II is a circle with a well-kept garden in its center, adorned with colored flowers and enclosed by a fence painted in Easter egg hues. A former **church** now houses the courthouse. Next door is the now-deserted **Spanish consulate,** built in a stunning semicircular design. Across the circle and down the street, next to the Hôtel de Ville (town hall), is the Spanish cinema, which may reopen as a cultural center. Facing the Hôtel Belle Vue, take the small Rue Ibn Toumart on your left toward a stocky **lighthouse,** now integrated into a family compound but still lighted every evening. The wall alongside the light-house is a perfect place to watch the sun set.

From here you can also see vestiges of the **Spanish port** farther down the coast. The Spaniards, who ruled Sidi Ifni from 1934 to 1969, hauled in their daily catch with a gondola system: boats parked at a station out in the ocean and unloaded fish into a cable car that had been lowered from a station on the hillside. The crane that anchored the overhead cable car mid-trip still rises from the water, but local authorities, declaring this system too expensive, closed it for several years in the 1970s and came up with a **new port,** now accessible from the beach farther south. You can walk to the port along the beach below town, or follow the signs from the center of town past the deserted airfield that now hosts the annual weeklong almuggar celebrating its 1969 independence. Activity at the port heats up between around 2 and 4 in the afternoon, when a boisterous auction for large fish takes over the port hall. Follow the action to the town's **central market** any afternoon between 6 and 8, when locals complete the food chain by selecting their fish suppers.

Dining and Lodging

Accommodations in Ifni are limited. Repeat visitors reserve their rooms weeks in advance, and in the summer you should follow suit. Note that, beyond café-restaurants, all of Ifni's restaurants outside hotels are open only in summer.

$ ✕⌆ **Hotel Suerte Loca.** Family-run and English-friendly, the hotel, whose name means "blind luck," is a favorite not only with surfers, independent travelers, and families but also with local young men, who mingle with travelers over pool tables, chess games, and impromptu guitar jam sessions. The rooms are clean and comfortable, and some have private baths; there is also a spacious roof terrace. The staff can help organize excursions into nearby villages on market days, as well as beach trips for small groups, and is extremely helpful with general regional information. Even if you don't stay here, order dinner from the restaurant ahead of time and stop in for baked fish or paella. ⊠ *Rue Moulay Youssef,* ☎ *08/87–53–50,* ⅛ℵ *08/78–00–03. 16 rooms. Restaurant. No credit cards.*

$ ⌆ **Hôtel Belle Vue.** What the Belle Vue lacks in charm it makes up for in facilities, location, and solitude, especially if you're not up for the sociability of the Suerte Loca. Double beds and a full bar are particular pluses. All of the clean, comfortable guest rooms have hot showers and walk-in closets, and some have ocean views. ⊠ *Place Hassan II,* ☎ *08/87–50–72 or 87–52–42,* ⅛ℵ *08/78–04–99. 25 rooms. 2 restaurants, bar, disco. V.*

Mirleft

⑲ *25 km (15 mi) north of Ifni.*

The beaches south of Ifni require a sturdy vehicle to navigate the pistes, though the Plage Blanche is gratifyingly quiet and calm. The massive **red-sandstone arches** over the beach at Al Jazira, north of Ifni, are worth a quick visit or an afternoon jaunt; just watch your odometer, as the turn is not signposted. Take the Tiznit road north 10 km (6 mi) and turn left onto the piste that dead-ends in a flat spot where, in high season, you might join European camper vans. Walk down to the beach below and head south to reach the arches. Other beach options are clustered around the village of Mirleft. The cinder-block storefronts between Tiznit and Ifni are deceptively drab, for the village inland (market day: Monday) is friendly and makes a pleasant overnight alternative to Ifni. Stock up on fishing tackle, poles, and beach toys at the shop neighboring the Café Restaurant Layachi.

To reach the imposing 1933 **French fort** hovering above town, follow the piste through town and up the hill. You'll see why the French wanted this vantage point: the beach just south of the center of Mirleft marked the meeting of the French and Spanish colonial territories, and Sidi Abdellah's tomb on the beach (now nearly swallowed by a new mosque) was considered the Spanish boundary. From the hillside you'll also see an inviting beach just north, accessible from the main road by a piste winding past fields of corn—with scarecrows made of black plastic bags—to stop at peaceful sands. A cement walkway links pedestrians to the neighborhood above. At Mirleft's annual Almuggar Issig, held the last Thursday in July, area girls seeking suitors assemble to sing and dance, with older, married women drumming in accompaniment around them. It's an interesting alternative to Imilchil's touristy marriage festival (held in September). In addition, Mirleft-area women celebrate the June festival of Ashura with a nighttime song to ward off pests that might spoil their flour supplies.

Lodging

$$ ⊞ **Albergo de la Plage–Cobratours.** Right on the beach, just 2 km (1 mi) south of the center of Mirleft, this Italian-run inn offers tastefully decorated rooms, a panoramic Moroccan salon, and sumptuous Italian dinners of fish and pasta. Michele and his wife, Sandra, an archaeologist, organize sophisticated tours emphasizing Moroccan archeology, geology, and geography. ⊠ *B.P. 27, Mirleft/Tiznit 85350,* ☎ FAX *08/71–90–56 or 71–91–85. Cobratours business office:* ☎ FAX *08/71–91–05 or 71–91–74. 5 rooms. V.*

ESSAOUIRA, THE SOUSS VALLEY, AND THE ANTI-ATLAS A TO Z

Arriving and Departing

By Bus

Numerous intercity buses connect Casablanca and Marrakesh to points south; the most reliable company is C.T.M. Check local bus stations for schedules, as they change frequently.

By Plane

Flying into Agadir or Essaouira allows you to bypass the congested roadways around Casablanca. Both Royal Air Maroc and the newer Regional Airlines offer inexpensive domestic flights to the southwest several days a week, for which you can almost always book tickets once you arrive at Casa's airport (if you haven't reserved in advance). Agadir handles several daily flights to and from Casablanca on both RAM and Regional, and seasonal international flights. Agadir's **Al Massira** Airport (☎ 08/83–91–22) is 35 km (21 mi) east of town on the road to Taroudant. *Grands taxis* between the airport and Agadir cost 100DH during the day, 150DH at night and in early morning (prices are totals for up to six passengers). Grands taxis also connect the airport to major towns; if you have light bags and are heading inland, take the bus (3DH) or a grand taxi (200DH total) to the Inezgane terminus, a local hub, and catch grands taxis or buses from there. The new **Aeroport Essaouira Mogador** (☎ 04/47–67–09 airport), 14 km (9 mi) south of Essaouira on the Agadir road, handles RAM flights to and from Casablanca on weekends. A grand taxi into Essaouira costs 100DH total. Bus and taxi service is also available.

By Train
Morocco has no train service south of Marrakesh.

Getting Around

By Car
Driving is the most flexible way to tour the Souss Valley and Anti-Atlas, as shared taxis sometimes fill slowly, and buses can leave hours apart. A small car, such as a Renault 205 or a Fiat Uno, is sufficient for flat pistes as well as most paved roads in this region. Get four-wheel drive for more adventurous driving. Good two-lane roads connect Essaouira, Agadir, Taroudant, Tafraoute, Tiznit, and Sidi Ifni; other towns are linked by 1½-lane roads that require one driver to cede the road when another passes.

Rental options are numerous in Agadir. Most major international companies allow you to pick the car up and drop it off in different cities; a local, less expensive agency is a good choice if you plan to stay in the Souss region. For the greatest flexibility, make arrangements before you come to Morocco so that your car is waiting for you at the airport. Make sure the price includes kilometers, insurance, and any drop-off fee, and get the agreement in writing. Reconfirm your car 24 hours before you pick it up. The major agencies are gathered along Avenue Mohammed V in Agadir; airport offices open only when a flight is arriving. **Avis** (☎ 08/84–17–55; airport 08/84–03–45). **Budget** (☎ 08/84–82–22; airport 08/83–91–01). **Europcar** (☎ 08/84–02–03; airport 08/83–90–66). **Hertz** (☎ 08/84–34–76; airport 08/83–90–71). **Imloc Cars,** walking distance from the grand-taxi stand, is a trustworthy local choice with an affable staff (✉ Kissariate El Kebbaj 40 bis, off Avenue Hassan II across from Hotel Cinq Parties du Monde; ☎ 08/82–07–83).

In Essaouira, outdoor public parking is available between the town and the port; follow Avenue Mohammed V and continue with the water on your left to find the lot. Walled, guarded parking is available outside Bab Doukkala.

By Grand Taxi
Shared taxis are the fastest means between urban destinations, providing the taxi fills quickly. You can hire a grand taxi for the price of six individual places; pay before you leave. Bus and taxi prices are similar and are standard; note that Essaouira drivers often try to charge more. Sample fares per person (if taxi is full): Agadir to Taroudant, 23DH; Taroudant to Inezgane, 20DH; Inezgane to Marrakesh, 70DH.

Contacts and Resources

Airlines
Royal Air Maroc (✉ Al Massira airport, Agadir, ☎ 08/83–90–01, 83–91–22, or 83–90–12; ✉ Rue du General Kettani, Agadir, ☎ 08/84–01–45 or 84–00–45).

Banks
In **Essaouira,** banks line the Place Moulay Hassan. Plans for an ATM are underway, but for now you must get dirhams during banking hours. The Credit du Maroc is open Saturday morning and afternoon as well as weekdays.

Church
Eglise Sainte Anne (✉ 115, Rue de Marrakech, Agadir, ☎ 08/82–22–51) holds a French mass Saturday at 6:30 PM and polyglot services Sunday at 10 AM and 7 PM.

Cybercafés

At **Essaouira**'s Espace Internet (✉ Rue de Caire), you can access the Web for 30DH an hour. **Agadir** has a cybercafé on Avenue Hassan II (near the Place La Fontaine). **Taroudant** has a small facility across from the Hotel Tiout.

Emergencies

Highway assistance: ☎ 177. **Police:** ☎ 19. **Fire:** ☎ 15.

Guided Tours

Southern Moroccan towns have their share of unofficial but insistent faux guides, who generally approach foreigners in larger cities. Feel free to ignore them. In towns where there is no tourist office, you can hire an official guide at one of the nicer hotels.

One of Essaouira's three official tour guides holds a university degree in English and is highly knowledgeable about Essaouira's political, architectural, and social history. Contact **Hassan Echatir** (✉ 30, Logement Economique, Essaouira, ☎ 04/78–46–52). The **Syndicat d'Initiative et de Tourisme** (✉ Rue du Caire, ☎ 04/47–42–47 or 04/47–42–48) has general information on travel and transport.

For guided tours of Souss flora, fauna, and geology, contact **Saïd Ahmoume** at Taroudant's Environmental and Cultural Centre (☎ 08/55–16–28). For sophisticated tours with archaeological, architectural, or geographical themes in the south, the High Atlas, or the whole of Morocco, contact **Cobratours** (✉ B.P. 27, Mirleft, Tiznit 85350, ☎ FAX 08/71–91–05 or 08/71–91–74).

Late-Night Pharmacies

One late-night pharmacy (*pharmacie de garde*) stays open in each Moroccan town; check the door of any pharmacy to see whose turn it is.

Sports and Outdoor Activities

Abdelaziz Tali arranges hikes in the western Atlas mountains for groups of all sizes and schedules. Ask about his Wonder Walk from Taroudant through the Tichka Plateau and on to Djebel Toubkal. Contact him directly (✉ B.P. 132, Taroudant, ☎ 08/85–35–01) or ask after him at the Hotel Taroudant on Place Assareg.

Visitor Information

Tourist offices: **Agadir** (✉ Place du Heritier Sidi Mohammed, ☎ 08/84–63–77).

Essaouira (✉ Syndicat d'Initiative et de Tourisme, Rue du Caire, ☎ 04/47–42–47 or 04/47–42–48).

10 THE SOUTHERN COAST AND WESTERN SAHARA

Morocco's chunk of the western Sahara Desert is a stark expanse of rocky plains and sand dunes, lined on one side by Atlantic beaches and coastal cliffs. Forming the tail end of this long, narrow country, it presents an entirely different face than the Morocco that precedes it.

By Angela
Scarfino

FEW TRAVELERS VENTURE this far south in Morocco, but those who do are rewarded with a slice of life in the great Sahara Desert. Vast dunes follow the coast from Tan-Tan south to Laayoune, broken by stretches of *hamada*—flat expanses of rocky desert, sometimes accented by scrub and by dunes of pure sand. On the desert's western edge, the Atlantic Ocean provides the fish that help support this region economically, meeting the land in surf that ranges from wild to calm. It's a sparse but striking landscape, and it forms Morocco's southernmost gateway to the rest of the African continent.

The few cities in the western Sahara seem to rise out of the sand as clumps of civilization between long stretches of empty road. Even in the cities themselves, tourist resources are slim, and the distances between stopping points make advance planning crucial. If you find time to make this journey, you'll experience a very different face of Morocco from all those farther north, one that puts on no airs and presents itself with stark and simple honesty.

The history of the western Sahara Desert was scantly recorded before the 19th century. There is evidence that the area was a great and fertile savanna in prehistoric times, with substantial wildlife. Archaeological evidence shows that the region was likely inhabited by hunter-gatherer hominids as early as a million years ago. The Sahara is said to have entered its desertification stage around 3000 BC, its dry borders spreading to overgrazed, sparsely watered areas nearby, at which point the hunter-gatherer civilizations migrated north to the more fertile and temperate pre-Saharan and High Atlas regions.

Local lore claims that native Saharans were nomads here for centuries, participating in caravans through Mali, Mauritania, and Niger. In the 19th and 20th centuries the coastline of the western Sahara was a minor stopping point for European trading vessels headed for Africa's Gold Coast. In the early 20th century it served as an overnight stopping place for French pilots en route to southern Africa.

The Moroccan sultan Moulay Ismail, who recruited many members of his legendary army guard by making forays into southern Morocco and Mauritania, is said to have established a post near Laayoune in the 1670s. The sultan Moulay el Hassan, known as Hassan I, ventured south in the 1880s on an expedition meant to pacify the local populations, i.e., bring them more firmly under the monarchy's control and arrange for them to be taxed. The activity of these two rulers gave Morocco a historical claim to this region, a claim that would come into greater focus in the second half of the 20th century.

In the 1960s, the Sahara's importance increased dramatically with the discovery of substantial phosphate deposits around Boukra. Around this time, the Spanish, who had already colonized northern Morocco and developed a very basic presence along the Atlantic coast, reinforced their erstwhile Saharan colonies of Rio de Oro and Seguiat el Hamra. Bringing more-advanced infrastructure and investment to the region, the Spanish created a series of small towns along the coast, including a capital city—Laayoune—and native nomadic peoples began settling here for good. Increased access to education and other amenities created a stronger sense of nationalism in the newly settled populations, much as it had in the formerly French colonies of the north prior to Moroccan independence in 1956. Somewhat ironically, Moroccans increasingly saw the western Sahara as part of their country, and resentment toward the Spanish presence grew.

Hassan II ascended to the throne in 1961, at a highly tumultuous time following Moroccan independence. The new king used the issue of the Sahara and the nationalistic spirit born of independence to rebuild and strengthen the institution of the monarchy and rally all Moroccans toward the Saharan cause. King Hassan II monitored Saharan progress very carefully, and in 1975 he sent nearly 400,000 Moroccans on Al Massira, the Green March—Morocco's official reclamation of the western Sahara. This manifestation of Moroccan strength gave the Spanish an ultimatum to fight or to withdraw from the Sahara. They withdrew, and the land was split between Moroccan and Mauritanian control. During the Moroccan advance—and certainly during the Moroccan occupation following the Green March—native Saharans, unhappy with anything less than a democratic republic, fled to neighboring Mauritania and Algeria. Algeria reacted by ceding a portion of desolate land southeast of its own Tindouf to Polisario, the Saharan independence front. Here the group established a series of camps, inhabited mostly by Saharan refugees. By the early 1990s more than 175,000 refugees inhabited these camps, and while their living conditions were not ideal, the Polisario established health-care centers and schools here, and delivered food aid from international organizations and several European nations.

The growing independence movement, led by the Saharan Arab Democratic Republic, used these camps as bases for anti-Moroccan activity. The pressure of guerrilla attacks and independence fighters caused Morocco to retreat, centering itself around the larger Saharan cities on the coast, and Mauritania to withdraw from its alliance with Morocco, a split that was mended only in a 1989 agreement to join the Maghreb Arab Union. Between 1981 and 1988, in a show of strength and self-protection against the guerrilla attacks, the Forces Armées Royales (FAR), Morocco's royal armed forces, built a series of enormous, heavily protected desert walls to seal off large portions of the western Sahara from bordering countries. With these obstructions in place, Morocco began to build up its Saharan cities and consider the western Sahara part of the Moroccan map.

An official U.N. cease-fire was declared in 1989, and since then, the western Sahara has seen no major conflict, though heated discussions between the Moroccan government and Polisario are frequent. A U.N.-sponsored referendum that would allow the Saharan population to vote on independence has been in the works for years, held up by questions about voting rosters, eligibility, and other political details.

The U.N. currently employs a large contingent of representatives here, a team known as MINURSO (a French acronym for Mission for Referendum in the Western Sahara). Despite political controversy, the only visible manifestations of the situation are the U.N. staff and vehicles in large cities and the presence of several military checkpoints. If you stick to the routes outlined below, you should encounter no problems other than filling out forms at police checkpoints.

Pleasures and Pastimes

Beaches
The Atlantic coast of the western Sahara has some of Morocco's finest and most pristine beaches. The stretch between Tan-Tan and Tarfaya is lined with long stretches of golden sand and good surf, which Europeans and Australians like to ride in the winter months. Try the area around Akhfenir for seaside solitude; continuing south, Laayoune Plage offers excellent surfing and windsurfing, and calmer areas for swimming. The windy coast continues to Boujdour, another well-

known surfing site. The almost-400-km (248-mi) route from Boujdour to Dakhla passes lovely swaths of beach, the finest of which are centered around Dakhla itself.

The region's coastal lagoons also attract many species of native and migratory birds as well as unique plants, all adapted to life in the consistently temperate southern-Moroccan climate.

Dining and Lodging

Restaurants and hotels in this region are concentrated in the largest cities, and even then they're few in number and fairly consistent in flavor. The major hotels in Laayoune and Dakhla have good restaurants, though, and you can dine well in the numerous small cafés and restaurants on the main avenues. Standard and enjoyable fare includes salads, soups, sandwiches, tagines, and grilled meats. Fresh seafood, hauled into most cities daily from nearby ports, is a sure bet; the local grilled sardines are particularly delicious.

Hotels in the western Sahara are not luxurious. Rooms are often small and spartan, with little in the way of decor or amenities. Phones and private baths cannot be expected. We indicate the availability of private baths wherever possible; some hotels offer a mixture of private and shared bath facilities, so if you want a private bath and are faced with a multilingual proprietor, by all means inquire. Accommodations tend to be clean, and they're reasonably comfortable in the larger cities, but you should still look at your room before you accept it. Note that members of the MINURSO team book most of the nicer urban hotels in blocks, so advance reservations are essential.

Dinner at any restaurant in this region costs 120DH or less per person, excluding drinks, service, and (when applicable) tax, so we classify all restaurants in this chapter as $. Hotels are categorized as follows:

CATEGORY	COST*
$$$	350–500DH
$$	200–350DH
$	under 200DH

All prices are for a standard double room, excluding tax.

Exploring the Southern Coast and Western Sahara

If you want to linger for several days, one of the most enjoyable ways to cover the territory is to organize a tour through one of several agencies based in Laayoune. These companies provide transport, arrange accommodations or camping in the desert, and arrange guided tours to sights of interest, often to places well off the beaten path. Because the Sahara's high points are so far apart, a tour can be the most efficient way to see them in a limited amount of time.

Great Itineraries

The distance between the western Sahara and other Moroccan destinations makes a trip to this region a time-consuming undertaking. Domestic flights to Tan-Tan, Laayoune, and Dakhla can cut down on transportation time.

IF YOU HAVE 2 DAYS

Fly into **Tan-Tan** ②. Enjoy a brief drive through the town and pick up the main coastal road south to Laayoune. Lunch on grilled fish in the small town of **Akhfenir** ④; stop in the coastal town of **Tarfaya** ⑤; and see the birds, beaches, and dunes of the nearby Naila Lagoon. Arrive in ⊡ **Laayoune** ⑥ that evening. The next day, explore Laayoune in the

242

The Southern Coast and Western Sahara

morning and travel south to **Boujdour** ⑧ and its nearby beaches in the afternoon. Return to Laayoune for a second night and fly out from Laayoune the next morning.

IF YOU HAVE 4 DAYS

Follow the itinerary above through the morning of day two. That afternoon, instead of going to Boujdour, travel to 🖼 **Smara** ⑦ to visit the Palace of Ma el Ainin and spend the night. Hit the road early on day three, going back to Laayoune and then south along the coastal road. Stop in the village of **Boujdour** ⑧ for lunch and some time on the beach. Continue south to 🖼 **Dakhla** ⑨ for the night. Spend day four exploring Dakhla and its surroundings, especially the pristine coastal areas. Fly out of Dakhla late in the day.

When to Go

The Atlantic coast keeps local temperatures lower than the name "Sahara" might imply; except in July and August, the area near the Atlantic route remains temperate. Inland towns, such as Smara and Boukra, tend to be much hotter. Summer brings Moroccans from the northern regions down to western-Saharan beaches, combining with the ever-present MINURSO members to make accommodations scarce indeed, so spring and fall are the ideal times to come. The cities are devoid of travelers then, the lagoons teem with migratory bird and plant life, and the warm sun hovers beneath its summer peak.

GUELMIM TO TARFAYA

This route takes you from the pre-Saharan plains, oases, and camel herds of Guelmim to the rocky hamada near Tan-Tan. It then opens onto the Atlantic coast, along sand dunes that stretch clear to the water, with only a few settlements and fishing villages breaking the sight line. Wide open and largely untouched, this unique blend of Sahara and Atlantic is one of Morocco's most memorable journeys.

Guelmim

❶ *107 km (66 mi) south of Tiznit.*

Guelmim is known as the Gateway to the Sahara, and the ensuing drive south to Tan-Tan—the first town in the western Sahara proper—illustrates why. It's an easy trip, shooting through empty stretches of flat hamada broken only by the occasional village or café and one gas station. You're likely to catch your first glimpse of large camel herds here. Camels bound for Guelmim's famous Saturday **camel souk**, as well as markets farther north toward Agadir, are often moved along this route, sometimes by the hundred. About 15 km (9 mi) north of Tan-Tan you'll cross the Oued Drâa: now dry virtually year-round, this river formed the border between the French and Spanish protectorates in colonial times.

You'll be hard-pressed to find anywhere to eat in Guelmim beyond dingy cafés and roast-chicken joints. In a pinch, see if the restaurant at the Hotel Salam is open. If you have time, follow the signs southwest from Guelmim to Plage Blanche to grab a bite and behold a fine sand beach that ultimately stretches 65 km (40 mi). There are no hotels here, but several cafés along the Tan-Tan road serve tagines, sandwiches, and salads; try the Café Jour et Nuit.

Lodging

$ 🖼 **Auberge Abaynou.** If you find yourself in Guelmim at day's end, settle into a cheerful courtyard room at this inn for the night. Between a natural hot spring and the *koubba* of Sidi Slimane, the inn is accessible by taking the Ifni road northwest from Guelmim 5 km (3 mi), then following the signs for 10 more km (6 mi). Hot springs are favorite vacation spots for Moroccan families; by day you can join them for a dip in sex-segregated pools of the naturally warm waters. After 7 PM, the pools open to foreign hotel guests of both sexes. ⊠ *Abaynou par Guelmim,* ☎ *08/87–04–22 or 08/87–04–23. 15 rooms. Restaurant, bar, pool. No credit cards.*

$ ⚏ **Hotel Salam.** Here you can sleep in spacious rooms with private bathrooms, but the restaurant only functions when a critical mass of tourists appears. ⊠ *Rue Youssef Ben Tachfine,* ☎ *08/87–20–57,* ⬛ *08/77–09–12. 20 rooms. No credit cards.*

$ ⚏ **Fort Bou-Jerif.** Unless you're in dire straits, don't be tempted to forge on to this old French fort on the road to Plage Blanche. It's more than 30 km (19 mi) northwest of Guelmim on a *piste* (track) along the Assaka River. The resident French management oversees a kitschy, stonewall faux-Moroccan administrative center that hosts primarily European tour groups, who pay disproportionate sums to brave the whipping winds in collective tents, or hunker down in the amazingly basic rooms and brave the curt staff. Bath facilities are shared in both cases. Omar, the German snake charmer down the road, completes the travesty. ⊠ *B.P. 504,* ☎ ⬛ *08/87–30–39. 5 rooms. Restaurant, bar. No credit cards.*

Tan-Tan

❷ *125 km (78 mi) south of Guelmim.*

As you approach Tan-Tan, you may think you're seeing a giant mirage. Fear not, for your eyes do not deceive you: there really are two enormous **kissing camels** forming an archway over the road into town. Carved out of stone in the 1970s, these affectionate creatures are one of Tan-Tan's chief claims to fame, and the subjects of many a western-Sahara postcard. The town makes a logical stop on a trip farther south and is a passable choice for an overnight stay, as long as you keep in mind that accommodations are often small and sparse, with little in the way of decor or amenities.

Tan-Tan is a very low-key administrative center whose main significance (beyond the kissing camels) is that it was the starting point for the Green March of 1975. The Royal Armed Forces building sits on the hill in the town center; spelled out on the hillside are the French words *Tous pour Hassan II* (All for Hassan II), a memorial to the march and the leader who made it happen. Note that you are technically forbidden to photograph government buildings.

At the town's lively **souks,** you're likely to see local men—many of them former Saharan nomads—dressed in enormous blue or white robes called *gondoras,* and head scarves like those worn in Mali and Niger. Women wear a sheer garment known as a *ml'hafa,* distinctive to the Sahara and traditionally made with local dyes. Dress here reflects the hot, dusty climate: garments are loose and lightweight, and each has a piece that can be held up to protect the face and eyes from wind and flying sand.

Tan-Tan comes to life in June with the moussem of **Sidi Loghdof,** a great holy man to southern-Saharan tribes. Worshipers flock here, many from the southern regions of Mauritania, Algeria, and West Africa, and pitch tents on the hamada. Festivities include camel races, trading, and dancing, including the famed *guedra* rendered by some of the Sahara's most talented performers. This traditional dance is executed by a woman on her knees, who drums on a clay pot (*guedra*) throughout the routine. It starts slow and speeds up until the performer eventually faints in a frenzy—think "dervish."

The town is organized around its main boulevard, Mohammed V, with Avenue Hassan II the main thoroughfare in and out of town. The northern end of Mohammed V, which you can pick up just past the Royal Armed Forces hill, holds a smattering of small banks, mosques, and cafés and the town souks. Here you can hire a taxi to Tan-Tan Plage, the town's nearby port and beach. Mohammed V continues south through a mainly residential area, with unpaved side streets leading up to modest, dusty dwellings, with the occasional small store or café peeking around a corner.

Tan-Tan's residential streets have a perceptible openness to them, in contrast with the traditionally private nature of North African living spaces. Doors are left open, and from windows and doorways women talk to each other unveiled. The streets are alive with women cleaning their quarters and carrying bread to be baked, children playing, and men gathering in groups on the road's edge. Locals are particularly friendly to travelers here, as so few come through.

The southern end of Boulevard Mohammed V is Tan-Tan's main square, **Place de la Marche Verte** (Green March Square). This is the main transportation hub for taxis and cars headed back to Guelmim and on to Laayoune. The plaza is ringed with cafés and Moroccan restaurants.

Dining and Lodging

Restaurants are scarce in Tan-Tan, and the existing options are very basic. For a good lunch, try any of the cafés around Place de la Marche Verte. **Café de Paris** fixes very good salads, beans, and roast chicken. **Jour et Nuit** prepares excellent charcoal tagines. The cafés near the Poste de Police, on the northern end of Mohammed V, serve equally good café fare; **Snack Seoul,** offering simple sandwiches, salads, and meats, and **Café le Jardin** are particularly recommended.

Tan-Tan's hotels leave a lot to be desired, but the long trip to Laayoune may necessitate an overnight stay. Accommodations have few to no amenities, but the best of the bunch are clean and comfortable. Just bring cash, as virtually none of the town's hotels takes credit cards.

$ 🏨 **Hotel Royal.** The Royal is the best choice in town. Centrally located near the markets at the northern end of town, it offers carpeted rooms with private baths and clean beds. The windows invite nice breezes in the evening. ⊠ *Avenue Mohammed V,* ☎ *08/87–71–86. 12 rooms, 3 with bath. No credit cards.*

$ 🏨 **Hotel Tafoukt.** Run by a cheerful Berber family, this is the best lodging near the Place de la Marche Verte. The rooms are clean and newly decorated, and some have private baths. You're near plenty of restaurants and cafés serving tasty tagines and other inexpensive local fare. ⊠ *98, Place de la Marche Verte,* ☎ *08/87–70–31. 13 rooms, 4 with bath. No credit cards.*

En Route There are two ways to travel from Tan-Tan to Laayoune. One is the coastal road, which passes through the towns of Tarfaya and Akhfenir before turning inland toward Laayoune. The other is a completely inland route, the new Saharan Road, which goes to Smara and on to Laayoune via P44. Together these routes form a circuit of more than 800 km (496 mi) around the region.

The Atlantic route follows the sea for some 170 km (105 mi) before turning inland near Tarfaya. It cuts through high sand dunes and rocky hamada, grants stunning views over natural gorges and basins, and opens up along unspoiled stretches of beach.

Tan-Tan Plage

❸ *28 km (17 mi) southwest of Tan-Tan.*

The Tan-Tan Beach area combines actual sand with a modern fishing port specializing in sardines for export. The area has begun to reimagine itself as an upscale vacation spot, and the four-star Hotel Ayoub has been under very slow construction since 1991. Marginal interest on the part of both investors and locals, however, has made some locals skeptical that this will ever become a full-fledged resort.

The small port town has several cafés, banks, and mosques, but no real sights and no accommodations. The beach, due to its close proximity to the port, is often littered with nets, seaweed, and litter; for superior Atlantic access, you'll do better to continue south.

Akhfenir

❹ *150 km (93 mi) south of Tan-Tan.*

This modest fishing village has the first gas station, cafés, and stores on the coastal route after Tan-Tan Plage. Several small cafés serve excellent grilled sardines; locals favor the Café Paris. Just behind the café strip is a small path to a beautiful coastal lookout. Footpaths down to a gorgeous beach make Akhfenir a good place for an en-route swimming stop.

Twenty kilometers (12 miles) south of Akhfenir, a piste branches toward the sea. Follow it for 5 km (3 mi), and you'll come upon the **Naila Lagoon,** surrounded by large dunes. An important stop for migratory birds, including pink flamingos, herons, swans, and ibis, the lagoon is also used for local fishing, algae collection, and aquaculture. The tourist office in Laayoune can provide more information and arrange guided tours.

Tarfaya

❺ *235 km (146 mi) south of Tan-Tan, 85 km (53 mi) south of Akhfenir.*

The approach to Tarfaya passes wonderfully flat strips of beach containing three large **shipwrecks,** all visible from the road. These piles of twisted metal and decaying wood, with large gashes in their sides, have fascinated travelers for years; many people park their cars on the side of the road and walk down to the beach to get a better look. The ships were most likely of British or Portuguese origin and probably ran afoul of the elements on trading missions to Africa's Gold Coast.

The largest of the few coastal towns on this route, Tarfaya offers panoramic ocean views, excellent seafood, and a nice place to explore before the road turns inland. Simple restaurants and cafés line the main street, where you can catch buses and taxis running between Tan-Tan and Laayoune or safely park your car to explore the town on foot or walk down to the beach. The streets are arranged in a gridlike pattern and feel very open, with whitewashed buildings, little stores selling food and sundries, and various nameless cafés. Quiet and unassuming, Tarfaya rarely sees visitors; people simply go about their business in the crisp sea air. The street along the water is full of pedestrians, bikes, cars, children playing, and fishermen hauling in their catch.

Sir Donald MacKenzie, a British trader, founded Tarfaya as Port Victoria in the late 1800s. His original fort, the **Casa Mar** (Sea House), rises from a small rocky outcrop off the coast, crumbling yet majestic. Tarfaya was also put on the map early in the 20th century as a staging post and overnight stop for the French Aéropostale Service flyers en route to West Africa. Antoine de Saint-Exupéry, author of the beloved children's book *The Little Prince* and a member of the service, was one of Tarfaya's most famous guests. A plane-shape monument on the beach commemorates him, and an annual fall aviation rally from France to West Africa still stops in Tarfaya for a night. The town served as a minor capital for Spain's protectorate until 1958.

LAAYOUNE TO DAKHLA

The trip south to Dakhla is the end of the road in Morocco. A total of almost 600 km (372 mi) of desert and sea road make this journey more memorable than any single point within it. The land along the way is barely inhabited, traditionally home only to Saharan tribes and nomads, European sultans, and rich phosphate deposits. It's every bit as alluring as it is immense, a true geographical discovery. The fishing just off the coast is renowned.

Laayoune

6 *115 km (71 mi) south of Tarfaya.*

Formerly known as El Aioun, the former capital of the Spanish Sahara, has thrived under Moroccan rule, expanding in size and benefiting from urban-development initiatives and drastic improvements in infrastructure. A calm and easy place to navigate, Laayoune makes the best base for trips around the western Sahara if your time is limited.

Laayoune is divided into upper and lower areas: Laayoune *fo'k* (upper), or the Ville Nouvelle, and Laayoune *te'ht* (lower). The Spanish built the lower area, which lies on the southern slope of a dry river valley, during colonial times. You can see the domed roofs of old Spanish barracks on the lower hillsides; these are used today as military and family housing for the Moroccan Royal Armed Forces (FAR) and form an interesting contrast to the city's more modern architecture.

The Moroccan government developed the Ville Nouvelle, which rises sharply from the older areas, after the Green March. The new houses and buildings are purely functional in style, their simplicity broken only by other modern features such as the new mosque, the huge soccer stadium, and the Place Mechouar and by such vestiges as the Spanish domed roofs of the *complexe artisanal,* a run-down collection of craft workshops a few paces from the new mosque.

Laayoune is best explored on foot. It's quite effective to look around at surrounding dunes and landscape and contemplate the very existence of a town this size in the middle of the Sahara Desert. A walking tour of Laayoune should start at the shockingly modern **Place Mechouar,** a stark open space lined with canopies and flanked by the Palais du Congrés. Across the street rises the minaret of the **Great Mosque,** one of Laayoune's surprisingly few mosques. The terra-cotta–color domed roofs just behind the mosque house the **complexe artisanal.** Vendors sell very little inside, but the stalls selling painted Saharan leather goods are interesting. From the great mosque, head downhill on Mohammed V, passing the **Colline des Oiseaux** (Bird Hill), near the Hotel Parador, a bird sanctuary of sorts, with several exotic species in large cages. Follow the road as it continues to wind downhill and opens onto a large plaza with a Spanish cathedral at one end. Now closed, the cathedral serves mainly to provide a nice backdrop for the small plaza, which fills with women and children in the late afternoon.

Across from the plaza from the cathedral begins **Souk Djej** (Chicken Market), Laayoune's old market section. It's pleasantly eclectic, with domed roofs, the occasional Spanish-tiled street sign, and mismatched market goods—everything from pots and pans to clothing and furniture.

Back at the cathedral, follow the road as it winds down to the Hotel Rif. Here a footpath winds down to the dry lagoon, with sand dunes rising on the other side. This area makes a pleasant place to stroll, with the high dunes your final destination: over the tops of the dunes you can see Laayoune and the long, dry road to Tan-Tan. Wind carries sand along the flat riverbed, and there's a general sense of seclusion.

Dining and Lodging

Laayoune has several very nice hotels with good restaurants on the premises. In addition, many small restaurants along Avenue Mohammed V, Avenue Hassan II, and Avenue de la Mekka serve simple cuisine. Popular with locals, **Restaurant Diament Vert** (⊠ Avenue de la Mekka) and **Restaurant La Marelka** (⊠ Avenue Hassan II) both offer a wide range of salads, soups, tagines, meats, and seafood. Both are good choices for something a little more upscale than the street-side cafés. Neither takes credit cards.

$ ✕ **Restaurant Marah–Big Fish.** This small, quaint indoor restaurant serves a wide choice of salads, soups, pizza, meats, and seafood. Breakfast, available after 7 AM, can include bread, croissants, pastries, omelets, and freshly squeezed juice in addition to coffee or tea. ⊠ *Avenue de la Mekka (next to Hotel Massira),* ☎ *no phone. No credit cards.*

$$$ 🏨 **Hotel Parador.** Laayoune's finest hotel, the Parador is centrally located between the old and new towns. Replete with a shady courtyard and *zellij* (mosaic) fountain, it's a charming place. Rooms are decorated in Moroccan style, and those overlooking the courtyard have balconies. All have private baths. ⊠ *Rue Okba Ivn Nafih,* ☎ *08/89–45–00, 28 rooms, 2 suites. Restaurant, bar, pool, 2 tennis courts, free parking. MC, V.*

$$$ 🏨 **Hotel Al Massira.** Run by the same company that manages the Parador, this is Laayoune's second most upscale lodging. Larger and less elaborately decorated than the Parador, it's just down the road from the Great Mosque. Rooms are very tasteful, with white walls, a big window, and minimal decoration, and have large, comfortable beds and private baths. ⊠ *12, Avenue de la Mekka,* ☎ *08/89–42-25. 72 rooms, 3 suites. 2 restaurants, bar, pool, 2 tennis courts, nightclub. MC, V.*

$$ 🏨 **Hotel Nagjir.** This downtown hotel has a friendly staff and quirky but comfortable rooms. Decor tends not to match—the floral curtains and bedspreads may not have been chosen with the print couches in mind—but rooms are carpeted and have phones, refrigerators, and private baths. ⊠ *Place Nagjir at Avenue de la Mekka,* ☎ *08/89–41–68. 104 rooms, 10 suites. Restaurant, bar, refrigerators, nightclub.*

$ 🏨 **Hotel Lakouara.** The Lakouara is very basic, but the staff is congenial, and the rooms are clean. The building is well located near restaurants and markets on Avenue Hassan II. ⊠ *Avenue Hassan II,* ☎ *08/89–33–78. 17 rooms, 5 with bath. No credit cards.*

En Route The trip from Laayoune to Smara takes you from the Atlantic coast into the Saharan mainland, a hot, rocky, and inhospitable place. The same characteristics that make the Sahara hard to navigate, however, make it such a unique and gratifying journey apart.

Twelve kilometers (7 miles) southeast of Laayoune is the oasis of **Lemseyed.** Here you have fine views over the impressively steep canyon of the Seguiat el Hamra (Red River). Continue on toward Boukra, noticing the CAMEL CROSSING signs along the way and the large **Boukra–Laayoune conveyor belt** just off the road. This electronic device carries phosphates from the mines around Boukra to Laayoune for export.

The road to Smara passes through very empty landscape. A stop at the village of Asli offers a look at some **prehistoric rock carvings,** best viewed in a casual walk around the large rocks off the road. Ask locals for the *azrou* (rock) and see if you can retain someone to guide you there. If not, look for large rock outcroppings just past the village on the right. About 50 ft from the road, walk amid these and look for small carvings of circles and what some say are gazelles.

A few miles before Smara, the colors of the stony landscape begin to darken slightly as the local basalt deposits come into focus.

Smara

❼   *240 km (149 mi) east of Laayoune.*

Smara's central site has long been an important Saharan caravan stop. The town itself was built in 1884 by Sheikh Ma el Ainin, known as the Blue Sultan for the fabrics he brought back from the Mauritanian trade route. El Ainin masterminded both Smara's situation (it sits higher on the plateau than other populated areas) and its fortification, the combination of which aided local resistance to French and Spanish colonization. The remains of the sheikh's palace are still visible. By the 1930s the area was deserted, used only as a stopping spot for nomads, and today it is mainly a military garrison town. Most of the fun, it must be said, is in getting here.

Once you *are* here, however, a visit to the **Palace of Ma el Ainin** is a must. Located near the Salouam River, which is usually all but dry, the palace is divided into four separate residences (for the sheikh's four wives), a mosque, and several other domestic areas. The property is maintained by a guardian and his family, who will be happy to show you around. Highlights include the domed *zaouia*, the original doors, and the remains of arches and structures of the mosque.

Look around Smara for buildings made of the local black basalt (most have been painted over). Spanish influence is obvious in the egg-shape domes and tubular barracks scattered around town, now used, as in Laayoune, as private homes.

Smara's souk, through the archway off Avenue Hassan II, gets lively in the evening. Try eating at one of the outdoor food stalls: the grilled meats are fresh (sausages, *kefta*, chicken, and sometimes fish), and you can accompany them with rice, salads, and soups (*harira* or the traditional tomato-based Ramadan soup, with lentils, vegetables, and chickpeas). Everything is cooked on the spot.

Dining and Lodging

Dining is a simple affair in Smara. Try any of the open-air grills near the souk, or the restaurant-cafés along Hassan II. Locals like **Restaurant Ezzerdda,** near the souk.

$$$ 🏨 **Hotel Maghreb El Arbi.** Smara's best hotel offers simple, comfortable accommodations and atmosphere, and a great location: you're a block from the souk, near restaurants and cafés, and a short walk from the Palace of Ma el Ainin. Guest rooms are carpeted, have simple white walls and wooden furniture, and are impeccably clean. The staff is friendly and knowledgeable. The U.N. books the hotel to near capacity, so reservations are a must. ⊠ *Avenue Hassan II,* ☎ *08/89–51–91. MC, V.*

$$ 🏨 **Hotel Chabab Sakia El Hamra.** Decor is minimal, and the overall look is slightly worn, but guest rooms at this hotel are larger than those at the neighboring Maghreb El Arbi. All rooms are carpeted, and some are hung with paintings. ⊠ *Avenue Hassan II,* ☎ *08/89–25–24. No credit cards.*

En Route The 550-km (341-mi) trip from Smara to Dakhla snakes inland and returns to the coast near Dakhla. The road is in good condition, and passes some lovely coastline with high cliffs. Strong surf pounds a rocky shore that occasionally opens up to long, sandy beaches. Fishermen either fish from the cliffs or use long bamboo poles to guide their small boats (*floukas*) out into the waves.

Boujdour

8 *420 km (260 mi) southwest of Smara.*

Forty-eight kilometers (30 miles) south of the small settlement of Lemsid, Boujdour is a small fishing port with several cafés, restaurants, gas stations, and even a small, no-frills hotel. The old **Portuguese lighthouse** on the coast is worth a visit; knock on the gate and see if the guardian, who lives inside with his family, is available to show you around. The beaches surrounding the quiet town are long ones, broken by dramatically protruding high cliffs. The road from Boujdour turns inland, stretching through vast hamada, and rejoins the coastal road at the tiny village of Skaymat before continuing on to Dakhla.

Dakhla

9 *303 km (188 mi) south of Boujdour, 545 km (338 mi) south of Laayoune.*

Dakhla is the last frontier for most travelers to the western Sahara, as those wishing to go farther south can only do so as part of a police-escorted convoy to the Mauritanian border. Known as Villa Cisneros during the Spanish colonial period, Dakhla served as a small administrative center for the Rio de Oro colony, and the city's Spanish cathedral and plaza are legacies of this period. Surrounded by functional, concrete military buildings, they now seem sadly out of place. Since the retreat of Spanish, Dakhla has mainly grown as a military hub and a fishing center, employing many Moroccans from northern areas as seasonal fishermen.

Dakhla's main attractions are its superb beaches and the surrounding cliffs. Whales and sea lions frequently surface off the coast, and the tourist office can organize fishing expeditions.

Moving on from Dakhla requires a special Mauritanian visa, available through the Mauritanian consulate in Casablanca. If you're interested, consult your embassy or the U.S. Embassy in Rabat for instructions. Once you've got your visa, the only way to continue south is to join the **convoys** that depart Dakhla for the Mauritanian border on Tuesday and Friday, escorted by Moroccan police. The 460-km (285-mi) drive takes you across the Tropic of Cancer to the Mauritanian border post at La Gouéra, from which Mauritanian police escort you to Nouadibhou. Contact Dakhla's tourist office for details (☞ The Southern Coast and Western Sahara A to Z, *below*).

Dining and Lodging

Small restaurants cluster around Dakhla's main avenue, Mohammed V, and near the souk. The simple **Hotel Sahara,** in the souk area, serves couscous, tagine, and very good fried fish. The salads here do not pique the imagination, but they're adequate for a light lunch.

$$ 🏠 **Hotel Doumss.** This simple hotel is Dakhla's best, with a good, quiet location and a friendly staff. Rooms are on the small side, but their windows let in cool sea breezes, and the beds are clean. There are plenty of cafés and restaurants nearby. ✉ *49, Avenue el Wallaa Dakhla,* ☎ *08/89–80–46. No credit cards.*

$ 🖫 **El Wahda.** El Wahda is small, with a very pleasant concierge, and cheaper than the Hotel Doumss. Rooms are basic, with little more to speak of than a bed and table or two, though renovations are in the works. Everything is very clean, including the bathrooms, which are all shared. ⊠ *Avenue el Wallaa,* ☏ *no phone. No credit cards.*

THE SOUTHERN COAST AND WESTERN SAHARA A TO Z

Arriving and Departing

By Bus

Buses serve Tan-Tan, Laayoune, Smara, and Dakhla once daily from Casablanca and several times daily from Marrakesh and Agadir. **CTM** and **SATAS** are the most comfortable lines.

By Plane

The distance between western Saharan cities, not to mention the distance from here to other hubs in Morocco, makes arriving by plane a logical and popular choice. The region has three airports. **Tan-Tan** (⊠ Plage Blanche, 9 km [6 mi] outside town, ☏ 08/87–71–43) serves Casablanca and Laayoune. **Laayoune** (2 km [1 mi] outside town, ☏ 08/89–33–46 or 08/89–33–47) serves Casablanca, Agadir, Tan-Tan, Dakhla, and Las Palmas, on the Canary Islands. **Dakhla** (5 km [3 mi] outside town, ☏ 08/89–70–49) serves Casablanca, Agadir, and Laayoune.

By Train

Morocco's national railway, the ONCF, does not offer train service south of Marrakesh. It does operate the **Supratours** bus line, which allows you to take the train to Marrakesh and connect with a bus for trips farther south, with stops as far as Laayoune. Supratours buses are comfortable, punctual, and reliable. Tourist offices and train stations have schedules for both the ONCF and Supratours.

Getting Around

By Bus

Regional buses connect Tan-Tan, Laayoune, Smara, and Dakhla.

By Car

Driving is the most efficient way to travel in the western Sahara, and because gas is subsidized throughout the region, fuel is cheaper here than it is up north. Local public transportation tends to whiz past interesting beaches, towns, and other sights, so a car is the ideal way to work in all the highlights. The coastal road and the Smara loop are both very safe; tourist offices can advise you on other roads.

Rental agencies: **Souabi** (⊠ Laayoune, ☏ 08/89–36–61). **Laayoune Cars** (☏ 08/89–47–44).

By Grand Taxi

Grand taxis are old Mercedes four-doors that can seat six if everyone squeezes in. They run between towns and are often faster than buses. To rent the taxi (and driver) for a day, you simply pay for all six seats. In this case, negotiate a price with the driver before you set out—bargain hard—and do not pay until the end of the trip. It's polite to buy the driver lunch and tea along the way.

A trip from Tan-Tan to Laayoune should cost about 100DH per person if you hop on, 600DH–900DH if you rent the whole taxi.

Contacts and Resources

Emergencies

Dial **15** from any public phone for an ambulance or urgent medical care.

Guided Tours

If you have any kind of time constraint, you'll probably find a guided tour a big help in this part of the country. The tourist offices in Laayoune and Dakhla (☞ *below*) can design tours to suit your personal interests.

Late-Night Pharmacies

All pharmacies in Guelmim, Tan-Tan, Laayoune, Smara, and Dakhla post the names of the ones on duty late at night.

Sports and Outdoor Activities

Travel agencies and tourist offices (☞ *below*) can both help arrange fishing trips, surfing excursions, and desert treks.

Travel Agencies

Two agencies, both in Laayoune, organize outdoor excursions of various stripes and can arrange for desert expeditions with Land Rovers and drivers. **Agence Massira Tours International** (✉ 20, Avenue de la Mekka, ☎ 08/89–42–29). **Bureau du Tourisme du Sahara** (✉ Oum Saad, ☎ 08/89–42–24).

Visitor Information

The Moroccan Tourist Office can arrange tours, suggest restaurants and hotels, and generally assist with regional travel plans. They're among the best resources in the area, so by all means consult them for help in making the most of a short stay. **Dakhla** (✉ 1, Rue Tiris, ☎ 08/89–82–28). **Laayoune** (✉ Avenue de l'Islam, across from Hotel Parador, B.P. 471, ☎ 08/89–16–94, ℻ 08/89–16–95).

11 PORTRAITS OF MOROCCO

Islam: Five Steps to a Life of Peace

Books and Films

French and Moroccan Arabic Vocabulary

ISLAM: FIVE STEPS TO A LIFE OF PEACE

Your daily life is your temple and your religion.

—Kahlil Gibran

Muslims view their religion as a blueprint
for a life of harmony in which faith and
practice become one and the same. Islam
is based on five principles, or "pillars,"
which guide the actions of every devout
Muslim. Observing the Five Pillars promises
a peaceful existence here on earth as well
as in the afterlife.

The first pillar of Islam is *shahada*—witness. Islam is monotheistic: The Muslim
must profess his faith by declaring, "There
is no God but Allah" and "Mohammed
is His Prophet." Mohammed was born
around AD 570 in the Arabian city of
Mecca, and Muslims believe that the word
of God was revealed to him by the angel
Gabriel over a period of 22 years beginning in 610. After the prophet's death in
632, these *sourat,* or teachings, were written down by *imams* (religious scholars) as
the Koran, now considered an infallible
source by Muslims. The Islamic oral tradition, called *hadith,* is based on the words
and practices of Mohammed, rather than
Allah himself, and are not considered infallible; the Five Pillars of Islam are based
on hadith rather than the Koran. Many of
the stories in the Torah and Bible are included in the Koran, which recognizes the
Judeo-Christian prophets who preceded Mohammed (such as Moses and Jesus) while
regarding him as the last. Tolerance of
other faiths is evident in Moroccan society; every large city has its share of churches
and synagogues.

There are two schools of Islam: Sunna
and Shia. Morocco subscribes to Sunna,
or orthodox, Islam, as do the majority of
Muslims worldwide. The Shiites are a mi-
nority who agree in principle with the
Sunni but differ on questions of leadership
and politics. Whereas the Sunni embrace
tolerance and are open to diverse inter-
pretations of the *hadith,* the Shiites believe
that the Koran is the sole valid source of
knowledge and trust their imam to provide them with infallible guidance. Idriss
ben Abdellah, a descendant of the Prophet
Mohammed, is credited with bringing
Islam to Morocco in 788: He settled in the
vicinity of Volubilis, near Meknes, and
was accepted by the local tribes as their
spiritual leader. Unlike some other religions,
Islam has no ordained clergy, but rather
prayer leaders and religious scholars. Es-
tablishing the Idrissid dynasty, Idriss ben
Abdellah created new cities and religious
centers, notably Fez, which even today is
considered Morocco's spiritual capital.

To observe the second pillar of Islam, *salat*
(prayer), a devout Muslim must pray five
times a day: just before sunrise, early afternoon, late afternoon, just after sunset,
and in the evening. The call to prayer is
chanted publicly from the mosque, the
Muslim place of worship, by a muezzin
(who traditionally used only his lungs,
but is nowadays aided by a microphone).
Before praying, the Muslim must remove
his shoes, perform ablutions, place a clean
mat on the ground, and face Mecca. In the
absence of soap and water, the ritual ablutions can be carried out symbolically in any
clean, quiet place, as their importance lies
in the purification of one's thoughts in
preparation for communion with God.
The prayers must be recited in Arabic,
the original language of the Koran (though
the Koran itself has been translated into
several languages for the various nationalities that subscribe to the faith). Friday
is the Muslims' day for congregational
worship in the mosque; non-Muslims are
forbidden from entering all Moroccan
mosques, though a few, such as the majestic Hassan II Mosque in Casablanca,
allow visitors into areas not used for
prayer. Worshipers must remove their
shoes before entering the mosque, and
women, who pray in separate rooms, must
cover their heads with a scarf. It is said that
anyone who builds a mosque, or con-
tributes in some way to its construction,
is assured a place in paradise.

Every Friday, a traditional Moroccan family serves couscous, a sort of granulated
pastina topped with a stew of meat and
vegetables, for lunch. As they finish their
pre-meal prayers (every Muslim meal begins with the recitation of the phrase "*Bis
m'Allah,*" "Through the Grace of God")
the family may send a platter of couscous

to the local mosque for distribution to the poor—a ritual that exemplifies the third pillar of Islam, *zakat* (alms). While alms are not legally required, Muslims are expected to give 2.5% of the value of their possessions to the less fortunate each year, traditionally at Moharrem, the beginning of the Muslim new year. Since there is no organized social-welfare system in Morocco, the needy depend solely on non-government organizations and the generosity of others. People do give coins to the beggars and infirm in the streets, but Moroccans concentrate much of their support on their extended family and local community.

The family is a vital part of Islamic culture. Family members come to the aid of any relative, young or old, who is passing through difficult times. A Muslim household often includes members of the extended family at one time or another, and all Muslims are taught to care for their parents as they age—there are no retirement homes in an Islamic society. By offering alms and helping others, the Muslim thanks God for his worldly blessings.

The ninth month of the Islamic calendar, Ramadan, is another opportunity for the Muslim to empathize with the poor and reflect on his good fortune. For the duration of Ramadan, all Muslims must refrain from eating, drinking, smoking, and sex from sunrise to sunset. This fasting, called *siyam*, is the fourth pillar of Islam, and culminates in Islam's second-most-important holiday, Äid el Fitr, the Feast of the Breaking of the Fast. The Koran was first revealed to the Prophet Mohammed on the 27th night of Ramadan, so Muslims believe that fasting on the 27th day, near the end of the month, is equivalent to fasting for 1,000 regular days. To ease them into the rigors of Ramadan, children begin their first fast on this day, usually when they reach adolescence; that evening, after *ftir*, the sunset meal, children are dressed in traditional clothes and paraded through the streets to mark their initiation to this rite.

Mealtimes take on special significance during Ramadan, with families and friends often inviting each other over to break the fast. After the meal, many people devote quiet time to prayer and contemplation. Muslims who are sick, pregnant, or traveling a great distance are excused from fasting, but they are expected to make up the days they missed another time. As a result of the various privations, people may be more nervous and irritable than usual during this time; driving is especially challenging, as some motorists lack sleep and sustenance.

Under threat from his polytheistic and mercantile enemies, Mohammed fled to Medina in 622. Successful in spreading Islam there, he soon raised an army, and later returned triumphantly to Mecca. The prophet's flight (*hegira*) from Mecca is commemorated in the fifth pillar of Islam: the *hajj* (pilgrimage). Muslims who are physically and financially able are required to make a pilgrimage to Mecca at least once in their lives. The hajj is marked by various rites and prayer sessions at Mecca's Great Mosque, particularly at its Kaaba—the most sacred shrine in all of Islam—and other sites in the vicinity. The pilgrimage takes place after the month of Ramadan and culminates in the most important Muslim holiday, Äid el Adha. This holiday honors the sacrifice of Ibrahim (Abraham), who is considered the founder of Islam. According to the Koran (and the Book of Genesis), Ibrahim was asked by God to sacrifice his firstborn son, Ismail. As he prepared to carry out God's will, an angel intervened and decreed that a lamb could be sacrificed instead. On Äid el Adha, every Moroccan family that can afford to do so sacrifices one or more lambs and gathers together for a traditional feast. Part of the meat is distributed to the poor. Because of the abundance of meat in most households at this time, many butchers stay closed for up to a week afterwards.

In addition to the five pillars, Muslims are guided by other religious mores, such as dietary laws that forbid eating pork and drinking alcohol. Like the Judeo-Christian Ten Commandments, Islamic law (*sharia*) prohibits such acts as murder, theft, adultery, and false witness. Men and women are both encouraged to dress modestly. In Morocco's larger cities, people wear a variety of clothing, from traditional veils and *djellaba*s (hooded robes) to contemporary Western-style dress, while traditional styles prevail in the outlying towns and villages.

Muslim society is heavily influenced by the belief that one's fate lies in God's hands, that one's life span and time of death are predetermined. A Moroccan never talks about the future without the qualifier *insh'Allah*—"God willing." This can be confounding at times to the foreigner who prefers to believe that he controls his own destiny. Islam does teach that people are responsible for their own actions and will be held accountable for them; Muslims strive to establish a balance between determinism (not to say fatalism) and accountability.

The Arabic word Islam comes from *salaam*—"peace." The followers of Islam constitute a community of the faithful, the core of which is the extended family. In concentric circles around this nucleus, the community reaches out to the neighborhood, the nation, and, ultimately, all humanity. Muslims seek not so much to subscribe to a religion as to incarnate their faith. In so doing, they bring peace not only to themselves, but to each member of their community.

—Eileen Colucci

BOOKS AND FILMS

Readings on Morocco in English begin and end with the works of the late Tangier-based American expatriate Paul Bowles and the many Moroccan writers whose work he has translated. Bowles's most famous novel, *The Sheltering Sky,* purports to take place in Algeria, but this tale of a doomed triangle of young Americans adrift in North Africa is quintessentially Moroccan in both tone and content. *The Spider's House* is a superb historical novel and portrait of Fez at the end of the French Protectorate. *Let It Come Down* paints a vivid portrait of life in Tangier's expatriate community, which Bowles has now inhabited for over half a century.

The most comprehensive collection of Bowles's short stories is *Collected Stories of Paul Bowles 1939–76.* Later collections include *Midnight Mass, Call at Corazón,* and *Unwelcome Words.* Some of the best single stories are "The Delicate Prey," "The Time of Friendship," "Things Gone and Things Still Here," and "A Distant Episode."

Days: Tangier Journal, 1987–1989 is the most recent addition to the Bowles bibliography, a series of musings and accounts of daily events that Bowles effortlessly (or so it seems) elevates to the level of artistic essays. All of Bowles's nonfiction is notable, but *Their Heads are Green and Their Hands Are Blue* is the most revealing and informative on Morocco. *Yallah!, Without Stopping,* and *Points in Time* also illuminate both Morocco and their author.

Bowles's translations from the Arabic and Berber canons include Driss ben Hamed Charhadi's *A Life Full of Holes;* Mohammed Mrabet's *Love with a Few Hairs, The Lemon, M'Hashish, The Boy Who Set the Fire & Other Stories, Harmless Poisons, Blameless Sins, The Big Mirror, The Chest,* and *Marriage with Papers;* Isabelle Eberhardt's *The Oblivion Seekers & Other Writings;* Rodrigo Rey-Rosa's *The Beggar's Knife;* and Mohammed Choukri's *Jean Genet in Tangier, Tennessee Williams in Tangier,* and *For Bread Alone.*

Writings by Jane Auer Bowles, Paul's wife, are no less interesting than her husband's. A Tangier resident from the 1940s until her 1973 death in a Spanish insane asylum, Auer Bowles's *Everything Is Nice: Collected Stories* is a flawless portrait of expatriate life in Morocco. Millicent Dillon's biography of Jane Auer Bowles, *A Little Original Sin,* has key insights into both Mr. and Mrs. Bowles and their adopted country.

Winner of France's Prix Goncourt, Moroccan author Tahar Ben Jelloun's novel *The Sand Child* tells the story of a girl brought up as a boy by her father. Also by Ben Jelloun are *Sacred Night* and *With Downcast Eyes.*

Highlights of modern travel literature include *Morocco: The Traveller's Companion,* edited by Margaret and Robin Bidwell; *The Voices of Marrakesh,* by Elias Canetti; *Tangier: City of the Dream,* by Ian Finlayson; and *A Year in Marrakesh,* by Peter Mayne. Among turn-of-the-20th-century accounts, French novelist Pierre Loti's *Voyage au Maroc* is a classic, as is Polish count Jean Potocki's *Voyage to Morocco.* Charles de Foucauld, a French nobleman, army officer, and missionary, chronicled his time as a Trappist monk in Morocco in his book *Voyage au Maroc.* For more historical and ethnographical accounts, find Edith Wharton's 1920 *In Morocco;* Antoine de Saint-Exupéry's *Wind, Sand and Stars* and *Southern Mail;* Walter Harris's 1921 *Morocco That Was;* Amin Malouf's *Leo the African;* Gavin Maxwell's *Lords of the Atlas;* and Wyndham Lewis's *Journey into Barbary.*

The question of the Moroccan woman's experience has given rise to some excellent social critiques. *Beyond the Veil: Male-Female Dynamics in a Modern Muslim Society* is a prominent work by the Moroccan feminist Fatima Mernissi, who spoke only Arabic until the age of 20 but went on to earn a master's degree at the Sorbonne and a Ph.D. from Brandeis University. Mernissi has also written *The Forgotten Queens of Islam,* biographical studies of female leaders in the Muslim world, and *Dreams on the Threshold,* a study of Moroccan women's hopes as their country begins to modernize. Sylvia Kennedy's *See Ouarzazate and Die,* a more general social rundown, was actually banned in Morocco. *Opening the Gates: A Century of Arab Feminist Writing,* edited by Margot Badran and Miriam Cooke, comprises three essays, one by Fatima Mernissi. Alison Baker's *Voices of Resistance: Oral Histories of Moroccan Women* documents interviews in which women speak freely about feminism, nationalism, and their own lives.

On food and the culinary arts, Paula Wolfert's *Good Food from Morocco* and Robert Carrier's *Taste of Morocco* are both excellent, the former for its prose and the latter for its photographs and background on the Moroccan social context. Both have fabulous recipes. *Traditional Moroccan Cooking: Recipes from Fez,* by Zette Guinaudeau-Franc et al. is a more recent (1995) take on classic Moroccan cooking.

Morocco, a large-format collection of photos with a preface by Paul Bowles and an introduction by Tahar Ben Jelloun, is a fine coffee-table choice, as is *Living in Morocco,* by Liesl and Landt Dennis.

A great many films that do not take place in Morocco were nonetheless shot there, most notably Orson Welles's *Othello,* David Lean's *Lawrence of Arabia,* David Cronenberg's *Naked Lunch,* Bernardo Bertolucci's *The Sheltering Sky,* and Martin Scorsese's *The Last Temptation of Christ* and *Kundun.* Recently, though, Morocco was featured in its own right: Gillies MacKinnon's 1999 film *Hideous Kinky,* based on the Esther Freud novel, stars Kate Winslet as an English hippie who drags her two young daughters to Marrakesh in the mid-'70s seeking she-knows-not-what. She finds it.

FRENCH AND MOROCCAN ARABIC VOCABULARY

Most Moroccans are multilingual. The country's official languages are classical Arabic and French; most Moroccans speak the Moroccan Arabic dialect, with many city dwellers also speaking French. Since the time of the French Protectorate, French has been taught to schoolchildren (not all children) starting in the first grade, resulting in several French-language newspapers, magazines, and TV shows. Spanish enters the mix in northern Morocco, and several Berber tongues are spoken in the south. In the medinas and souks of big cities, you may find merchants who can bargain in just about any language, including English and German.

A rudimentary knowledge of French and, especially, Arabic will get you far in Morocco. If you're more comfortable with French, by all means use it in the major cities; in smaller cities, villages, and the mountains, it's best to attempt some Moroccan Arabic. Arabic is always a good choice, as Moroccans will go out of their way to accommodate the foreigner who attempts to learn their mother tongue.

FRENCH

English	French	Pronunciation
Greetings and Basics		
Hello/ Good morning/ Good afternoon	Bonjour	bohn-**zhoor**
Good evening	Bonsoir	bohn-**swahr**
Goodbye	Au revoir	oh ruh-**vwahr**
Mr./Sir	Monsieur	muh-**syuh**
Mrs./Madam	Madame	mah-**dahm**
Miss	Mademoiselle	mahd-mwah-**zel**
Pleased to meet you	Enchanté	ahn-shahn-**tay**
How are you?	Comment ça va?	**koh**-mohn sa **va**?
Very well	Très bien	tray bee-ehn
And you?	Et vous?	ay **voo**?
yes/no	oui/non	wee/nohn
please	S'il vous plait	seal voo **play**
Thank you	Merci	mare-**see**
You're welcome	Je vous en prie	zhuh **voo** zahn **pree**
I'm sorry	Pardon	pahr-**dohn**
Excuse me	Je m'excuse	zhuh mex-**cues**
Useful Phrases		
Do you speak	Parlez-vous	par-lay-**voo**
English?	anglais?	ahn-**glay**?
I don't speak	Je ne parle pas	huhn parl **pah**
French	français	frahn-**say**
I don't understand	Je ne comprends pas	zhuhn **kohm**-prahn **pah**

I don't know	Je ne sais pas	zhuhn say **pah**
I am American	Je suis américain	zhuh **sweez** ah-may-ree-**kehn**
I am British	Je suis anglais	zhuz sweez ahn-**glay**
My name is . . .	Je m'appelle . . .	zhuh mah-**pell** . . .
What's your name?	Comment vous appelez-vous?	**koh**-mohn voo za-play **voo**?
Where is	Ou se trouve	**oo** suh **troov**
the train station	la gare	la **gahr**
the airport	l'aéroport	lehr-oh-**por**
the bus station	la gare routière	la **gahr** root-y-**air**
the rest room	la toilette	la twah-**let**

MOROCCAN ARABIC

English	Arabic Transliteration	Pronunciation

Greetings and Basics

Hello/Peace upon you	salaam ou alaikum	sa-**lahm** oo allah-ee-**koom**
(Reply:) Hello/And peace upon you	oua alaikum Salaam	wa allay-koom sa-**lahm**
Goodbye	baslamma	bess-**lah**-ma
Mr./Sir	saïd	**sah**-yeed
Mrs./Madam	saïda	sah-yeed-**ah**
Miss	anissa	ah-nee-**sah**
How are you? Fine, thank you	labass, alhamdul'Illah	la-**bahs**, al-**hahm**-doo-lee-**lah**
("No harm?") ("No harm, praise to be God")	labass	la-**bahs**
Pleased to meet you	misharafin	mish-arra-**feen**
Yes/No	naam/la	nahm/lah
Please	afek	**ah**-feck
Thank you	choukran	**chook**-rahn
God willing	insh'Allah	in-**shah**-ahl-lah
I'm sorry (to a man)	smahali	**sma**-hah-li
I'm sorry (to a woman)	smahailia	sma-high-**lee**-a

Days

Today	el yum	el **youm**
Yesterday	el barah	el-**bar**-a
Tomorrow	ghedaa	ghe-**dah**
Sunday	el had	el **had**
Monday	tneen	t'**neen**
Tuesday	thlat	ktlet
Wednesday	larbaa	lar-**bah**
Thursday	el khamis	el kha-**mees**
Friday	el jemaa	el j'**mah**
Saturday	sebt	sebt

Numbers

1	wahad	**wa**-hed
2	jouj	jewj
3	thlata	**tlet**-ta
4	rbaa	ar-**bah**
5	khamsa	**khem**-sa h
6	sta	stah
7	sbaa	se-**bah**
8	taminia	ta-**min**-ee-ya
9	tseud	tsood
10	aachra	**ah**-she-ra
11	hadash	ha-**dahsh**
12	tanash	ta-**nahsh**
20	aacherine	ah-**chreen**
50	khamsine	khum-**seen**
100	milla	**mee**-yah
200	millatein	mee-ya **tayn**

Useful Phrases

Do you speak English?	ouesh tat tkelem belinglisia	**wesh** tet te- **kel**-lem **blin**-gliz-ee-yah?
I don't understand	ma fahemtsh	ma-**f'emtch**
I don't know	ma naarf	ma **nahr**-ef
I'm lost	ana mouddar	ahna mo-**wa**-dahr
I am American	ana amiriqui	ahna **ameeri**-key
I am British	ana inglisi	anna in-ge-**lee**-zee
What is this?	shnou hada	**shnoo** ha-da
Where is?	Fein?	fay-**en**?
the train station	mahatat al ketar	ma-ha-**tat** al **ket**-tar
the city bus station	mahatat tobis	**ma-ha**-tat **toh**-beese
the intracity bus station	mahatat al cairan	**ma**-ha-tat al kah-ee-rahn
the airport	l'matar	**al**-ma-**tarr**
the hotel	al foundouk	**al**-fun-**duck**
the café	l'kkhaoua	**al**-kah-**hou**-wah
the restaurant	mataam	mat-**ahm**
the telephone	tilifoon	**til-lee**-foon
the hospital	sbitar	sbee-**tar**
the post office	l'bosta	**al**-bost-**a**
the rest room	bit al ma	**beet**-el-ma
the pharmacy	pharmacien	far-**ma-cienn**
the bank	l'banca	**al** bann-**ka**
the embassy	sifara	**see**-far-**ra**
I would like a room	bghit bit	**bgheet**-beet
I would like to buy	bghit nechri	bgheet nesh-**ree**
cigarettes	garro	**gahr**-oh
a city map	kharretta del medina	kha-**ray**-ta del m'**dee**-nah
a road map	kharretta del bled	kha-**ray**-ta del blad
How much is it?	besh hal hada?	be-**shal hah**-da?
It's expensive.	ghaliya	**gha**-lee-ya

A little	shwiya	**shwee**-ya
A lot	bezzaf	be-**zef**
Enough	baraka	**ba**-rah-ka
I am ill. (a man)	ana ayen	ah-na a-**yen**
I am ill. (a woman)	ana ayena	**ah**-na a-**yen**-a
I need a doctor.	bghit tbib	bgeet t'**beeb**
I have a problem.	aandi mouchkila	**ahn**-dee moosh-**kee**-la
left	lessar	**lis**-sar
right	leemen	**lee**-men
Help!	atkhoruh!	aat-kho-**rouh**!
Fire!	laafiya	**lah**-fee-ya
Caution!/Look out!	aindek!	**aann**-deck

Dining

I would like	bghit	bgeet
water	l'ma	l'mah
bread	l'khobz	l'khobz
vegetables	khoudra	**khu**-dra
meat	l'hamm	l'hahm
fruits	l'fawakeh	el **fah**-wah-keh
cakes	l'haloua	el **hahl**-oo-wa
tea	atay	**ah**-tay
coffee	kahoua	**kah**-wa
a fork	m'tikka	me-**tick**-a
a spoon	maalka	**mahl**-ka
a knife	mousse	moose
a plate	ghtar	gtar

INDEX

NOTES

Looking for a different kind of vacation?

Fodor's makes it easy with a full line of specialty guidebooks to suit a variety of interests—from adventure to romance to language help.

Fodor's. For the world of ways you travel.

Fodor's
ESCAPE

One-of-a-kind travel experiences

The perfect companions to **Fodor's** Gold Guides, these exquisite full-color guidebooks will inspire you with their unique vacation ideas, help you plan with detailed contact information, and safeguard your memories with their gorgeous photographs.

At bookstores everywhere.

Smart Travelers Go with **Fodor's**®